Read SAP PRESS online also

With booksonline we offer you online access to leading SAP experts' knowledge. Whether you use it as a beneficial supplement or as an alternative to the printed book – with booksonline you can:

- Access any book at any time
- Quickly look up and find what you need
- Compile your own SAP library

Your advantage as the reader of this book

Register your book on our website and obtain an exclusive and free test access to its online version. You're convinced you like the online book? Then you can purchase it at a preferential price!

And here's how to make use of your advantage

1. Visit www.sap-press.com
2. Click on the link for SAP PRESS booksonline
3. Enter your free trial license key
4. Test-drive your online book with full access for a limited time!

Your personal **license key** for your test access including the preferential offer

7ry4-u35w-bfig-tvdj

E-Recruiting with SAP® ERP HCM

SAP PRESS is a joint initiative of SAP and Galileo Press. The know-how offered by SAP specialists combined with the expertise of the Galileo Press publishing house offers the reader expert books in the field. SAP PRESS features first-hand information and expert advice, and provides useful skills for professional decision-making.

SAP PRESS offers a variety of books on technical and business related topics for the SAP user. For further information, please visit our website: *www.sap-press.com*.

Richard Haßmann, Christian Krämer, Jens Richter
Personnel Planning and Development Using SAP ERP HCM
2009, 564 pp.
978-1-59229-187-8

Jeremy Masters, Christos Kotsakis
Enterprise Compensation Management with SAP ERP HCM
2009, 405 pp.
978-1-59229-207-3

Sven Ringling, Jörg Edinger, Janet McClurg
Mastering HR Management with SAP ERP HCM
2009, 664 pp.
978-1-59229-278-3

Prashanth Padmanabhan, Christian Hochwarth, Sharon Wolf Newton, Sankara Bharathan, Manoj Parthasarathy
SAP Enterprise Learning
2009, 347 pp.
978-1-59229-269-1

Jeremy Masters, Christos Kotsakis, and Venki Krishnamoorthy

E-Recruiting with SAP® ERP HCM

Bonn • Boston

Galileo Press is named after the Italian physicist, mathematician and philosopher Galileo Galilei (1564–1642). He is known as one of the founders of modern science and an advocate of our contemporary, heliocentric worldview. His words *Eppur se muove* (And yet it moves) have become legendary. The Galileo Press logo depicts Jupiter orbited by the four Galilean moons, which were discovered by Galileo in 1610.

Editor Jenifer Niles
Copyeditor Ruth Saavedra
Cover Design Jill Winitzer
Photo Credit Image copyright Thomas Mounsey. Used under license from Shutterstock.com.
Layout Design Vera Brauner
Production Editor Kelly O'Callaghan
Assistant Production Editor Graham Geary
Typesetting Publishers' Design and Production Services, Inc.
Printed and bound in Canada

ISBN 978-1-59229-243-1

1st Edition 2010

Library of Congress Cataloging-in-Publication Data
Masters, Jeremy.
E-recruiting with SAP ERP HCM / Jeremy Masters, Christos Kotsakis, Venki Krishnamoorthy. -- 1st ed.
p. cm.
Includes bibliographical references and index.
ISBN-13: 978-1-59229-243-1 (alk. paper)
ISBN-10: 1-59229-243-7 (alk. paper)
1. SAP ERP. 2. Employees — Recruiting — Computer programs. 3. Personnel management — Computer programs.
I. Kotsakis, Christos. II. Krishnamoorthy, Venki. III. Title.
HF5549.5.R44M377 2010
658.3'111028553 — dc22

2010000623

Contents at a Glance

Contents

Acknowledgments

This project draws inspiration from the efforts and support of many individuals. Without these friends and colleagues, this book would not have been possible.

Thank you to our friends at Galileo Press – for their guidance, patience and support. We would especially like to thank Jenifer Niles who made this book possible and has encouraged us to get the words onto the printed page (once again).

We owe the utmost gratitude to our families, who supported us during the writing of this book. Thank you for your love and patience throughout this project.

We would also like to thank our colleagues who have dedicated countless hours to the success of key initiatives. Without their dedication to solving impossible problems, we would have never achieved the successes that we did. We owe a big thanks to Venkat Challa, Rinaldo Condo, Matt Miller, John Wunderlich, Brad Chilcoat, Vidyasagar Guntur, Jimmy Kalivas, Michel Chamoun, Rahmat Jaffari, Patrick Rabbat, Dan Stein, Wayne Harmon, Beth Solomon, Yasmine Abdallah, Bongisa Mahlulo, and Carlos Gutierrez.

We hope you find this book informative and easy to read. We are hopeful that we will provide you with new perspectives, practical anecdotes, and "food for thought" as you embark on your recruitment implementation.

Sincerely,
Jeremy Masters, **Christos Kotsakis**, and **Venki Krishnamoorthy**
New York, NY
2010

Preface

Acquiring and retaining the right talent is critical to a company's success. With the changing business landscape, finding and retaining the right talent has become increasingly difficult. It requires effective hiring strategies that include both internal and external candidates along with the ability to leverage other sources, such as vendors, alumni, and even social media platforms.

Recruitment is one of the essential functions that the human resources department performs because it directly correlates to the performance of the organization. Poor recruiting decisions can impact morale, production, and labor costs as organizations fail to recognize internal resources and hire unqualified resources.

The design and implementation of a recruiting strategy and an effective approach to hiring the right talent can directly influence a company's ability to achieve their goals. They can also dramatically increase morale and retention of current talent while continuing to leverage institutional knowledge.

As technology has improved, so have the tools that are available to human resources organizations. Tools such as SAP E-Recruiting enable the strategic aspects of recruiting by integrating the talent management processes, introducing talent relationship management, and enabling companies to leverage the platform to identify and select the right resources.

As part of our series on talent management, we have written this book to address both the functional and technical needs of SAP E-Recruiting. Throughout the book, we provide examples and best practices on common business requirements for SAP E-Recruiting implementations. In some cases, we have expanded the content to include functionality that extends beyond the standard solution to show what enhancements are possible within the flexible SAP NetWeaver® platform. We also discuss considerations in the form of lessons learned for a successful rollout of SAP E-Recruiting.

This book has been written as a complete reference to cover the recruiting processes and the associated SAP E-Recruiting features that enable the process. We have dedicated a chapter to lessons learned from past SAP E-Recruiting implementations and have highlighted recommended approaches and solutions to address key gaps within the functionality.

This book is targeted to both customers and consultants who are implementing SAP E-Recruiting or considering its implementation. If you have comments or questions relating to SAP E-Recruiting or the contents of this book, feel free to contact the authors by email at *jmasters@worklogix.com*, *christos.kotsakis@emedianet.com*, or *venki.krish@ymail.com*.

SAP E-Recruiting enables companies to source key talent to the organization. This book explains how to implement and support the critical recruitment processes, including candidate and requisition management using SAP's recruitment functionality. SAP E-Recruiting is part of SAP's larger Talent Management strategic umbrella and provides the tools and controls necessary to efficiently manage recruitment processes within the corporation. This chapter gets us started on our journey. Here we introduce the book, its target audience, and its layout.

1 Introduction

A solid recruitment strategy is a vital part of any company's talent management initiatives. Attracting the right talent to the organization is possibly the most important of all human capital management functions. Without key positions staffed with capable individuals, a company will never be successful. Although developing and executing a solid talent management relationship strategy is at the top of many executives' agendas today, many organizations fall short in its delivery. In some cases, a sound approach may be developed and ready for implementation, but there is no tool with which to execute the strategy.

The SAP E-Recruiting application provides a comprehensive set of recruitment tools to improve how the organization attracts key talent from both outside (external candidates) and inside (internal candidates) the enterprise. External candidates can elect to register within the talent warehouse or remain unregistered. Internal candidates (i.e., employees) are already set up and integrated in the system. Robust functionality around requisition and candidate management — along with its integration capabilities with core human resources (HR) data — make SAP E-Recruiting an attractive offering for companies using SAP ERP Human Capital Management (HCM). Enhanced authorization management features ensure that data privacy and security concerns are addressed. Reporting tools — including capability through the SAP NetWeaver Business Warehouse — provide robust analytics for managers, recruiters, and talent leaders.

1.1 Target Audience

This book is written for human resources professionals including recruitment specialists, information technology professionals, and SAP ERP HCM consultants interested in understanding the steps needed to deliver and operationally support a successful SAP E-Recruiting implementation using the latest SAP software versions (In this book, our focus will be on SAP ERP 6.0, enhancement pack 4).

Project and program managers of recruiting implementations and upgrades will also find this book helpful. We expect that the information in this book will resonate with both project leaders and team members because the lessons discussed throughout the book can provide immediate value — especially for those implementing the application for the first time. For customers already using SAP E-Recruiting, we also believe this book will provide value because we review both the latest functionalities available in the enhancement packs and offer a preview of the SAP E-Recruiting roadmap.

1.2 Book Layout

We have organized the book in a logical sequence to help you explore the components of SAP E-Recruiting and to assist in its implementation. The book begins with an introduction to general recruitment processes and then covers more technical topics such as SAP configuration and implementation specifics. The book reviews a wide range of functional and technical subjects including configuration, portal, search, security, vendor services, and integration. The book concludes with lessons learned from other SAP E-Recruiting implementations and a resources chapter that contains useful information for your project team's reference.

Let's take a quick look at what will be covered in each chapter:

Chapter 2 presents a high-level overview of the various processes within recruiting. The chapter breaks down the processes and discusses the elements that make up each process. Important topics are covered such as requisition management, applicant tracking, and the candidate offer.

Chapter 3 provides an overview of the basic configuration and related infotypes (including the data model) that are available with SAP E-Recruiting. The chapter reviews concepts such as requisitions, candidates, and talent groups. We also review the new functionalities available in enhancement pack 4 and provide an inventory of portal content necessary to get started.

Chapter 4 covers requisition management and the various tools available to support requisitions within the organization. Topics within this chapter include requisition creation, requisition maintenance, job postings, publications, questionnaires, scales, proficiencies, process templates, activity management, correspondence management, and manager involvement (through Manager Self-Service).

Chapter 5 discusses candidate management, including internal and external candidates. The chapter explores registration and its interplay with the talent warehouse. It covers many important topics including data privacy, the candidate profile, the applicant cockpit, job search, favorites, the application wizard, internal and external applications, application groups, job agents, hot jobs indicator, tell a friend service, talent groups, ranking, and talent warehouse setup.

Chapter 6 reviews the three core functionality components of the recruitment administrator: user management, central system administration, and transaction data management. This chapter covers the maintenance of support teams, talent groups, application groups, and process templates.

Chapter 7 focuses on the search functionality available in SAP E-Recruiting. Topics include configuration and support on the SAP search engine, TREX, and the new SES (search engine service) interface. This chapter also covers search profiles and search profile types.

Chapter 8 provides a perspective on the integration points between SAP E-Recruiting and other components within SAP ERP HCM. Components discussed include personnel administration, organizational management, qualifications, business partners, and user management. The focus is on the data transfer scenario from SAP E-Recruiting to SAP ERP HCM to hire employees based on candidate data.

Chapter 9 discusses vendor services typically involved in SAP E-Recruiting implementations, including background and drug checks, job board postings, and resume parsing.

Chapter 10 reviews the important topic of authorization management. This chapter reviews specific recruitment authorizations and the standard-delivered roles.

Chapter 11 highlights the standard reporting capability that is provided within SAP E-Recruiting. We also provide an overview of the reports available if you want to implement any analytics using SAP NetWeaver Business Warehouse.

Chapter 12 reviews lessons learned from previous SAP E-Recruiting implementations. The chapter is divided into four sections: recruitment process and system design, change management, social media and mobile platforms, and system implementation.

Chapter 13 covers helpful resources for your SAP E-Recruiting implementation, including where to find solutions to common problems either online or on the SAP network.

Appendices include an article, *Talent Groups in SAP E-Recruitment Target the Right Candidates*, SAP E-Recruiting Terms, and details on business function HCM_ERC_CI_3.

1.3 Product Releases

Although many of the concepts and configuration elements we discuss apply to all versions of SAP E-Recruiting, this book is based on the latest version of SAP ERP. (At the time of this book's writing, the latest version is SAP ERP 6.0 with enhancement pack 4). All customers using SAP E-Recruiting can benefit from the contents of this book, because the core functionality has not fundamentally changed from its original version. In the appendix, we will also preview the functionality that will be available in enhancement pack 5.

1.4 Summary

This book serves as a comprehensive guide for understanding and implementing the SAP E-Recruiting solution. It highlights important recruitment process constructs and key implementation components and provides best practices for implementation. We hope you enjoy the book.

The recruiting process is dynamic by nature and should be designed to enable a series of activities to take place concurrently with the identification of key activities that determine which candidates move to the next phase of the process.

2 The Process of Recruiting

Recruitment is defined as the process of creating a pool of potential candidates from which a selection process can refine the pool to the right talent to fill vacant positions.

This basic description distills the essence of recruiting for talent, but anyone who has been involved with staffing the right talent for the right role knows that it is an incredibly challenging process to find, identify, and select the right talent.

This chapter presents a view of the recruiting process and various strategies related to parts of the process that require additional focus during blueprinting. Most organizations use the implementation of a recruitment system as an opportunity to refine recruiting strategies and processes.

2.1 Budgeting and Managing Headcount

Organizations start the process at the beginning of the year by planning for the number of resources they need to achieve the company's objectives. This includes accounting for the existing resources in the company and the additional resources that will be hired during the year.

Once this process is completed, departments have a target number of resources for the year. Managers can start planning on hiring for key positions based on when they will be needed and can also plan the associated workload.

2.1.1 Leveraging the SAP System for Tracking Approved Headcount

To enable the recruitment process in SAP E-Recruiting, some companies have opted to leverage SAP positions to represent the approved headcount. The output from the budgeting process is represented in the SAP system by creating vacant positions and setting the vacancy status with a date at which the position can be filled.

Using vacant positions to represent budgeted headcount can also provide the ability to report on potential headcount and the associated costs. Any position that is vacant can now be calculated based on vacancy status and compensation range to determine when those costs may become realized.

The recruiting teams can also leverage the vacant position status to review which positions will need to be filled in the upcoming period. And, recruiters can be more proactive because they are able to meet with managers and/or department heads to put a plan in place for finding and hiring the right talent.

2.1.2 Accounting for Transfers and Terminations

The movement of resources between departments and departures from the company present a dynamic scenario for managers and recruiters.

Many organizations are now linking the process of transfers (which includes promotions, demotions, and lateral moves) and terminations to the recruitment process by moving these actions to Manager Self-Service.

Managers and HR generalists are provided with online forms that enable them to request the transfer or termination of an employee. Each of these forms is enhanced with an indicator that allows the initiator to indicate if the position needs to be closed or filled with a new candidate.

This indicator can now serve as a trigger to change the budgeted headcount through the necessary approval chain and for the recruiters to track new demand for resources.

2.1.3 Requesting Additional Headcount

Organizations deal with incremental headcount in different ways. Once a budget has been approved, the addition of resources is considered unbudgeted and usually requires an approval process based on justification provided by the hiring manager.

The most common process is for managers to open a headcount request form that captures the information related to the position they need to fill, the justification, and the estimated compensation range. This form is usually routed for senior manager approval and then collected by HR for review with senior leadership.

As companies become more cautious about hiring additional resources, they can take a more aggressive approach by requiring that approved headcount be subjected to the same process as requesting additional headcount. This approach enables companies to review the assumptions and current market conditions and allows leaders to make changes to current staffing levels.

Tip

If you are implementing a form or process for handling new headcount requests, consider enhancing the process to optionally accommodate the review of approved headcount.

2.2 Assessing and Preparing Jobs

At the core of the recruiting process are the jobs that a company needs to operate. These jobs provide the framework for the type of skills, responsibilities, and compensation ranges that define positions in the organization.

Jobs are the foundation on which positions are based. Once a position becomes vacant or is newly created, it is to be posted so that it can be filled. Jobs typically go through an annual review process that is designed to ensure that companies are competitive in the marketplace.

2.2.1 Job Pricing

To facilitate recruiting, companies go through a process of creating and managing jobs so that the attributes serve as a basis to create positions. Jobs are also standardized so that they can be compared to similar jobs in the same and across different industries.

The compensation department selects jobs that are key to the organization and submits them to a service that provides comparison data. The data is used to determine how well the company's compensation structure is positioned against competitors and other industries that are looking to hire the same resources.

The process of comparing or pricing jobs against external data allows companies to determine the latest compensation ranges, which are used to create competitive offers to potential employees.

2.2.2 Skills and Qualifications

Part of the process of assessing jobs in an organization includes determining the required skills and qualifications and the competency levels.

This is a critical part of the process because it allows the detailed list of skills and qualifications to be attached to a job and ultimately define each related position. Having the job explicitly defined in the system enables the development of detailed job descriptions, development of questionnaires to filter candidates, and comparison of candidates to determine which candidate is the best fit for the job.

2.3 Recruiting Process

The core recruiting process is very dynamic in that it requires a series of activities to be performed for various candidates at various stages in the process. This dynamic nature of the recruiting process is often underestimated in the blueprinting phase because the team is usually not accustomed to processes that are not linear.

2.3.1 Requisitions

The recruiting process is usually triggered by a request for a position to be filled. Managers can call an HR generalist or in many cases open a requisition form online. The requisition is routed to the manager for approval and depending on the process may go directly to the compensation team for review.

The compensation team reviews the position being requested and determines or verifies the proposed compensation range that will be offered. Having a process step that incorporates the compensation team can reduce rework and provides the recruiter with an idea of how and where to market this position.

Once the requisition is approved, the recruiting team can begin to assess the request. Recruiters often meet with the manager to better understand the requirements, refine the job description, and understand the specifics about the job.

2.3.2 Posting Jobs

The recruiter looks at the type of job that needs to be recruited for and determines the best approach for advertising the job. The recruiter can look at many options including posting the job externally on the company's career site, posting on various job boards, and/or leveraging the talent relationship system to find candidates that previously worked at the company, have expressed interest in working at the company, or have been referred by existing employees.

Certain jobs that are difficult to find candidates for and/or require specific industry experience require a much more aggressive approach. Recruiters may post the job to one or more external recruiters that can find specific candidates.

Certain jobs are also posted internally for employees to consider applying. Many companies choose to post all jobs internally first, which promotes opportunities for employees. This part of the process should be highlighted during blueprinting, because it can present challenges with processing internal candidates.

Advertising jobs and recruiting strategies are also important to many organizations and can determine the success or failure of the recruiting process. It is important to understand and discuss strategies when completing the blueprinting phase to ensure that the implementation covers the requirements.

2.3.3 Processing Candidates

Once the job has been posted, candidates begin to submit applications for consideration. They begin by opening a profile and providing applicable information that includes contact information, skills, previous employment, and their resume. Applications can be submitted by both internal and external candidates.

Candidates can also be asked to complete one or more questionnaires that capture specific information about the candidate and filter out candidates that don't meet the job requirements. For example, companies can embed specific questions that serve as knockout questions.

The recruiter begins to assess the candidates that have applied by filtering and sorting the candidates that meet the criteria for the job. This is a critical part of the process because recruiters can save time by selecting the most qualified candidates to move forward. Once the candidates are selected to move forward, they are contacted and begin to go through the interview and selection process.

2.3.4 Candidate Interview and Selection

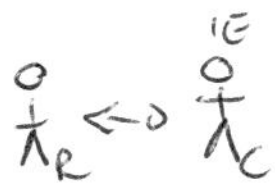

The process of selecting a candidate to hire can vary depending on the job being filled. Depending on the job, the interview process can require several phone screenings by the recruiters, verification of references, and several levels of internal interviews by company employees.

Interviews can also vary depending on the job. For example, some jobs require a peer interview or an interview by a panel of people who must evaluate the candidate.

The recruiter has to manage the process of getting the candidate through the process and requires a robust application that helps track the status of each candidate. The recruiter must also gather feedback from each person in the interview process and coordinate the feedback to determine which candidate will be offered a job or if the search should continue.

Once a candidate is selected to receive an offer, the recruiter kicks off the process of making sure that candidate compliance is part of the process.

2.3.5 Compliance

Compliance is a critical part of the process and is the part of the process that requires as many of the elements to be automated as possible.

The compliance part of the process includes a set of activities designed to verify that the candidate should be hired into the company. Many of the activities are required, but this process can be tailored to specific jobs.

Compliance activities include background checks to verify education, previous employment, and criminal records and can also include drug testing, behavior tests, and health exams.

Once the candidate has completed the compliance activities, he is cleared to receive an offer letter.

2.3.6 Offer to Hire

The offer letter is the last part of the process and is typically generated from the system. Recruiters work with the HR team and the manager to create an offer letter that will be submitted to the employee. Many systems can generate the offer letter based on predefined templates, and HR then edits the letter.

Depending on the job being filled, it is also recommended that you have legal review the offer letter before it is sent to a candidate. This is not always required, but depending on the changes made during negotiation, legal, compensation, and HR should review the letter.

2.4 Summary

With this chapter we have reviewed the recruitment process that many organizations leverage to find, select, and hire the right candidates. It is important to recognize that the recruiting process is not linear in nature and requires that many activities happen concurrently.

The following chapters will provide detailed information on how to leverage SAP E-Recruiting to design the activities that will support your process.

In today's economy, recruiting the right candidate within the allotted recruiting budget has become even more important. At some point, all recruiters have experienced the difficulty of identifying the right candidate for a vacant position. But with SAP E-Recruiting, implementing an efficient recruiting process is possible. With functionalities such as process template, talent pool, and talent relationship management, recruiters can attract the top talent and recruit them for vacant positions in the organization. This chapter explains the basics of SAP E-Recruiting, the new features in enhancement pack 4, and the best practices.

3 SAP E-Recruiting Basics

Recruiting is an important function for many organizations. Recruiters are tasked with the responsibility of filling vacant positions with top talent in the shortest possible time — all within the budget allotted. Recruiters need to network with candidates, keep candidates informed of the vacant positions, and seek referrals. Recruiters also need to target candidates with specific skills for many of the vacant positions.

During an economic boom, recruiters have difficulty finding highly talented candidates; during an economic downturn, recruiters have difficulty finding the right talent in an overcrowded candidate market. This chapter explains the basics of SAP E-Recruiting and how the application supports the full recruiting lifecycle in an organization.

After explaining the basics of the application, we will discuss the data model, the infotypes, and the terminology that are commonly used. We will also consider the implementation requirements and the new features that are available in enhancement pack 4.

Let's start with an overview of SAP E-Recruiting and how you can efficiently use it in the recruiting process.

3.1 SAP E-Recruiting Overview

Organizations spend a large amount of money on recruiting budgets to attract top talent in the marketplace. Implementing SAP E-Recruiting is an example of such an investment. SAP E-Recruiting is a Web-based e-recruiting solution. It provides a suite of tools to create and approve job requisitions, allow recruiters to make job postings and source for candidates, and allow candidates to register and apply for job postings. In SAP E-Recruiting, you can monitor each step in the recruiting process. For example, the recruiter can monitor the status of the candidacy they are working with. The application provides the tools necessary to maintain correspondence with the candidates, thereby enabling an enhanced and efficient talent relationship management platform.

3.2 SAP E-Recruiting Basics

The recruiting lifecycle follows a four-step process from requisition creation through the hiring of the candidate and closure of the requisition. Understanding and managing the recruiting process using the procedures in the four-step process will help your recruiting team and hiring managers effectively manage the recruiting process from end to end. The four-step process consists of the following stages:

- Requisition
- Candidate preselection
- Candidate assessment
- Candidate hiring and requisition closing

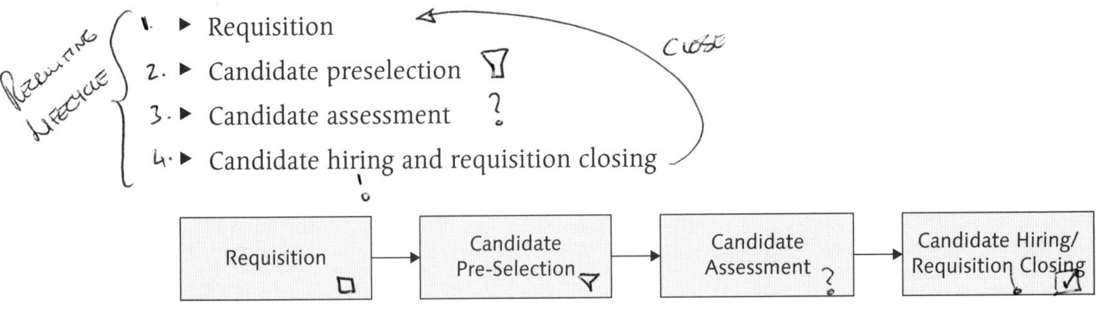

Figure 3.1 Recruiting Lifecyle

Figure 3.1 shows the typical recruiting lifecycle which is fully supported by SAP E-Recruiting. Let's discuss each step in the process, starting with the requisition process.

3.2.1 Requisition

Requisition may be the most important activity in the recruiting process. An approved and released requisition is a prerequisite to a job posting and the publication of the requisition on any job boards. A requisition should be released before a recruiter can start the recruiting process. In anticipation of the requisition, a recruiter can do a preliminary search in the talent warehouse to check if any qualified candidates are available, but the recruiter cannot start recruiting candidates unless a requisition is approved and released for recruiting.

The steps involved in the requisition process are the following:

- Requisition creation
- Requisition approval
- Job posting and publication
- Candidate application

In the requisition process, the main actors are:

- Recruiter
- Hiring manager
- Approver (in many situations, the hiring manager might be the approver.)
- Candidate (after the requisition is approved and posted)

SAP standard delivered roles exist for each of these actors. We will discuss more about standard delivered roles and authorization in Chapter 10, Authorization Management.

For now let's explain the requisition creation process and how SAP E-Recruiting supports the business process.

Requisition Creation

As the first step in the requisition creation, the hiring manager collects the requirements for the position and creates a draft requisition.

Figure 3.2 shows a typical requisition creation process in an organization. As shown in Figure 3.2, the hiring manager can email the draft requisition to the assigned recruiter. The recruiter creates the requisition in the SAP E-Recruiting system.

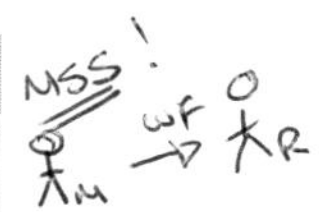

> **Note**
>
> In SAP E-Recruiting EP4, the manager can create the requisition in Manager Self-Service. The recruiter will be informed of the draft requisition on the SAP E-Recruiting system via a workflow. We will discuss more about management involvement in Chapter 4, Requisition Management.

During the requisition creation process, the recruiter might meet the hiring manager for a requisition briefing. During the requisition briefing the support team for the requisition is formed. We will discuss the concept of the support team later in the chapter. The other important topic that needs to be discussed during the requisition briefing is the qualifying questions or the job-related questions. The qualifying questions for a requisition are different from the general questions and the Equal Employment Opportunity (EEO) questions.

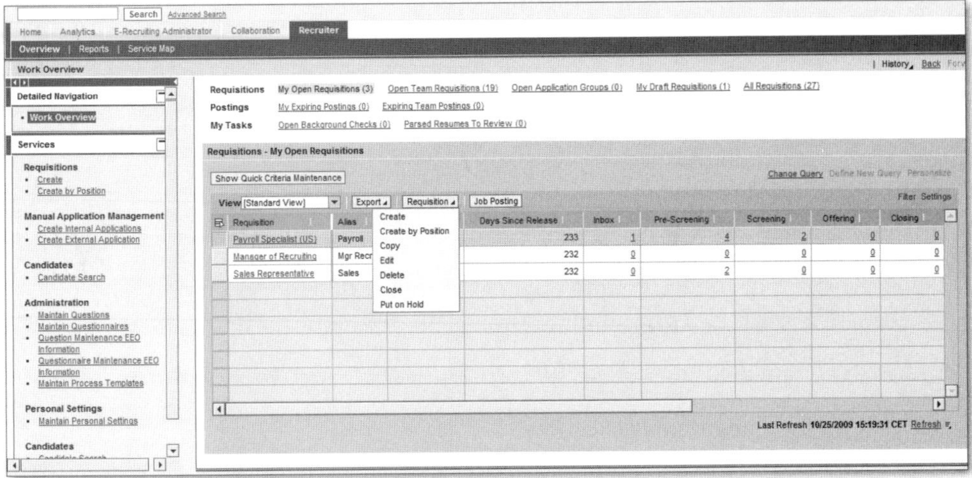

Figure 3.2 Requisition Creation

The qualifying questions form part of the questionnaires that are relevant to the position that the requisition is created to fill. The qualifying questions should be chosen and drafted to attract the most qualified candidates from the talent pool and the job marketplace. The hiring manager can draft the qualifying questions and provide them to the recruiter.

In the SAP E-Recruiting system, the recruiter can create qualifying questions that are related to the position for which the requisition is created and posted. The recruiter can make answering the qualifying questions mandatory, if desired. Based on the responses to the qualifying questions, the candidate can be screened in or screened out. If the candidate's responses to the qualifying questions are not satisfactory (based on the points scored), the SAP E-Recruiting system automatically screens out the candidate.

The recruiter maintains the questions and questionnaires in the recruiter work center. You can customize the different questionnaire groups such as the job-related and candidate-related questionnaires in the IMG. The menu path to configure the questions is IMG • SAP E-RECRUITING • APPLICANT TRACKING • QUESTIONNAIRES.

Figure 3.3 shows the screen in the recruiter work center where the qualifying questions are maintained. The tabs in the screen correspond to the questionnaire groups that you customized in the IMG.

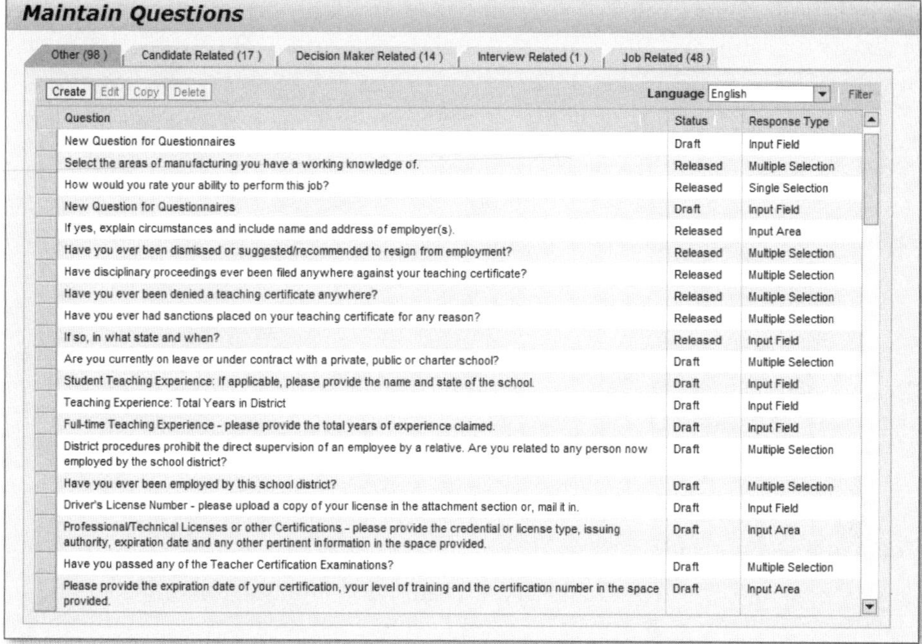

Question	Status	Response Type
New Question for Questionnaires	Draft	Input Field
Select the areas of manufacturing you have a working knowledge of.	Released	Multiple Selection
How would you rate your ability to perform this job?	Released	Single Selection
New Question for Questionnaires	Draft	Input Field
If yes, explain circumstances and include name and address of employer(s).	Released	Input Area
Have you ever been dismissed or suggested/recommended to resign from employment?	Released	Multiple Selection
Have disciplinary proceedings ever been filed anywhere against your teaching certificate?	Released	Multiple Selection
Have you ever been denied a teaching certificate anywhere?	Released	Multiple Selection
Have you ever had sanctions placed on your teaching certificate for any reason?	Released	Multiple Selection
If so, in what state and when?	Released	Input Field
Are you currently on leave or under contract with a private, public or charter school?	Draft	Multiple Selection
Student Teaching Experience: If applicable, please provide the name and state of the school.	Draft	Input Field
Teaching Experience: Total Years in District	Draft	Input Field
Full-time Teaching Experience - please provide the total years of experience claimed.	Draft	Input Field
District procedures prohibit the direct supervision of an employee by a relative. Are you related to any person now employed by the school district?	Draft	Multiple Selection
Have you ever been employed by this school district?	Draft	Multiple Selection
Driver's License Number - please upload a copy of your license in the attachment section or, mail it in.	Draft	Input Field
Professional/Technical Licenses or other Certifications - please provide the credential or license type, issuing authority, expiration date and any other pertinent information in the space provided.	Draft	Input Area
Have you passed any of the Teacher Certification Examinations?	Draft	Multiple Selection
Please provide the expiration date of your certification, your level of training and the certification number in the space provided.	Draft	Input Area

Figure 3.3 Maintain Questions

Assume the recruiter is posting a requisition to fill the position of an SAP ERP Human Capital Management (HCM) functional consultant. One of the prerequisites for the position is a minimum experience of at least two years as an SAP HCM functional consultant. The qualifying question can be something like "How many years of experience do you have as an SAP ERP HCM consultant?" The candidate is asked to pick from possible responses such as:

A. 1-2 years experience

B. 2-5 years experience

C. More than 5 years experience

If the candidate chooses response A, SAP E-Recruiting may determine the candidate to be "not qualified," and the candidate is screened out of the application process. The candidate can still continue to respond to the remaining questions and complete the online application. At the backend, SAP E-Recruiting identifies this candidate as "not qualified" based on the candidate's response to the qualifying question.

On the frontend, the candidate will not be aware of this screening-out process. By creating qualifying questions for a requisition, the recruiter is able to attract qualified candidates for the requisition.

The recruiter can also maintain a template of the qualifying questions. One of the easier ways to develop the qualifying questions is to do a profile match between the position and the qualification catalog. By doing a profile match, the recruiter gains a better understanding of the requirements for the position. Additional job-related questions can be developed after consulting the hiring manager.

Note

If your SAP E-Recruiting system is integrated with your SAP ERP HCM system, a current organizational structure is important. In SAP E-Recruiting 604, you can create the job requisition for the vacant position directly from your organization structure.

Requisition Approval

Once the recruiter has created the requisition in the SAP E-Recruiting system, it is typically sent to the hiring manager for the requisition approvals. The hiring manager can approve the requisition or suggest changes to the requisition. On approval of the requisition, the recruiter creates the job posting and identifies the publication channels where the job posting can be published.

If the requisition is being created for a vacancy in a future line of business, ensure that the vacancy is properly budgeted. In many organizations, the requisition process involves the requisition being approved by the compensation team. This process called the *requisition leveling* and usually involves a compensation analyst reviewing the requisition and ensuring that the salary offered for the position is within the range offered for that position (or job) in the organization. If the requisition is for a position in a new line of business, the compensation analyst might refer to the organization job pricing prior to the requisition approvals.

Currently, there is no integration between SAP E-Recruiting and SAP Enterprise Compensation Management (ECM). The requisition leveling is done outside the SAP system. The recruiter emails the draft requisition to the compensation analyst for approvals.

After receiving the approvals from the compensation analyst, the recruiter creates the requisition in the system. In SAP E-Recruiting enhancement package 4, the requisition can be created either by the recruiter or by the hiring manager. The recruiter can create the requisition by logging into the recruiter work center. The hiring manager can create the requisition directly from the Manager Self-Service capability on the SAP Portal.

Job Posting and Publication

As shown in Figure 3.4, the recruiter, in consultation with the hiring manager, decides on the publication channels and the time duration the posting needs to be active.

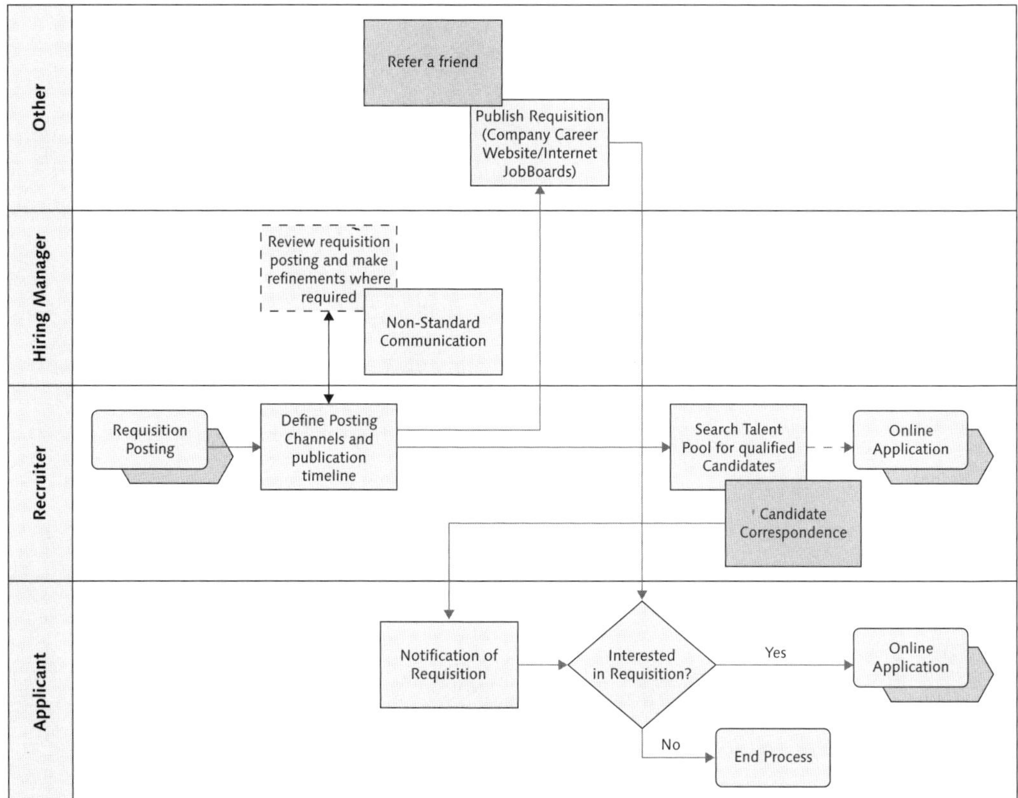

Figure 3.4 Job Posting Channels

The *publication channels* in SAP E-Recruiting are external job boards and internal career websites in the portal in which the recruiter chooses to publish the requisition. A recruiter might decide to publish the requisition in all of the job boards the recruiter has access to or might decide to publish the requisition in a certain job board based on past experience in attracting the right candidate in the shortest possible time.

Note

Web 2.0 websites such as Facebook and LinkedIn are very popular with recruiters targeting candidates and seeking referrals. SAP E-Recruiting currently does not offer integration with any of the Web 2.0 websites.

Simultaneously, the recruiter might do a search in the talent pool to identify any potential external or internal candidates. The recruiter might send communication about the requisition to the qualified candidates in the talent pool. The recruiter might invite the qualified candidate to apply for the position. If the candidate is not available or is not interested, the recruiter might seek referrals of friends who might be qualified and interested in the job opportunity.

The recruiter can create the job posting text and publish the job posting to the different publication channels from the recruiter work center. We will explain more about the requisition creation and the requisition posting in Chapter 4, Requisition Management.

Candidate Application

As shown in Figure 3.5, the candidate registers in the talent warehouse. As a registered candidate, he starts the application process for the requisition. The candidate answers the qualifying questions for the requisition and completes the online application.

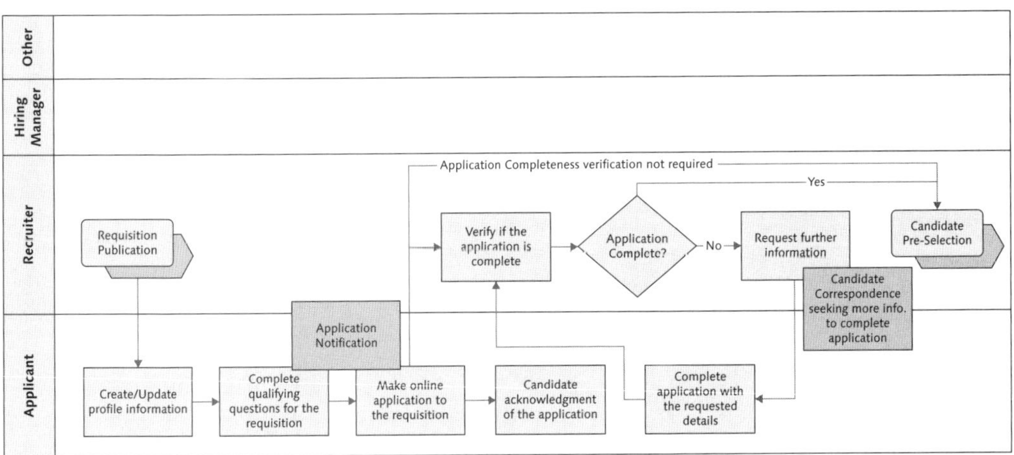

Figure 3.5 Candidate Application

In SAP E-Recruiting, you can configure whether or not the candidate receives an acknowledgment that the recruiter has received his application. The candidate acknowledgment letter can be configured to mention the requisition number and the recruiter's contact details. By mentioning the recruiter's name and contact details, the candidate can touch base with the recruiter to follow up on the application at any time during the process.

On receipt of the application, the recruiter can verify if the application has all of the required details. If any details are missing from the job application, the recruiter can speak to the candidate to get the additional details.

You can configure SAP E-Recruiting to allow registered and unregistered candidates to apply to a job requisition. Many organizations prefer to have candidates register in the talent pool prior to applying to a requisition. This is primarily done to build the talent pool and maintain talent relationship management. Some organizations allow registered and unregistered candidates to apply for requisitions. In the candidate acknowledgment letter, the company may encourage the unregistered candidate to register in the talent pool and to search for all open positions in the organization.

If a candidate is registered in the talent pool, the candidate can receive periodic communications from the company, for example, an invitation to a job fair. Registered candidates can also set up job agents to receive periodic notification of open positions that match the candidate's interests and qualifications.

The talent pool is a collection of all candidates available to recruiters who have the required authorization to access the talent pool. The recruiting administrator creates and maintains the talent groups.

Note

We will explain about the talent pool in detail in Chapter 5 when we discuss candidate management.

3.2.2 Candidate Pre-selection

Figure 3.6 shows the process for candidate pre-selection and screening. Your organization's business process for candidate pre-selection might vary from what is depicted in this figure.

As shown in Figure 3.6, the recruiter reviews the candidate ranking generated by the SAP E-Recruiting system. The recruiter may do a candidate pre-selection by conducting telephone prescreening with the candidate. The recruiter can further rank the candidate manually based on the conversation with the candidate; this new ranking is based on the recruiter's understanding of the candidate's qualifications, interest in the position, and willingness to join the organization if a job offer is made.

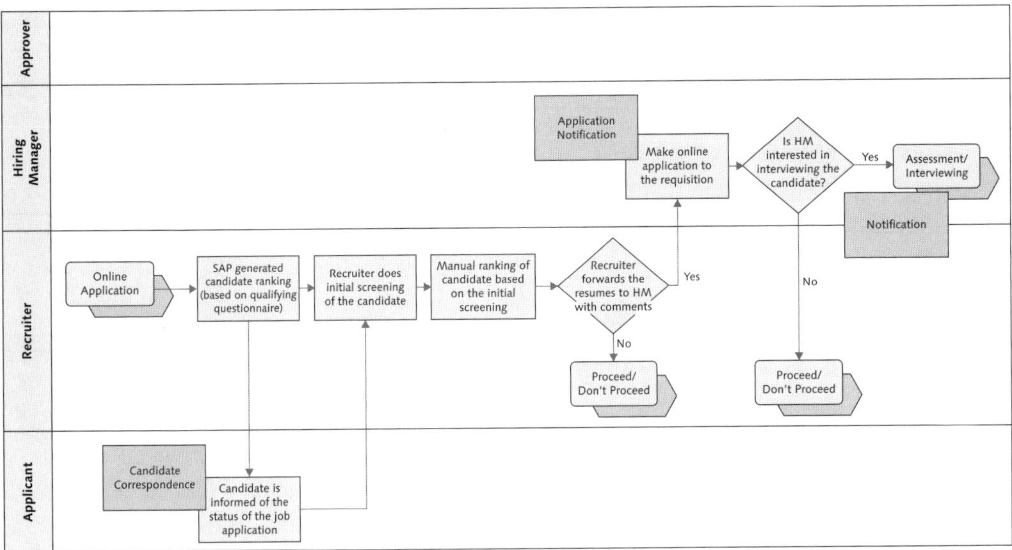

Figure 3.6 Candidate Pre-selection

If the recruiter is interested, he might review the applications that were received for the requisition but were not ranked high by SAP E-Recruiting. It is always a good idea to scan these applications because the recruiter may come across some resumes that might be interesting. The recruiter can conduct a pre-selection on such candidates by calling them and getting more details. Many recruiters have found this practice to be very helpful.

Depending on the requisition and your organization's best practices, the recruiter can use several criteria to manually rank these candidates. Some of the criteria can be:

- Educational qualification
- International experience
- Competitive edge

After manually ranking the candidate, the recruiter might set up a pre-selection telephone screening.

You can configure SAP E-Recruiting to send a notification to the candidate for a pre-selection screening. The candidate notification can include details such the requisition number, the position title, and the pre-selection screening being requested. The recruiter can include any other information that might be relevant to the requisition. In the notification, the recruiter can request a suitable date and time to discuss more about the opportunity.

With SAP E-Recruiting enhancement pack 4, the recruiter can create notes about the candidate as well. This is a very useful feature, especially during the pre-selection process. The recruiter can enter details such as any additional qualifications and work experience that may not be highlighted in the resume. These notes can also be made available to members of the requisition's support team.

Figure 3.7 shows the screen of the Notes feature in SAP E-Recruiting. You create additional notes by clicking on the Add button.

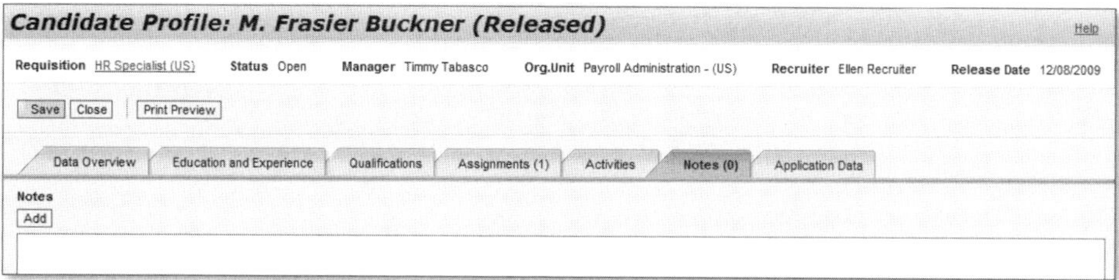

Figure 3.7 Notes Functionality

The recruiter forwards the resumes and the candidates' profiles to the hiring manager with his comments. The hiring manager reviews the resumes and the candidacy profiles and identifies the candidates to be short-listed. These candidates may be called for a job interview and be subject to further assessment. From SAP E-Recruiting, you can send notification to the short-listed candidate about the next steps in the job selection process.

Note

We have noticed organizations using psychometric tests for further assessment of candidates. SAP E-Recruiting currently does not provide vendor services or integration with any psychometric test provider. If you are interested in integrating SAP E-Recruiting with a psychometric test vendor, you will need custom development.

> The workaround to the custom development would be to conduct the psychometric test outside SAP E-Recruiting. You could then upload the results of the test to the system as an attachment to the candidate profile.
>
> SAP is planning to provide integration to a psychometric test vendor in a future release of SAP E-Recruiting.

After the recruiter receives comments from the hiring manager about the candidates to be called for assessment, the recruiter typically sets up a date and time with the candidate for a candidate assessment.

3.2.3 Candidate Assessment

The candidate assessment is an important phase in the recruiting process. The recruiter has to plan for the interview with the hiring manager and other staff who might be involved in the interviewing process. If the candidate is to be brought onsite for an in-person interview, further planning may be required to coordinate the candidate's travel plans.

> **Note**
>
> SAP E-Recruiting does not provide integration with MS Office for calendar scheduling. If you are interested in integrating SAP E-Recruiting with MS Office, you can consider implementing a solution using Duet® (*www.duet.com*).
>
> Duet is a solution jointly developed and marketed by SAP and Microsoft. Duet provides seamless integration with SAP E-Recruiting and MS Office.

As shown in Figure 3.8, the recruiter coordinates with the hiring manager and the candidate to schedule an interview. The interview schedule is done via a telephone conversation and email correspondence.

For situations like these, the recruiter can capture these correspondences as notes in SAP E-Recruiting. The hiring manager and interview team conduct the candidate assessment and provide the interview feedback to the recruiter and to the support team. The feedback from the hiring manager and the other staff who have interviewed the candidate can be captured and retained as notes in the system. This feedback becomes more important during the consensus meeting — when the support team meets to make decisions on the candidate who interviewed for the position.

The recruiter might also enter his feedback as notes in the candidacy profile.

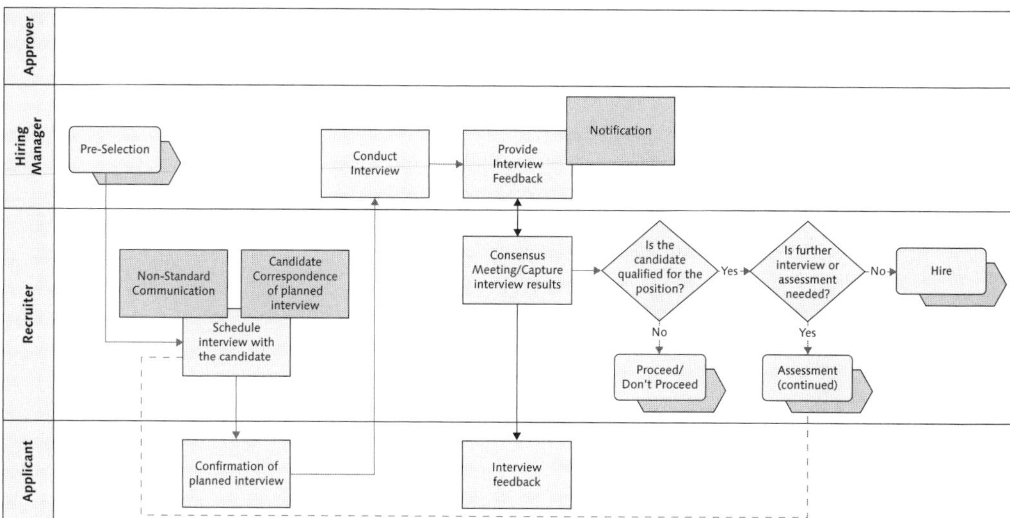

Figure 3.8 Candidate Assessment and Job Interview

Such notes might also help other recruiters know more about the candidate, including the candidate's strengths and weaknesses and how the candidate could possibly be better suited for other positions in the company.

Based on the interview feedback from the hiring manager, the recruiter can speak to the candidate about the job offer if a green light is given to move forward with the candidate. The recruiter also can make decisions about the unsuccessful candidates if these candidates should be retained in the talent pool and considered for future job openings.

Note

It is a best practice for the recruiter (not the manager) to inform the candidate about the status of the interview. The recruiter can have this conversation by telephone.

The recruiter should always encourage candidates to continue to search for job openings in the talent pool. As a follow-up to the telephone conversation, the recruiter can send a standard correspondence from SAP E-Recruiting. In that correspondence, the recruiter can mention any upcoming job fairs and company recruiting events. Also, the recruiter should encourage candidates to provide referrals.

Such talent relationship management activities are very important to attract top talent in the organization. As part of talent relationship management, the recruiter can even create a talent group called "Candidates Interviewed," for example. Because the recruiter knows the candidates' strengths, he can better position such candidates with the hiring manager for future openings.

3.2.4 Candidate Hiring and Requisition Closing

Figure 3.9 shows the process for candidate hire. After a candidate has been identified as the most suitable for a position, the recruiter typically speaks to the successful candidate and initiates the discussion about the job offer. After the candidate accepts the verbal offer made by the recruiter, the recruiter generates the offer packet from the SAP E-Recruiting system. The "extend offer" is an activity type that can be configured in the SAP E-Recruiting and is a simple correspondence. (We will explain correspondences in detail in later chapters).

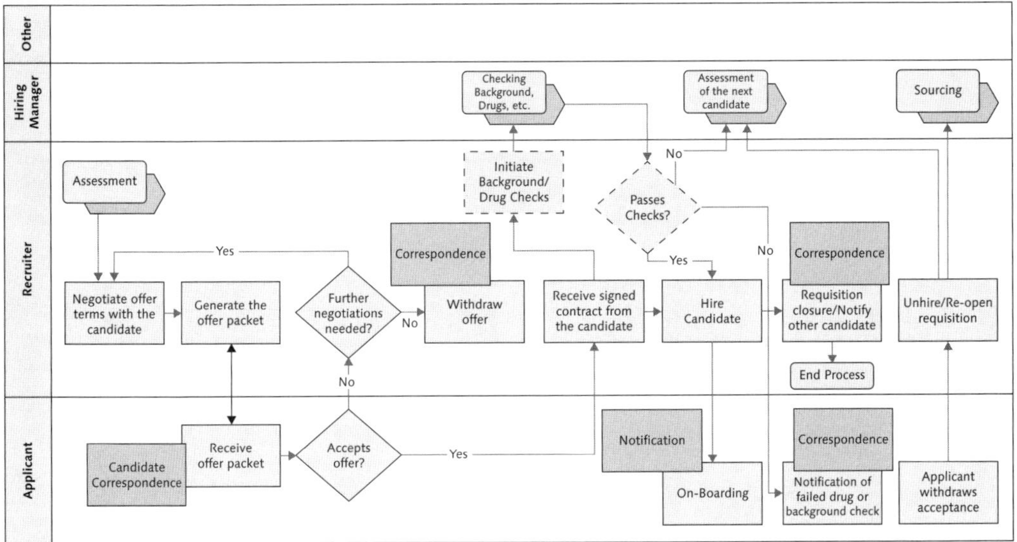

Figure 3.9 Candidate Hire

After the recruiter receives the offer acceptance from the candidate, the recruiter typically initiates a background check and/or drug test. While it is a best practice to initiate these tests only after offer acceptance, under certain circumstances, these tests can be initiated prior to receiving the offer acceptance from the candidate. In enhancement pack 4, SAP E-Recruiting offers vendors' services where the system can be integrated to the vendor providing background checks and drug tests. We will discuss more about these services in Chapter 9, Vendor Services.

If no negative results are received from the background checks and the drug tests, the recruiter initiates the on-boarding process. As part of the on-boarding process, the candidate details are transferred to the SAP ERP HCM system and queued for the hiring action. Use Transaction code PA48 to transfer data from SAP E-Recruiting to SAP ERP HCM. To initiate the PA48 action, an RFC connection should exist between the SAP E-Recruiting and SAP ERP HCM systems. (This assumes that your E-Recruiting system and SAP ERP HCM system are on two separate systems. We will discuss single-instance and dual-instance set-up later).

Note

During the pre-selection process, it is a common practice for the recruiter to discuss with the candidate both the salary expectations and the benefits offered. The candidate will likely try to renegotiate the salary. Another challenge the recruiter might face during the hiring process is when the candidate suddenly becomes unavailable either because he had decided to continue in his current job or because he has accepted an offer from another organization.

When a candidate becomes unavailable or withdraws the offer acceptance, the recruiter can work with the hiring manager to identify the next "best" candidate from the list of candidates who were interviewed for the position. If the hiring manager is not interested in any other candidates, the recruiter may need to repost the requisition (assuming the requisition posting is retired) and continue sourcing for suitable candidates. The process is similar if the organization rescinds the job offer owing to a failed drug test or background check.

After the candidate is entered as an employee in the SAP ERP HCM system, the recruiter closes the requisition. Concurrent to the hiring process, the recruiter makes decisions about the unsuccessful candidates, how these candidates should be positioned for future requirements, and talent relationship management activities, if desired.

3.2.5 Proceed/Don't Proceed

Figure 3.10 shows the process via which the recruiter decides about a candidate who is unsuccessful during the interview process for an open position. As shown in this process flow, if the candidate has received good feedback from the hiring manager during the interview process, the recruiter might make a "proceed" decision and continue to consider the candidate for other open positions. The invite to apply is a simple correspondence that is configured as an activity type in the system.

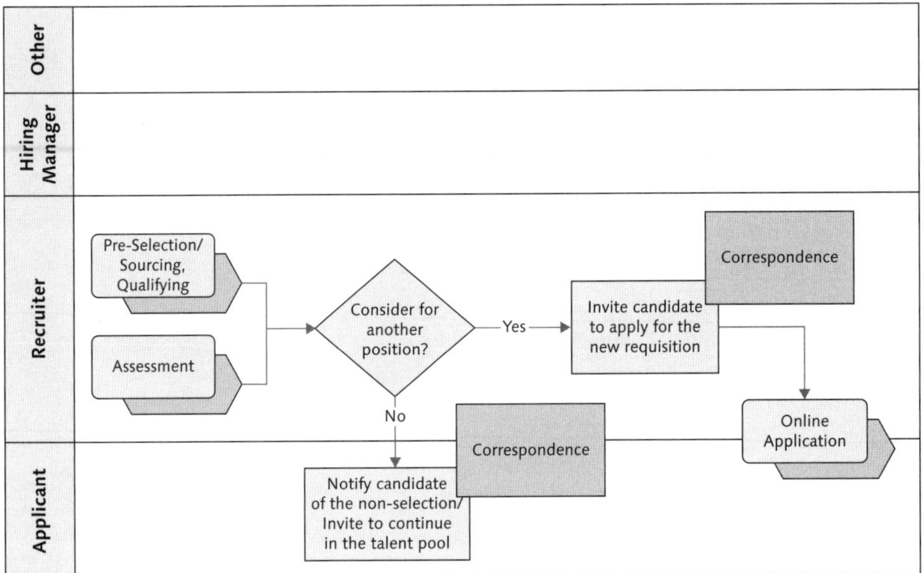

Figure 3.10 Proceed/Don't Proceed

The recruiter might decide not to proceed with the particular candidate with any of the open requisitions on which he is currently working. In such circumstances, the recruiter might send the candidate a simple correspondence inviting the candidate to continue to search for open positions and to continue in the talent pool.

You should now have a high-level understanding of how you can implement SAP E-Recruiting to meet your organizations' recruiting needs. In the next section, we will explain the data model to get a deeper understanding of the different objects, their associated infotypes, and how the objects are related to each other.

3.3 SAP E-Recruiting Data Model

SAP E-Recruiting uses objects, relationships, and infotypes to deliver a robust data model.

In EP4, SAP introduced Support Group (Object type NG) as a new object. In Figure 3.11, you can see the infotypes associated with each of the objects. In the following sections, we will explain about the different objects in SAP E-Recruiting, the infotypes associated with these objects, and the SAP standard delivered roles.

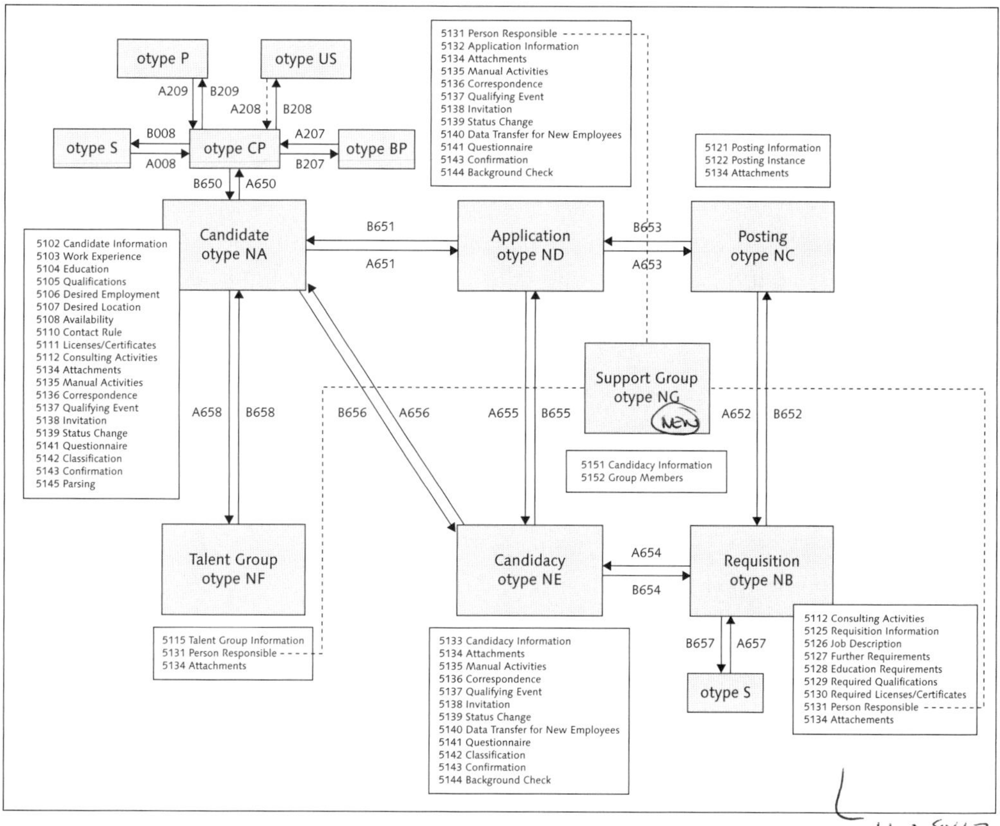

Figure 3.11 SAP E-Recruiting Data Model

3.3.1 Candidate

A candidate is any person who registers in the organization's talent warehouse. This person is interested in joining the organization as an employee and is currently searching for open positions for which he can apply. SAP E-Recruiting creates a Candidate object (Object type NA) when any of the following happens:

- The person registers in the talent warehouse.
- The person applies to a job posting.
- The person applies to a job posting by mail.

Then on behalf of the applicant, the recruiter could enter the application in the SAP E-Recruiting system. The recruiter might also register the applicant in the talent warehouse. (Even if the recruiter does not register the applicant in the talent warehouse, the system would automatically create the candidate).

In SAP E-Recruiting, the candidate is classified as either an internal candidate or an external candidate. The internal candidate is a person who is currently an employee of the organization. The SAP E-Recruiting system can be configured so that internal candidates need not register in the talent warehouse. The internal candidate's data can be automatically transferred from the SAP ERP HCM system to the SAP E-Recruiting system.

- If SAP ERP HCM and SAP E-Recruiting are on two different systems, the data is transferred from SAP ERP HCM to SAP E-Recruiting by application link enabling (ALE). The employee then already exists as an internal user in E-Recruiting.
- If SAP ERP HCM and SAP E-Recruiting are on the same system, the system uses the method CONV_HR_DATA_TO_EREC to create a candidate for each employee. The employee's data from the following infotypes are then transferred to SAP E-Recruiting:
  - 0000 (Actions)
  - 0001 (Organizational Assignment)
  - 0002 (Personal Data)
  - 0006 (Addresses)
  - 0105 (Communication)
  - 1001 (Relationships) including qualifications (Q object)

The data is stored in the infotypes for the candidate object.

Figure 3.12 shows the IMG path used to configure the candidate object in SAP E-Recruiting.

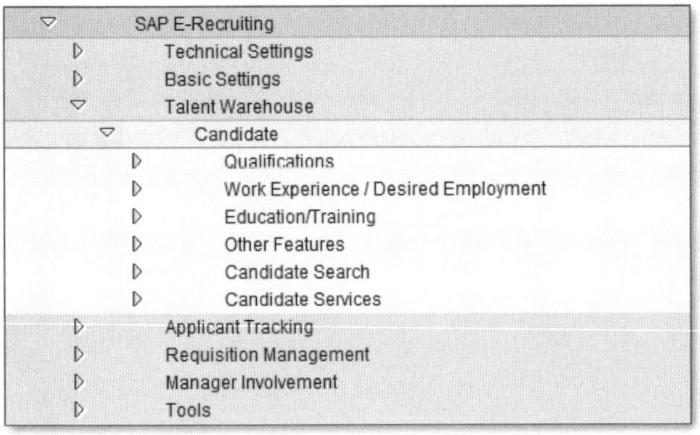

- SAP E-Recruiting
  - Technical Settings
  - Basic Settings
  - Talent Warehouse
    - Candidate
      - Qualifications
      - Work Experience / Desired Employment
      - Education/Training
      - Other Features
      - Candidate Search
      - Candidate Services
  - Applicant Tracking
  - Requisition Management
  - Manager Involvement
  - Tools

Figure 3.12 Configuring the Candidate Object in the IMG

The candidate object has the following structure:

- **Personal data**
  First name, last name, date of birth, and any other personal data
- **Communication data**
  Mailing address, telephone numbers, and email address

Note

Many organizations use a combination of the candidate's last name and the email address to identify if the candidate is present or registered in the talent warehouse. However, some public sector organizations do not use the email address as the unique identifier. In such circumstances, you can use the candidate's date of birth or mother's maiden name as the unique identifier.

- **Work experience**
  The candidate's past and current work experience
- **Qualifications**
  The candidate's qualifications and/or competencies (the candidate can also be required to rate each qualification)
- **Attachments**
  Documents such as the resume, references, and certificates

In SAP E-Recruiting, you can configure valid attachments that are permitted for your implementation. The IMG path used to configure the attachments is IMG • SAP E-Recruiting • Basic Settings • Attachment Types.

Figure 3.13 shows the list of attachments that are configured in the system. Providing valid attachment types is helpful because it will discourage candidates from uploading attachments that are not useful for the requisition or candidate assessment. After you have configured the attachment types, you can assign them to the SAP E-Recruiting objects such as Candidate (NA), Requisition (NB), Posting (NC), Application (ND), and Talent Group (NF).

You perform the customizing in the IMG under the menu path SAP E-Recruiting • Basic Settings • Attachment Types • Determine Use Of Attachment Types.

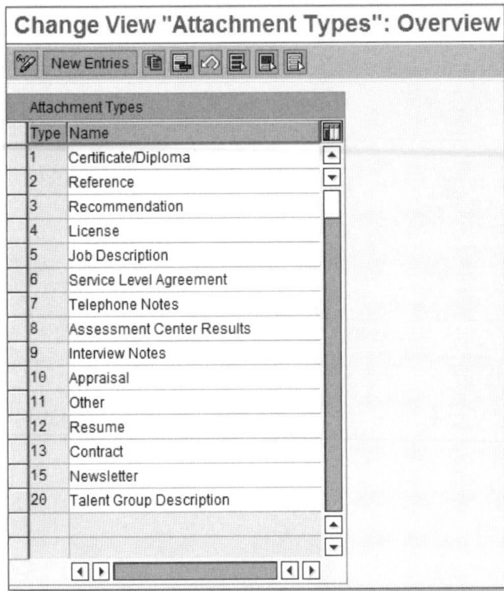

Type	Name
1	Certificate/Diploma
2	Reference
3	Recommendation
4	License
5	Job Description
6	Service Level Agreement
7	Telephone Notes
8	Assessment Center Results
9	Interview Notes
10	Appraisal
11	Other
12	Resume
13	Contract
15	Newsletter
20	Talent Group Description

Figure 3.13 List of Attachments

After you have completed the customizing steps, Define Attachment Types and Determine Use of Attachment Types, you can define the attachment type that indicates the resume that candidates upload and the attachment types the resume parsing vendors use to upload the formatted resumes. You perform this customizing in the IMG under the menu path SAP E-RECRUITING • BASIC SETTINGS • ATTACHMENT TYPES • IDENTIFY ATTACHMENT TYPE AS RESUME. The table here contains all attachment types that can be assigned to the attachment subtype resume for the SAP E-Recruiting object Candidate (NA).

If you want to have a request form on the requisition, you should define the attachment type. As a prerequisite you should have completed the customizing steps DEFINE ATTACHMENT TYPES • DETERMINE USE OF ATTACHMENT TYPES and have assigned this attachment type to the attachment subtype Requisition Management for the SAP E-Recruiting object requisition (NB). This customizing is performed in the IMG under the menu path IMG • SAP E-RECRUITING • BASIC SETTINGS • ATTACHMENT TYPES • IDENTIFY ATTACHMENT TYPE AS REQUEST FORM.

In the data overview for the requisition, you might not want all attachments to be visible and accessible by everyone in the process. In SAP E-Recruiting, the default is that all attachments are visible and can be viewed by all users. You can implement and activate the BAdI HRRCF00_DATAOVR_ATTACHMENTS to restrict the view of the links and the attachments in the data overview.

Other data stored on the Candidate object include:

- **Desired job**
  Data such as whether the candidate is looking for a full time job, part time job, internship, and so on.
- **Work location**
  If your organization has branches, the candidate can specify his location preferences.
- **Profile release**
  After the candidate has registered in the talent warehouse, he has to release his profile. If the candidate wants to keep his profile private, he will not be visible to the recruiter when the recruiter does a search in the talent pool.

> **Note**
>
> Work location is very important data to capture. If your organization is trying to fill a position in a location that does not attract lots of applications, the recruiter can use this data to track candidates who might be interested in working in that particular location. Work location can also be used to track candidates who might be interested in overseas assignments or are open to relocation.

As shown in the data model, the Candidate object (type NA) has a relationship to the following objects:

- **Application (object type ND)**
  A candidate can be linked to multiple applications.
- **Candidacy (object type NE)**
  When a candidate is related to a requisition, a Candidacy object is created in the system. The candidate can be linked to multiple candidacies.
- **Business partner (object type BP)**
  Data such as the candidate's name is linked to the Business Partner object.
- **Talent group (object type TF)**
  A candidate can be linked (assigned) to one or more talent groups. A candidate can exist in the talent warehouse and not be assigned to any talent group. The recruiter manually assigns a candidate to a talent group. A candidate can be present in one or more talent groups simultaneously.

3.3.2 Requisition

The requisition is a document giving requirements of and details about the position the organization is planning to fill. The assigned recruiter creates the requisition in

SAP E-Recruiting in consultation with the hiring manager. SAP E-Recruiting creates the requisition object (object type NB) when any of the following happens:

- A requisition is created for internal posting, where only employees can apply.
- A requisition is created for external posting, where only ex-employees or external candidates can apply.
- A requisition is created for internal and external posting, where both employees and external candidates can apply.

A requisition can be created to fill one vacant position or multiple vacant positions.

Figure 3.14 displays the Recruiter Work Center the recruiter uses to create requisitions. We will discuss more about the process of creating requisitions in SAP E-Recruiting in Chapter 4, Requisition Management.

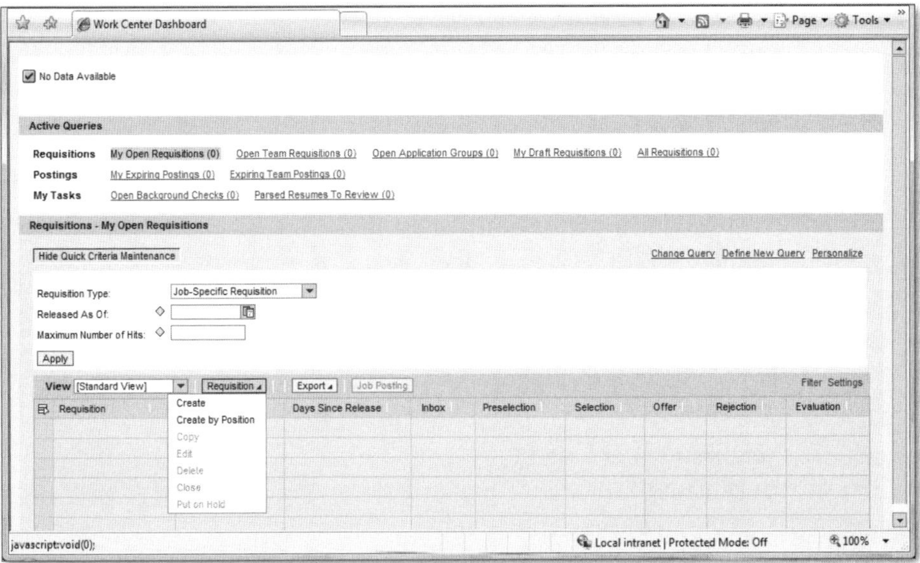

Figure 3.14 Recruiter Work Center

The requisition object has the following structure:

- **General information area**
    - **Requisition title and alias**
      This defines the title and short name of the requisition. A suggested best practice is to choose a title to reflect the position that the organization is planning to fill. The recruiter can use the alias as an internal naming convention.

- **Interest group**
  When the candidate is registering in the talent warehouse, he is asked to indicate his interest group. You configure interest groups under the IMG path SAP E-Recruiting • Talent Warehouse • Candidate • Other Features • Define interest groups.

> **Note**
>
> Interest groups are different from talent groups. Recruiters maintain talent groups to segment the talent profiles available in the talent warehouse. Talent groups are very dynamic; they reflect the recruiting requirements of the organization. Candidates can be assigned and removed from talent groups.
>
> Interest groups, however, are available to candidates to indicate their areas of interest. An example of an interest group is executive-level positions, R&D, finance, accounting, and so on. While creating requisitions, you can assign an interest group to a requisition.

- **Application close**
  This denotes the last date to receive the application. The application close and the last date of the posting should be the same. If the requisition is available in the posting channels well past the application close date, the candidates would still be able to apply to the requisition. Therefore, the application close date and the last date of the posting should be same.
- **Hiring manager**
  The name of the manager for whom the requisition is created. The hiring manager is typically an employee of the organization.
- **Recruiter**
  The recruiter assigned to work on the requisition.
- **Process template**
  Every requisition should have a process template assigned to it. The process template contains the processes and the activities required for this requisition.
- **Job details**
  Details about the position.
- **Payment information**
  This indicates how much the position pays. The recruiter can also mention the minimum and maximum ranges.
- **Positions and organizations units**
  This gives details about the organizational unit and the vacant position the requisition is trying to fill.

- **Account assignment**
  This is for information only. Currently, SAP E-Recruiting does not offer any integration with SAP ERP Financial Accounting for cost center posting.
- **Attachments**
  Any additional details the recruiter would like to provide regarding the requisition.

- **Requirements Area**
  - **Education requirements**
    The requisition document displays the education requirements for the position. If the position requires a PhD in a particular subject or field of study, it should be mentioned here.
  - **Qualifications**
    This indicates all of the qualifications that are required for the position. It is best practice that the qualifications catalog (Q object) be updated to reflect the requirements of all of the positions in the organization. The qualifications mentioned in the requisition document should be similar to the requirements mentioned for the position in the qualifications catalog.
  - **Questionnaires**
    This contains the qualifying and the general questionnaires for this position. The questionnaires are made available in the application wizard.
  - **Support team**
    This defines employees on the requisition's support team. An employee must be a member of the support team to work on the requisition.
  - **Print preview**
    This provides a data overview of the requisition.

Figure 3.15 displays the data overview of the requisition. An attachment to the requisition outlines the recruiting strategy for the requisition. This attachment is displayed in the requisition as a URL. You can implement the BAdI HRRCF00_DOC_UPLOAD to run a virus check of the attachments, check size of the attachments, and so on.

- **Status**
  The following are the valid and standard delivered statuses: Draft, Released, Closed, To Be Deleted, and On Hold.

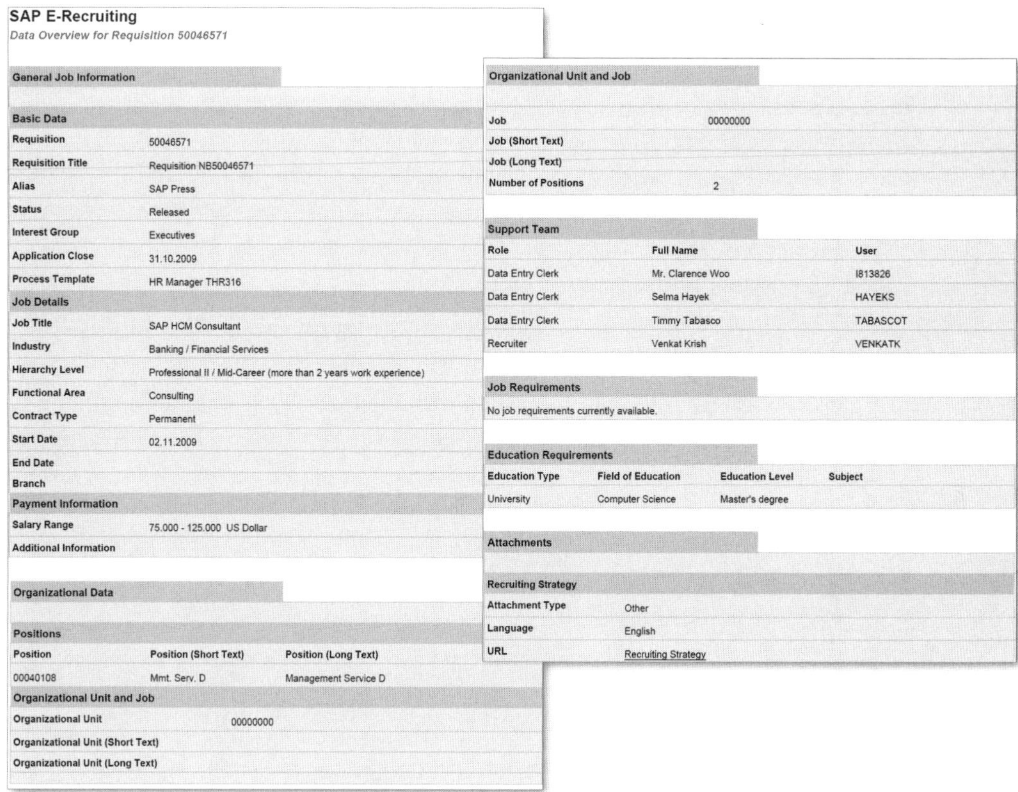

SAP E-Recruiting

Data Overview for Requisition 50046571

General Job Information

Basic Data

Requisition	50046571
Requisition Title	Requisition NB50046571
Alias	SAP Press
Status	Released
Interest Group	Executives
Application Close	31.10.2009
Process Template	HR Manager THR316

Job Details

Job Title	SAP HCM Consultant
Industry	Banking / Financial Services
Hierarchy Level	Professional II / Mid-Career (more than 2 years work experience)
Functional Area	Consulting
Contract Type	Permanent
Start Date	02.11.2009
End Date	
Branch	

Payment Information

Salary Range	75.000 - 125.000 US Dollar
Additional Information	

Organizational Data

Positions

Position	Position (Short Text)	Position (Long Text)
00040108	Mmt. Serv. D	Management Service D

Organizational Unit and Job

Organizational Unit	00000000
Organizational Unit (Short Text)	
Organizational Unit (Long Text)	

Organizational Unit and Job

Job	00000000
Job (Short Text)	
Job (Long Text)	
Number of Positions	2

Support Team

Role	Full Name	User
Data Entry Clerk	Mr. Clarence Woo	I813826
Data Entry Clerk	Selma Hayek	HAYEKS
Data Entry Clerk	Timmy Tabasco	TABASCOT
Recruiter	Venkat Krish	VENKATK

Job Requirements

No job requirements currently available.

Education Requirements

Education Type	Field of Education	Education Level	Subject
University	Computer Science	Master's degree	

Attachments

Recruiting Strategy

Attachment Type	Other
Language	English
URL	Recruiting Strategy

Figure 3.15 Data Overview of a Requisition

As shown in the data model, the requisition (object type NB) has a relationship to the following objects:

- **Job posting (object type NC)**
  A requisition is related to multiple job postings. A job posting is always based on a requisition.
- **Candidacy (object type NE)**
  A candidacy can be related to multiple requisitions. A requisition can be related to multiple requisitions.

3.3.3 Job Posting

Once a requisition is created, it has to be communicated to job seekers. Job posting is the communication mechanism of the requisition. A job posting is always associated with a requisition. The job posting can be configured for internal and external posting channels.

We suggest that you customize job postings for internal and external posting channels. For example, with internal postings, you might want to include additional details such as "discuss with your current manager prior to applying for this requisition." In an internal posting, recruiters can request employees to refer their friends for the requisition. If your organization has a referral policy, employees can be paid for successful referrals.

You can customize the posting channels in the IMG. The path to configure the posting channels is SAP E-RECRUITING • REQUISITION MANAGEMENT • JOB POSTING • DEFINE POSTING CHANNELS. As shown in Figure 3.16, if you define the posting channels, you must assign an ABAP class to the channel. This ABAP class is required for the publication and the withdrawal of the job posting. It must implement the publisher class IF_HRRCF_PUBLISHER.

Change View "Posting Channels": Overview

New Entries

Posting Channels

Chanl	Name	Publisher Class	Cand.Class	Identific
1	For Internal Candidates	CL_HRRCF_PUBLISHER_INT	I Interna	
2	For External Candidates	CL_HRRCF_PUBLISHER_EXT	E Externa	
6000	Application Groups	CL_HRRCF_PUBLISHER_EXT_U	E Externa	
6001	Application Groups	CL_HRRCF_PUBLISHER_INT_U	I Interna	
9000	JobViper	ZCL_HRRCF_PUBLISHER_JOBVIPER	E Externa	

Figure 3.16 Customizing the Posting Channels in the IMG

The job posting object (object type NC) has the following structure:

- **General posting information**
  Any information the recruiter wants to share with the candidate. The recruiter can include details about the organization, the work location, and advantages to working for the organization. When a candidate does a search in the Internet job board, one of the search criteria might be the work location. (If the position is in a location not mentioned in the Internet job board, mention the closest city as the job location).
- **Posting texts**
  Details on the position such as job requirements, qualifications, experience, tasks, and responsibilities. A candidate gathers details about the requisition from the posting text.

Note

A job posting can be published only if it is associated with a requisition and the requisition is in Released status. The posting text needs to be saved prior to the publication of the job posting.

Figure 3.17 displays the data overview of the posting text. This posting text is published in the different publication channels. You can create one posting text for internal publication and a different posting text for external publication.

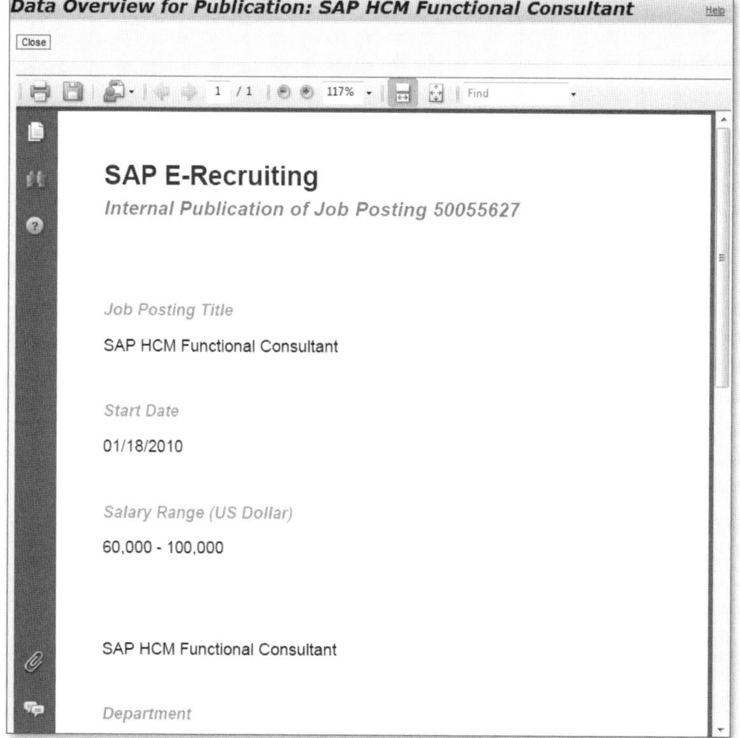

Figure 3.17 Data Overview of the Job Posting

As seen in the data model, the Job Posting (object type NC) has a relationship to the following objects:

- **Requisition (object type NB)**
  A job posting is always related to a requisition.
- **Publication**
  One or many publications can be assigned to a job posting.

3.3.4 Candidacy

When a candidate applies to a requisition, the system creates a candidacy object. A Candidacy object (object type NE) is created in any of the following scenarios:

- A candidate applies online to a requisition. The system creates a candidacy object when the candidate completes the online application.
- A recruiter creates an online application for a paper resume she might have received.
- A recruiter includes the candidate in the Favorites list of a requisition.
- Based on the candidate's qualifications, the recruiter assigns the candidate to open requisitions. SAP E-Recruiting creates a candidacy for these assignments.

Many of the activities that are performed on a candidate object are created for the candidacy by the SAP E-Recruiting. The candidacy can have the following statuses:

- **In Process**
  The candidate is being considered for the requisition.
- **Withdrawn**
  The candidate withdraws his application for a requisition.
- **Rejected**
  The candidate is rejected for the requisition.
- **To Be Hired**
  The candidate is found suitable for the requisition, and a job offer has been made.

Note

In SAP E-Recruiting, the status of the candidacy object is maintained for each requisition for which the candidate has submitted a job application. This status is maintained independently of the status of the candidacy for the other requisitions.

For example, let's assume the candidate has applied to two different requisitions; his candidacy might be rejected in one of the requisitions. This candidacy status has no relationship to the candidacy status in the other requisition.

As shown in the data model, the Candidacy (object type NE) has a relationship to the following objects:

- **Requisition (object type NB)**
  When a candidate applies to a requisition or is assigned to a requisition by the recruiter, a candidacy is created on the requisition.
- **Application (object type ND)**
  When the candidate submits an application, the application is linked with the candidacy; the candidate is linked to the requisition through the candidacy object that was created on the requisition.
- **Candidate (object type NA)**
  A candidacy is created for the candidate who has submitted the job application for a requisition.

3.3.5 Application

An application is an expression of interest by the candidate to be employed by the organization. The application can be in response to a requisition, or it can be an unsolicited application. In SAP E-Recruiting, both registered and unregistered candidates can apply to a job requisition. If the candidate sends a paper application, the recruiter can create a profile for the candidate in the system, assign the candidate to a talent group, and create an online application on behalf of the candidate.

The Application object (object type ND) has the following structure:

- **Application cover letter**
  The candidate submits a cover letter with his application expressing his interest in an open requisition or makes an unsolicited application requesting his application be considered for a suitable position that might be vacant.
- **Resume**
  The resume contains details such as the candidate's work experience, educational qualifications, and current role and responsibilities.

If the candidate is registered in the talent warehouse, the application cover letter and the resume can be uploaded as attachments to the candidate profile. It is important that the resume and the application cover letter be valid attachment types.

The application can have the following status:

- **Draft**
  The candidate is still working on the application and has not submitted it.
- **In Process**
  The candidate has completed and submitted the application, which is currently being processed.

- **Withdrawn**
  The candidate withdrew his application.
- **Rejected**
  The recruiter or the hiring manager has rejected the application.
- **To Be Hired**
  The candidate is to be hired.

As shown in the data model, the application (object type ND) has a relationship to the following objects:

- **Job Posting (object type NC)**
  An application is always linked to a job posting. A candidate submits an application in response to the job posting.
- **Candidate (object type NA)**
  A candidate submits an application. Through the application and the candidacy objects, a candidate is linked to the requisition to which the job posting belongs.
- **Candidacy (object type NE)**
  An application can be linked to one or multiple candidacies.

3.3.6 Talent Groups

Talent groups (object type NF) are created to classify the candidates in the talent warehouse based on certain characteristics, qualifications, or skills. Talent groups are dynamic and should reflect the current recruiting strategy and requirements. For example, let's assume your organization is planning to hire college graduates for internships in the different departments in your organization. The recruiting manager can create a talent group called Interns or College Graduates. The resumes of new graduates and candidates with less experience (less than two years) can be assigned to this talent group.

In Figure 3.18, we see the screen used to create a talent group. In SAP E-Recruiting, the recruiting administrator creates and maintains talent groups.

The advantage of using talent groups is that talent relationship management can be customized to meet the specific needs of the talent groups. For example, new graduates would like to know what training and mentoring opportunities are available in the organization. This specific need of the new graduates is different from that of an experienced professional whose career requirement might be, "What additional responsibilities can I have?"

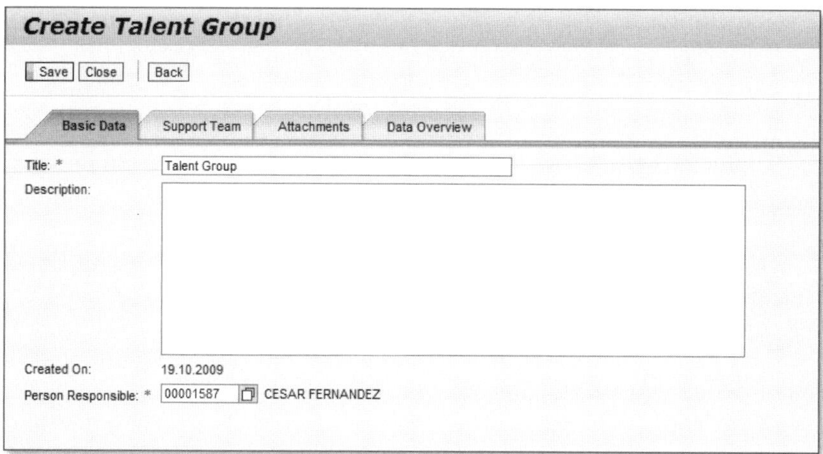

Figure 3.18 Talent Group Creation

Once the recruiting requirement to hire new graduates is met, this particular talent group can be deleted. All of the candidates in that talent group can be assigned to another talent group or distributed to the talent warehouse. The talent groups object has the following structure:

- **Basic Data**
  - **Title**
    The title of the talent group. (Keep the title meaningful so it reflects the qualifications of the candidates in that talent group.)
  - **Description**
    The purpose of the talent group.
  - **Creation date**
    The date the talent group was created.
  - **Person responsible**
    The name of the person who created the talent group. This person is usually the recruiting manager or the recruiting administrator and is responsible for maintaining the talent group. He is also responsible for assigning members to the support team.
- **Support team**
  The support team needs to be assigned to a talent group for recruiters to be able to search for candidates in that talent group. The support team can include the

recruiters and the hiring manager who are working on a requisition and are looking for qualified candidates to fill the requisition.

- **Attachments**
  This includes any additional documents that might be required to further describe the purpose of the talent group. The attachment type should be valid and should correspond to one of the attachment types configured in the IMG.

One of the ways to best utilize the attachments in the talent groups is to upload talent relationship management strategy documents as attachments. The support team can review these documents and formalize and follow the talent relationship management strategy while working with the candidates in that talent group. We also suggest that templates be created, targeting the specific needs and requirements of the candidates in the talent group. The support team can use those templates for candidate correspondence.

For example, if your organization is interested in hiring former employees of your organization, you can create a talent group called Former Employees. The recruiting administrator can create templates that meet the interests and requirements of this talent group. The candidate correspondence can provide links to an alumni website if it exists. The candidate correspondence can provide details on why it is a good idea to return to the organization and continue where they left.

As shown in the data model, the talent group (object type NF) has a relationship to the following objects:

- **Candidate**
  One or more candidates can be assigned to a talent group. A candidate can be assigned to one or more talent groups.

Talent groups are an exciting feature in SAP E-Recruiting, and we strongly recommend that your organization leverages this feature effectively.

3.3.7 Support Groups

In ehnancement pack 4, the Support Group is a new object (object type NG). The recruiting administrator can create support groups to assign as a support team to a requisition, talent groups, an application, application groups, or agencies. A support group consists of people the recruiting administrator wants in a support team. Support groups are an efficient way of forming support teams. For a requisition, the recruiting administrator can assign members of the support group as a support team in a single step. You can also assign a certain support group as the support team for certain type of requisition.

When you assign a support group as the support team, you can delete individual members of the support group from the support team if that is a requirement. When a support team is assigned to a requisition, the recruiting administrator can also assign people who are not members of a support group to be part of the support team for the requisition.

Figure 3.19 shows the screen used to create the support group. The recruiting administrator creates and maintains the support group. To create a support group, the recruiting administrator logs in to the portal using his assigned role. While creating the support group, the recruiting administrator assigns the members and their roles. The support group must be in a Released status before they can be assigned to a requisition.

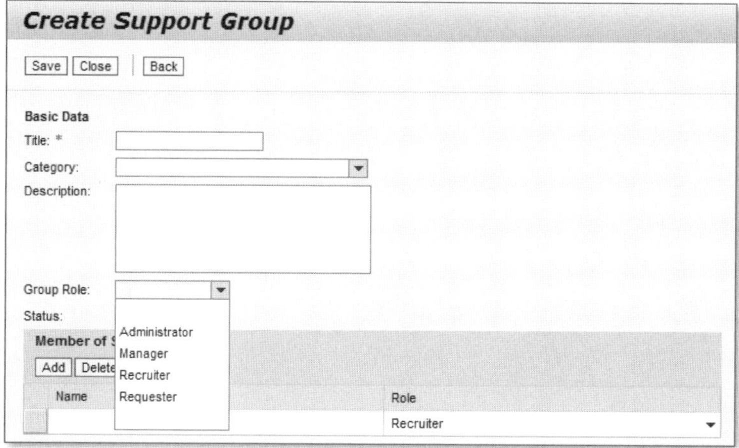

Figure 3.19 Create Support Group

The Support Group object (Object Type NG) has the following structure:

- **Basic data**
  - **Title**
    Contains the title of the support group.
  - **Category**
    The support group can be categorized according to the tasks (support groups for requisition, for talent groups, etc). In the IMG, you can customize different categories for support groups. For example, you can create categories to

reflect your different lines of business or office locations. You can assign support groups to any of these categories. The IMG activity is found under the IMG path SAP E-Recruiting • Technical Settings • User Administration • Define Categories for Groupings.

- **Description**
  The description of the support group. The description should be meaningful and communicate the purpose and use of the support group.
- **Group role**
  The roles of the individual members of the support group.

- **Members of the support group**
  The names of the individual members of the support group. The roles of the individual group members are also mentioned.

The support group can be assigned to the support teams of a requisition, talent groups, an application, or application groups. If the support group is to be assigned to an agency, you must have assigned the role Date Entry Clerk to the group role of that support group.

Now that you have a good understanding of the data model within SAP E-Recruiting, let's explore the new features available in enhancement pack 4.

3.4 What's New in SAP E-Recruiting Enhancement Pack 4 (E-Recruiting 604)?

In this section, we will summarize the new features introduced in SAP E-Recruiting enhancement pack 4.

3.4.1 Recruiter Administrative Services

In enhancement pack 4, SAP has provided a new user interface (UI) for the recruiter role. The services for the recruiter role are based on Web Dynpro for ABAP technology. In the delivered system, the services can be accessed through the recruiter work center in the SAP Portal. To use this functionality, you need to activate business function `HCM_ERC_CI_2`.

In Figure 3.20, you can see the new services that need to be activated. You can reach the Switch Framework screen using Transaction code SFW5 from SAP Easy Access. In the Switch Framework screen, expand the folder Enterprise_Business_Functions. In the displayed tree structure, activate the business function HCM_ERC_CI_2

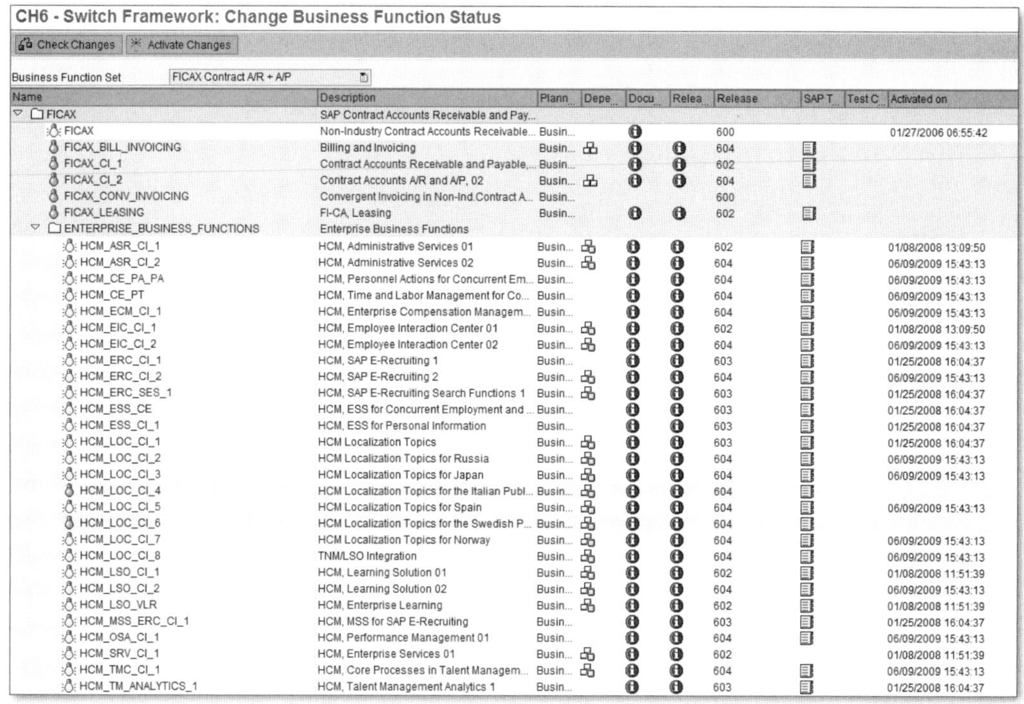

CH6 - Switch Framework: Change Business Function Status

Check Changes | Activate Changes

Business Function Set: FICAX Contract A/R + A/P

Name	Description	Plann...	Depe...	Docu...	Relea...	Release	SAP T...	Test C...	Activated on
FICAX	SAP Contract Accounts Receivable and Pay...								
FICAX	Non-Industry Contract Accounts Receivable...	Busin...				600			01/27/2006 06:55:42
FICAX_BILL_INVOICING	Billing and Invoicing	Busin...				604			
FICAX_CI_1	Contract Accounts Receivable and Payable,...	Busin...				602			
FICAX_CI_2	Contract Accounts A/R and A/P, 02	Busin...				604			
FICAX_CONV_INVOICING	Convergent Invoicing in Non-Ind.Contract A...	Busin...				600			
FICAX_LEASING	FI-CA, Leasing	Busin...				602			
ENTERPRISE_BUSINESS_FUNCTIONS	Enterprise Business Functions								
HCM_ASR_CI_1	HCM, Administrative Services 01	Busin...				602			01/08/2008 13:09:50
HCM_ASR_CI_2	HCM, Administrative Services 02	Busin...				604			06/09/2009 15:43:13
HCM_CE_PA_PA	HCM, Personnel Actions for Concurrent Em...	Busin...				604			06/09/2009 15:43:13
HCM_CE_PT	HCM, Time and Labor Management for Co...	Busin...				604			06/09/2009 15:43:13
HCM_ECM_CI_1	HCM, Enterprise Compensation Managem...	Busin...				604			06/09/2009 15:43:13
HCM_EIC_CI_1	HCM, Employee Interaction Center 01	Busin...				602			01/08/2008 13:09:50
HCM_EIC_CI_2	HCM, Employee Interaction Center 02	Busin...				604			06/09/2009 15:43:13
HCM_ERC_CI_1	HCM, SAP E-Recruiting 1	Busin...				603			01/25/2008 16:04:37
HCM_ERC_CI_2	HCM, SAP E-Recruiting 2	Busin...				604			06/09/2009 15:43:13
HCM_ERC_SES_1	HCM, SAP E-Recruiting Search Functions 1	Busin...				603			01/25/2008 16:04:37
HCM_ESS_CE	HCM, ESS for Concurrent Employment and ...	Busin...				603			01/25/2008 16:04:37
HCM_ESS_CI_1	HCM, ESS for Personal Information	Busin...				603			01/25/2008 16:04:37
HCM_LOC_CI_1	HCM Localization Topics	Busin...				603			01/25/2008 16:04:37
HCM_LOC_CI_2	HCM Localization Topics for Russia	Busin...				604			06/09/2009 15:43:13
HCM_LOC_CI_3	HCM Localization Topics for Japan	Busin...				604			06/09/2009 15:43:13
HCM_LOC_CI_4	HCM Localization Topics for the Italian Publ...	Busin...				604			
HCM_LOC_CI_5	HCM Localization Topics for Spain	Busin...				604			06/09/2009 15:43:13
HCM_LOC_CI_6	HCM Localization Topics for the Swedish P...	Busin...				604			
HCM_LOC_CI_7	HCM Localization Topics for Norway	Busin...				604			06/09/2009 15:43:13
HCM_LOC_CI_8	TNM/LSO Integration	Busin...				604			06/09/2009 15:43:13
HCM_LSO_CI_1	HCM, Learning Solution 01	Busin...				602			01/08/2008 11:51:39
HCM_LSO_CI_2	HCM, Learning Solution 02	Busin...				604			06/09/2009 15:43:13
HCM_LSO_VLR	HCM, Enterprise Learning	Busin...				602			01/08/2008 11:51:39
HCM_MSS_ERC_CI_1	HCM, MSS for SAP E-Recruiting	Busin...				603			01/25/2008 16:04:37
HCM_OSA_CI_1	HCM, Performance Management 01	Busin...				604			06/09/2009 15:43:13
HCM_SRV_CI_1	HCM, Enterprise Services 01	Busin...				602			01/08/2008 11:51:39
HCM_TMC_CI_1	HCM, Core Processes in Talent Managem...	Busin...				604			06/09/2009 15:43:13
HCM_TM_ANALYTICS_1	HCM, Talent Management Analytics 1	Busin...				603			01/25/2008 16:04:37

Figure 3.20 Switch Framework to Activate Business Functions

In enhancement pack 4, SAP has introduced the concept of the recruiter work center. The work center provides an overview of the open tasks on which the recruiter is currently working. The recruiter can customize the query and the view of the display screen. Refer to Figure 3.14 for a display of the recruiter work center. The recruiter work center can be accessed by recruiters who are assigned the recruiter role. You can access the screen through the work overview of the recruiter portal in Employee Self-Service (ESS).

Some improvements have also been made to the questions and questionnaires functionality:

- You can display questions and questionnaires by category.
- You can translate questions and questionnaires with Draft status.
- You can build questionnaires for internal and external use.
- You can build instructions for each question.
- The questionnaire screen provides a new field called Alias. The Alias field can be used to identify questionnaires by region, country, or any other characteristics that you might have customized.

Enhancements have been made to the process template. In enhancement pack 4, you can select multiple activities and add them to a process all at once.

Improvements have been made to requisition administration:

- You can create requisitions by position.
- You can add a questionnaire to the requisition.
- The lead recruiter information is defaulted to the requisition.
- Compared to the earlier versions, the posting text and the job posting process is greatly simplified.

The following enhancements have been made to the candidate selection process in enhancement pack 4:

- You can personalize the candidate selection screen, defining which fields are visible and hidden and in what sequence you would like the fields to be displayed.
- You can propose candidates from the talent pool to the requisition.
- Features such as Print Version, Export to Excel, Decline, and Delete Assignment are available in the assignment screen.
- You can filter candidates based on statuses such as Rejected, To Be Hired, Withdrawn, and Date. These selection criteria are available in the All tab of the Candidate Selection screen.

3.4.2 Customizing Activities

You can now customize the following in the IMG activities:

- **Assign columns for candidate shortlists**
  You can specify for each process or work area which columns are available, which columns are visible, and the position where the columns will be displayed. The IMG path for the customizing is SAP E-Recruiting • Technical Settings • User Interfaces • Administrator and Recruiter • Settings for Candidate Selection • Assign Columns for Candidate Shortlists.
- **Define pushbuttons for fast access to activity types**
  This is an exciting feature in enhancement pack 4. As shown in Figure 3.21, in this customizing step, you define the buttons to be displayed in the tab page of the respective processes. For each button, you assign an activity type that is assigned to the respective process.

The recruiter uses these buttons for fast access, to execute the activity types in the respective process, and to create activities for one or multiple candidates.

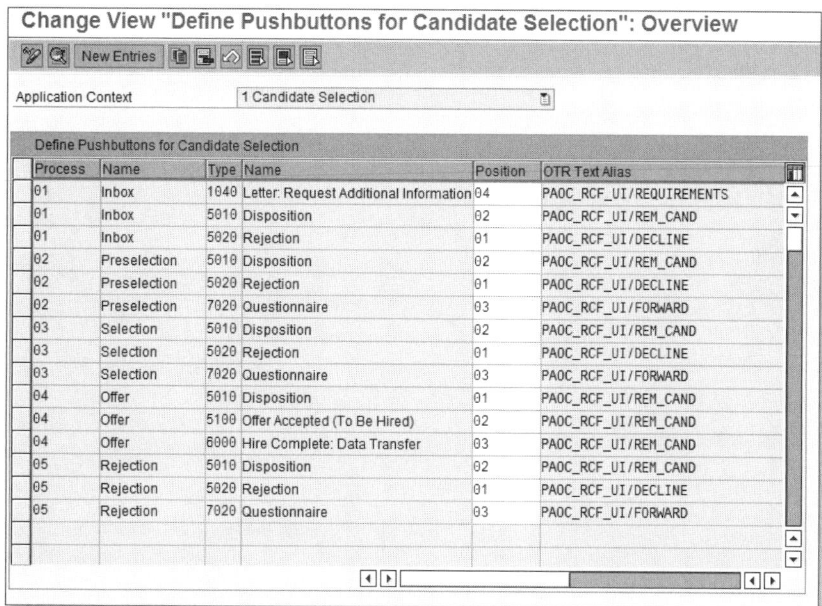

Change View "Define Pushbuttons for Candidate Selection": Overview

New Entries

Application Context: 1 Candidate Selection

Define Pushbuttons for Candidate Selection

Process	Name	Type	Name	Position	OTR Text Alias
01	Inbox	1040	Letter: Request Additional Information	04	PAOC_RCF_UI/REQUIREMENTS
01	Inbox	5010	Disposition	02	PAOC_RCF_UI/REM_CAND
01	Inbox	5020	Rejection	01	PAOC_RCF_UI/DECLINE
02	Preselection	5010	Disposition	02	PAOC_RCF_UI/REM_CAND
02	Preselection	5020	Rejection	01	PAOC_RCF_UI/DECLINE
02	Preselection	7020	Questionnaire	03	PAOC_RCF_UI/FORWARD
03	Selection	5010	Disposition	02	PAOC_RCF_UI/REM_CAND
03	Selection	5020	Rejection	01	PAOC_RCF_UI/DECLINE
03	Selection	7020	Questionnaire	03	PAOC_RCF_UI/FORWARD
04	Offer	5010	Disposition	01	PAOC_RCF_UI/REM_CAND
04	Offer	5100	Offer Accepted (To Be Hired)	02	PAOC_RCF_UI/REM_CAND
04	Offer	6000	Hire Complete: Data Transfer	03	PAOC_RCF_UI/REM_CAND
05	Rejection	5010	Disposition	02	PAOC_RCF_UI/REM_CAND
05	Rejection	5020	Rejection	01	PAOC_RCF_UI/DECLINE
05	Rejection	7020	Questionnaire	03	PAOC_RCF_UI/FORWARD

Figure 3.21 Define Pushbuttons for Candidate Selection

The activity for the customizing can be found under the IMG path SAP E-RECRUITING • TECHNICAL SETTINGS • USER INTERFACES • ADMINISTRATOR AND RECRUITER • SETTINGS FOR CANDIDATE SELECTION • DEFINE PUSHBUTTONS FOR FAST ACCESS TO ACTIVITY TYPES.

3.4.3 Activity Management

In enhancement pack 4, SAP E-Recruiting also now provides the following activity management enhancements:

- Guided navigation tells you what activities you need to create.
- The activity screen has a new UI layout.
- You can maintain histories of the activities.

3.4.4 Candidate Profile

UI changes have also been made to the candidate profile. There is a now short overview of the candidate profile with the option of storing the candidate's picture. The Assignments tab provides an overview of all of the requisitions for which the candidate has applied. You can also get an overview of all of the activities by requisition.

As shown in Figure 3.22, when you conduct a candidate search, you can assign individual candidates to a requisition or to a talent group. Also, the recruiter can now do a profile matchup for the requisition requirements. Lastly, you can store notes about the candidate. This is particularly useful when you are on a call with the candidate and doing a pre-assessment or during the offer process and you are negotiating pay with the candidate.

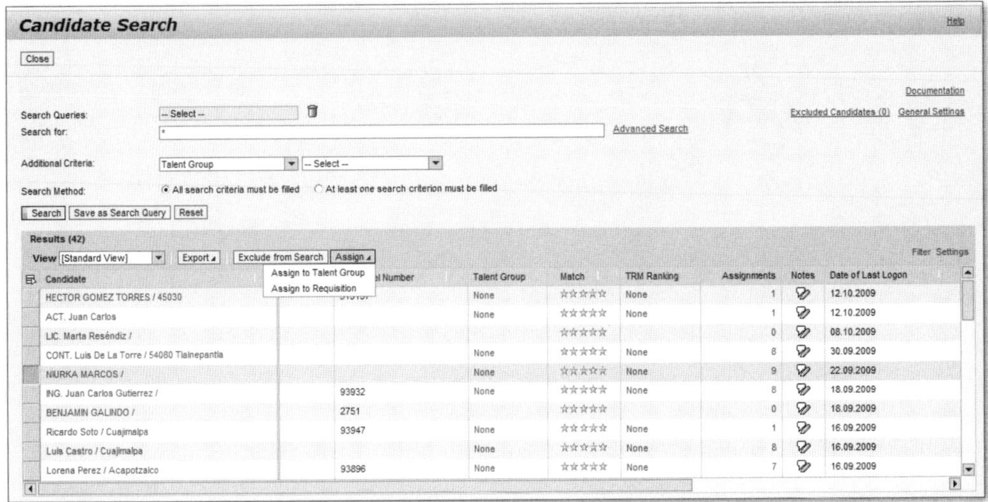

Figure 3.22 Assignment of a Candidate to a Talent Group or Requisition

3.4.5 New System Parameters

In enhancement pack 4, SAP has introduced six new parameters for E-Recruiting. In customizing via Transaction SM30, you can maintain the following parameters in table T77S0.

- **Activity changes process assignment (RECFA ACTPA)**
  This parameter determines if you can change a candidate from one process to another through an activity.
- **Duplicate checking for background check order (RECFA BGCDC)**
  This parameter defines the time period in which repeated background checks are considered duplicates.
- **No maintenance of HR data in E-Recruiting (RECFA HRDAT)**
  This parameter determines if the data for internal candidates can be changed in the candidate profile or in the SAP E-Recruiting or if these can be maintained in SAP ERP HCM only.

- **Period with duplicates for candidate profiles (RECFA PRODC)**
  This parameter determines in days, in which candidate profiles are considered duplicates, based on the last candidate profile update.
- **Concurrent employment active in E-Recruiting (RECFA RECCE)**
  This parameter determines if concurrent employment is active in E-Recruiting. This parameter is not valid in an integrated environment.
- **Role of provider in business partner (RECFA VENRO)**
  This defines the vendor partners such as the resume parsing service provider and the background checks service provider as business partners.

The IMG path to set this parameter is IMG • SAP E-RECRUITING • TECHNICAL SETTINGS • SET SYSTEM PARAMETERS.

Figure 3.23 shows a list of the parameters and the delivered values.

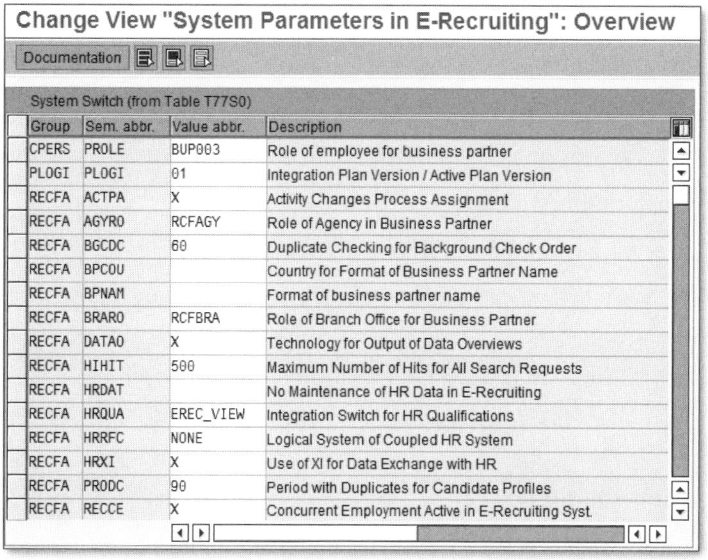

Change View "System Parameters in E-Recruiting": Overview

Documentation

System Switch (from Table T77S0)

Group	Sem. abbr.	Value abbr.	Description
CPERS	PROLE	BUP003	Role of employee for business partner
PLOGI	PLOGI	01	Integration Plan Version / Active Plan Version
RECFA	ACTPA	X	Activity Changes Process Assignment
RECFA	AGYRO	RCFAGY	Role of Agency in Business Partner
RECFA	BGCDC	60	Duplicate Checking for Background Check Order
RECFA	BPCOU		Country for Format of Business Partner Name
RECFA	BPNAM		Format of business partner name
RECFA	BRARO	RCFBRA	Role of Branch Office for Business Partner
RECFA	DATAO	X	Technology for Output of Data Overviews
RECFA	HIHIT	500	Maximum Number of Hits for All Search Requests
RECFA	HRDAT		No Maintenance of HR Data in E-Recruiting
RECFA	HRQUA	EREC_VIEW	Integration Switch for HR Qualifications
RECFA	HRRFC	NONE	Logical System of Coupled HR System
RECFA	HRXI	X	Use of XI for Data Exchange with HR
RECFA	PRODC	90	Period with Duplicates for Candidate Profiles
RECFA	RECCE	X	Concurrent Employment Active in E-Recruiting Syst.

Figure 3.23 System Parameters in E-Recruiting

The following two parameters are no longer available from enhancement pack 4 on:

- Call garbage collector explicitly (RECFA GARBC)
- Individual correspondence with/without web editor (RECFA INDCO)

3.4.6 Search Functionality

The recruiter work center provides a quick search. You can enter the search criteria and do a search. You can use the search to conduct a prospecting search for candidates from the talent pool and from the candidate assignment list.

A dynamic query builder is now provided with guided navigation. The output of the query can be personalized so you can choose which category or query needs to be set as the default query. Figure 3.24 shows a screenshot from building a query.

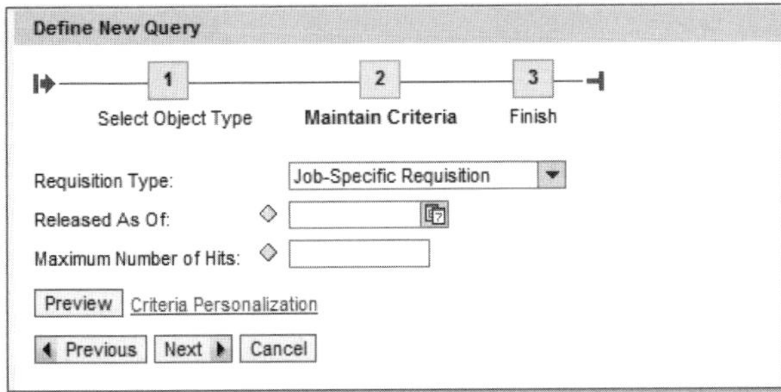

Figure 3.24 Define New Query

Other enhancements include the following:

- You can personalize the layout to be in either the matrix or tab format.
- During the candidate search, you can build the query to search only internal or external candidates.
- For internal candidates, the search is possible by personnel number.
- You can exclude candidates during a candidate search.

3.4.7 Concurrent Employment

In enhancement pack 4, SAP E-Recruiting supports concurrent employment. In the SAP ERP HCM system, if an employee exists with multiple work contracts, then one candidate (NA) object is created in the SAP E-Recruiting system with assigned objects Central Person (CP) and Business Partner (BP). In a concurrent employment scenario, an internal candidate is active if at least one work contract exists for the candidate in the SAP ERP HCM system. The customizing settings required for a concurrent employment scenario depend on the implementation model of SAP E-Recruiting. SAP E-Recruiting can be implemented as a separate instance or as an integrated instance. Later in this chapter (Section 3.6), we will briefly intrc the implementation scenarios. We will discuss more about the implementation scenarios in Chapter 8, Integration.

If the SAP E-Recruiting system is implemented as a stand-alone system, you need to complete the following customizing:

- Activate the switch RECFA RECCE to switch on the concurrent employment functionality. On the SAP ERP HCM side, activate the switch CCURE MAINS.
- After you have activated the switch RECFA RECCE, execute ALE distribution for all candidates already available in the SAP E-Recruiting system for whom there is an entry in the table Bookmark Employee Status Based on HR Data (T77RCF_P_STAT).

If the SAP E-Recruiting implementation is in an integrated environment, then you need to activate the switch CCURE MAINS on the SAP ERP HCM side. SAP uses the switch CCURE MAINS to control the concurrent employment for both SAP ERP HCM and SAP E-Recruiting. The customizing step to activate the switch RECFA RECCE is not required in an integrated environment.

To implement concurrent employment in SAP E-Recruiting, the system requires a decoupled infotype framework in the SAP ERP HCM system.

3.4.8 Other Enhancements

Enhancement pack 4 also comes with the following enhancements:

- The recruiting administrator portal role is delivered standard.
- The UI for the recruiting administrator is in Web Dynpro for ABAP (WD4A).
- The recruiter can parse resumes while entering applications (for internal and external candidates) manually.
- Background checks can be initiated asynchronously.

As you have seen, SAP has introduced a number of new functionalities in enhancement pack 4 in SAP E-Recruiting. These functionalities provide an enhanced user experience and better integration with vendor services such as drug testing and background checks. In enhancement pack 4, SAP has delivered the recruiter and the administrator UI in WD4A, whereas the earlier versions were in Business Server Pages (BSPs). In the next section, we will provide a list of iViews that are required to implement SAP E-Recruiting 604.

3.5 iViews Required to be Implemented in SAP E-Recruiting 604

In this section, we provide a list of iViews that you need to activate and implement in SAP E-Recruiting.

- **Recruiting Administrator**

Roles and Worksets for the Administrator are shown in Table 3.1

Object	Technical Name
Role: Recruiting Administrator	com.sap.pct.erp.erecadmin
Workset: Recruiting Admin	com.sap.pct.erp.erecadmin.administration
Workset: Work Overview	com.sap.pct.erp.erecadmin.work_overview

Table 3.1 Roles and Worksets for Recruiting Administrator

iViews for the Administrator are shown in Table 3.2

Object	Technical Name
Requisitions To Be Deleted	com.sap.pct.erp.erecadmin.requisitions_to_be_deleted
Maintain Internal Users	com.sap.pct.erp.erecadmin.maintain_internal_user
Delete Registrations	com.sap.pct.erp.erecadmin.delete_registration
Delete External Candidates	com.sap.pct.erp.erecadmin.delete_external_candidates
Maintain Support Groups	com.sap.pct.erp.erecadmin.maintain_support_groups
Adjust Support Teams	com.sap.pct.erp.erecadmin.adjust_support_team
Maintain Companies and Branches	com.sap.pct.erp.erecadmin.maintain_company_branches
Maintain Agencies	com.sap.pct.erp.erecadmin.maintain_agencies
Requisition Management	com.sap.pct.erp.erecadmin.requisition_administration

Table 3.2 iViews for Recruiting Administrator

Object	Technical Name
Maintain Process Templates	com.sap.pct.erp.erecadmin.maintain_process_templates
Maintain Talent Groups	com.sap.pct.erp.erecadmin.maintain_talent_groups
Maintain Application Groups	com.sap.pct.erp.erecadmin.maintain_application_groups
Access Audit Trails	com.sap.pct.erp.erecadmin.access_audit_trail
Personal Settings	com.sap.pct.erp.erecadmin.personal_settings

Table 3.2 iViews for Recruiting Administrator (Cont.)

- **Recruiter**

Roles and Worksets for the Recruiter are shown in Table 3.3

Object	Technical Name
Role: Recruiter	com.sap.pct.erp.recruiter.recruiter
Workset: Work Overview	com.sap.pct.erp.recruiter.work_overview
Workset: Reports	com.sap.pct.erp.recruiter.reports

Table 3.3 Roles and Worksets for Recruiter

iViews for the Recruiter are shown in Table 3.4

Object	Technical Name
Dashboard	com.sap.pct.erp.recruiter.dashboard
Search	com.sap.pct.erp.recruiter.search
Reports	com.sap.pct.erp.recruiter.reports
Create	com.sap.pct.erp.recruiter.create
Create by Position	com.sap.pct.erp.recruiter.create_by_position
Create Internal Applications	com.sap.pct.erp.recruiter.maintain_internal_applications

Table 3.4 iViews for Recruiter

Object	Technical Name
Create External Applications	com.sap.pct.erp.recruiter.maintain_external_application
Candidate Search	com.sap.pct.erp.recruiter.search_for_candidates
Maintain Questions	com.sap.pct.erp.recruiter.maintain_questions
Question Maintenance EEO Information	com.sap.pct.erp.recruiter.maintain_eeo_Questions
Maintain Questionnaires	com.sap.pct.erp.recruiter.maintain_questionnaire
Questionnaire Maintenance EEO Information	com.sap.pct.erp.recruiter.maintain_eeo_questionnaires
Maintain Process Templates	com.sap.pct.erp.recruiter.maintain_process_templates
Maintain Personal Settings	com.sap.pct.erp.recruiter.maintain_personal_settings

Table 3.4 iViews for Recruiter (Cont.)

These iViews are SAP standard-delivered. All of the roles in the enhancement pack 4 require access to the portal and the iViews. You can develop custom iViews to meet your specific business requirements, if necessary.

Note

For more information on how to implement ESS and MSS, refer to the SAP PRESS book, *Implementing Employee and Manager Self-Services in SAP ERP HCM*, by Jeremy Masters and Christos Kotsakis, 2008.

3.6 Getting Started

One of the questions we are frequently asked is, "How is SAP E-Recruiting deployed?" SAP E-Recruiting is considered an add-on to SAP ERP HCM and is based on the SAP NetWeaver architecture. You can deploy SAP E-Recruiting in one of the three ways:

- As a stand-alone system with no integration to SAP ERP HCM
- As a stand-alone system with integration to SAP ERP HCM
- As an integral part of SAP ERP HCM

SAP recommends deploying SAP E-Recruiting as a stand-alone system with integration to SAP ERP HCM. In this type of deployment, firewalls are set up to protect access from the Internet to the SAP E-Recruiting system and from the SAP E-Recruiting system to SAP ERP HCM.

All internal users are behind the SAP E-Recruiting firewall.

Figure 3.25 shows how SAP E-Recruiting is deployed as a stand-alone system with integration to SAP ERP HCM. In this deployment, after the completion of the recruiting activities, the data of the new hire is sent to SAP ERP HCM for the actual hiring. The data transfer is done either by using RFC (ALE) or by SAP NetWeaver Exchange Infrastructure (SAP XI).

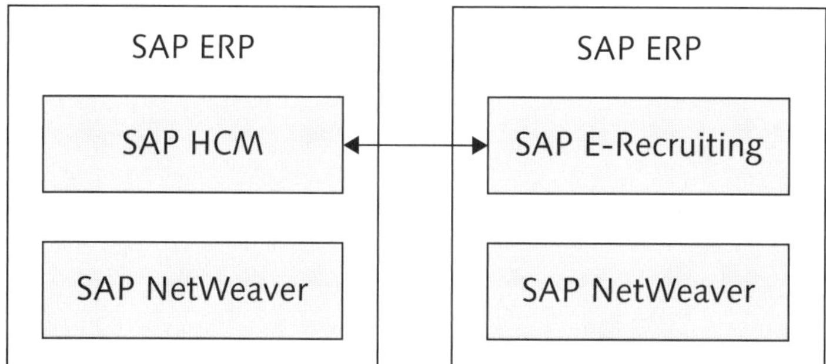

Figure 3.25 SAP E-Recruiting as a Stand-Alone Implementation

Using ALE makes the enterprise architecture and objects such as the qualifications catalog available to the SAP E-Recruiting system. An employee in the SAP ERP HCM system is automatically created in SAP E-Recruiting as a business partner (Object type BP). We will discuss the deployment options in detail in Chapter 8.

3.6.1 Determine E-Recruiting Services

In this customizing activity, you can activate the services that are required for the roles of recruiter and recruiting administrator. The menu path in the IMG for this activity is SAP E-RECRUITING • TECHNICAL SETTINGS • USER INTERFACES • ADMINISTRATOR AND RECRUITER • GENERAL SETTINGS • DETERMINE E-RECRUITING SERVICES.

Figure 3.26 lists services that have to be activated. Alternatively, you can activate these services by using Transaction code SICF.

```
/default_host/sap/bc/webdynpro/sap/ERC_A_ADJUST_REQ_RET
/default_host/sap/bc/webdynpro/sap/ERC_A_ADJ_SUPP_TEAM
/default_host/sap/bc/webdynpro/sap/ERC_A_ADMIN_ATRL
/default_host/sap/bc/webdynpro/sap/ERC_A_ADMIN_DEL_REQUI
/default_host/sap/bc/webdynpro/sap/ERC_A_ADMIN_SUPP_GROUP
/default_host/sap/bc/webdynpro/sap/ERC_A_AGENCY
/default_host/sap/bc/webdynpro/sap/ERC_A_APPL_GRP
/default_host/sap/bc/webdynpro/sap/ERC_A_APPL_MGMT
/default_host/sap/bc/webdynpro/sap/ERC_A_BGC_ACTIVITY_DETAIL
/default_host/sap/bc/webdynpro/sap/ERC_A_BRANCH_COMPANY
/default_host/sap/bc/webdynpro/sap/ERC_A_CAND_OVERVIEW
/default_host/sap/bc/webdynpro/sap/ERC_A_CAND_OVERVIEW_DISPLAY
/default_host/sap/bc/webdynpro/sap/ERC_A_CAND_SELECT
/default_host/sap/bc/webdynpro/sap/ERC_A_CAND_SRCH
/default_host/sap/bc/webdynpro/sap/ERC_A_DATAOVERVIEW
/default_host/sap/bc/webdynpro/sap/ERC_A_DEL_EXT_CAND
/default_host/sap/bc/webdynpro/sap/ERC_A_DEREG_CAND
/default_host/sap/bc/webdynpro/sap/ERC_A_MNT_USER
/default_host/sap/bc/webdynpro/sap/ERC_A_PERS_SETTINGS
/default_host/sap/bc/webdynpro/sap/ERC_A_PROC_TEMPL_MAINTAIN
/default_host/sap/bc/webdynpro/sap/ERC_A_QUESNR_MAINTAIN
/default_host/sap/bc/webdynpro/sap/ERC_A_QUEST_MAINTAIN
/default_host/sap/bc/webdynpro/sap/ERC_A_QUICK_SEARCH
/default_host/sap/bc/webdynpro/sap/ERC_A_REQ_CAND_SRCH
/default_host/sap/bc/webdynpro/sap/ERC_A_REQ_MGMT
/default_host/sap/bc/webdynpro/sap/ERC_A_SEARCH_SETTS
/default_host/sap/bc/webdynpro/sap/ERC_A_TG
/default_host/sap/bc/webdynpro/sap/ERC_A_WORKCENTER
```

Figure 3.26 New Services in SAP E-Recruiting EP4

3.6.2 Technical Settings

Having the correct technical settings and system parameters is essential for an efficient implementation of SAP E-Recruiting. You can customize the system parameters in the IMG, using the menu path SAP E-Recruiting • Technical Settings • Set System Parameters. We strongly recommend that you check and validate the following parameters:

- **RFC connection to TREX**
  Use Transaction code SM59 and navigate to the screen Configuration of RFC Connections. Select TCP/IP connections and open the tree structure. In the displayed RFC connections, select IMSDEFAULT and test this RFC connection. (TREX is the search engine used in E-Recruiting. We will discuss TREX and the search functionality more in Chapter 7.)
- **CPERS/PROLE**
  Specifies the role of an employee as a business partner (BP). We recommend that you use the SAP standard delivery and do not make any changes.
- **PLOGI/PLOGI**
  Specifies the active plan variant. Leave as 01.

- **RECFA/AGYRO**
  Specifies the roles of an agency as a business partner. We recommend that you use the SAP standard delivery and do not make any changes.
- **RECFA/BRARO**
  Specifies the role of a branch as a business partner. We recommend that you use the SAP standard delivery and do not make any changes.
- **RECFA/HRQUA**
  Specifies the integration of the qualifications catalog maintained in the SAP ERP HCM system to the SAP E-Recruiting system.
- **RECFA/HRRFC**
  This setting is important if you deploy SAP E-Recruiting as a stand-alone system with integration to the SAP ERP HCM system. Enter the name of the RFC connection in the system parameters table. This setting will be required when you transfer the data of the new hire to the SAP ERP HCM system.

This concludes our review of the preliminary steps required to get started in implementing SAP E-Recruiting. Let's look at some basic settings.

3.6.3 Basic Settings

In this section, we will explain the basic settings (see Figure 3.27) that are required for an SAP E-Recruiting implementation.

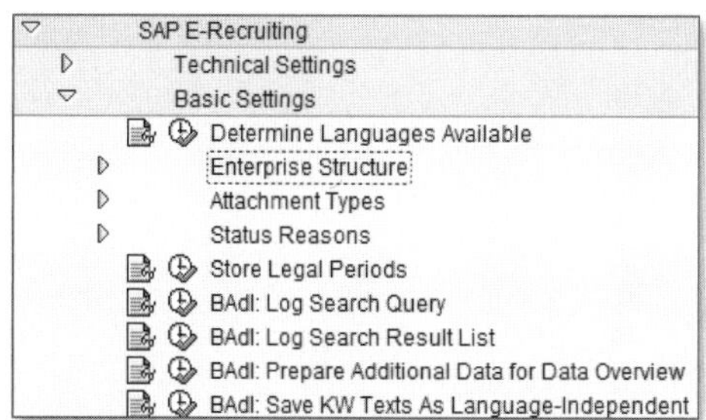

Figure 3.27 Basic Settings in the SAP IMG

- **Determine Languages Available**
  In this customizing activity, you specify the languages that are available in the SAP E-Recruiting system. You perform the customizing activity in the IMG under the menu path SAP E-RECRUITING • BASIC SETTINGS • DETERMINE LANGUAGES AVAILABLE. The attachments in SAP E-Recruiting, text in questions and questionnaires, and text in job postings can be saved in these languages only. Searches in SAP E-Recruiting can be performed in these languages only.

- **Define Company**
  In this customizing activity, you define the individual companies in your enterprise. You can customize the application process to meet the individual company requirements. Candidates can use individual companies as search criteria while searching for jobs. The menu path in the IMG is SAP E-RECRUITING • ENTERPRISE STRUCTURE • DEFINE COMPANY. SAP recommends that you maintain individual companies and branches in the SAP E-Recruiting application, rather than customizing them in the SAP IMG. We will explain more about creating and maintaining individual companies and branches, in Chapter 6, Administration.

- **Define Business Partner Role for Branches**
  In this customizing activity, you define the business partner role SAP E-Recruiting, which you can use in branches. In the customizing activity (see Figure 3.28), you create the business partner role RCFBRA and assign RCFBRA to the BP Role Cat. field. The menu path for the customizing activity is IMG • SAP E-RECRUITING • BASIC SETTINGS • ENTERPRISE STRUCTURE • DEFINE BUSINESS PARTNER ROLE FOR BRANCHES.

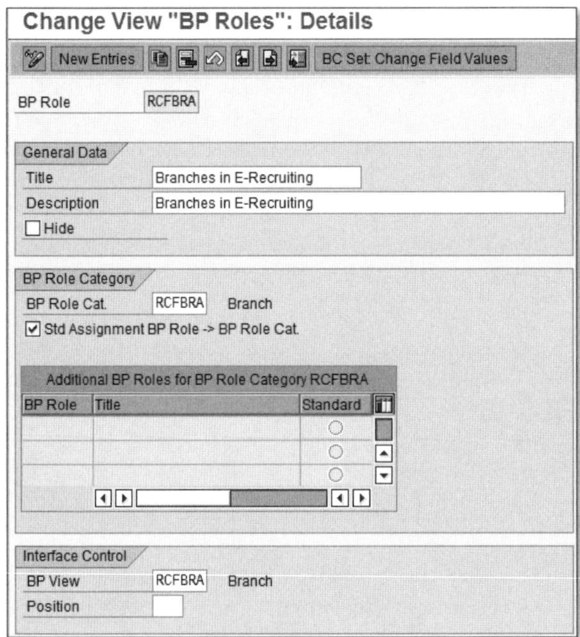

Figure 3.28 Business Partner Roles

The prerequisite for this customizing activity is that you have assigned the parameter RCFBRA to the switch RECFA/BRARO. In this customizing activity, you define the time periods for the retention or the expiration of the requisitions and applications data in the SAP E-Recruiting system after the recruiting process is completed. The menu path in the IMG for this customizing activity is SAP E-RECRUITING • BASIC SETTINGS • STORE LEGAL PERIODS.

- **Define and Assign Branches to Companies**
  In this customizing activity, you define the branches and assign them to the companies in your enterprise. The menu path in the IMG for the customizing activity is SAP E-RECRUITING • BASIC SETTINGS • ENTERPRISE STRUCTURE • DEFINE AND ASSIGN BRANCHES TO COMPANIES. As a prerequisite for this customizing activity, you should have completed the customizing activities Define Company and Define Business Partner Role for Branches.
- **Store Legal Periods**
  Many countries require that requisitions and the application data be retained in the SAP E-Recruiting system for a certain period of time, even after the requisition is closed.

Note

In the United States, check the OFCCP website (*www.ofccp.org*) for the definition of Internet applications and the regulatory time period for retaining the requisitions and application data.

3.6.4 Personalization

In SAP E-Recruiting, the recruiter, the recruiting administrator, and the candidate can maintain personal settings. For the recruiter role, personal settings (see Figure 3.29) can be maintained in the Recruiter Work Center, which can be found in the Services group of the Work Overview. Some of the settings that can be maintained include the data format, decimal notation, preferred language, and the default print device.

In SAP E-Recruiting, you can personalize many of the Web Dynpro screens. You can select which columns to be displayed and the sequence of the display. Figure 3.30 shows the Personalization screen used to personalize the Assignment for Requisition Screen. In a Web Dynpro screen, if you do not see the link for Settings, you should see the Personalization icon. Click the icon and select personalize.

Save | Close

Basic Settings
Date Format: MM/DD/YYYY
Decimal Notation: 1,234,567.89
General Settings
Preferred Language: English
Printer Settings
Output Device: LP01 DO NOT DELETE (default print device w/o physical destination)

Figure 3.29 Maintain Personal Settings

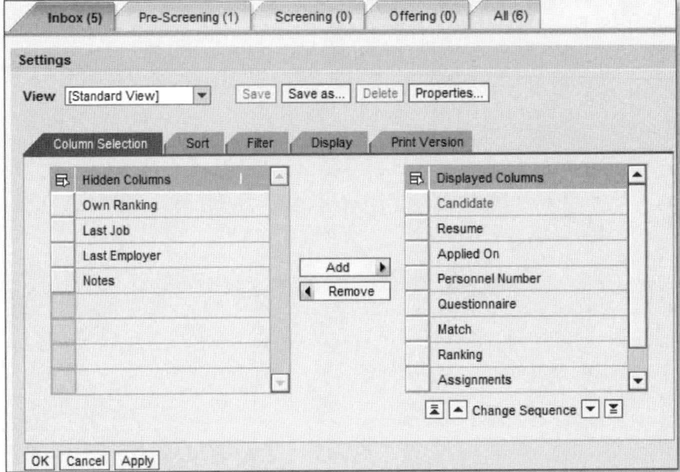

Figure 3.30 Personalization

Users can define their own personal view for the columns to be displayed and the sequence of display. In the personalization, users can define the sort order, the filter columns, and the display interface. In the personalization of the recruiter dashboard, users can define if the dashboard is displayed as tabs or links.

3.6.5 Important SAP Notes

The following SAP Notes are important for you to get started:

- SAP Note 1241014 describes all changes and restrictions for SAP E-Recruiting customers who want to use the business function HCM SAP E-Recruiting 2 (HCM_ERC_CI_2) to activate enhancement pack 4.

- SAP Note 105148 provides details about a decoupled infotype framework in the SAP ERP HCM system, which is required for implementing concurrent employment in SAP E-Recruiting.
- SAP Note 997181 offers details regarding integration between SAP E-Recruiting and SAP ERP HCM.
- SAP Note 830591 provides information on the prerequisites for implementing SAP E-Recruiting and SAP ERP HCM on one instance.

3.7 Summary

In this chapter, we explained the basics of SAP E-Recruiting, the deployment options, and the new functionalities in enhancement pack 4. As you have seen, the important actors in the recruiting process are the recruiter and the candidate. SAP provides standard delivered roles for both the recruiter and the candidate.

In the next chapter, we will look in detail at the requisition process, the recruiter work center, and one of the most important functionalities within E-Recruiting — the process template and the activities involved in requisition. Later in the chapter, we will explain how to create and activate a job posting.

Requisition management is one of the core functionalities within the recruiting process. SAP E-Recruiting provides a number of capabilities such as process templates, activities, and candidate correspondence to aid in requisition management. With enhancement pack 4, SAP has introduced the Recruiter Work Center, which provides an overview of all requisitions that the recruiter is currently working on as well as the status of candidacies and postings. In this chapter, we will discuss the steps involved in requisition management.

4 Requisition Management

The topic of requisition management within SAP E-Recruiting is one of the most important, because the creation of the requisition document and the identification of the posting channels play a vital role in attracting qualified candidates. Adherence to a recruiting budget becomes a critical piece of the recruiting cycle for many companies, especially in harder economic times. This chapter provides a comprehensive review of the requisition management functionality available in SAP E-Recruiting. After providing an overview of the functionality, we will dive deep into the requisition management tasks — from creating requisitions to creating qualifying questionnaires to job postings — that the process requires. We will also show the customizing steps you need to perform while using the functionality and discuss best practices. To begin, we will provide an overview and describe the process steps involved in requisition management.

4.1 Overview of Requisition Management

A requisition is a formal announcement by the hiring manager that there is a vacant position to be filled. The vacant position can be an existing position or a forecasted position. This vacant position should be budgeted in headcount. Figure 4.1 gives an overview of requisition management and the roles of the various actors such as the hiring manager, the recruiter, and the candidate.

In the requisition document, the hiring manager notes the number of positions to be filled, the education qualifications, the work experience required for the position, and the roles and responsibilities of the position. The requisition document should also mention the job classification and the organizational unit the position will belong to in the organization structure.

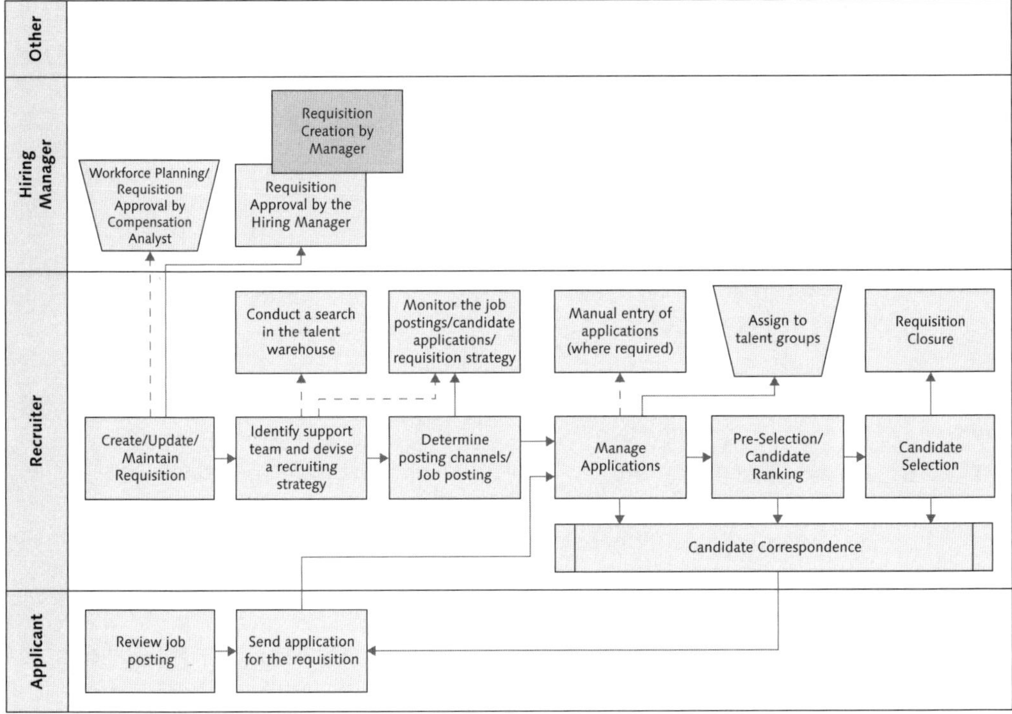

Figure 4.1 Requisition Management Process Flow

The hiring manager sends the requisition document to the recruiter with a request to find qualified candidates for the position. When the recruiter receives the requisition request from the hiring manager, he creates the requisition in the SAP E-Recruiting system. While creating the requisition in the SAP E-Recruiting system, the recruiter can assign the support team to this requisition. The support team is the group of individuals who will be involved in recruiting a suitable candidate for the requisition. During requisition creation, the recruiter assigns a process template (and thereby the associated activities) to the requisition. The process template also contains the qualifying questionnaire associated with the requisition (if one exists).

For the job posting, the recruiter creates the posting text, which includes the description of the position and the required qualifications and work experience.

For publication of the requisition, the different posting channels such as external, internal, or Internet job boards are created and saved.

> **Note**
>
> In SAP E-Recruiting, either a manager or a recruiter can create the requisition. The requisition is an internal document and can be viewed and maintained by the members of the support team.

Next, we will explain the functionality available within the recruiter work center. In enhancement pack 4, SAP has provided a role-based, task-specific work center. The recruiter work center is a "one-stop" dashboard for the recruiter to perform activities such as creating requisitions, assigning candidates to a requisition, reviewing candidate profiles, and engaging in talent relationship management activities.

4.2 Recruiter Work Center

In enhancement pack 4, the recruiter role and the user interface have been greatly enhanced with the introduction of the recruiter work center. To implement the recruiter role, you need to perform the following tasks:

- Activate the business function HCM_ERC_CI_2 using the switch framework SWF5. (Again, you must be on enhancement pack 4.)
- Install the business package for the recruiter component version 1.40. Prior to using the business package for the recruiter, you must have activated the business function above.
- Create a user account in the enterprise portal.

Let's now discuss the dashboard for the Recruiter Work Center.

4.2.1 Dashboard

The Recruiter Work Center contains the services and information required for recruiters to accomplish their day-to-day activities — all on one screen (see Figure 4.2). The Recruiter Work Center has many important functionalities, which we will describe for you now.

The Active Queries section contains queries that show the number of open requisitions, requisitions that are in draft status, and all of the requisitions on which the recruiter is currently working. This section also displays the open application groups, expiring job postings, expiring job postings of the team, the number of open background checks, and the number of parsed resumes to review.

Home
Analytics
Collaboration
E-Recruiting Administrator
Recruiter
Overview | Reports | Service Map
Work Overview
History, Back Forward
Detailed Navigation
Work Overview
Services
Requisitions
Create
Create by Position
Manual Application Management
Create Internal Applications
Create External Application
Candidates
Candidate Search
Administration
Maintain Questions
Maintain Questionnaires
Question Maintenance EEO Information
Questionnaire Maintenance EEO Information
Maintain Process Templates
Personal Settings
Maintain Personal Settings
Search
Search for:
Search
Dashboard
Active Queries
Requisitions
My Open Requisitions (4)
Open Team Requisitions (19)
Open Application Groups (0)
My Draft Requisitions (1)
All Requisitions (27)
Postings
My Expiring Postings (0)
Expiring Team Postings (0)
My Tasks
Open Background Checks (0)
Parsed Resumes To Review (0)
Requisitions - My Open Requisitions
Show Quick Criteria Maintenance
Change Query
Define New Query
Personalize
View [Standard View]
Requisition
Job Posting
Assignments
Export
Filter Settings
Requisition | Alias | Manager | Days Since Release | Inbox | Pre-Screening | Screening | Offering | Closing
Payroll Specialist (US) | Payroll | Timmy Tabasco | 311 | 1 | 4 | 2 | 0 | 0
HR-Spezialist/in | HR_SPEZ | Ellen Rilke | 66 | 1 | 0 | 0 | 1 | 0
Sales Representative | Sales | Gary Dahl | 310 | 0 | 2 | 0 | 0 | 0
Manager of Recruiting | Mgr Recrt | Mark Taylor | 310 | 0 | 0 | 0 | 0 | 0

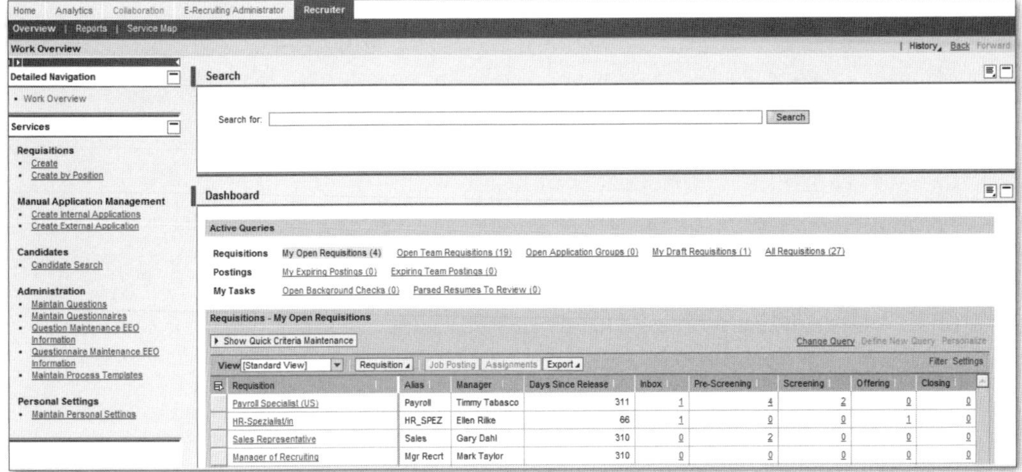

Figure 4.2 Recruiter Work Center

The Requisitions – My Open Requisitions section shows all requisitions in released status and the number of candidates in each step of the recruiting cycle. When you click on the requisition title, it displays the requisition. You can get more details about the requisition, the job requirements, and the support team from the requisition screen. We will explain more about the requisition in the next section. When you click on the candidate total displayed in any of the process step columns, it displays the Assignments for Requisition screen (see Figure 4.3).

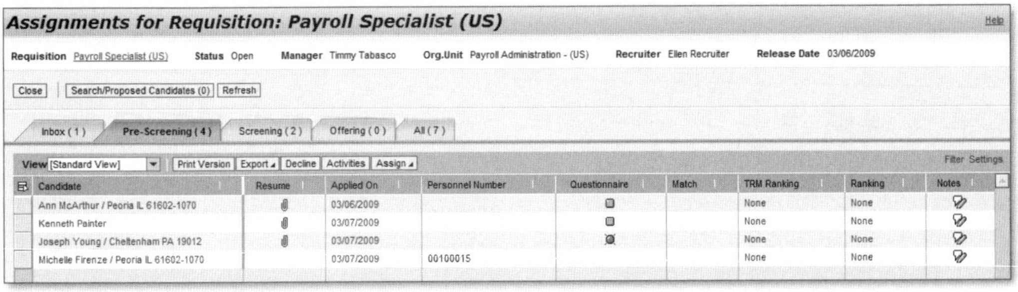

Assignments for Requisition: Payroll Specialist (US)
Help
Requisition Payroll Specialist (US)
Status Open
Manager Timmy Tabasco
Org.Unit Payroll Administration - (US)
Recruiter Ellen Recruiter
Release Date 03/06/2009
Close
Search/Proposed Candidates (0)
Refresh
Inbox (1)
Pre-Screening (4)
Screening (2)
Offering (0)
All (7)
View [Standard View]
Print Version
Export
Decline
Activities
Assign
Filter Settings
Candidate | Resume | Applied On | Personnel Number | Questionnaire | Match | TRM Ranking | Ranking | Notes
Ann McArthur / Peoria IL 61602-1070 | 03/06/2009 | None | None
Kenneth Painter | 03/07/2009 | None | None
Joseph Young / Cheltenham PA 19012 | 03/07/2009 | None | None
Michelle Firenze / Peoria IL 61602-1070 | 03/07/2009 | 00100015 | None | None

Figure 4.3 Assignments for Requisition

In the Assignments for Requisition screen, you can see the candidates who have applied for the requisition and the status of each within the recruitment process.

The different statuses in the recruiting process are displayed as tabs on the screen. When you highlight and click on the candidate, it displays the candidate profile. You can enter notes about the candidate in the notes section of the candidate profile.

In the Assignments screen, you can review candidates' resumes, review their responses to qualifying and general questionnaires, and decline the candidate for the current requisition. When you click on the Assign button, you can assign a candidate to another requisition, an application group, or a talent group. You can also assign the candidate to the next step in the recruitment process.

When you click on the Search/Proposed Candidates button in the Assignment screen, it displays all of the candidates who are a match for the requisition (see Figure 4.4).

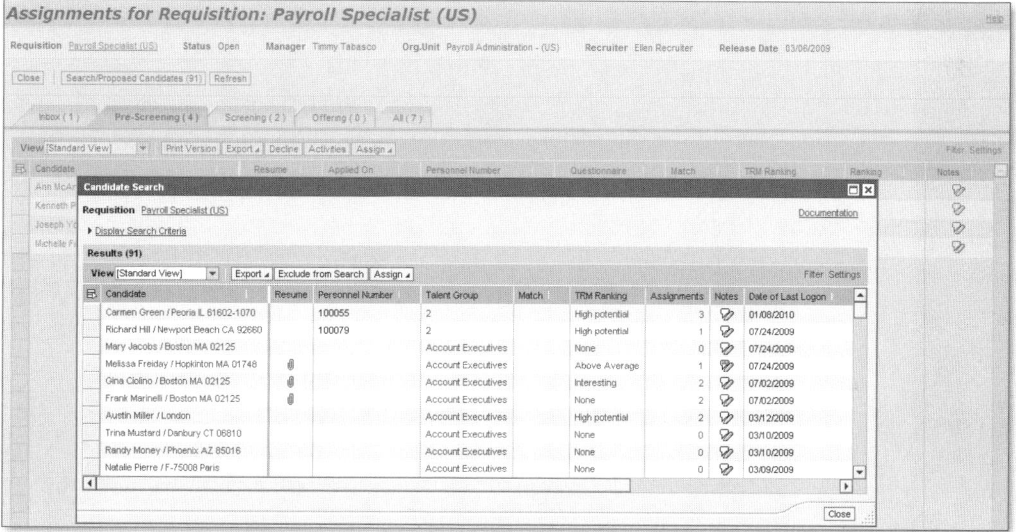

Figure 4.4 Candidate Search

The Candidate Search screen (shown in Figure 4.4), displays a candidate's personnel number if he is an internal candidate (i.e., an existing employee). This screen displays any talent groups and requisitions to which the candidate is currently assigned. Clicking on any of the hyperlinks takes you to the candidate profile, where you can obtain more details about the candidate.

In the Candidate Search screen, you can click on the Display Search Criteria link to display the search criteria used in the query. In these search criteria, you can select if you want all or at least one search criterion to be filled. Based on the search criteria, the matching candidates available in the talent warehouse are displayed.

In the Candidate Search screen, the Exclude from Search button excludes a candidate from the search. To use it, select the Candidate and click on the Exclude from Search button.

> **Tip**
>
> During the candidate search, if you want to exclude internal candidates (current employees) from the search, you can highlight the candidates who have a personnel number displayed and click on the Exclude from Search button.

You can click on the Export button and export the displayed candidates to an Excel worksheet.

4.2.2 Search

In the Search section, you can enter a search term for the system to search for candidates, requisitions, and posting that match the search term. For example, you could enter "payroll" in the search area and click on the Search button.

As shown in Figure 4.5, SAP E-Recruiting totals the number of candidates, requisitions, and published job postings that match the search criteria. In this example, 32 candidates, 5 requisitions, and 3 published job postings match the term "payroll." The search functionality is particularly useful if the recruiter wants to know the types of requisitions or publications that are currently in Released or Draft status.

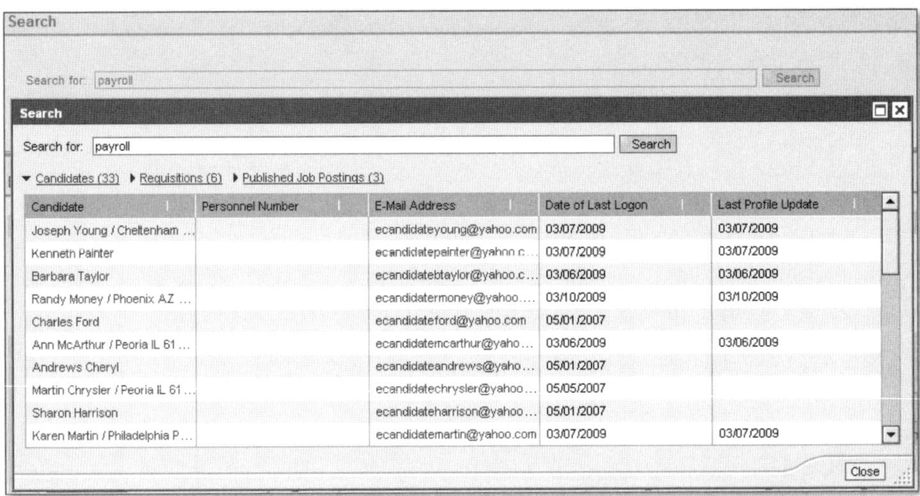

Figure 4.5 Search Results

If required, the recruiter can work with the lead recruiter of those requisitions and share the candidate or gain better insight on the candidates who are being considered for those requisitions.

Now that we have covered an overview of the recruiter work center, let's see how to create a requisition.

4.3 Create a Requisition

Users assigned the role of a recruiter can log into the recruiter work center to create a requisition in SAP E-Recruiting.

As shown in Figure 4.6, the recruiter can create a requisition by clicking on the Requisition button in the recruiter work center. You can create a requisition by selecting Create or Create by Position. You can also create a requisition by selecting an existing requisition and selecting Copy in the dropdown list.

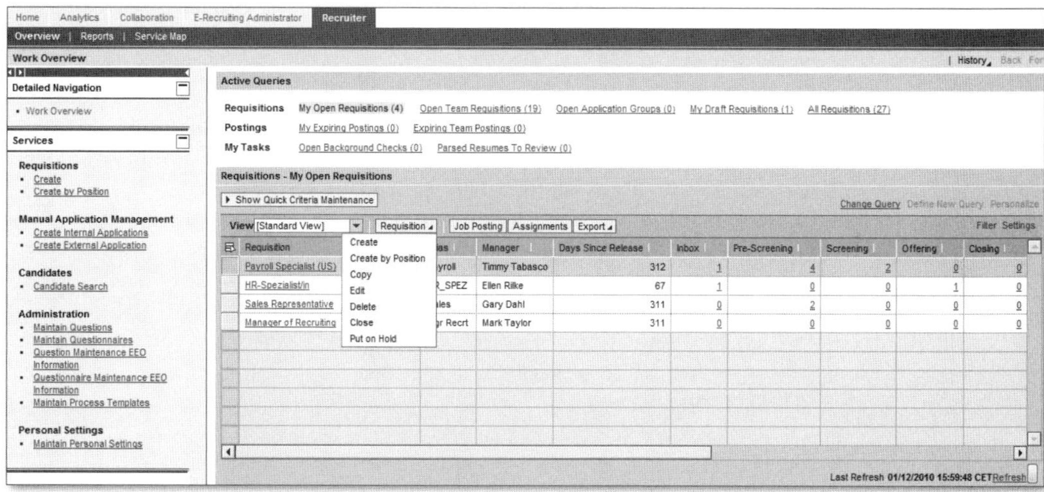

Figure 4.6 Create a Requisition from the Recruiter Work Center

4.3.1 Create a Requisition by Position

Figure 4.7 displays the screen that appears when you create a requisition by position. In the dialog box Select Position, selecting the Org. Tree option allows you to enter the organizational unit. Alternatively, you can press the F4 key to bring up the search for the organizational unit.

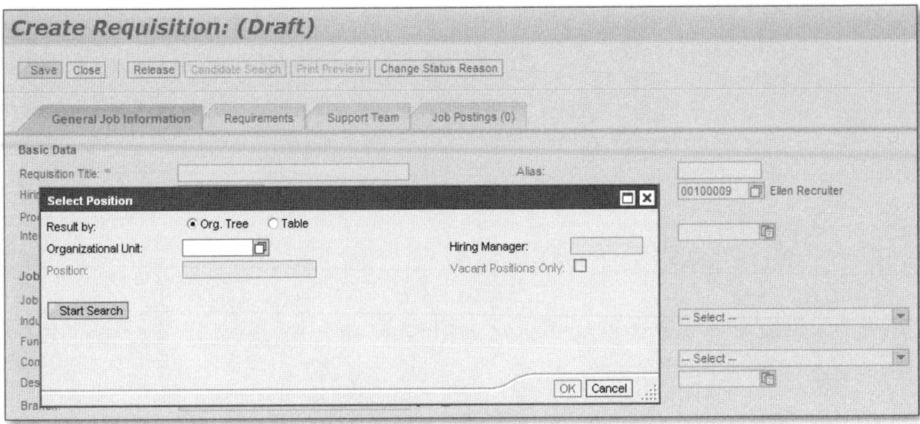

Figure 4.7 Create a Requisition by Position

After you have entered the organizational unit, click on the Start Search button. In the displayed results list, select the position ID for which you would like to create this requisition. When you click on the OK button, the requisition title and the position section are filled with the selected position title and the position details.

In the Select Position screen, if you select the option Table, the fields Hiring Manager, Position, and Vacant Positions Only are enabled. You can enter the values for these fields or press the F4 key to enter the search term and select the value from the displayed search list.

Note

If the hiring manager you enter does not belong to the organizational unit that you enter, the search does not return any values. The position ID for which you are creating the requisition may or may not be vacant. If the position is currently occupied, it will not display the holder of the position.

After you have entered the values in the Select Position dialog box, click on the Start Search button. In the displayed results list, select the position ID for which you are creating the requisition. When you click the OK button in the displayed results, the requisition screen is filled with the details of the position.

4.3.2 Create a Requisition by Copy

You can also create a new requisition by copying an existing requisition. If your organization creates many requisitions, we recommend that you create templates of common requisition types. Once it's created, you can make a copy of this requisition template and speed up processing time and reduce errors. From the recruiter work center in the Requisitions – My Open Requisitions section, you can select a requisition that you want to copy to create the new requisition.

Figure 4.8 shows a new requisition that is copied from an existing requisition. The details of the selected requisition are copied. In the requisition screen, the requisition title is displayed as Copy of <Requisition that you copied>. The requisition screen also displays the assigned job postings of the requisition that you copied. You can select those job postings for your new requisition or create new job postings.

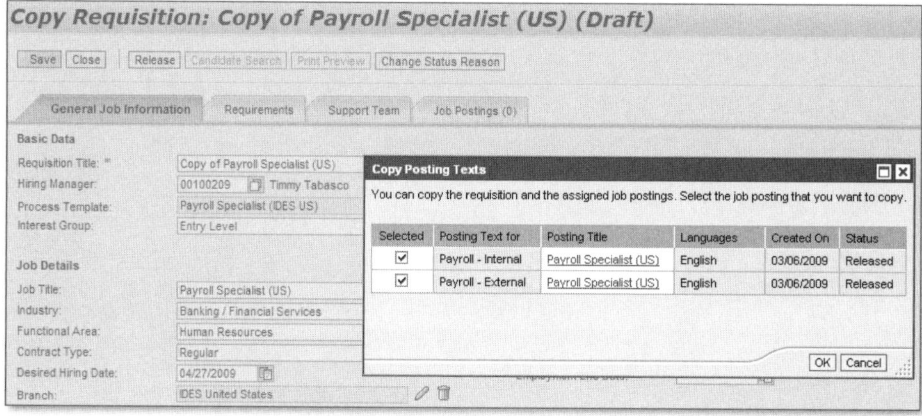

Figure 4.8 Create a New Requisition by Copy Method

In this section, we explained the different methods to create a new requisition. We do not have a preference for one method or the other; choose the method that best suits your business requirements. In the next section, we will explain the different data that needs to be entered to create a new requisition. Later in the section, we will also explain how to create and publish a job posting.

4.4 Requisition Document

To complete a requisition, the following information is available:

- General job information
- Organizational data
- Support team
- Job requirements

- Education requirements
- Attachments
- Status
- Data overview

In the next section, we will discuss each of these in detail. The first subject is general job information.

4.4.1 General Job Information

Figure 4.9 shows the General Job Information tab that is available when you create the requisition in SAP E-Recruiting.

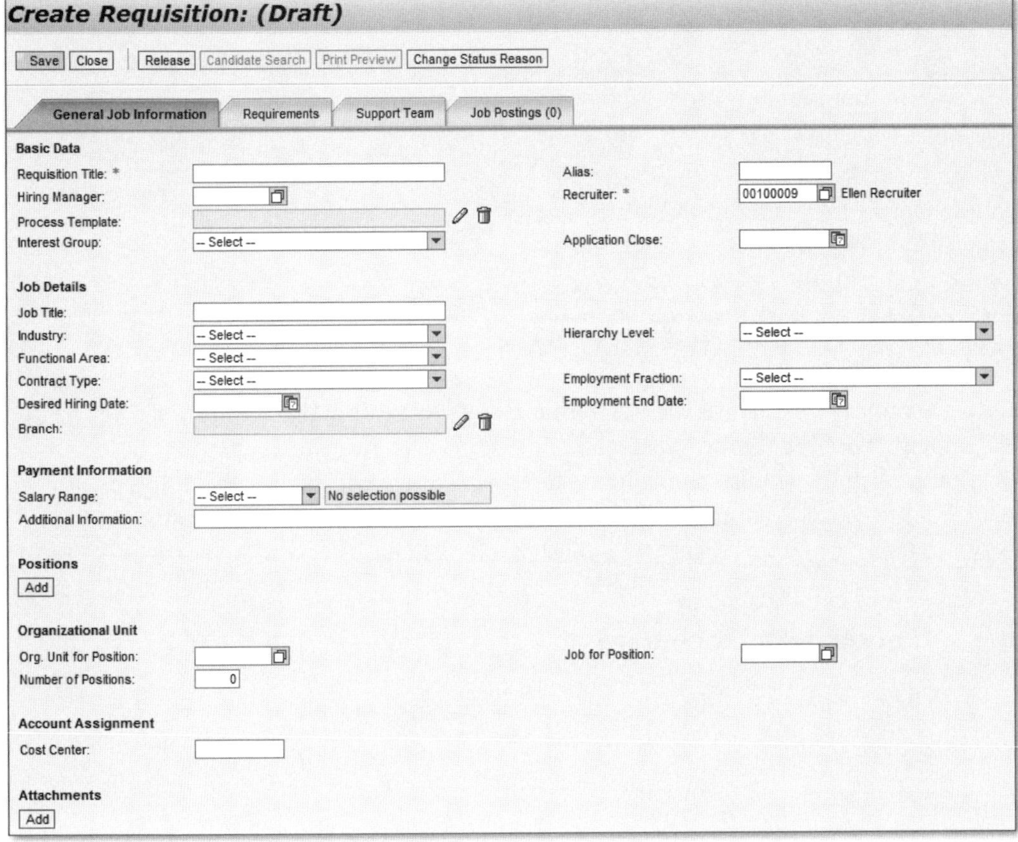

Figure 4.9 General Job Information Tab

You can enter the following data on the General Job Information tab:

- **Basic Data**
  - **Requisition Title**
    Enter the title of the requisition. This title will be displayed in the requisition lists.
  - **Alias**
    You can enter an alias for the requisition title. This alias is used to define additional sorting criteria.
  - **Hiring Manager**
    The name of the hiring manager who is responsible for filling this requisition.
  - **Recruiter**
    The name of the lead recruiter who is responsible for sourcing candidates for this requisition.
  - **Process Template**
    You assign a process template and the associated activity to the requisition.
  - **Interest Group**
    While creating a requisition, you can assign an interest group to it and broadcast the requisition to this interest group.
  - **Application Close**
    The last day the requisition can receive applications. Because the requisition is an internal document, this data is for informational purposes only.

Note

When a candidate registers in the talent warehouse, he selects an interest group to which he would like to be assigned. By assigning an interest group to a requisition and broadcasting the requisition to an interest group, you can receive faster responses to requisitions. The recruiter can also seek and receive referrals from the candidates who receive these requisitions.

- **Job Details**
  - **Job Title**
    The position title the requisition is to fill.
  - **Industry**
    The industry with which your business is associated. This can also refer to the business for which the new hire will be working.

- **Functional Area**
  The department that is planning to fill the position.
- **Hierarchy Level**
  The hierarchy level of the position, for example, executive-level management, mid-level management, trainee, and trainee/intern.
- **Contract Type**
  Whether the position is permanent, temporary, an internship, or union-based.
- **Employment Fraction**
  If the position is full-time or part-time.
- **Start Date**
  The date when the new hire is planned to start.
- **End Date**
  If the position is for a certain time period, you can enter the planned end date. Usually, the end date is populated with 12/31/9999.
- **Branch**
  The branch where the position will be located.

- **Payment Information**
  - **Salary Range**
    The salary range this position will pay. You can also enter the currency.
  - **Additional information**
    Any additional information you would like to add about the position or the requisition from a compensation perspective.
- **Positions**
  - **Positions area**
    Here you can use your organizational structure to fill in details such as the organizational unit and job of the position.
  - **Number of Positions**
    The number of positions the requisition is meant to fill.

> **Note**
>
> If the position requirements are similar, you can create one requisition to fill multiple positions. For example, if you are planning to start an IT project and require five SAP ERP HCM consultants with two to five years of SAP ERP HCM implementation experience, you can create one requisition to fill the five positions.

- **Account Assignment**
  The cost center that will be responsible for this requisition. This field is for informational purposes only. SAP E-Recruiting does not post the cost of the requisition to this assigned cost center.
- **Attachments**
  You can upload as attachments any additional information that you would like to provide to the support team about this requisition. For example, you can upload the recruiting strategy that you have devised to fill this requisition. The members of the support team can refer to this attachment to understand more about this requisition and what the plans are for sourcing.

Please note that every tab page has a Save button. After you have entered the required information, click on the Save button to save the entries.

4.4.2 Requirements

Figure 4.10 displays the Requirements tab for creating the requisition.

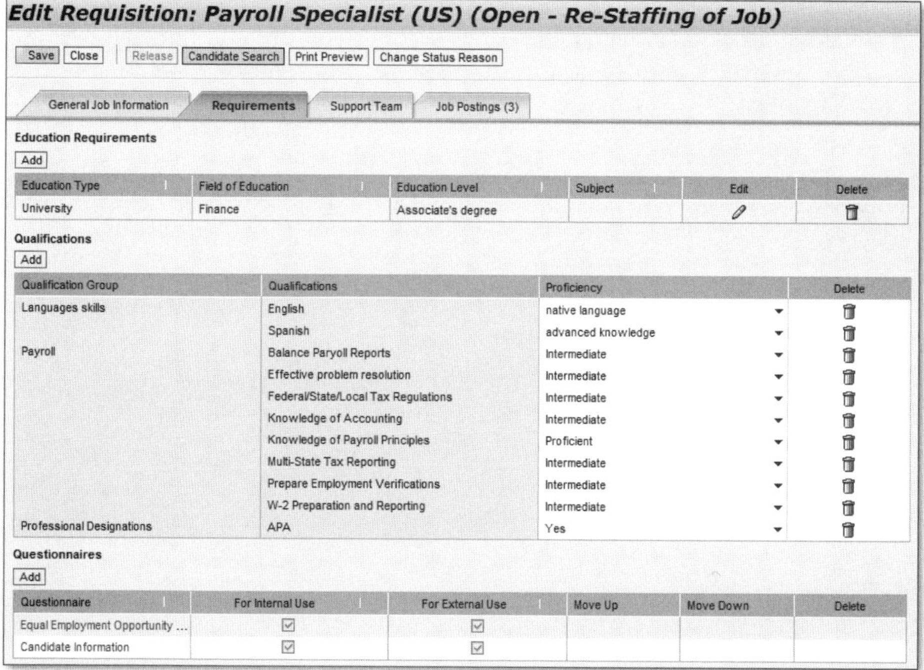

Figure 4.10 Requirements Tab

The Requirements tab contains the following data:

- **Education Requirements**
  - **Education Type**
    Specify what education type is required for the position. Some possible values are High School, Vocational Institute, University, and Other College.
  - **Field of Education**
    Specify what field of study is required for this position. If the requisition is for a position in your IT department, you might list computer science as an educational requirement for this position.
  - **Education Level**
  - **Subject (i.e., major)**
  - **Qualifications**
    You can add qualifications to the requisition from the qualifications catalog. In customizing, you can configure the system so that position requirements are displayed for that particular position only.

  Figure 4.11 displays the qualifications catalog you use to add the qualifications to the requisition. In the qualifications section, you can add the qualifications group, the qualifications in the group, and the proficiency required for each of the qualification.

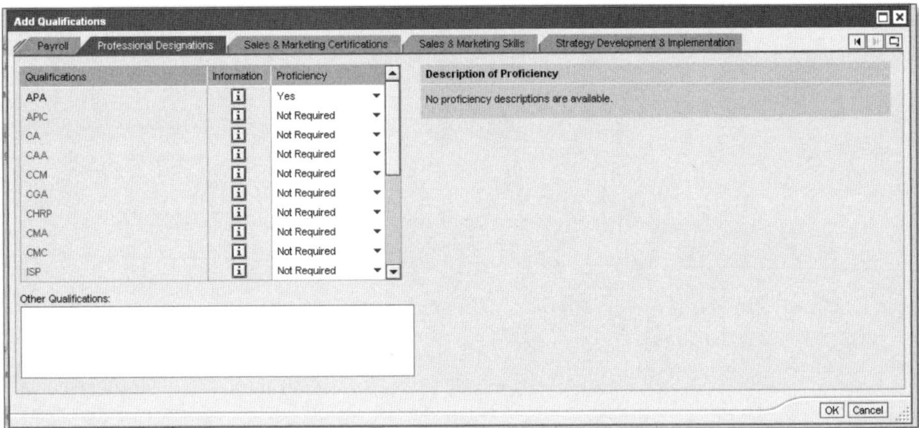

Figure 4.11 Qualifications Catalog

- **Questionnaires**
  In the application wizard, you can add the questionnaires to which candidates need to respond. In the Questionnaires section, you can add the general ques-

tionnaire, qualifying questionnaire, and the EEO questionnaire. For each questionnaire, you can select which questionnaires are for internal or external candidates only or for both.

Note

In the United States, an Equal Employment Opportunity (EEO) questionnaire is mandatory for every requisition. The data from the EEO questionnaire is required for Office of Federal Contract Compliance Programs (OFCCP) (*www.ofccp.org*) federal filing. In some implementations, we have seen customers collect EEO data when the candidate is registering in the talent warehouse. The suggested best practice is to collect EEO data for an application. Therefore, you should have the candidate respond to the EEO questionnaire when applying to a requisition. In this way, EEO data can be collected from both the registered and the unregistered candidate.

4.4.3 Requisition Management – Customizing

You perform the following settings for requisition management within the IMG. To perform this customizing, look for these activities under the IMG menu path SAP E-Recruiting • Requisition Management • Requisition.

- **Define Hierarchy Levels**
  In this customizing activity, you define the hierarchy levels that exist in your organization. For example, apprentice, senior professional, and top management/executive could be different hierarchy levels.
- **Define Work Contract Types**
  In this customizing activity, you define the different types of work contract that exist in your organization, for example, regular, part-time, and temporary.
- **Define Industries**
  In this customizing activity, you define the industries in which your organization is currently doing business. The industries you customize in this activity can also reflect the industries in which the candidate needs to have experience, for example, retail, real estate, or technology.
- **Define Functional Areas**
  In this customizing activity, you define the different work areas in your organization, for example, human resources, sales, and research and development.
- **Define Employment Fractions**
  In this customizing activity, you define the minimum number of working hours for the different employment fractions, for example, full-time/threshold 40 hours and part-time/threshold 20 hours.

Salary ranges configuration is performed under these two activities:

- **Determine Currencies for Salary Ranges**
  In this customizing activity, you define the currencies that are used in the salary ranges. You can also specify if the currency is a reference currency.
- **Define Salary Ranges**
  In this customizing activity, you define the currency and the salary ranges. You can customize multiple salary ranges for a particular currency, depending on the requisition requirements. You should have customized Determine Currencies for Salary Ranges prior to customizing Define Salary Ranges.

4.4.4 Support Team

For every requisition, a support team should be assigned. The support team is responsible for working on the requisition. The members of the support team have roles assigned to them depending on their responsibility in filling the requisition.

As shown in Figure 4.12, you can add individual members to the support team. When adding individual members, you must also define the role of the member in the support team. You can customize the roles in SAP E-Recruiting to meet your business requirements. The menu path to customize the roles in the IMG is SAP E-RECRUITING • TECHNICAL SETTINGS • USER ADMINISTRATION • ROLES IN E-RECRUITING. When you create a user in this customizing step, you need to add a reference user to the newly created role. We will discuss more about roles and reference users in Chapter 10, Authorization Management.

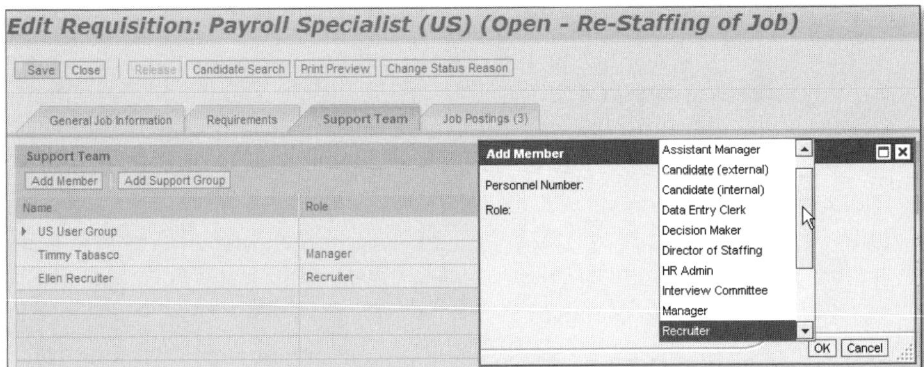

Figure 4.12 Adding a Member to the Support Team

If your recruiting administrator has created support groups, then you can add a specific support group as the support team to the requisition as well.

Figure 4.13 shows how to add a support group to the support team of a requisition. If you want to delete the support group assigned to the requisition, click on the Trash icon. When you click on the Disband Group link, it disbands the group, but the members of the support group are retained as members of the support team.

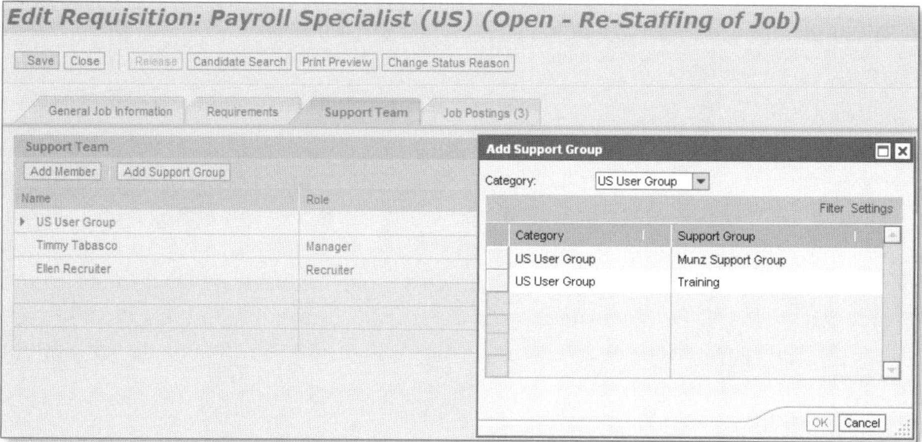

Figure 4.13 Adding a Support Group to the Support Team

While creating the support group, you can also categorize the support group based on branch locations, lines of business, or any subject that meets your business requirements. The customizing activity is performed in the IMG under the menu path SAP E-RECRUITING • TECHNICAL SETTINGS • USER ADMINISTRATION • DEFINE CATEGORIES FOR GROUPINGS.

The person who creates the requisition or who enters the candidate application manually is automatically assigned to the support team. A requisition should have at least one person assigned to the support team so that the requisition can be maintained.

4.4.5 Print Preview

You can click on the Print Preview button to display the data overview of the requisition. This displays a summary of the information on the requisition and can be controlled via your Smart Form template.

4.4.6 Requisition Status

In SAP E-Recruiting, the requisition has an assigned status. What activities can be performed on the requisition depends on the status of the requisition. The following are the standard delivered statuses for requisitions:

- **Draft**
  When a requisition is created, it is set in Draft status.
- **Released**
  A requisition should be in Released status if it is to be published in different publication channels.
- **Closed**
  A requisition can be closed if the vacancy is filled or if the requisition will no longer be used. There can be several business reasons why a requisition is closed, even before the vacancy is filled. One of the reasons might be that the forecasted headcount is no longer required.
  If the requisition is closed after publication, the candidates who applied to the requisition can still be retained in the talent warehouse. The recruiter can assign those candidates to talent groups or other requisitions and continue with talent relationship management (TRM) activities.
- **On Hold**
  A requisition can be put on hold pending some business decisions. A business scenario where a requisition can be on hold could be when the candidates are in the assessment phase and a decision is pending on their status. If a suitable candidate is not identified or if the candidate does not accept the offer, the requisition can be put back to Released status, and the candidate sourcing can continue. When a requisition is in the On Hold status, the recruiter could consider the candidates (who applied to this requisition) for other open requisitions.
- **To Be Deleted**
  When a requisition is in the To Be Deleted status, only a recruiting administrator can see it. A requisition can be set to the To Be Deleted status when it is filled and is no longer required or if the requisition was created by mistake.

Requisition statuses in SAP are standard delivered and cannot be changed or customized. However, when you change the status of the object, you can assign a reason for the status change. You can create custom status reasons to meet your business requirements. To perform this customizing, follow the IMG menu path SAP E-Recruiting • Basic Settings • Status Reasons • Define Status Reasons.

After you have created the custom status reasons, you need to assign the reasons to the status of the specific SAP E-Recruiting objects. The status reasons that are assigned to the status of the SAP E-Recruiting objects appear for the assigned objects only. The same status reason can be assigned to multiple objects. To perform this customizing, follow the IMG menu path SAP E-RECRUITING • BASIC SETTINGS • STATUS REASONS • ASSIGN STATUS REASONS TO STATUSES FOR RECRUITMENT.

4.4.7 Releasing a Requisition

To release a requisition, click on the query My Draft Requisitions. This displays all of the requisitions that are in Draft status in the display list. Select the requisition that you would like to move to the Released status. In the requisition screen, click on the Release button. When you make a status change, you can assign a reason for it.

As shown in Figure 4.14, select a status reason and click the OK button to accept your selection. The requisition is now in the Released status. After a requisition is moved to the Released status, if you edit or make any changes to the requisition, the SAP E-Recruiting system automatically moves the requisition to the Draft status. A recruiter would have to again manually move it back to the Released status when ready.

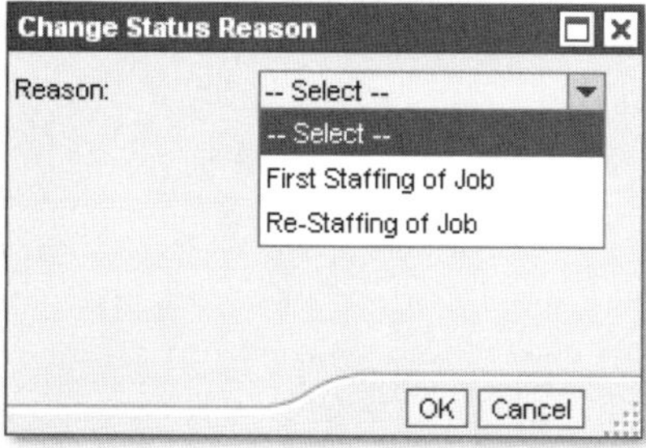

Figure 4.14 Status Reasons

4.4.8 Job Postings

A job posting is an announcement with details about a vacant position to which interested candidates can apply. Either the manager or the recruiter can create a job posting. The job posting contains the general posting information and the posting text. To access the Job Postings screen, you can do one of the following:

- In the recruiter work center, you can select and display the appropriate requisition. In the requisition screen, click on the Job Postings tab to display the job postings screen.

- In the recruiter work center, highlight the requisition and click on the Job Posting button.

Figure 4.15 displays the job posting screen. In the General Posting Information area, you can create the following:

- **Work Location**
  To add a work location, click on the Add button. This creates a new row and displays the values required for the work location as a dropdown list. If required, you can add more than one work location to the job posting. To add additional work locations, click on the Add button and select the required value from the dropdown list.
- **Functional Area**
- **Hierarchy Level**

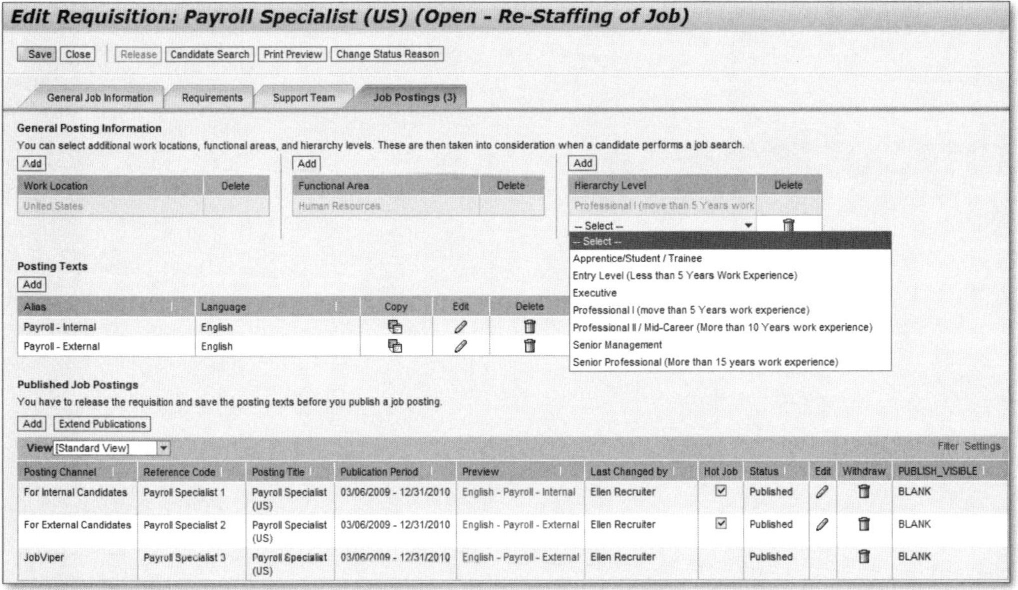

Figure 4.15 Job Posting Tab

> **Note**
>
> To create the Functional Area and Hierarchy Level, the steps are similar to work locations. The work location, functional area, and hierarchy level that you create in the job posting screen supplement the information that is already stored on the requisition. The interested candidates can use this additional information while searching for jobs.

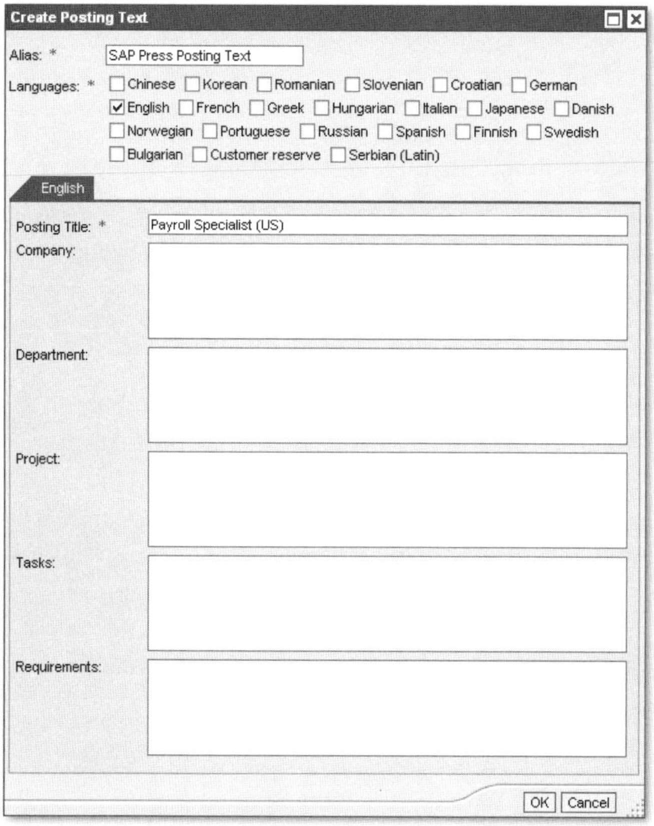

Figure 4.16 Create Posting Text

- **Posting Texts**
  To create the posting texts, click on the Add button. In the Create Posting Text screen displayed in Figure 4.16, enter the alias and select the language in which you want to develop the posting text. Click on the OK button. This displays the screen where you can enter the following details:
  - **Company**
    A brief introduction to the company
  - **Department**
    The department in your organization that is planning to fill this vacant position
  - **Project**
    A brief description of the job and its role

- **Tasks**
  The responsibilities of the position
- **Requirements**
  The educational requirements, work experience, and additional requirements that are needed for this position.

If required, you can change the Job Posting text to meet the requirements of different publication channels such as internal, external, or the application groups.

Let's now discuss publications.

4.4.9 Publications

To publish your job posting, click on the Add button in the Published Job Postings area.

In the Add Job Posting dialog box (see Figure 4.17), select the channels and specify the publication duration. Click the OK button to accept your selection. This displays the Further Specifications dialog box (see Figure 4.18).

Add Job Posting

Internal Posting Channels

Selected	Channel	Alias	English	Published From	Published To
☐	For Internal Candidates	-- Select --	☐	/ /	/ /
☐	Application Groups	-- Select --	☐	/ /	/ /

External Posting Channels

Selected	Channel	Alias	English	Published From	Published To
☐	For External Candidates	-- Select --	☐	/ /	/ /
☐	JobViper	-- Select --	☐	/ /	/ /

OK Cancel

Figure 4.17 Add Job Posting

As shown in Figure 4.18, the Further Specifications dialog box displays the posting channel and the reference code for each of the posting channels. You can also set any of the postings as a *hot job*. When you identify a posting as a hot job, the hot job duration defaults to the publication period. You can edit the duration of the hot job to suit your requirements. Remember, the hot job's publication duration cannot be longer than the job posting publication period.

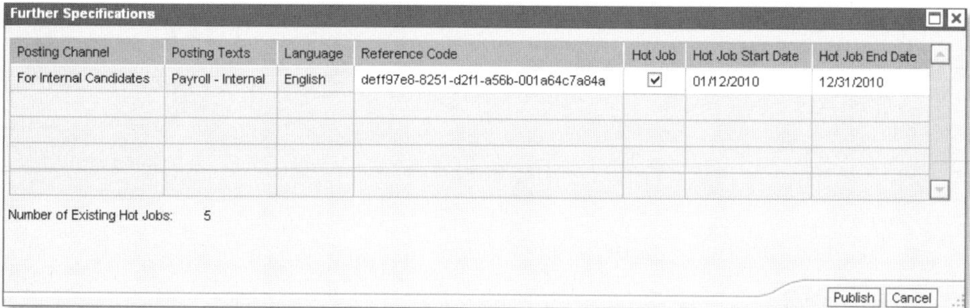
Posting Channel	Posting Texts	Language	Reference Code	Hot Job	Hot Job Start Date	Hot Job End Date
For Internal Candidates	Payroll - Internal	English	deff97e8-8251-d2f1-a56b-001a64c7a84a	☑	01/12/2010	12/31/2010

Number of Existing Hot Jobs: 5

Publish Cancel

Figure 4.18 Further Specifications

> **Note**
>
> You can implement and activate the BAdI HRRCF00_GET_EXT_CODE to create a custom reference code. You can customize the reference code to meet your business requirements and your current recruiting strategy of generating reference codes. For example, all HR-related postings can start with HR, all Finance department related postings can start with FIN, and so on.

You can customize the posting channels where you would like your job posting to be published. To perform this customizing, follow the IMG menu path SAP E-Recruiting • Requisition Management • Job Posting • Define Posting Channels. In the customizing activity, after you have created a posting channel, you need to specify the candidate class and assign a publisher class to the channel. The publisher class defines the publishing and the withdrawal of the publication. The publisher class must implement the method IF_HRRCF_PUBLISHER. The WITHDRAW_POSSIBLE method checks if a status change of Released to Withdrawn is possible for the posting channel. If the status change to withdrawn is possible, then the method WITHDRAW initiates the process to change the status of the publication. The REPUBLISH_REQUIRED method checks if a republication is possible in the publisher class that is used for the posting channel. If the republication is possible, the method REPUBLISH initiates the process to update the publication. The prerequisite for the republication is that the publication period must still be valid.

You can activate the standard implementation of BAdI HRRCF00_GET_EXT_CODE to have SAP E-Recruiting generate the reference code for the publication. If the BAdI implementation is active, the recruiter can click on the Generate Reference Code button for the system to generate the reference code. Interested candidates use the reference code to apply to the requisition. Managers and recruiters also can use the reference code to manage the applications. In the standard delivery, the BAdI implementation is not active.

You can activate the standard implementation of BAdI HRRCF00_GET_DEFAULTS_TEXTS to have SAP E-Recruiting default text in the job posting. If the BAdI implementation is activated, buttons are displayed in the screen where the job posting is created. The recruiter can click on the button to default the texts. In the standard delivery, the BAdI implementation is not active.

- **Status**
  The valid statuses for the publications are:
  - **Published**
    This is similar to the Released status. A job posting can be in Published status *only* if the assigned requisition is in Released status and the posting text has been created.
  - **Withdrawn**
    You can withdraw a publication by clicking on the Withdraw icon displayed for the publication.

    You can withdraw a publication only if its publication period is valid and has not expired. Also, to be able to withdraw a publication in the customizing, you must have configured the publication class for the channel to be able to withdraw a publication.

    When you withdraw a publication, the Hot Job designation is also removed. When the publication is withdrawn, its status cannot be reset to published. If you have a business need to publish the posting in the same channel, you have to create a new publication. Once you withdraw a publication, the publication will continue to be displayed with the status as Withdrawn in the publication list.

Note

If your organization creates many job postings, there might be a temptation to identify every job posting as a hot job. To every recruiter, his job posting is important and is a hot job. The suggested best practice is to identify as hot jobs only job postings that have an immediate business need. You can also circulate the job postings as hot jobs; every week identify a few job postings as hot jobs and set the duration for a week or so. The following week you can retire these hot jobs and identify a new set of job postings as hot jobs.

Editing the Publication

After a job posting is published, you can edit certain information on it. If you have published a job posting and you would like to make it a hot job, click on the Edit icon of the publication. In the displayed dialog box (see Figure 4.19), you can select the Hot Job checkbox and make the publication a hot job. The hot job publication period defaults to the same period as the publication period. You can change the hot job duration as well if required.

You can also change the publication duration if required. The Published From field is disabled and you cannot make changes. The Published To period is enabled, and you can change the last day of the publication if required.

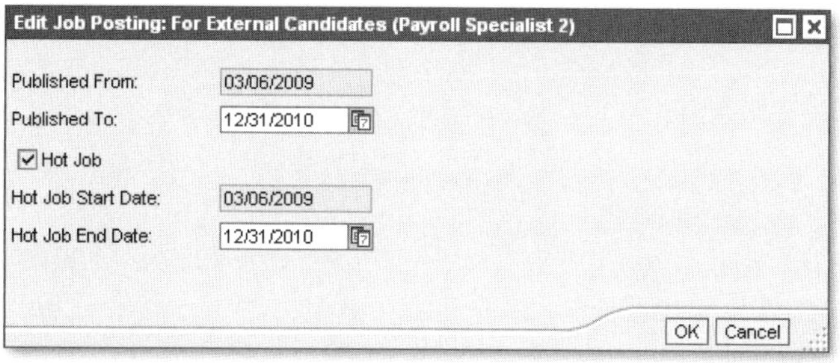

Figure 4.19 Edit Job Postings

> **Note**
>
> You cannot edit the publication if the publication channel is for an application group. You also cannot make the publication for an application group a hot job.

Extending Publications

If you have multiple publications for the same requisition and you would like to change the end date of the publications simultaneously, the Extend Publications functionality is a good option.

- When you click on the Extend Publications button, a dialog box is displayed (see Figure 4.20). In the displayed dialog box, select the publications that you want to adjust. Enter the new Publication End date click on OK to accept your changes.
- In the next section, we will explain questionnaire and question management. In SAP E-Recruiting, you can attach a questionnaire to the application wizard and have candidates respond to this questionnaire. SAP E-Recruiting can rank the candidates based on their responses to the questionnaire. Many SAP E-Recruiting customers use questionnaires to prequalify candidates and source top prospects.

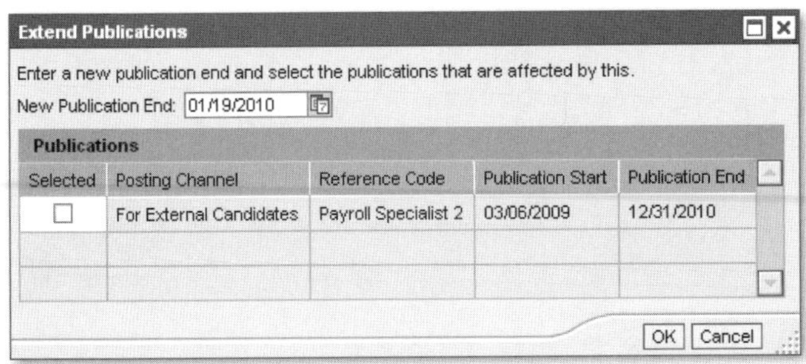

Figure 4.20 Extending Publications

4.5 Question and Questionnaire Management

In SAP E-Recruiting, you can develop questionnaires to meet the specific requirements of your requisition. While developing the questionnaire, you can develop:

- General criteria questions
- Knock-out questions
- EEO questions

In this section, we will explain how to create and maintain questionnaires and questions. Later in the section, we will explain how to use the questionnaire to prequalify the candidate for a requisition and how to use the questionnaire for TRM activities.

4.5.1 Questionnaire Categories

SAP E-Recruiting provides two types of questionnaire categories:

- **Evaluable information**
  The system uses questionnaires in this category to rank candidates based on their responses to the questions. These questionnaires contain both general questions and knock-out questions.
- **Equal Employment Opportunity information**
  Questionnaires in this category are used to collect EEO data from the candidate. The collected data is used for OFCCP filing. EEO questionnaires are specific to the United States.
  - You can execute the report RCF_QA_CREATE_CATEGORY or use Transaction code OO_HRRCF_CAT_CREATE to make the settings and generate the table entries for questionnaire maintenance. You need to execute this report only once before starting your configuration.

4.5.2 Questionnaire Groups

In SAP E-Recruiting, you can group the questions and the questionnaires based on business need. Grouping questionnaires enables easy maintenance. Creating questionnaire groups is a customizing activity. To create a questionnaire group, follow the IMG menu path SAP E-RECRUITING • APPLICANT TRACKING • QUESTIONNAIRES • DEFINE QUESTIONNAIRE GROUPS.

In the customizing activity (see Figure 4.21), each questionnaire group needs a group ID, name, and category. SAP recommends not using 0 as a group ID because it might lead to problems in the flexibilization. After you have created your questionnaire groups, you need to categorize them as either evaluable information or Equal Employment Opportunity information.

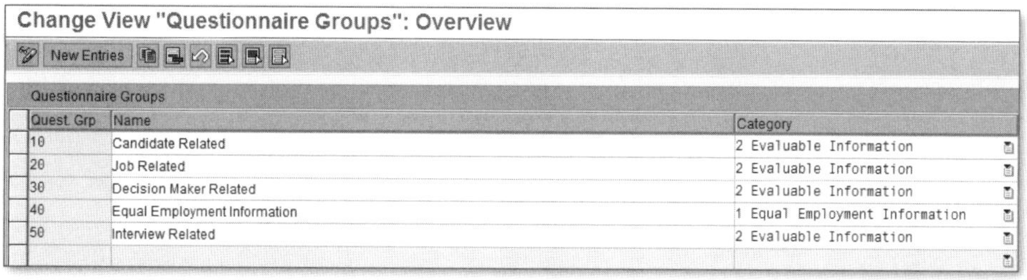

Change View "Questionnaire Groups": Overview

New Entries

Questionnaire Groups

Quest. Grp	Name	Category
10	Candidate Related	2 Evaluable Information
20	Job Related	2 Evaluable Information
30	Decision Maker Related	2 Evaluable Information
40	Equal Employment Information	1 Equal Employment Information
50	Interview Related	2 Evaluable Information

Figure 4.21 Create Questionnaire Groups

The groups that are created in this customizing activity are displayed as tabs in the question and questionnaire maintenance screen.

4.5.3 Question Management

A questionnaire consists of a question or multiple questions. You can access the Maintain Questions screen (see Figure 4.22) from the Recruiter Work Center. In the Recruiter Work Center, the Maintain Questions screen is under Administration in the Services section of the work overview.

The structure of the questions consists of the following:

- **Question**
  Enter the question as free text. This is a mandatory field.
- **Status**
  The question has three possible statuses. They are SAP standard delivered and cannot be changed:
  - **Draft**
    The question is still being constructed and is not ready for use.

- **Released**
  The questions is released and can be used in a questionnaire.
- **Do Not Use**
  The question should no longer be used in questionnaires. If the question has a status of Do Not Use, you *cannot* change the status of the question to Draft or Released.

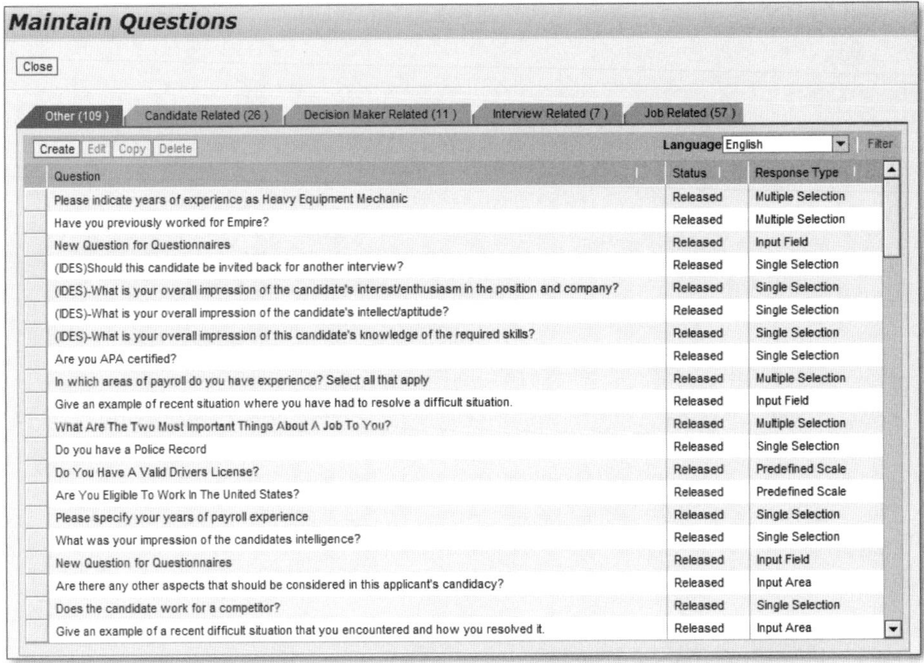

Figure 4.22 Maintain Questions

- **Language**
  The languages in which you want the questions to be displayed.
- **Response Type**
  How the candidate responds to the question. The different response types are:
  - **Predefined scale**
    Prior to using the predefined scale as a response type, you need to define the scales for the questionnaire. This is a customizing activity in the IMG. To create a scale for the questionnaire, follow the menu path SAP E-RECRUITING • APPLICANT TRACKING • QUESTIONNAIRES • DEFINE SCALES FOR QUESTIONNAIRES.

In the customizing activity (see Figure 4.23), you create a new scale by configuring a scale ID and a name for the scale. SAP recommends not using 0 as the scale ID because it might lead to problems in the flexibilization. Once you have created the scale, you need to define the proficiencies of the scale. In the Change View "Scaling": Overview screen, select the newly created scale. Double-click on Proficiencies. In the Change View "Proficiencies": Overview screen (see Figure 4.24), create the proficiencies that you want to associate with this scale.

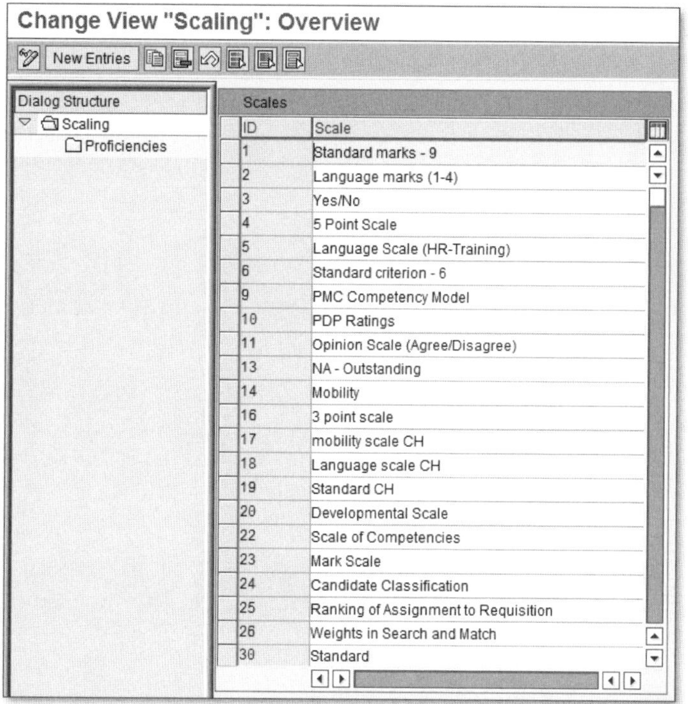

Figure 4.23 Define Scales for Questionnaires

At least one proficiency should be associated with every scale for the questionnaire. Keep the proficiencies meaningful. Also, do not change the scale or the proficiencies associated with the scale after you have used them in a question or questionnaire.

More response types include:

- **Input field**
  In this response type, you expect a response in the form of free text up to 40 characters.

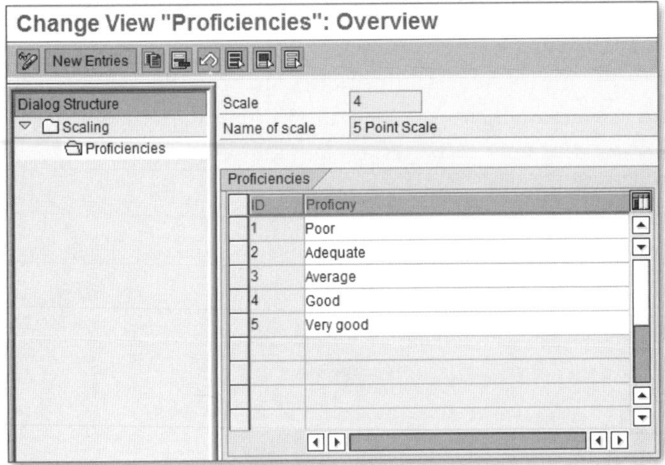

Figure 4.24 Define Proficiencies for Questionnaire Scales

- **Input area**
  This is similar to the input field except that the free text can be of any character length.
- **Single selection**
  The possible responses are offered to the candidate in a dropdown list. The candidate can select one of the responses as a valid response to the question. In a single selection, the candidate can select only one response.
- **Multiple selection**
  This is very similar to the single selection. In response to the question using a multiple selection, the candidate can select multiple responses from the dropdown list.
- **Group**
  In this field, you can group the questions based on the subject or the topic. The created question would then appear under that group in the Maintain Questions screen.

Let's discuss how to create a question in the next section.

4.5.4 Creating a Question

In the main screen for maintaining questions, different questionnaire groups are displayed as tabs. Each tab contains the questions that you have grouped under that topic. You can perform the following activities:

- **Create new question by standard method**
  You can create a new question by clicking on the Create button, or you can create a new question by copying an existing question.
- **Edit a question**
  To edit a question, highlight it and click on the Edit button. If the question is in Released status, you cannot edit it. To edit the question, you have to change its status to Draft. When the question is in Draft status, all of the fields except the Language field are displayed. In the Maintain Questions screen, if required, you can reorder the responses, delete a response, or add a new response. You can also change the other fields such as Response Type or Questionnaire Group.
- **Delete a question**
  To delete a question, highlight it and click on the Delete button. The question should not be in use. If the question is in Released status, you will get an error message saying, "Question does not have status Draft. Not possible to delete." To delete a released question, click on the Edit button and change the status to Draft. If the question is not in use, you can delete it. You cannot delete a question if the status is Do Not Use.

Note

When you are in the Maintain Questions screen and you want to return to the Maintain Questions Listing screen, click on the Back button. If you click the Close button, the system will take you back to the recruiter work center.

- If you want to create a new question, click on the Create button in the Maintain Questions Listing screen. In the Create Question screen (see Figure 4.25), enter the basic data.

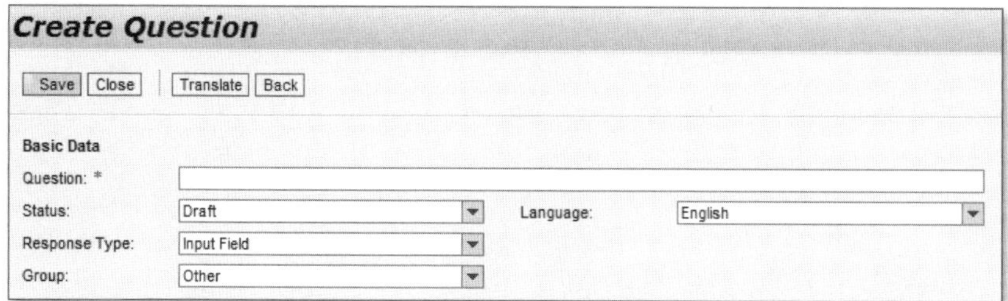

Figure 4.25 Create Question

- In the Create Question screen, the Response Type usually defaults to Input field. For the response types Input Field and Input Area, you cannot add any responses in the Create Question screen. You can select a response type from the dropdown list. If you select the option Predefined Scale, the field Scale is displayed. Select the required scale from the dropdown list, and the scales are displayed in the Responses group of the Create Question screen.

- When you select Single Selection or Multiple Selection, you can create the responses by clicking on the Add button in the Responses area (see Figure 4.26). In the Assign Response dialog box, you can create a new response or select an existing response by pressing the F4 key or selecting the Help icon displayed in the Assign Response dialog box. After you have created a response, you can delete it by clicking the Trash Can icon.

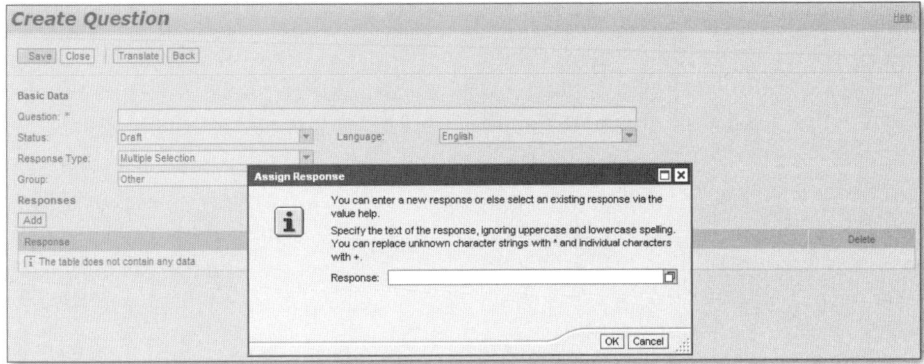

Figure 4.26 Create Response

- When a question is initially created, the status will be in Draft. You need to change the status to Released to be able to use the question and make it available for assignment to a requisition or to a questionnaire.

4.5.5 Creating a Question by the Copy Method

You can also create a question by copying an existing question. Select the question you want to copy and click on the Copy button. In the Copy Question screen (see Figure 4.27), the question field has the phrase "Copy of" appended to the question text. If you want to change the response type, you will see a warning message as a dialog box. Click on OK and you can add responses to the new response type you have just selected. Once you have created the question, click on the Save button to accept your changes.

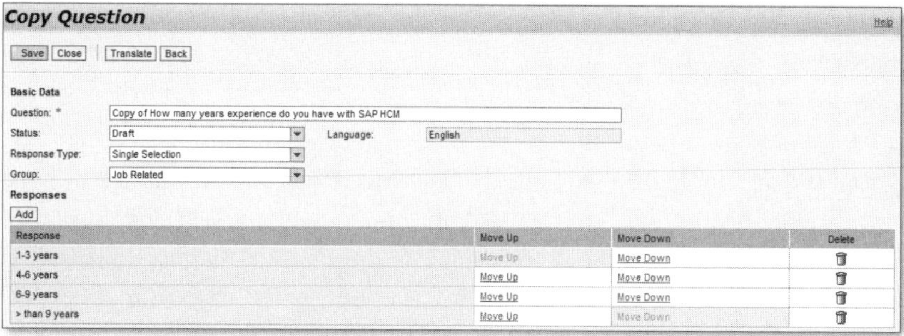

Figure 4.27 Create a New Question by the Copy Method

In this section, we gained a better understanding of question management and how to create and maintain questions. In the next section, we will explain questionnaire management and the structure of a questionnaire.

4.5.6 Questionnaire Management

A questionnaire consists of questions that the candidate is required to answer. Questions are the building blocks of questionnaires. You can access the Maintain Questionnaires link from the recruiter work center under Administration in the Services section of the work overview.

The questionnaire is an essential tool that recruiters and hiring managers can use during the recruiting process. While creating a questionnaire, the recruiter can determine which questions are required. When the candidate responds to a question, the ratings for that question can be saved in the SAP E-Recruiting application. SAP E-Recruiting uses these ratings to rank the candidates by implementing the ranking by questionnaire functionality.

The structure of the questionnaire consists of (see Figure 4.28):

- **Title**
  In this field, you enter the title of the questionnaire. The title is a mandatory field. If you assign the questionnaire in the application wizard, the system will use the questionnaire title to label the link in the navigation toolbar.
- **Alias**
- **Status**
  The questionnaire has three standard delivered statuses: Draft, Released, and Do Not Use.
- **Languages**
  The language in which you want the questionnaire to be created and maintained.

- **Relevance**
  In enhancement pack 4, you can create a questionnaire for internal candidates only, external candidates only, or for both.
- **Group**
  The group is the questionnaire group to which the questionnaire will be attached. In the Maintain Questionnaires Listing screen, the questionnaire appears in the tab of that particular group.
- **Instructions**
  This is a free text field where you can provide instructions to complete the questionnaire and the individual questions in the questionnaire. You can create instructions for every questionnaire group and for the available languages.
- **Assigned Questions**
  When you create the questionnaire, you can add questions to it. The prerequisite is that the questions be created and exist in the SAP E-Recruiting system.

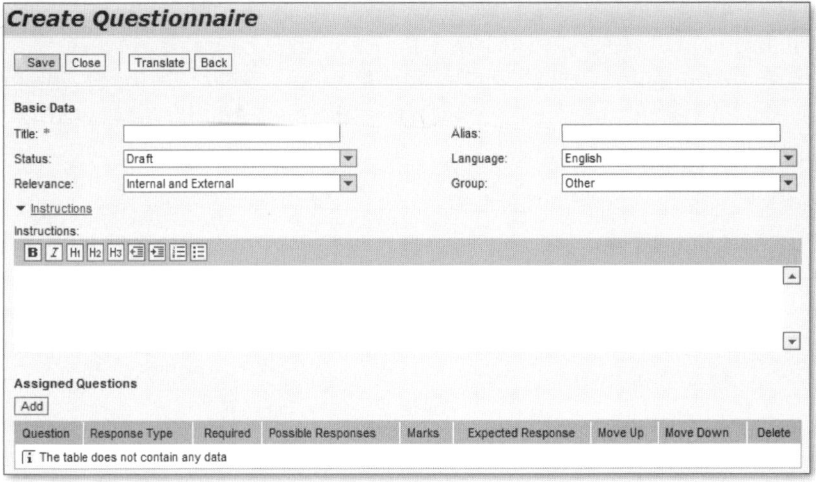

Figure 4.28 Structure of the Questionnaire

In the Maintain Questionnaires screen (see Figure 4.29), the questionnaires are displayed in the different questionnaire groups to which they are assigned. The questionnaire listing also displays if the questionnaire is for internal use, external use, or both. You can filter the listing by clicking on the Filter link and setting the filters for the For Internal Use or For External Use columns. You can use the buttons Create, Edit, Copy, and Delete to create the questionnaire and for questionnaire management. The functionalities of these buttons are similar to those in question management.

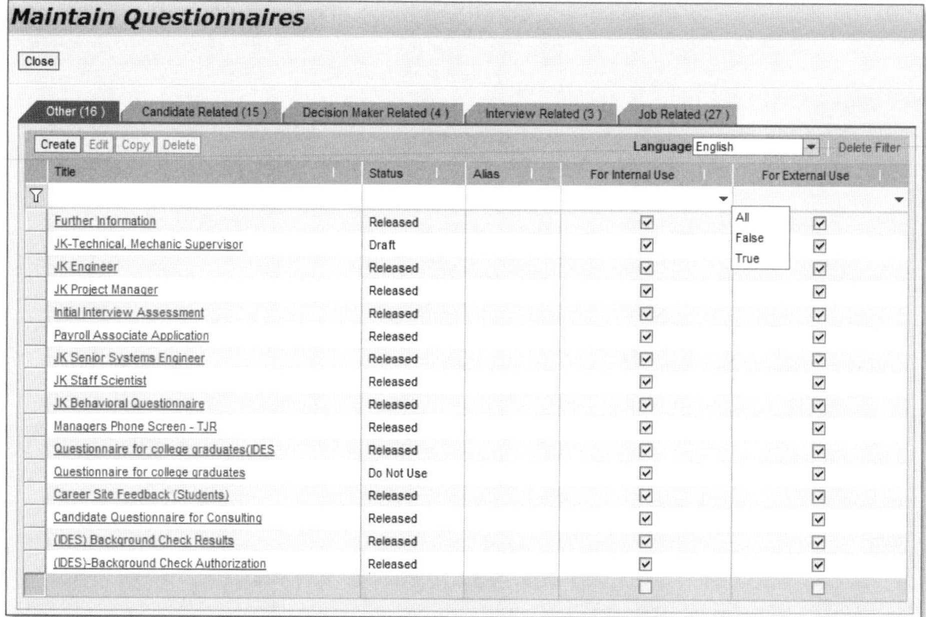

Figure 4.29 Maintain Questionnaires

Now let's look at how to create a questionnaire and how to add a question and explore the different methods by which the questionnaire can be sent to the candidate.

4.5.7 Create a Questionnaire

To create a questionnaire, click on the Create button in the Maintain Questionnaires Listing screen. In the Create Questionnaire screen, enter the basic data that is required for your business requirements.

A questionnaire consists of one or more questions. In the Assigned Questions group, click on the Add button to assign questions to the questionnaire (see Figure 4.30). When you assign questions to a questionnaire, you can select questions that belong to a different questionnaire group than the group to which the present questionnaire is assigned. For example, if the questionnaire belongs to the Other category, you can select questions from Other, Candidate Related, Decision Maker Related, Interview Related, and Job Related categories for assignment to the questionnaire.

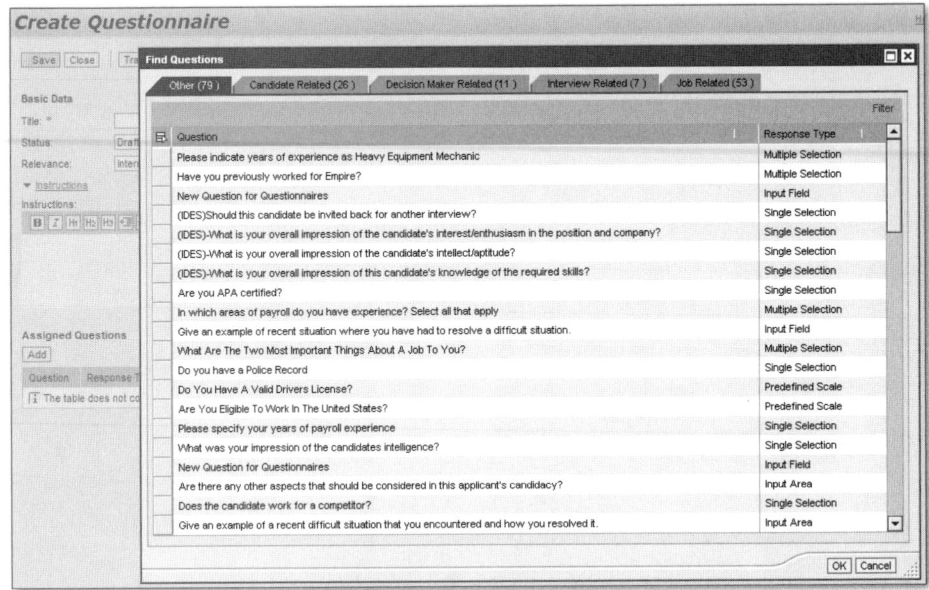

Figure 4.30 Add Questions to the Questionnaire

Assigned Questions

In the Assigned Questions group (see Figure 4.31), you can reorder the questions by clicking on the Move Up and Move Down links. You can delete an assigned question by clicking on the Trash Can icon.

Assigned Questions

Add

Question	Response Type	Required	Possible Responses	Marks	Expected Response	Move Up	Move Down	Delete
What interest you about this job?	Single Selection	☐	Compensation	000	☐	Move Up	Move Down	🗑
			The Benefits	000	☐			
			The Challenge of Learning a New Area	040	☐			
			Expanding My Skillset	050	☐			
			Other	010	☐			
If you responded 'Other' to the previous question, please expand on that response	Input Area	☐	No Response Predefined	000	☐	Move Up	Move Down	🗑
Do you prefer to work independently or as part of a team?	Single Selection	☐	Independently	030	☐	Move Up	Move Down	🗑
			Team	030	☐			
			A Mixture of Both	050	☐			
What motivates you as an employee	Multiple Selection	☐	Challenging Work	050	☐	Move Up	Move Down	🗑
			Compensation	010	☐			
			Growth Potential	040	☐			
			Rewarding Work.	040	☐			
			Recognition	030	☐			
			Work Life Balance	030	☐			
			Flextime	020	☐			
			Benefits	010	☐			
Why are you the best person for this job?	Input Area	☐	No Response Predefined	000	☐	Move Up	Move Down	🗑
What are you goals for the next 2 to 3 years?	Input Area	☐	No Response Predefined	000	☐	Move Up	Move Down	🗑

Figure 4.31 Sequencing the Questions in a Questionnaire

You can select the checkbox in the Required column for the question to make it mandatory for candidate response. If the question is set as required, the candidate *must* respond to the question. If the mandatory question is not answered, then the questionnaire cannot be saved, or if the questionnaire is attached to the application wizard, the application cannot be completed.

If the response type is single selection, multiple selection, or a predefined scale, you can select the expected response to the question. These expected responses will score the maximum rating for the candidate, and SAP E-Recruiting will rank the candidate higher if the ranking by questionnaire functionality is used. Also, if the response type is single selection, multiple selection, or a predefined scale, you can assign marks for each of the responses. The expected response should have the highest mark. For the other responses, you can either assign marks or leave them as 000 (the default).

4.5.8 Equal Employment Opportunity (EEO)

Collecting Equal Employment Opportunity (EEO) data is mandatory in the United States. It is required for annual reporting to the OFCCP (*www.ofccp.org*). In SAP E-Recruiting, you can assign your questionnaire as evaluable information or Equal Employment Opportunity.

If the questionnaire is assigned to the Equal Employment Opportunity category, the system does not do any ranking of the candidates. The data collected for EEO reporting should be evaluated and viewed by authorized personnel only. The process to create the EEO questions and the questionnaire are very similar to what we explained in the earlier sections.

Note

The OFCCP suggests the following text be displayed prior to the candidate responding to the EEO questionnaire:

<Your Organization Name> is an Equal Opportunity Employer and does not discriminate in hiring or employment against any individual on the basis of race, religion, color, gender, national origin, ancestry, age, physical or mental disability, veteran status or status within any other group protected by anti-discrimination laws.

You are invited to complete the following information to assist us in complying with Federal record-keeping requirements. Your response shall remain confidential, be kept separate from your application and shall in no way reflect any decision regarding your employment.

This information is voluntary and refusal to provide this information will not adversely affect your consideration for employment.

- Responding to an EEO questionnaire is voluntary and should not be considered in the assessment of the candidate.
- In 2007, OFCCP made changes to the race and the ethnicity categories.

The revised EEO-1 report is summarized below:

- Adds a new category titled "two or more races"
- Divides "Asian or Pacific Islander" into two separate categories: "Asian" and "Native Hawaiian or other Pacific Islander"
- Renames "Black" as "Black or African American"
- Renames "Hispanic" as "Hispanic or Latino"
- Strongly endorses self-identification of race and ethnic categories as opposed to visual identification by employers

It is a suggested best practice to check the OFCCP website (*www.ofccp.org*) for any updates regarding EEO data collection. Whenever the OFCCP announces changes to the EEO definitions or the requirements, SAP releases SAP Notes to handle the changes for annual mandatory reporting. SAP E-Recruiting provides standard delivered EEO reports for the OFCCP filing. We will explain in detail the standard delivered reports in Chapter 11.

You can access the question maintenance EEO information and the questionnaire maintenance EEO information from the Recruiter Work Center In the Services section of the work overview, this information is under the Administration section.

If your country's laws require you to collect EEO or a similar type of information, you need to create the questions and the questionnaire under the Equal Employment Opportunity category.

In this section, we explained questionnaire and question management. It is a suggested best practice to use questionnaires to prequalify your candidates as part of the recruiting process. Many SAP E-Recruiting customers gain experience and develop best practices from using questionnaires to qualify and assess candidates. You can use such experience to refine your questions and use the questionnaires more effectively. In the next section, we will explain process templates and how they can be used to define the recruiting process for a requisition.

4.6 Process Templates and Activity Types

A process template consists of a defined set of processes and the activities assigned to the individual processes. The processes can be defined in a specified sequence to meet your business requirements. A process template can be assigned to a requisition or to an application group. This guides the recruiter and the support team through the recruiting process. A process template can be assigned to multiple requisitions if the recruiting processes for the requisitions are similar.

4.6.1 Process Template

You can access the Maintain Process Template screen (see Figure 4.32) from the Recruiter Work Center. In the Services section of the work overview, the Maintain Process Template screen is under the Administration section.

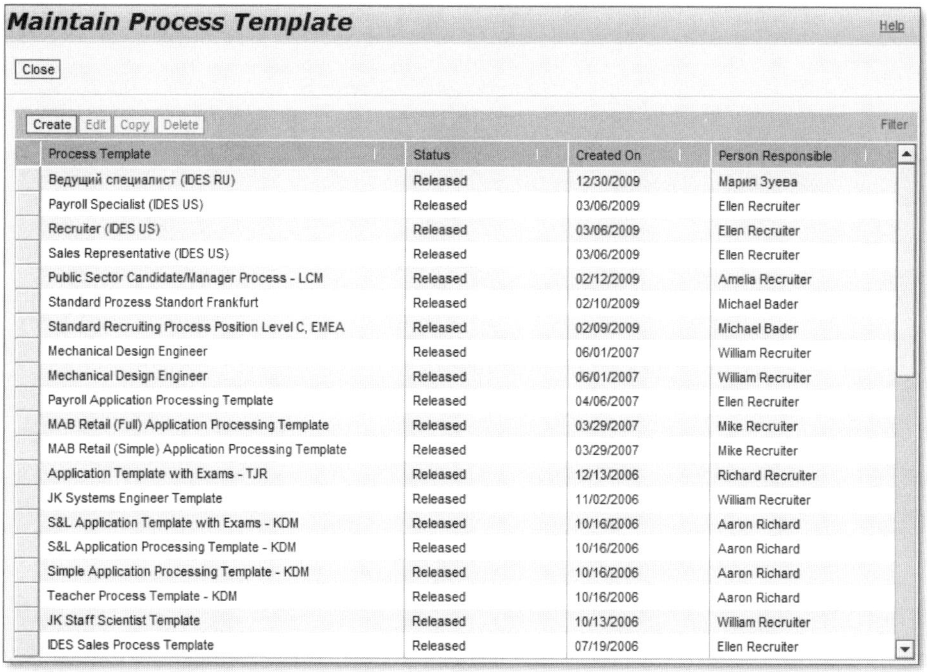

Maintain Process Template Help

Close

Create | Edit | Copy | Delete — Filter

Process Template	Status	Created On	Person Responsible
Ведущий специалист (IDES RU)	Released	12/30/2009	Мария Зуева
Payroll Specialist (IDES US)	Released	03/06/2009	Ellen Recruiter
Recruiter (IDES US)	Released	03/06/2009	Ellen Recruiter
Sales Representative (IDES US)	Released	03/06/2009	Ellen Recruiter
Public Sector Candidate/Manager Process - LCM	Released	02/12/2009	Amelia Recruiter
Standard Prozess Standort Frankfurt	Released	02/10/2009	Michael Bader
Standard Recruiting Process Position Level C, EMEA	Released	02/09/2009	Michael Bader
Mechanical Design Engineer	Released	06/01/2007	William Recruiter
Mechanical Design Engineer	Released	06/01/2007	William Recruiter
Payroll Application Processing Template	Released	04/06/2007	Ellen Recruiter
MAB Retail (Full) Application Processing Template	Released	03/29/2007	Mike Recruiter
MAB Retail (Simple) Application Processing Template	Released	03/29/2007	Mike Recruiter
Application Template with Exams - TJR	Released	12/13/2006	Richard Recruiter
JK Systems Engineer Template	Released	11/02/2006	William Recruiter
S&L Application Template with Exams - KDM	Released	10/16/2006	Aaron Richard
S&L Application Processing Template - KDM	Released	10/16/2006	Aaron Richard
Simple Application Processing Template - KDM	Released	10/16/2006	Aaron Richard
Teacher Process Template - KDM	Released	10/16/2006	Aaron Richard
JK Staff Scientist Template	Released	10/13/2006	William Recruiter
IDES Sales Process Template	Released	07/19/2006	Ellen Recruiter

Figure 4.32 Maintain Process Template

The structure of the process template consists of the following (see Figure 4.33):

- **Basic data**
  - **Process Template**
    The title of the process template. This is a mandatory field.
  - **Person Responsible**
    The person who creates and maintains the process template. This person is usually the lead recruiter. This field is also a mandatory field.

- **Status**
  The process template has three standard delivered statuses: Draft, Released, and Closed.

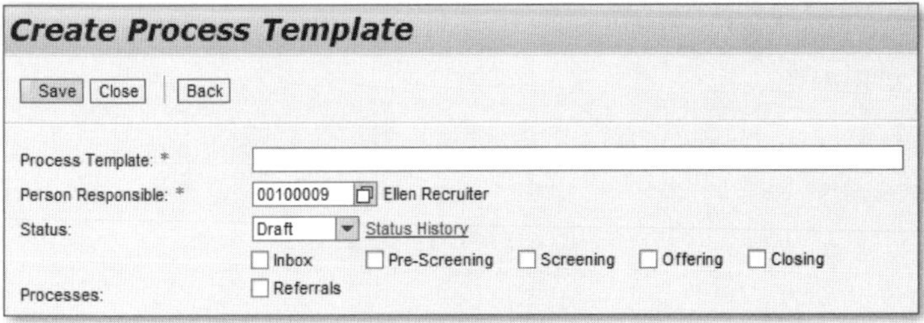

Figure 4.33 Basic Data of a Process Template

- **Processes and activity types**
  - Processes are assigned to a process template. You can define the sequence of the processes in a process template.

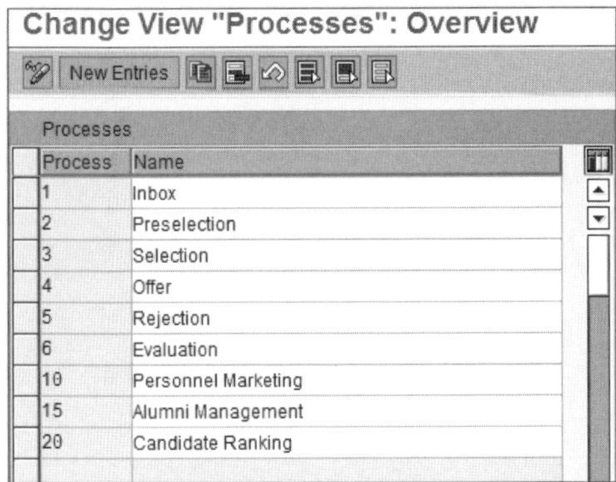

Figure 4.34 Defining Processes

In enhancement pack 4, SAP E-Recruiting provides the following processes as standard delivered (see Figure 4.34):

- Inbox
- Preselection
- Selection
- Offer
- Rejection
- Personnel Marketing

- Alumni Management
- Candidate Ranking

If you need additional processes in SAP E-Recruiting to meet your business requirements, you can create the processes in the IMG. The menu path for the customizing activity is SAP E-RECRUITING • APPLICANT TRACKING • ACTIVITIES • DEFINE PROCESSES. In this customizing activity, you must specify the process ID and the name of the process. SAP recommends not using 0 as a process ID to avoid possible problems during the flexibilization.

After you have created the processes, you need to assign them to the process group. The standard delivered process groups are:

- **Candidate Shortlist**
  The processes assigned to this group are used in processing the candidate of a requisition or the candidates belonging to an application group.
- **TRM Talent Relationship Management**
  The processes assigned to the TRM are used in processing TRM activities.

Processes are assigned to process groups in the IMG. In the customizing, you specify if the process needs to be used for the recruiting or for the talent relationship management activity. The menu path for the customizing activity is SAP E-RECRUITING • APPLICANT TRACKING • ACTIVITIES • ASSIGN PROCESSES TO RECRUITMENT.

Change View "Assignment of Processes to Recruitment": Overview

New Entries

Assignment of Processes to Recruitment

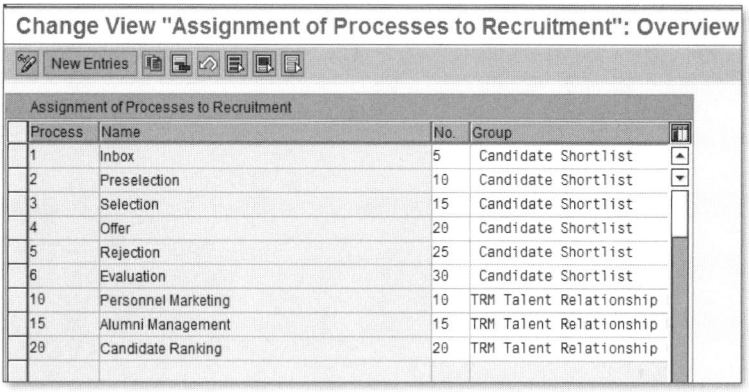

Process	Name	No.	Group
1	Inbox	5	Candidate Shortlist
2	Preselection	10	Candidate Shortlist
3	Selection	15	Candidate Shortlist
4	Offer	20	Candidate Shortlist
5	Rejection	25	Candidate Shortlist
6	Evaluation	30	Candidate Shortlist
10	Personnel Marketing	10	TRM Talent Relationship
15	Alumni Management	15	TRM Talent Relationship
20	Candidate Ranking	20	TRM Talent Relationship

Figure 4.35 Assign Processes to Recruitment Area

As shown in Figure 4.35, when you assign a process to recruitment, you specify in the No. column the sequence in which a recruiter can execute the process. For example, in Figure 4.35, the Candidate Shortlist process group has Inbox, Pre-selection, Selection, Offer, Rejection, and Evaluation assigned to it. The No.

column denotes the sequence in which the recruiter or support team can execute the process. The Inbox process should be executed first, followed by the Preselection process. Therefore, you cannot execute the Selection process before executing the Preselection process.

Having gained an understanding of the process template and the data that has to be entered in the process template, in the next section we will explain activity management and the different activity categories.

4.6.2 Activity Categories

In SAP E-Recruiting, you execute various activities in different steps of the recruitment cycle and to support talent relationship management initiatives. The activity types contain data that the system uses to execute different steps during the process. Each activity type contains the following data:

- **Activity type status**
  The activity types have two standard delivered statuses: Planned and Completed.
- **Due date**
  Expected due date of the activity.
- **Processor**
  The person who executes this activity.
- **Notes**
  You can enter notes about the candidate. If the activity type is attached to a recruitment process, the recruiter and the support team have access to the notes. If it is for TRM, an authorized recruiter has access.
- **Attachments**
  Any additional attachments that be might required.
- **Email attachments**
  For activity types where the simple correspondence is executed, attachments can be uploaded with the letter to the candidate.

Similar types of activities are grouped into categories (see Figure 4.36). The following are the standard delivered activity categories:

1. **Simple activities**
   Activity types in this category contain general tasks that the recruiter and by the support team need to complete during the recruiting cycle. The simple activities category does not support any system functions. Examples of the activity types in this category include Add to Referral list, Contact with Candidate, and Find Suitable Requisitions.

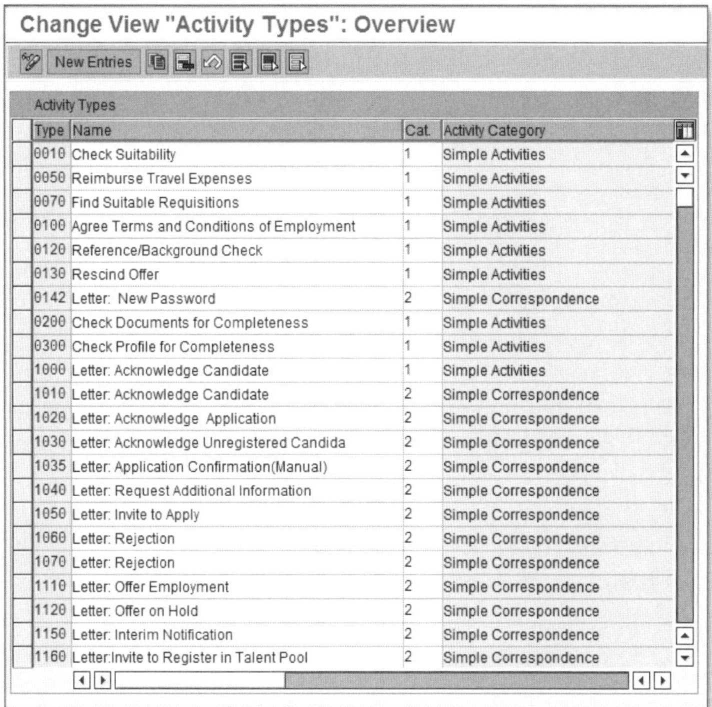

Change View "Activity Types": Overview

New Entries

Activity Types

Type	Name	Cat.	Activity Category
0010	Check Suitability	1	Simple Activities
0050	Reimburse Travel Expenses	1	Simple Activities
0070	Find Suitable Requisitions	1	Simple Activities
0100	Agree Terms and Conditions of Employment	1	Simple Activities
0120	Reference/Background Check	1	Simple Activities
0130	Rescind Offer	1	Simple Activities
0142	Letter: New Password	2	Simple Correspondence
0200	Check Documents for Completeness	1	Simple Activities
0300	Check Profile for Completeness	1	Simple Activities
1000	Letter: Acknowledge Candidate	1	Simple Activities
1010	Letter: Acknowledge Candidate	2	Simple Correspondence
1020	Letter: Acknowledge Application	2	Simple Correspondence
1030	Letter: Acknowledge Unregistered Candida	2	Simple Correspondence
1035	Letter: Application Confirmation(Manual)	2	Simple Correspondence
1040	Letter: Request Additional Information	2	Simple Correspondence
1050	Letter: Invite to Apply	2	Simple Correspondence
1060	Letter: Rejection	2	Simple Correspondence
1070	Letter: Rejection	2	Simple Correspondence
1110	Letter: Offer Employment	2	Simple Correspondence
1120	Letter: Offer on Hold	2	Simple Correspondence
1150	Letter: Interim Notification	2	Simple Correspondence
1160	Letter:Invite to Register in Talent Pool	2	Simple Correspondence

Figure 4.36 Activity Types

2. **Simple correspondence**
   The recruiter and the support team use the activity types in this activity category to send letters (correspondence) to the cadidate. They can use different types of letter templates for candidate correspondence. You can customize these letter templates for each simple correspondence activity. Simple correspondence supports the following functions:
   - **Add attachments**
     You can upload additional documents about the candidate.
   - **Add to email**
     You can upload additional documents that you would like to send with the correspondence to the candidate.
   - **Send email**
     This functionality is executed to send simple correspondence and any additional document to the candidate email listed in the candidate profile.
   - **Change letter section**
     In this functionality, you can customize the changeable letter section.

Examples of simple correspondence activity types include Invite to Register in Talent Pool, Invite to Apply to a Requisition, and Acknowledge Application.

3. **Qualifying event**
   The qualifying event category contains data that the recruiter and the support team require to plan a qualifying event. A qualifying event activity category contains data about the date and time when the qualifying event begins and ends. It also contains the address where the qualifying event will take place. You can use the simple correspondence activity type to notify the candidate about the qualifying event. Examples of qualifying event activity types include telephone interview, assessment center, and background check.
4. **Status change**
   You execute the activities in this activity category when the objects such as the candidate, candidacy, or applications require a status change. The activities in this category are executed within TRM to lock or release a candidate profile for the candidate search. The activity types in the status change category contain the field where you can state the reason for the status change. Examples of status change activity types include Disposition, Rejection, and Offer Accepted.
5. **Data transfer new employees**
   This activity type is available only for the recruitment process and is not available for TRM. It is executed to transfer data of the successful candidate (new hire) to the HR system (the external system can be a non-SAP HR system). You execute this activity type only when the candidate is to be hired.

   You can transfer the following candidate data to the HR system out-of-the-box:

   - Hiring date
   - Organizational unit
   - Job
   - First and last name
   - Academic title
   - Initials
   - Gender
   - Date of birth
   - Correspondence language
   - Address type
   - Street
   - City

- Postal code
- Country
- Region
- Applicant ID
- Employee ID (transferred initially)

The activity types in this category contain data about the position the new hire will be occupying and the organizational unit that is hiring the new employee. The data transfer new employee activity type supports the following functions:

- **Data transfer**
  The data transfer of the new hire is facilitated. For this function to be executed, the data connection between the HR system and SAP E-Recruiting should be established.
- **Add attachments**
  Any attachments associated with this activity are also transferred to the HR system.

6. **Resume parsing**
   You use this activity type to collect parsed resumes from an external vendor.
7. **Background check**
   You use this activity type to collect background check data from an external vendor.
8. **Questionnaire**
   You can execute this activity type when the recruiter or the support team wants to record the candidate's questionnaire. This activity type can be executed for both recruitment and TRM activities. Prior to executing this activity type, the questionnaire should be assigned to the activity type.

   When you assign the questionnaire to the activity, you can execute the activity types in any of the following ways:

   - The recruiter fills out the questionnaire for the candidate and sets the status to Complete.
   - The hiring manager fills out the questionnaire for the candidate. The name of the processor is changed to the manager's name, and the status is set to Complete.
   - The questionnaire is emailed to the candidate. Prior to this, the questionnaire activity type should be coupled to the activity in the invitation activity category.

The activity types in the questionnaire category contain the following data:

- **Questionnaire Completed**
  This indicator is selected when the questionnaire is completed.
- **Questionnaire Visible to Applicants**
  When this indicator is selected, the completed questionnaire is visible to the candidate when the candidate displays the application to which the questionnaire is assigned.
- **Complete Questionnaire**
  This function is executed when the recruiter completes the questionnaire.
- **Correspondence**
  The questionnaire can be sent to the candidate using the letter templates assigned for questionnaires.

Examples of questionnaires activity types include EEO questionnaire, questionnaire for interviews, and request for more information.

9. **Ranking**
   You can execute the activity types in this category to rank a candidate or to assign a candidate to a requisition based on the ranking. The activity type contains the rankings, that is, the rankings by recruiters and the overall, calculated ranking.
10. **Confirmation**
    You use activity types in this category to collect confirmations from the candidate.
11. **Invitation**
    You cannot execute the activity types in this category independently. The invitation activity types must be linked to the activity types of the activity categories Questionnaire or Status Change or the Qualifying event. You can create the link as a customizing activity in the IMG by following the menu path SAP E-Recruiting • Applicant Tracking • Activities • Link Activity Types with Referencing Activity Types.

    In Figure 4.37, you can see some of the activity types that are linked to the invitation activity types. The data of the linked activities is stored in the coupled invitation activity category. In the portal, the linked activities are displayed as activities of the invitation activity type category. You can activate or deactivate this activity type. Once you have activated the invitation activity type, the linked activity is executed and sent to the candidate.

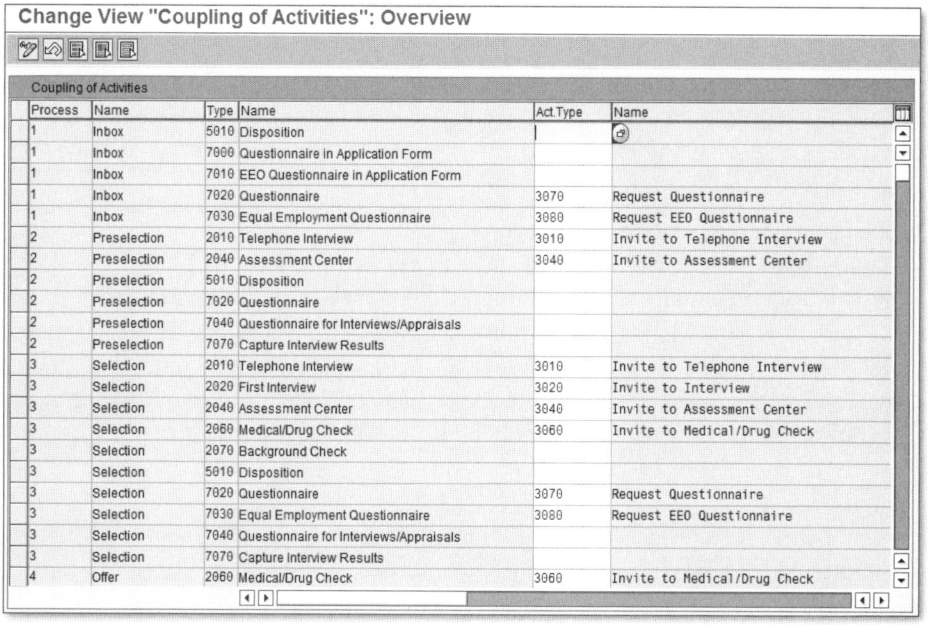

Change View "Coupling of Activities": Overview

Coupling of Activities

Process	Name	Type	Name	Act.Type	Name
1	Inbox	5010	Disposition		
1	Inbox	7000	Questionnaire in Application Form		
1	Inbox	7010	EEO Questionnaire in Application Form		
1	Inbox	7020	Questionnaire	3070	Request Questionnaire
1	Inbox	7030	Equal Employment Questionnaire	3080	Request EEO Questionnaire
2	Preselection	2010	Telephone Interview	3010	Invite to Telephone Interview
2	Preselection	2040	Assessment Center	3040	Invite to Assessment Center
2	Preselection	5010	Disposition		
2	Preselection	7020	Questionnaire		
2	Preselection	7040	Questionnaire for Interviews/Appraisals		
2	Preselection	7070	Capture Interview Results		
3	Selection	2010	Telephone Interview	3010	Invite to Telephone Interview
3	Selection	2020	First Interview	3020	Invite to Interview
3	Selection	2040	Assessment Center	3040	Invite to Assessment Center
3	Selection	2060	Medical/Drug Check	3060	Invite to Medical/Drug Check
3	Selection	2070	Background Check		
3	Selection	5010	Disposition		
3	Selection	7020	Questionnaire	3070	Request Questionnaire
3	Selection	7030	Equal Employment Questionnaire	3080	Request EEO Questionnaire
3	Selection	7040	Questionnaire for Interviews/Appraisals		
3	Selection	7070	Capture Interview Results		
4	Offer	2060	Medical/Drug Check	3060	Invite to Medical/Drug Check

Figure 4.37 Coupling of Activities

The structure of the coupled invitation activity type contains the following:

- **Letter template**
  The template of the letters that are used to correspond with the candidate
- **Email address**
  The email address of the candidate as maintained in the candidate profile
- **Email subject**
  Short text of the letter template

The invitation activity type supports a Changeable Letter section. This function can be executed to customize the changeable section of the letter template. Examples of the invitation activity type include Invite to Telephone interview, Invite to Assessment center, and Request EEO Questionnaire.

Having gained an understanding of the different activity categories and the data structure of the activity types, in the next section we will explain the customizing steps that are required to use these activity types in the process templates.

4.6.3 Activity Management – Customizing

It is important to perform the following customizing activities for effective activity management.

- **Define new activity types**
  In SAP E-Recruiting, you can create new activity types to meet your business requirements. You need to assign the newly created activity types to an activity category. You can create new activity types as a customizing activity in the IMG via the menu path SAP E-RECRUITING • APPLICANT TRACKING • ACTIVITIES • DEFINE ACTIVITY TYPES.

- **Assign object types to activity types**
  Before you use the activity types, you should assign them to SAP E-Recruiting objects. Assigning the activity types to the E-Recruiting objects is a customizing activity performed in the IMG.As shown in Figure As shown in Figure 4.38, you select the activity type and assign it to the SAP E-Recruiting Object. Prior to this customizing activity, you should have created the activity type and assigned it to an activity category. The menu path for this customizing activity is SAP E-RECRUITING •APPLICANT TRACKING • ACTIVITIES • ASSIGN HR OBJECTS TO ACTIVITY TYPES.

Change View "Assignment of Activity Type to Object Types": Overview

New Entries

Assignment of Activity Type to Object Types

Type	Name	O	Object type text
0010	Check Suitability	NE	Candidacy
0011	Negotiate Offer	NE	Candidacy
0050	Reimburse Travel Expenses	NE	Candidacy
0070	Find Suitable Requisitions	ND	Application
0100	Agree Terms and Conditions of Employment	ND	Application
0100	Agree Terms and Conditions of Employment	NE	Candidacy
0120	Reference/Background Check	NE	Candidacy
0130	Rescind Offer	NE	Candidacy
0142	Letter: New Password	NA	Candidate
0200	Check Documents for Completeness	ND	Application
0300	Check Profile for Completeness	NE	Candidacy
1000	Letter: Acknowledge Candidate	ND	Application
1000	Letter: Acknowledge Candidate	NE	Candidacy
1010	Letter: Acknowledge Candidate	NA	Candidate
1020	Letter: Acknowledge Application	ND	Application
1030	Letter: Acknowledge Unregistered Candida	ND	Application
1035	Letter: Application Confirmation(Manual)	ND	Application
1035	Letter: Application Confirmation(Manual)	NE	Candidacy
1040	Letter: Request Additional Information	NE	Candidacy
1050	Letter: Invite to Apply	NE	Candidacy
1060	Letter: Rejection	ND	Application
1060	Letter: Rejection	NE	Candidacy

Figure 4.38 Assign HR Objects to Activity Types

- **Assign a status to status-changing activity types**
  In this customizing activity, you assign a status to the status-changing activity types. The status changing activity types should be specific to the SAP E-Recruiting objects AND should be assigned only to the Candidate (NA), application (ND), Candidacy (NE), Requisition (NB), and Posting (NC) objects. Prior to this customizing activity, you should have defined the activity types and assigned them to the SAP E-Recruiting objects. The menu path for the customizing activity is SAP E-RECRUITING • APPLICANT TRACKING • ACTIVITIES • ASSIGN A STATUS TO STATUS-CHANGING ACTIVITY TYPES.

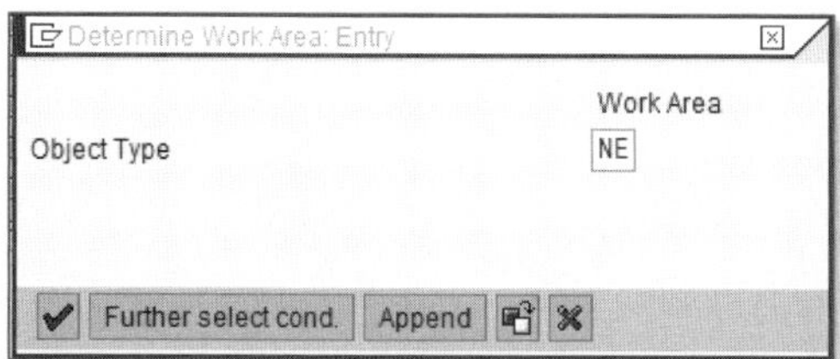

Figure 4.39 Determine Work Area

In this customizing activity, you select the SAP E-Recruiting object whose status will be affected by the status changing activity type. As shown in Figure 4.39, in the Determine Work Area dialog box, you select the SAP E-Recruiting object. In the Assignment Activity Type Object Status screen (see Figure 4.40), you assign the status to the activity types.

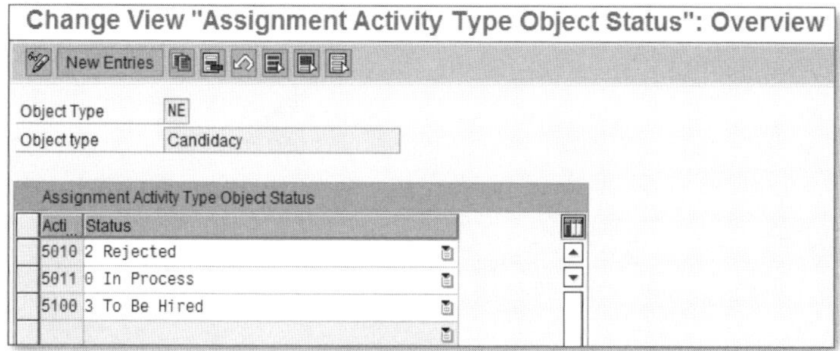

Figure 4.40 Assign Activity Type Object Status

- **Questionnaire categories (assign categories to activity types)**
  In this customizing activity, you assign the questionnaire category to each of the activity types in the questionnaire activity category. The standard delivered questionnaire categories are equal employment information and evaluable information. The menu path in the IMG to use to perform this customizing

activity is SAP E-RECRUITING • APPLICANT TRACKING • QUESTIONNAIRES • ASSIGN CATEGORIES TO ACTIVITY TYPES.

As shown in Figure 4.41, you can select the checkbox in the Application Wizard column if you want the questionnaires belonging to the activity type to be displayed in the application wizard. If you select the `Rank. Cand.` column, the questionnaires belonging to the activity type are included in the automatic ranking of the candidate.

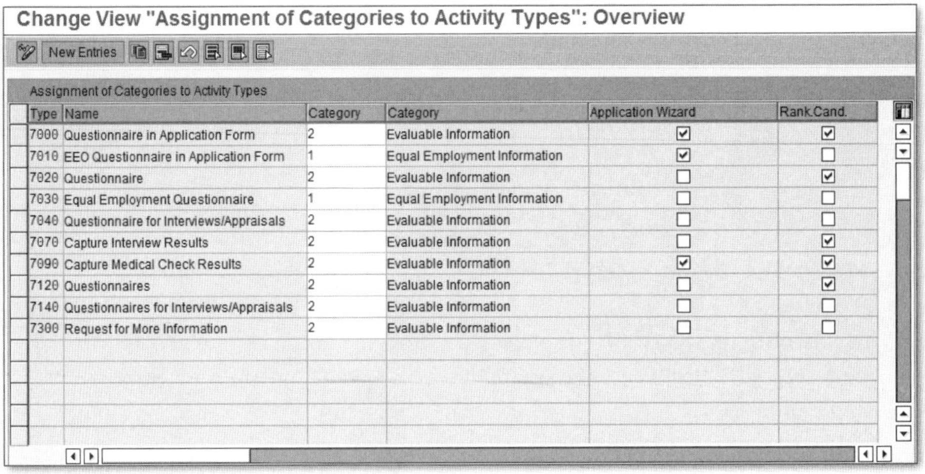

Change View "Assignment of Categories to Activity Types": Overview

New Entries

Assignment of Categories to Activity Types

Type	Name	Category	Category	Application Wizard	Rank.Cand.
7000	Questionnaire in Application Form	2	Evaluable Information	☑	☑
7010	EEO Questionnaire in Application Form	1	Equal Employment Information	☑	☐
7020	Questionnaire	2	Evaluable Information	☐	☑
7030	Equal Employment Questionnaire	1	Equal Employment Information	☐	☐
7040	Questionnaire for Interviews/Appraisals	2	Evaluable Information	☐	☐
7070	Capture Interview Results	2	Evaluable Information	☐	☑
7090	Capture Medical Check Results	2	Evaluable Information	☑	☑
7120	Questionnaires	2	Evaluable Information	☐	☑
7140	Questionnaires for Interviews/Appraisals	2	Evaluable Information	☐	☐
7300	Request for More Information	2	Evaluable Information	☐	☐

Figure 4.41 Assign Categories to Activity Types

- **Letter Templates**

  You can create templates and assign them to the activity types in the simple correspondence and invitation activity categories. To create the templates, use SAP Smart Form Builder. With these forms, you can create the letters that are used in the candidate correspondence activity types. The menu path to perform this customizing activity is SAP E-RECRUITING • APPLICANT TRACKING • ACTIVITIES • CORRESPONDENCE • CREATE LETTER TEMPLATES • CREATE FORMS AND CHANGEABLE LETTER SECTIONS.

  It is a suggested best practice to copy the SAP standard delivered forms and customize them for your requirements. For example, you can use these SAP standard delivered forms to create templates for the letters and invitations:

  - HRRCF_CS_IT_APPLICANT for letters
  - HRRCF_CS_IT_APPL_INVITATION for invitations
  - When you create the forms using the SAP Smart Form Builder, you can customize the look and feel of the template to suit your business requirements

and branding needs. For example, you can include your organization's logo in the form.

- When you create the form, it is a best practice to create texts that the recruiters and the support team can customize to meet their requirements in their correspondence with the candidate.
- The SAP standard delivered forms have the prefix HRRCF_CS_IT_*.
  The SAP standard delivered text modules for the forms have the prefix HRRCF_CS_MT_*.

After you have created the forms, you can assign the text modules that the recruiters and support team can customize for their simple correspondence activity. To perform this customizing activity, follow the menu path SAP E-Recruiting • Applicant Tracking • Activities • Correspondence • Create Letter Templates • Assign Changeable Letter Sections to Forms.

As shown in Figure 4.42, in the Form column, enter the form that can be used as a template in the simple correspondence or the invitation activity. In the Text Module column, enter the text module of the changeable letter section of the letter template. Click on the Save button to accept your entries. After you have completed these customizing activities, you need to assign the forms to activity types. The menu path to perform this customizing activity is SAP E-Recruiting • Applicant Tracking • Activities • Correspondence • Create Letter Templates • Assign Forms To Activity Types.

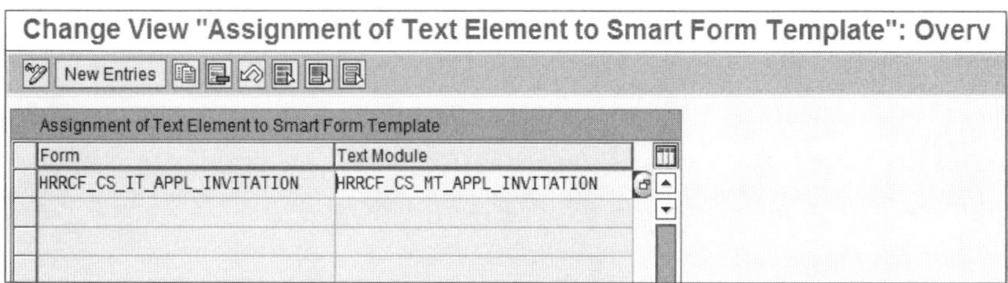

Figure 4.42 Assign Changeable Letter Sections to Forms

As shown in Figure 4.43, you assign the template letters to the activity types. In the Activity Type column, enter the activity types (or select them using the F4 key). You can indicate if this template should be used for a particular interest group or if it can be used for all candidates. In the Cand. Class field, specify if this template is for internal candidates only, external candidates only, or both internal and external candidates. In the Form column, specify the template that you are assigning to the activity. This template can be standard delivered or a customized form that your team has created. You can assign different templates for the same activity type by entering the sequence number in the No. column. When the recruiter or the support team is creating a simple correspondence, the different templates that are assigned to the activity are displayed in a dropdown list. The recruiter can then choose the template that is best suited for the communication.

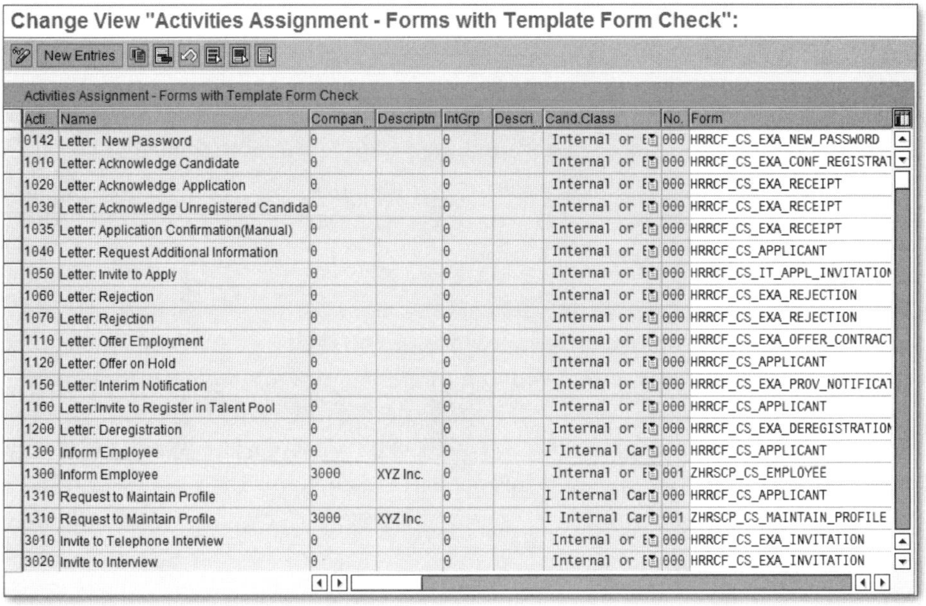

Change View "Activities Assignment - Forms with Template Form Check":

New Entries

Activities Assignment - Forms with Template Form Check

Acti	Name	Compan	Descriptn	IntGrp	Descri	Cand.Class	No.	Form
0142	Letter: New Password	0		0		Internal or E	000	HRRCF_CS_EXA_NEW_PASSWORD
1010	Letter: Acknowledge Candidate	0		0		Internal or E	000	HRRCF_CS_EXA_CONF_REGISTRAT
1020	Letter: Acknowledge Application	0		0		Internal or E	000	HRRCF_CS_EXA_RECEIPT
1030	Letter: Acknowledge Unregistered Candida	0		0		Internal or E	000	HRRCF_CS_EXA_RECEIPT
1035	Letter: Application Confirmation(Manual)	0		0		Internal or E	000	HRRCF_CS_EXA_RECEIPT
1040	Letter: Request Additional Information	0		0		Internal or E	000	HRRCF_CS_APPLICANT
1050	Letter: Invite to Apply	0		0		Internal or E	000	HRRCF_CS_IT_APPL_INVITATION
1060	Letter: Rejection	0		0		Internal or E	000	HRRCF_CS_EXA_REJECTION
1070	Letter: Rejection	0		0		Internal or E	000	HRRCF_CS_EXA_REJECTION
1110	Letter: Offer Employment	0		0		Internal or E	000	HRRCF_CS_EXA_OFFER_CONTRACT
1120	Letter: Offer on Hold	0		0		Internal or E	000	HRRCF_CS_APPLICANT
1150	Letter: Interim Notification	0		0		Internal or E	000	HRRCF_CS_EXA_PROV_NOTIFICAT
1160	Letter:Invite to Register in Talent Pool	0		0		Internal or E	000	HRRCF_CS_APPLICANT
1200	Letter: Deregistration	0		0		Internal or E	000	HRRCF_CS_EXA_DEREGISTRATION
1300	Inform Employee	0		0		I Internal Car	000	HRRCF_CS_APPLICANT
1300	Inform Employee	3000	XYZ Inc.	0		Internal or E	001	ZHRSCP_CS_EMPLOYEE
1310	Request to Maintain Profile	0		0		I Internal Car	000	HRRCF_CS_APPLICANT
1310	Request to Maintain Profile	3000	XYZ Inc.	0		I Internal Car	001	ZHRSCP_CS_MAINTAIN_PROFILE
3010	Invite to Telephone Interview	0		0		Internal or E	000	HRRCF_CS_EXA_INVITATION
3020	Invite to Interview	0		0		Internal or E	000	HRRCF_CS_EXA_INVITATION

Figure 4.43 Assign Forms to Activity Types

Changeable Letter Functionality

After you have completed the customization for the correspondence, you can implement the changeable letter functionality. In the Recruiter Work Center, select the candidate to whom you want to send the simple correspondence. In the Candidate Profile screen, click on the Activities tab and select the Simple Correspondence activity. As shown in Figure 4.44 in the Edit Activity dialog box, click on the Change Letter Section link. In the displayed free text area, enter the text that you would like to add to the letter template. For example, you can personalize your correspondence. You can click on the Send E-Mail button to send the letter or the Print Letter button to print the letter.

When you click on the Reset Letter button, the customized text is removed and the template is reset to the default.

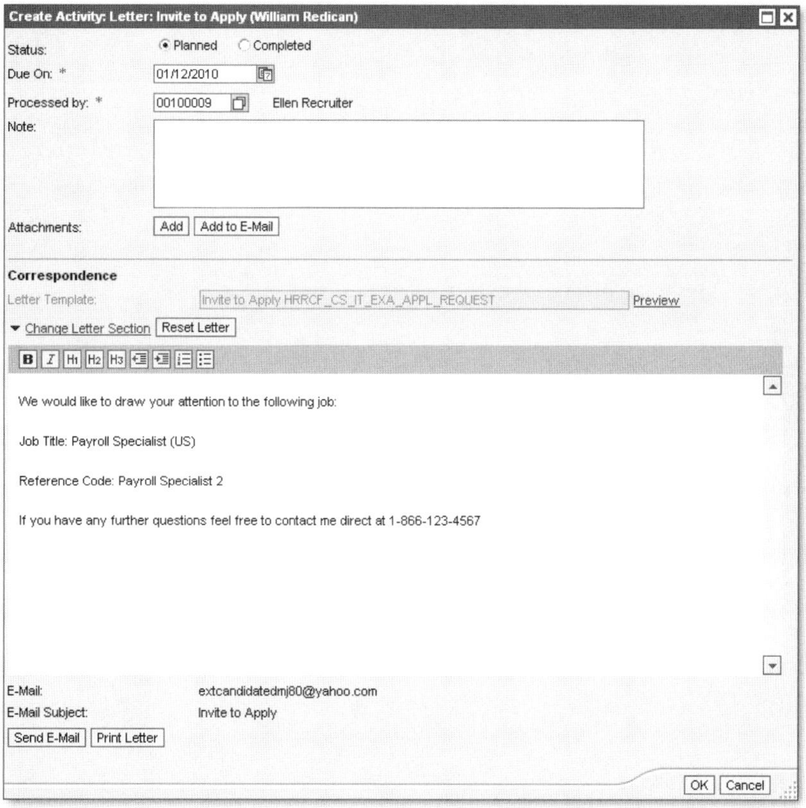

Figure 4.44 Enter Text for the Changeable Letter

Workflow

SAP E-Recruiting includes several SAP standard delivered workflows to which the activity types are assigned. These workflows are required to process these activity types. For example, if a registered candidate forgets his password, he can request a new one from the system. A new password is created and sent to the candidate using the Assign New Password workflow (ERCSendPwd). You can create and customize the workflows to suit your business requirements. The customizing is done in the IMG under the menu path SAP E-Recruiting • Technical Settings • Workflow.

- After you have created various activity types, you need to assign them to the recruitment processes. To perform this customizing activity, follow the menu path SAP E-Recruiting • Applicant Tracking • Activities • Assign Activity Types to Recruitment Processes.

- As shown in Figure 4.45, for the customizing activity, you enter the process ID and activity type that you want to assign to the particular process. The activity types that are customized and assigned to the recruitment work area are available when you create the process template and add activities to the processes. Please note that a prerequisite for the customizing activity Assign Activity Types to Recruitment Processes is that you have completed the customizing activities Define Activity Types and Define Processes.

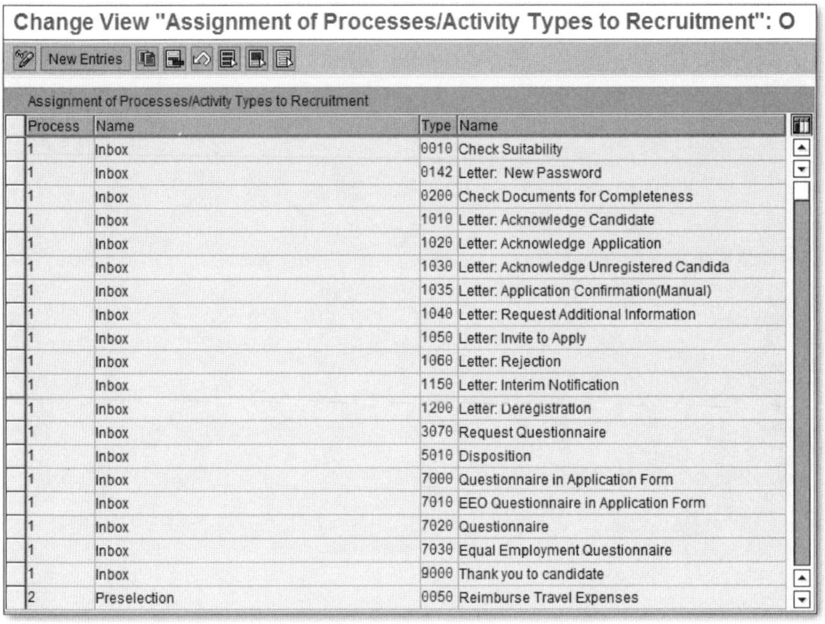

Change View "Assignment of Processes/Activity Types to Recruitment": O

New Entries

Assignment of Processes/Activity Types to Recruitment

Process	Name	Type	Name
1	Inbox	0010	Check Suitability
1	Inbox	0142	Letter: New Password
1	Inbox	0200	Check Documents for Completeness
1	Inbox	1010	Letter: Acknowledge Candidate
1	Inbox	1020	Letter: Acknowledge Application
1	Inbox	1030	Letter: Acknowledge Unregistered Candida
1	Inbox	1035	Letter: Application Confirmation(Manual)
1	Inbox	1040	Letter: Request Additional Information
1	Inbox	1050	Letter: Invite to Apply
1	Inbox	1060	Letter: Rejection
1	Inbox	1150	Letter: Interim Notification
1	Inbox	1200	Letter: Deregistration
1	Inbox	3070	Request Questionnaire
1	Inbox	5010	Disposition
1	Inbox	7000	Questionnaire in Application Form
1	Inbox	7010	EEO Questionnaire in Application Form
1	Inbox	7020	Questionnaire
1	Inbox	7030	Equal Employment Questionnaire
1	Inbox	9000	Thank you to candidate
2	Preselection	0050	Reimburse Travel Expenses

Figure 4.45 Assign Activity Types to Recruitment Processes

In this section, we reviewed the customizing required to create activities and perform effective activity management. In the next section, we will explain how to create the process template and assign activity types to it. We will also discuss how to assign the process template to a requisition.

4.6.4 Creating a Process Template and Assign Activity Types

Now that we understand process templates and activity types, let's step through creating a process template and assigning it activity types. You can access the Maintain Process Template Listing screen from the Recruiter Work Center. In the Services section of the Work Overview, the Maintain Process Template Listing screen is under the Administration section.

- In the Maintain Process Template Listing screen, click on the Create button to create a new process template. In the Create Process Template screen, enter the basic data of the process template and then select the processes that you want to include in your process template.
- As shown in Figure 4.46, selecting the assigned processes adds a new group where you can add the activity types assigned to the particular process. The processes that are displayed in the Create Process Template screen are the processes that you customized in the Assign Processes to Recruitment customizing activity.

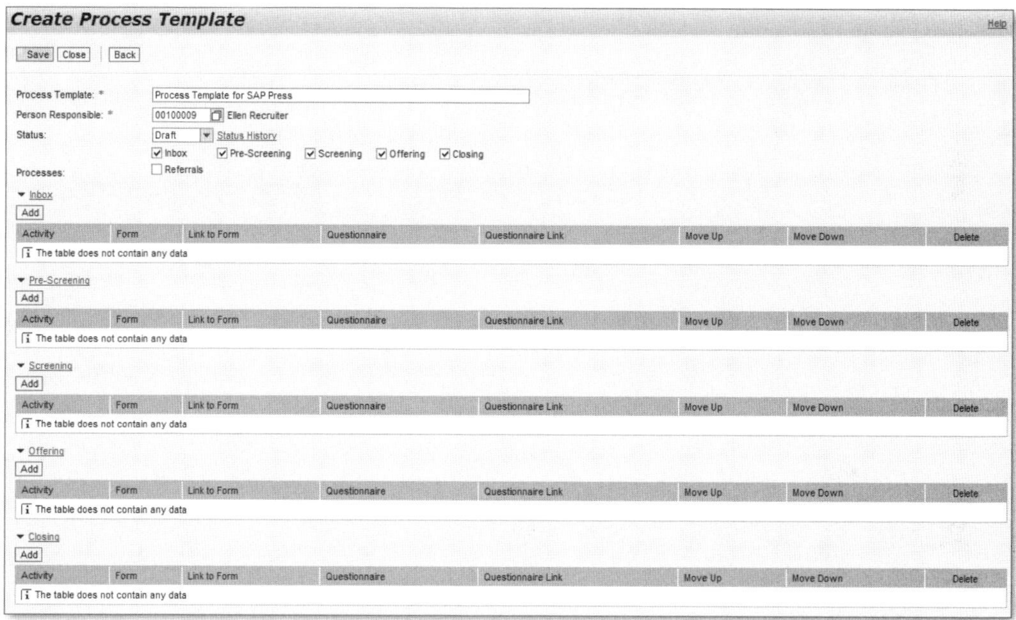

Figure 4.46 Add Processes to the Process Template

- If you want to assign an activity type to the process, click on the Add button of that process. In the displayed dialog box (see Figure 4.47), select the activity type that you want to assign to the process in this process template. As shown in Figure 4.47, the activity types that are displayed in the dialog box are the activity types that you have customized in the Assign Activity Types to Recruitment Processes customizing activity. Once you select an activity type and assign it to an activity process, that activity type is removed from the dialog box.

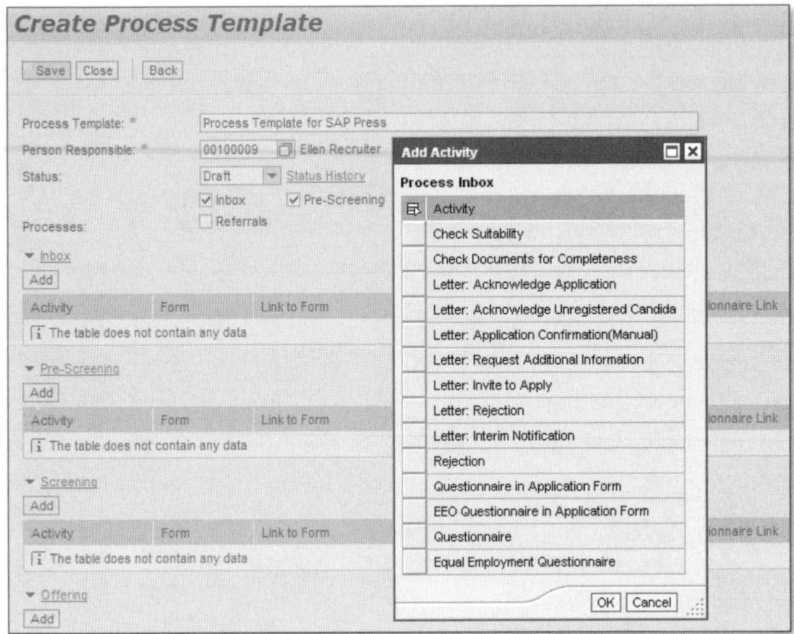

Figure 4.47 Add Activity Types to the Process

- You can reorder or sequence the activity types in a process by using the Move Up and Move Down links for the activity types. The sequence of the activity types in the activity process should be determined by your business requirements and the recruitment process for this requisition. If the activity has a Smart Form Template attached to it, you can view the template by clicking on the Display link. You can also delete a activity type at any time by clicking on the Trash Can icon. After you have completed assigning the activity types to the processes, you can change the status of the process template to Released and click on the Save button to accept your entries.

Note

While creating the process template, if you select the processes but do not assign any activity types to them, these processes are deselected when you click on the Save button to save the process template.

The process template should be in Released status if you want to assign it to a requisition or to an application group. If the process template is in Closed or Released status, it cannot be deleted. The process template should be in Draft status if you want to delete it. You can also create a new process template by copying an existing template. The template that you want to copy can have any of the standard delivered statuses.

In this section, we explained about the process template and activity management. In the next section, we will explain how to assign a process template to a requisition.

4.6.5 Assigning a Process Template to a Requisition

In the Recruiter Work Center, select the requisition to which you wish to assign the process template.

- Click on the Requisition button and select Edit.
- In the Edit Requisition screen, click on the Pencil icon next to the Process Template field.
- As shown in Figure 4.48, select the process template from the dialog box.
- In the dialog box, click on the OK button to confirm your selection.

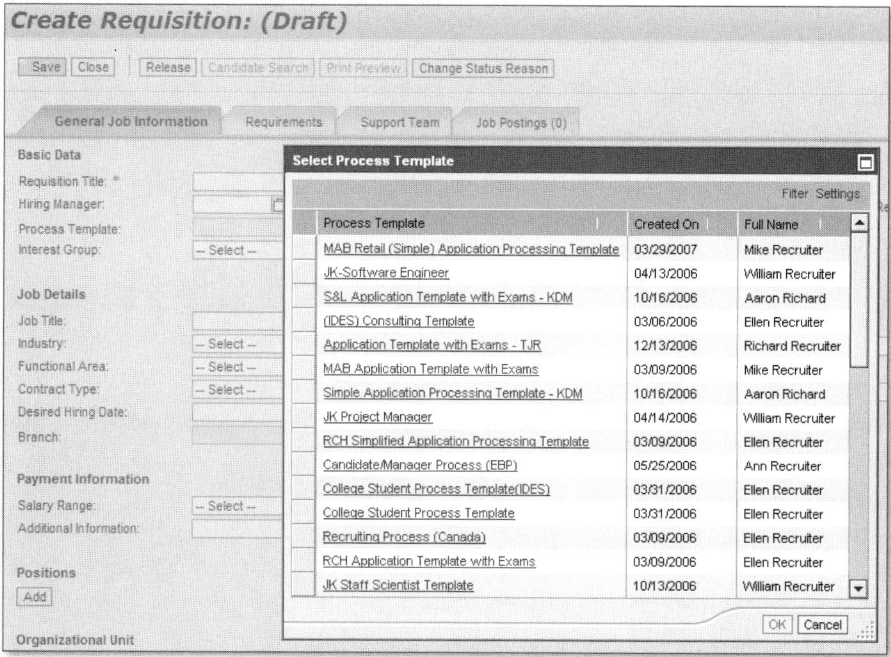

Figure 4.48 Assign Process Template to a Requisition

You will now notice the selected process template is assigned to the requisition.

- Click on the Save button in the Edit Requisition screen to confirm your entries.

Note

When you assign a process template to a requisition, ensure that the selected process template is suitable for this requisition and for the recruitment process that is selected for the requisition.

Process templates and activity types play an important role in requisition management because they guide the recruiter and the support team through the recruitment process. If the process template is constructed well, it can make your recruitment process extremely efficient. An organization can have multiple process templates depending on the type of requisition and the recruitment strategies supported. A process template can be assigned to multiple requisitions also, if the recruitment processes are similar.

In the next section, we will explain how the hiring manager can create a requisition in Manager Self-Service (MSS).

4.7 Management Involvement

In this section, we will explain the services available for the manager. SAP refers to this capability as management involvement in SAP E-Recruiting. In the system, the manager can perform the following activities from MSS:

- Create requisitions
- Maintain substitutes

In the MSS Recruiting page (see Figure 4.49), two iViews are provided for the manager:

- **Process Browser**
  This iView provides the manager with an overview of all of the requisitions that he has initiated.
- **Requisition Monitor**
  This iView provides managers with an overview of all of the requisitions they are associated with, the requisitions they have created, the requisitions they are supporting as substitutes, and the requisitions for which they are part of the support team.

Using the Requisition Monitor (see Figure 4.50), managers can get an overview of the shortlisted candidates for a requisition. They can also access the candidate assessments and the publications from this iView.

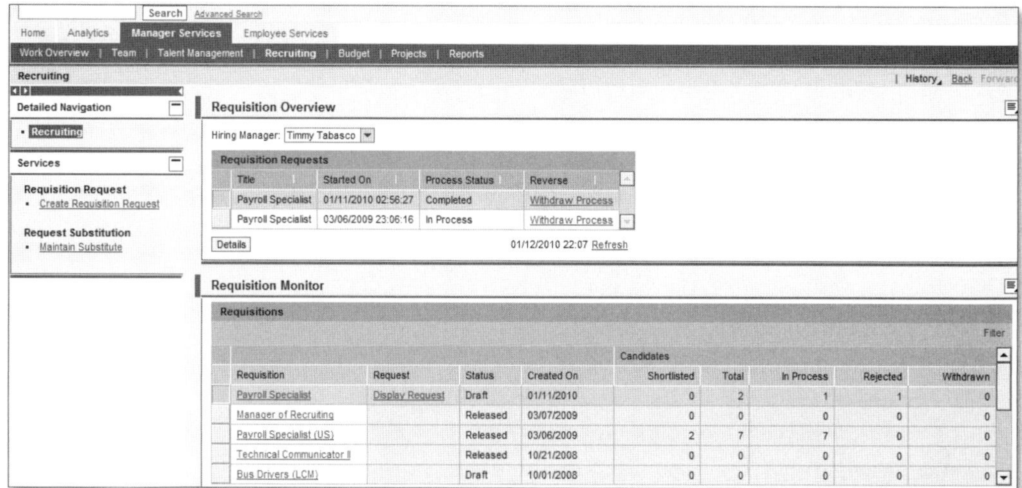

Figure 4.49 Recruiting Page in the Manager Portal

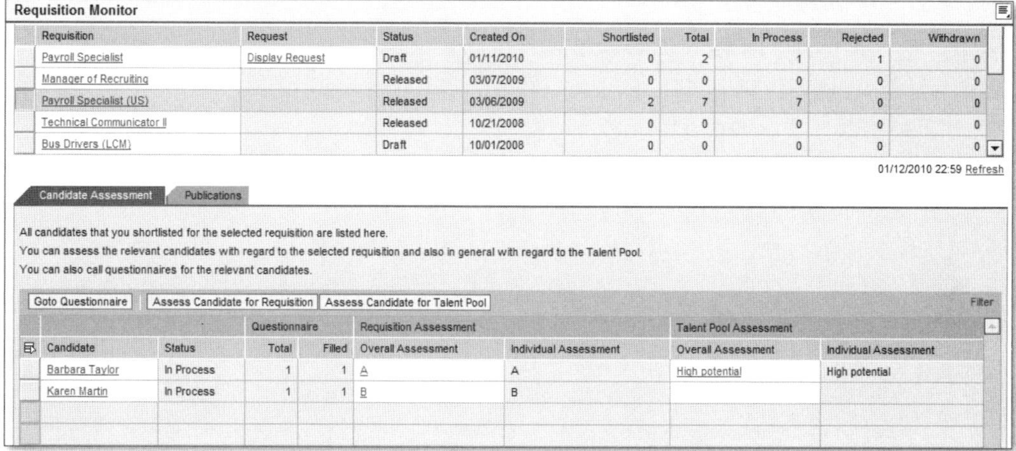

Figure 4.50 Requisition Monitor

4.7.1 Creating a Requisition

SAP E-Recruiting provides two standard delivered forms for the manager to use to create a requisition:

- **Simple requisition request**
  Using this form, the manager needs to enter a minimal amount of data to create a requisition. This form does not require approval by a higher-level manager.

The delivered workflow creates the requisition object (NB) in the background and sets the requisition to status to In Process. Any missing information on the requisition form can be completed by a recruiter.

- **Extended requisition request**
  Using this form, the manager enters the details required to create the requisition and requires approval by a higher-level manager. Via workflow, the requisition request is sent to the higher-level manager, who receives the request in the Universal Work List (UWL) on the portal. On approval by this manager, the system creates the requisition object (NB) with the status In Process.

The hiring manager can create a requisition by any of the following means:

- **Create requisition based on an exisiting position**
  The manager selects the position he is planning to fill. The system fills out the requisition form with the position data.
- **Create requisition based on existing job**
  The manager selects the job, and the system fills out the requisition form with the job data.
- **Create requisition based on previous request**
  This is similar to the copy method. The requisition form is filled in with data from a previous requisition form.
- **Create requisition using start without reference**
  The requisition is filled in with the manager's name and other system data.

The hiring manager can create the requisition in MSS by clicking on the Create Requisition Request link. The Create Requisition Request service is found in the Services section of the recruiting overview under the Requisition Request and an SAP Interactive Adobe form. The manager completes the form with the required information. On completion of the form, workflow routes the requisition to a higher-level manager and/or to a recruiter for approval. On approval from the required personnel, the requisition request with the information is transferred to the SAP E-Recruiting system.

In the Create Requisition Request screen (see Figure 4.51), you can see the "bread crumbs" (i.e., the informational trail of navigation history) that guides the manager through the completion of the form.

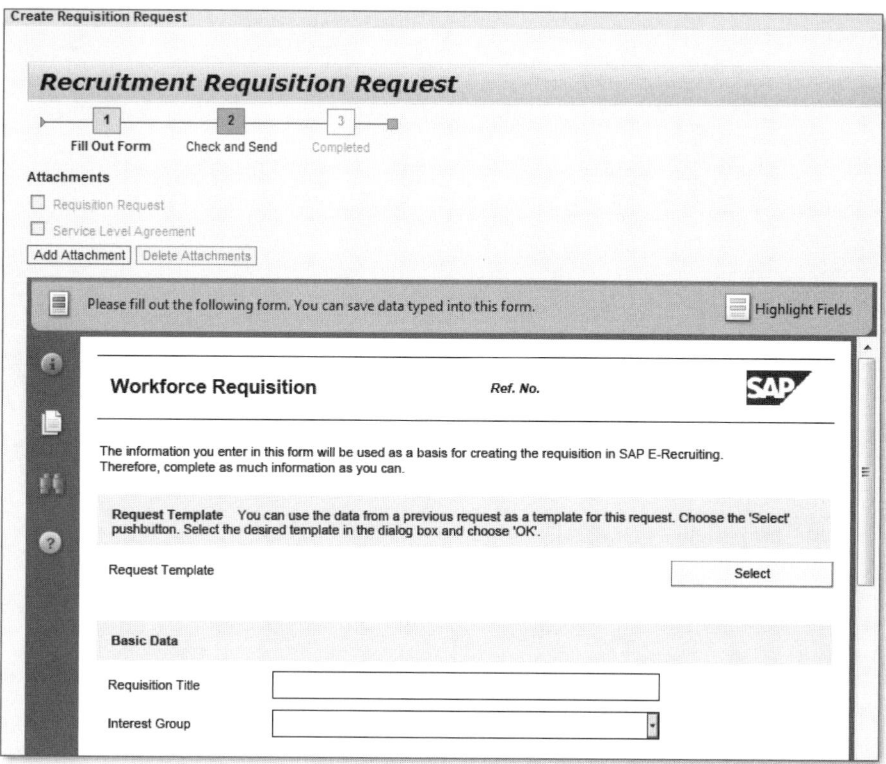

Figure 4.51 Requisition Request by the Manager

In the Adobe Interactive Forms screen, you can click on the Select button next to Request Template to use the data from a previous requisition request as a template to create a new request (see Figure 4.52). In the dialog box, click on the requisition that you want to use as the template for the new requisition request. Click on OK to accept your selection. The form is now filled with the data from the selected requisition. If needed, you can modify the data to suit your new requirements. For example, the earlier requisition for a payroll specialist might be for only one position. Now you have same requirement in a different branch office and need two positions to be filled. In such a scenario, you can use the data from the previous request and change the Location and Number of Positions fields.

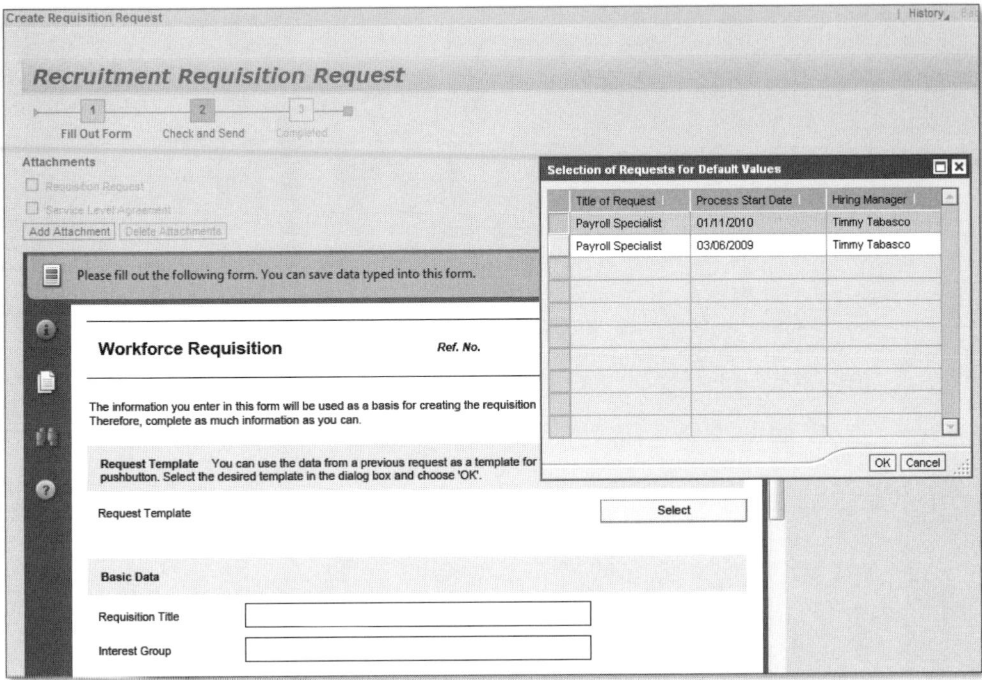

Figure 4.52 Creating a New Requisition by the Copy Method

To fill the organizational data group, you can click on the Select Position button. If your SAP E-Recruiting system is integrated with the SAP ERP HCM system, this will display the positions in your organization structure (see Figure 4.53). You can select the position by displaying:

- Directly subordinate positions
- Positions from organizational structure
- Position search

The positions are displayed in the dialog box. You highlight the position and click on the OK button to accept your selection. The data that is stored in the position object is used to enter the data in the form. Enter the required data in the form and click on the Check and Send button at the bottom of the form. You will see Check and Send highlighted in the "bread crumbs" (i.e., the informational trail of navigation history) displayed at the top of the form.

Check and Send is a service that checks if the required data and the mandatory fields are complete. If any data is missing, an appropriate error message is displayed as shown in Figure 4.54.

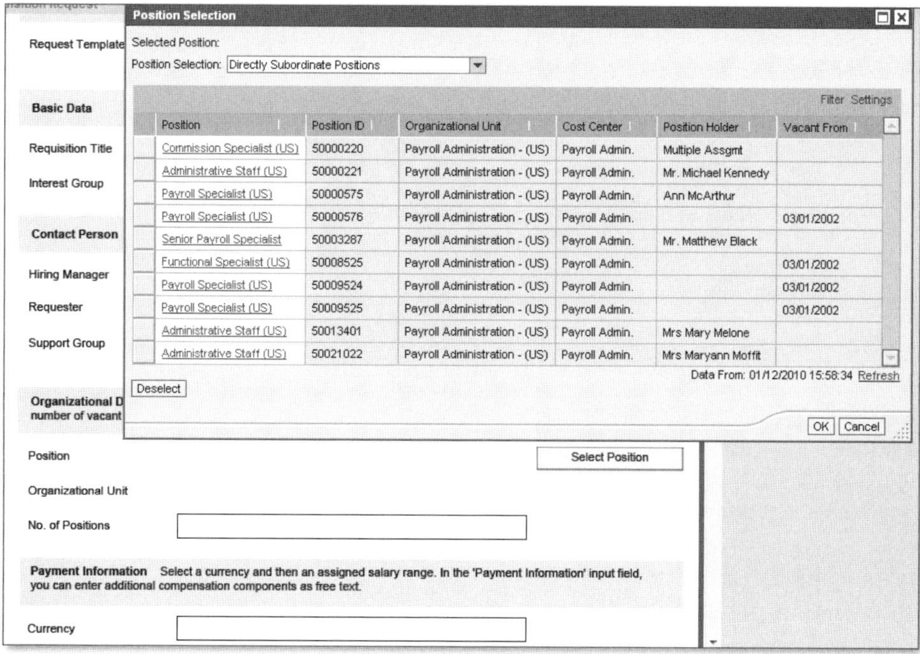

Figure 4.53 Position Selection to Fill the Organizational Data

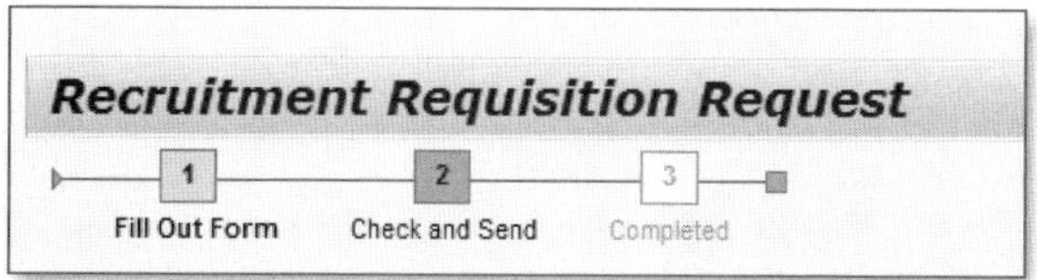

Figure 4.54 Error Message in the Requisition Request

After completing the form, click on the Send button. The data is saved, and the workflow (WS16900009-MSS_EREC_0: Process requisition request (0) / WS16900010-MSS_EREC_1:Process requisition request (1)) is initiated for requisition approval.

Note

The requisition request forms are based on the Internal Service Request (ISR) framework. The ISR enables you to organize internal requests for business services and related services. It supports default data for forms, workflows, and input validations.

The Requisition Request form uses Object and Data Provider (OADP) to display the data entries in a table format. It is a prerequisite that you have created and maintained the required data in Organizational Management.

4.7.2 Customizing Activities – Manager Involvement

In the IMG, you can make the following customizing settings for manager involvement via the menu path SAP E-RECRUITING • MANAGER INVOLVEMENT (see Figure 4.55).

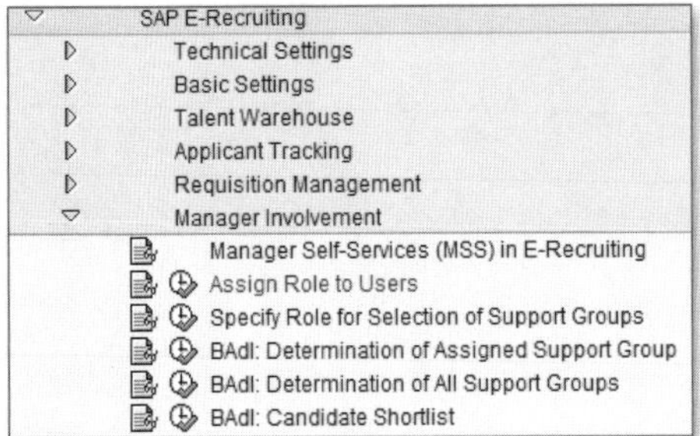

Figure 4.55 Customizing Activities for Manager Involvement

- **Assign Role to Users**
  In this customizing activity, you create the service and the reference users for the manager. (We will explain more about roles and authorizations in Chapter 10, Authorization Management.) The prerequisite for this customizing activity is that a valid RFC connection is established between the SAP ERP HCM and SAP E-Recruiting systems.
- **Specify Role for Selection of Support Groups**
  For this customizing activity, the default role of recruiter is assigned as an SAP standard delivered role. Perform this customizing activity only if you want to assign a different role for the manager involvement scenario. The suggested best practice is to use the SAP standard role.

If you want to use this functionality, you are also required to perform customizing settings for Manager Self-Service (MSS). The menu path to perform this customizing activity in the IMG is INTEGRATION WITH OTHER MYSAP.COM COMPONENTS • BUSINESS PACKAGES/FUNCTIONAL PACKAGES • MANAGER SELF-SERVICE (MYSAP ERP) • RECRUITMENT.

4.7.3 Management Involvement – Business Add-Ins (BAdIs)

For manager involvement processes, the following BAdIs are provided in the SAP standard delivery.

The BAdI HRRCF00_GET_ASSIGNED_SGR (Determination of Assigned Support Group) provides the manager with a default support group based on certain attributes such as role, organizational unit, or job. In the standard system, this BAdI is not implemented. The menu path to perform this customizing activity is SAP E-RECRUITING • MANAGER INVOLVEMENT • BADI: DETERMINATION OF ASSIGNED SUPPORT GROUP.

The BAdI HRRCF00_GET_SUPPORT_GROUPS (Determination of All Support Groups) provides the manager with a list of support groups as a dropdown list. These support groups are displayed in the Adobe Interactive Form when the manager creates a requisition request from the Create Requisition Request service. In the standard system, this BAdI is activated and implemented. You can customize this BAdI if there is a business requirement via the menu path SAP E-RECRUITING • MANAGER INVOLVEMENT • BADI: DETERMINATION OF ALL SUPPORT GROUPS.

The BAdI HRRCF00_SHORTLIST (Candidate Shortlist) determines the list of shortlisted candidates for the requisition that can be provided to the manager. In the standard system, this BAdI is activated and implemented. In the standard delivery, the candidate should have the status of In Process, the manager is in the support team of the requisition, and the manager is assigned a questionnaire to assess the candidate (if the assessment is for the talent group). You can customize this BAdI if there is a business need by following the menu path SAP E-RECRUITING • MANAGER INVOLVEMENT • BADI: CANDIDATE SHORTLIST.

4.7.4 Requisition Monitor

The manager can use the Requisition Monitor to get an overview of all requisitions and track the progress of the requisitions with which the manager is involved.

You implement the Requisition Monitor through the iView hrrcf_a_requi_monitor. Table 4.1 gives the technical details of this iView.

Technical name of iView	com.sap.pct.erp.mss.requisition_monitor
Technical name of application	hrrcf_a_requi_monitor
Runtime technology	iView: Java; application: Web Dynpro ABAP

Table 4.1 Technical Details of Requisition Monitor iView

The requisitions iView displays all of the requisitions the manager is currently working with either as a hiring manager, a substitute, or a support team member. The requisitions iView also provides details such as the number of candidates, the status of the candidates, and the number of shortlisted candidates.

In the requisition iView, if the manager selects a requisition, the Candidate Assessment tab page provides details about the shortlisted candidates. In the Candidate

Assessment tab page, the manager can click on the Questionnaire button and provide feedback about the candidate to the recruiter (see Figure 4.56). Within the Requisition Monitor, the manager can select a particular candidate and select Assess Candidate for the Requisition (see Figure 4.57) or Assess Candidate for the Talent Pool.

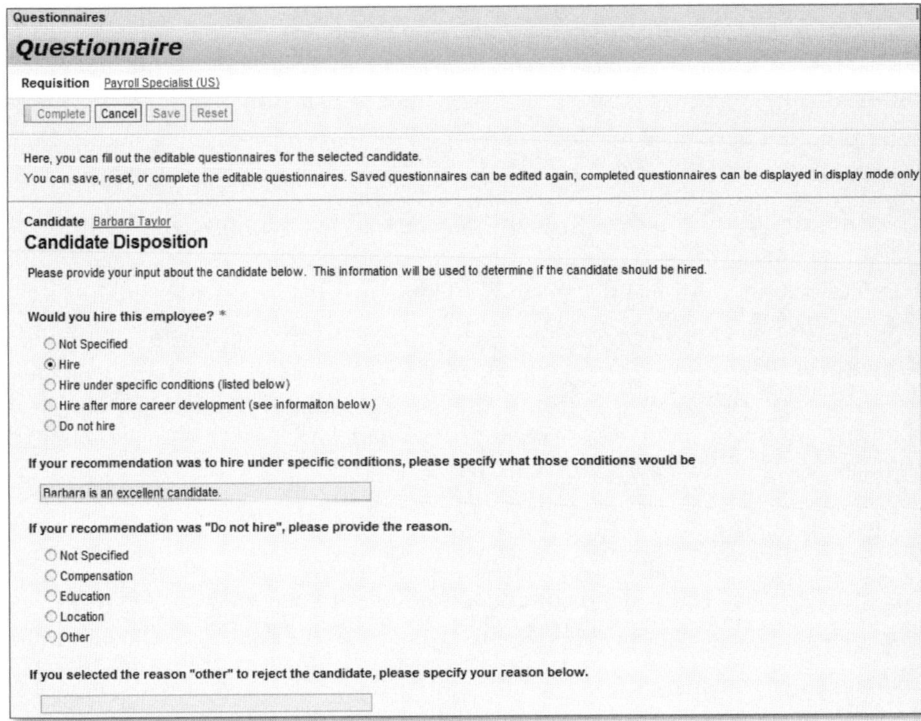

Figure 4.56 Manager Completing a Questionnaire

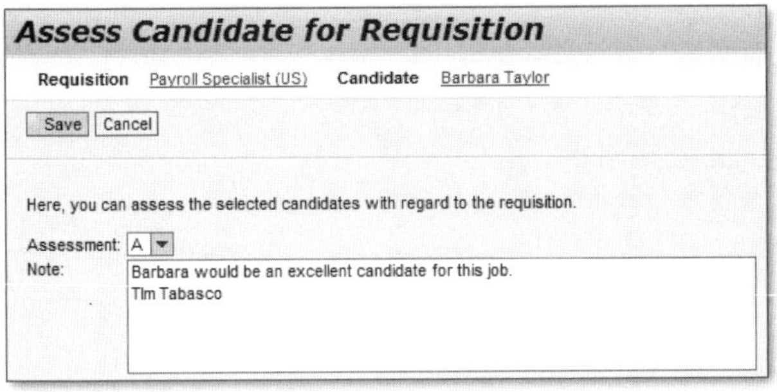

Assess Candidate for Requisition

Requisition Payroll Specialist (US) Candidate Barbara Taylor

Save Cancel

Here, you can assess the selected candidates with regard to the requisition.

Assessment: A

Note: Barbara would be an excellent candidate for this job.
Tim Tabasco

Figure 4.57 Assess Candidate for Requisition

This type of feedback is important during the requisition consensus meeting when the recruiter and the hiring manager need to make a decision on the candidates and whom to hire. In the Publications tab page, the manager obtains an overview of the publications and the channels where the job posting is published.

4.7.5 Maintain Substitute

The manager can create and maintain substitutes who can assume his responsibilities in SAP E-Recruiting in his absence. In SAP E-Recruiting, the manager can use the iView HRRCF_A_SUBSTITUTION_MANAGER to create and maintain a substitute.

Table 4.2 gives the technical details of the iView.

Technical name of iView	com.sap.pct.erp.mss.maintain_substitute
Technical name of application	hrrcf_a_substitution_manager
Runtime technology	iView: Java; application: Web Dynpro ABAP

Table 4.2 Technical Details of iView for Maintain Substitute

You can find the menu path for the Maintain Substitute service under the Request Substitution. To maintain a substitute, click on the link Maintain Substitute to display the Edit Substitutes screen (see Figure 4.58). In this screen, you can create and maintain your substitutes. Enter the name of the substitute, the type of the substitution, and the duration of the substitution. The manager can add, edit, or delete substitutes.

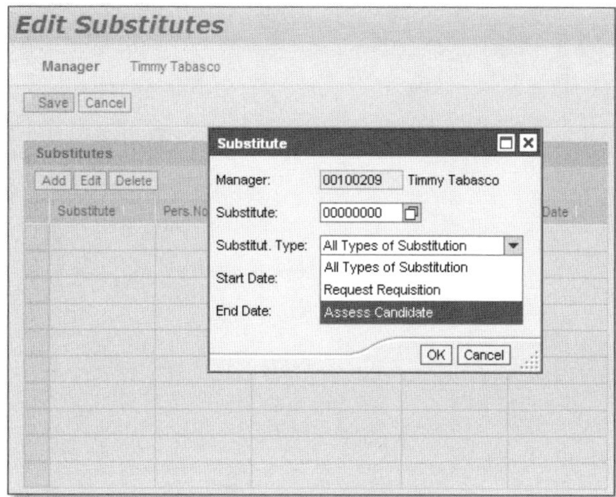

Figure 4.58 Create and Maintain Substitutes

4.8 Correspondence

Correspondence is a crucial activity in any recruiting process. Candidate correspondence aids in maintaining contact with the candidate and in TRM activities. In SAP E-Recruiting, a candidate correspondence template is maintained in SAP Smart Forms, and you can maintain correspondence with the candidate either by simple correspondence or by invitation activity. You can edit and maintain the correspondence template using SAP Smart Form Builder. When you create a letter, SAP E-Recruiting automatically fills in the candidate address data. You need to maintain at least one template for each correspondence activity.

4.8.1 Activity Types

Earlier in the chapter, we discussed process templates and activity types. We also discussed the customizing steps required to create those activity types. Table 4.3 shows the SAP standard delivered activities for the simple correspondence and invitation activity categories. You can attach the correspondence templates to these activities and then use the templates to maintain correspondence with the candidate.

Activity Type	Name	Activity Category
0142	New Password	Simple correspondence
1010	Acknowledge Candidate	Simple correspondence
1020	Acknowledge Registered Application	Simple correspondence
1030	Acknowledge Unregistered Candidate	Simple correspondence
1035	Application Confirmation (Manual)	Simple correspondence
1040	Request for More Information	Simple correspondence
1050	Invite to Apply	Simple correspondence
1060	Correspondence: Rejection	Simple correspondence
1110	Extend Offer	Simple correspondence
1120	Rescind Offer	Simple correspondence
1150	Interim Notification	Simple correspondence
1160	Propose Talent Pool Participation	Simple correspondence

Table 4.3 SAP Standard Delivered Activity Types

Activity Type	Name	Activity Category
1200	Deregistration	Simple correspondence
1300	Inform Employee	Simple correspondence
8520	Circular	Simple correspondence
3010	Invite to Telephone Interview	Invitation
3020	Invite to Interview	Invitation
3040	Invite to Assessment Center	Invitation
3060	Invite to Medical Check	Invitation
3070	Request Questionnaire	Invitation
3080	Request EEO Questionnaire	Invitation
3090	Correspondence: Rejection	Invitation

Table 4.3 SAP Standard Delivered Activity Types (Cont.)

4.8.2 Create Forms

Earlier in the chapter, we discussed the customizing activities Create Forms and Changeable Letter Sections, Assign Changeable Letter Sections to Forms, and Assign Form to Activity Types. In SAP E-Recruiting, you can copy the standard delivered templates to create custom forms. You can copy the standard delivered template HRRCF_CS_IT_APPLICANT and use it for simple correspondence activities. You can copy the standard delivered template HRRCF_CS_IT_APPL_INVITATION and use it for invitation type correspondence activities. Table 4.4 shows the SAP standard delivered copy templates and letter templates.

There is an SAP standard delivered cover letter template that you can assign to letter templates. When you use a cover letter, the email correspondence includes the cover letter and the actual letter correspondence. In this way, the content of the cover letter is different from the actual letter correspondence. You use the template HRRCF_CS_COV_IT_APPLICANT as the cover letter template for all simple correspondence letter templates. You use the template HRRCF_CS_COV_IT_INVITATION as the cover letter template for all invitation type letter templates.

Perform the customizing activity in the IMG by following the menu path SAP E-RECRUITING • APPLICANT TRACKING • ACTIVITIES • CORRESPONDENCE • CREATE LETTER TEMPLATES • ASSIGN TEMPLATES FOR COVER LETTER TO LETTER TEMPLATES.

Name	Description
HRRCF_CS_IT_APPLICANT	Letter to candidate (copy template)
HRRCF_CS_IT_APPL_INVITATION	Letter to candidate (copy template)
HRRCF_CS_IT_EXA_APPL_REQUEST	Invite to apply
HRRCF_CS_IT_EXA_CONF_REGISTER	Acknowledge candidate
HRRCF_CS_IT_EXA_DEREGISTRATION	Deregistration
HRRCF_CS_IT_EXA_INVITATION	Invitation
HRRCF_CS_IT_EXA_NEW_PASSWORD	Access authorization
HRRCF_CS_IT_EXA_OFFER_CONTRACT	Extend offer
HRRCF_CS_IT_EXA_PROV_NOTIF	Interim notification
HRRCF_CS_IT_EXA_QUESTIONAIRE	Request questionnaire
HRRCF_CS_IT_EXA_RECEIPT	Confirmation of receipt
HRRCF_CS_IT_EXA_REJECTION	Correspondence: rejection

Table 4.4 SAP Standard Delivered Letter Templates

4.8.3 Assign Document Formats to Output Channels

In SAP E-Recruiting, you can display a document in different formats in different output channels. In customizing, you assign the document formats to the output channels. You can perform the customizing activity in the IMG under the menu path SAP E-Recruiting • Applicant Tracking • Activities • Correspondence • Output Channels • Assign Document Formats to Output Channels.

Table 4.5 lists the output channels and the document formats that you can assign to these output channels.

Output Channel	Document Format	Effect
Editor	SSF_HTM	All documents are displayed in the editor in HTML format. This is the only selection available.
E-Mail	SSF_HTM	The document in the email is in HTML format.

Table 4.5 Output Formats and Possible Assignment to Output Channels

Output Channel	Document Format	Effect
E-Mail	SSF_PDF	The document in the email is in PDF format.
E-Mail	SSF_ASC	The document in the email is in ASCII format.
Front-End	SSF_PDF	The document is displayed in the frontend in PDF format.
Printer	SSF_OTF	The document is sent to printer in Output text format (OTF). This is the only selection available.

Table 4.5 Output Formats and Possible Assignment to Output Channels (Cont.)

4.9 Summary

In this chapter, we reviewed requisition management functionality within SAP E-Recruiting. We showed how to create a requisition and how to create and publish a job posting. We explained how to create a process template, assign activity types to the process template, and assign the process template to a requisition, which guides the recruiter and the support team through the recruitment process. We reviewed questionnaire and question administration and how to use the questionnaire in prequalifying candidates. Later in the chapter, we explained manager involvement and the different ways the manager can create a new requisition in SAP E-Recruiting.

Now that you have gained a deep understanding of requisition management, in the next chapter we will explain candidate management. We will discuss details about talent groups, application groups, and talent relationship management (TRM). We will show how an internal candidate and an external candidate can register in the talent warehouse and apply for a requisition, and we will revisit the process template, questionnaires, and activity types and show how to send a simple correspondence or create a qualifying event.

Companies implement SAP E-Recruiting so they can hire the right candidate using a set budget. Candidate management is an important functionality in SAP E-Recruiting for obvious reasons. The concepts of both talent groups and talent relationship management form an important component in Candidate Management. In this chapter, we will explain candidate management and the different functionalities that SAP E-Recruiting provides for sourcing the right talent.

5 Candidate Management

The topic of candidate management is important in any recruitment process. Companies invest and allot a large recruiting budget to attract the best candidates from the marketplace. Recruiters need to develop and maintain relationships with candidates, inform them of new requisitions, keep them updated on the status of their applications, and seek referrals. In this chapter, we will explain the features available in SAP E-Recruiting for candidate management including functionalities such as tell-a-friend and job agents. We will revisit questionnaires and the activities related to candidate management. Later in the chapter, we will explain about the talent warehouse, application groups, and talent relationship management. We will also show the customizing steps available for implementing the functionality and share best practices.

To begin, we provide an overview of candidate management and the process steps that are involved.

5.1 Overview of Candidate Management

In SAP E-Recruiting, a candidate is a person interested in joining your organization as an employee, contractor, and so on. Candidates are maintained as either internal candidates or external candidates. External candidates can be either registered or unregistered. All internal candidates are registered because the candidate's SAP ERP HCM master data is transferred to the SAP E-Recruiting application. When an external candidate registers in your organization's database, his details are stored in the SAP E-Recruiting talent warehouse. The talent warehouse also contains internal candidates. The talent pool consists of all candidates (internal or external) who are present in the talent warehouse.

Note

If you have a large team of recruiters, you can divide the talent warehouse into several talent pools. The talent pools can be distributed to the recruiters so that each recruiter has access to a particular talent pool or multiple talent pools. This suggested best practice prevents recruiters from competing for the same talent.

Let's now discuss external candidates in more detail including the activities they can perform in the talent warehouse and how they register in the application.

5.1.1 External Candidates

Depending on your business requirements, you can invite applications to a requisition from a registered or unregistered external candidate.

Note

Some organizations prefer only registered candidates to apply to a requisition. Unregistered candidates can still search for job openings in your organization's website. If they find a vacancy that suits their skills or experience and if they try to apply to that requisition, they receive a notice encouraging them to register in the talent warehouse prior to applying to the requisition.

After receiving an application from an unregistered candidate, the recruiter can send a simple correspondence to the candidate, inviting him to register in the talent warehouse. In the simple correspondence, the recruiter can highlight the benefits of being registered in the talent warehouse, for example receiving invitations to job fairs, utilizing job agents, and receiving notifications of upcoming requisitions. Alternatively, after sending his application to a requisition, an unregistered candidate can return and register in the talent warehouse prior to receiving from the recruiter any invitation to register in the talent warehouse.

Figure 5.1 displays the screen where an external candidate can register in the talent warehouse. The candidate enters the basic data such as first and last name, username, password, and email address.

Once registered, a candidate can perform any of the following activities:

- Create a candidate profile in the talent warehouse. If the candidate is interested he can release the candidate profile so recruiters can access it.

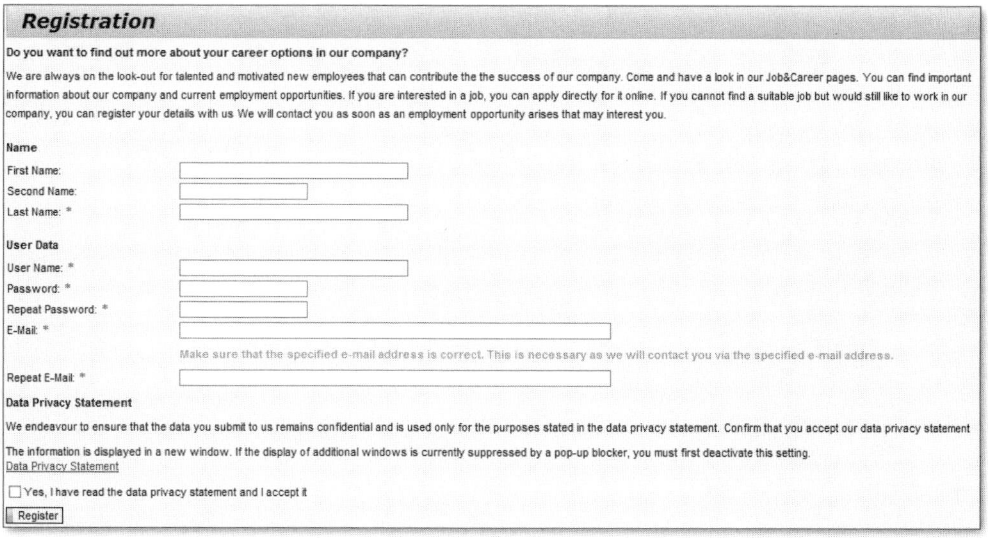

Figure 5.1 Registration Screen for an External Candidate

- Register for TRM activities, for example, receiving requisitions pertaining to the candidate's interest group, receiving simple correspondence from the recruiter inviting to a job fair, or requesting candidate referrals.
- Search job postings and apply to a suitable requisition.
- Request a new password if the candidate forgets his old password.
- Delete registration and the candidate profile, if desired.

After a candidate has registered in the talent warehouse, if the candidate is inactive for a certain period of time (say the candidate has not applied to any requisition in the past 12 months), the recruiter can send a simple correspondence inviting the candidate to apply to a requisition. If the candidate does not respond, the recruiter can delete the candidate's profile from the talent warehouse. A correspondence can be sent to the candidate informing him that the profile has been deleted and inviting him to register again in the talent warehouse if he wants.

Note

If a registered candidate has applied to a large number of requisitions and if his applications have not received favorable responses or if the applications are rejected, the recruiting administrator can enter appropriate notes about the candidate.

In the United States and other countries, a data privacy statement is an important requirement for online applications. Candidates may be required to read and accept a data privacy statement when they register in the talent warehouse. Let's look at the data privacy statements and see how you can upload them in different languages.

5.1.2 Data Privacy Statements

When a candidate enters the information required to register in the talent warehouse, he needs to review and accept the data privacy statement (see Figure 5.2).

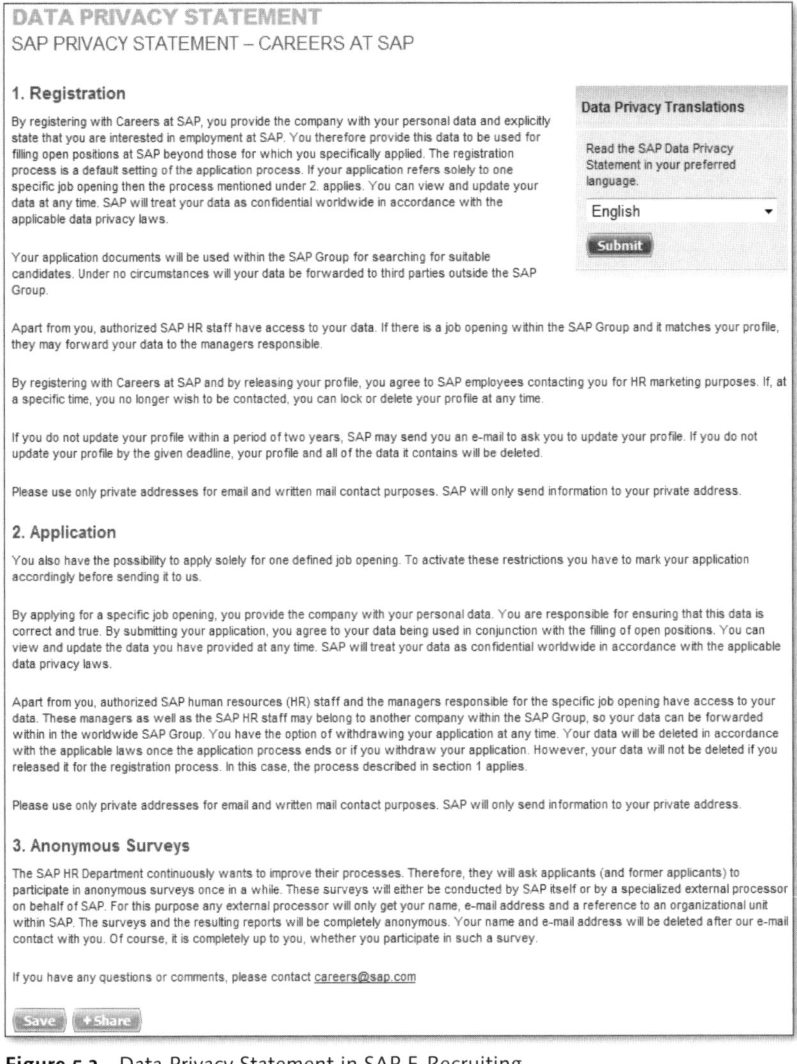

Figure 5.2 Data Privacy Statement in SAP E-Recruiting

The candidate *cannot* register in the talent warehouse without accepting the data privacy statement. The organization provides the data privacy statement to inform the candidate that the details provided while registering in the talent warehouse will be kept confidential.

The data privacy statement is mandatory in many countries. The content and the verbiage of the statement may differ from country to country. You should check with your local labor department for the content that is required.

In SAP E-Recruiting, you can store the data privacy statement in multiple languages. The customizing can only be performed if you use Web Dynpro for ABAP (WD4A) in your system. As shown in Figure 5.3, to perform this customizing in the IMG, follow the menu path SAP E-RECRUITING • TECHNICAL SETTINGS • USER INTERFACES • CANDIDATE • BACKEND CANDIDATE • STORE URLS FOR LANGUAGE-DEPENDENT DATA PRIVACY STATEMENTS.

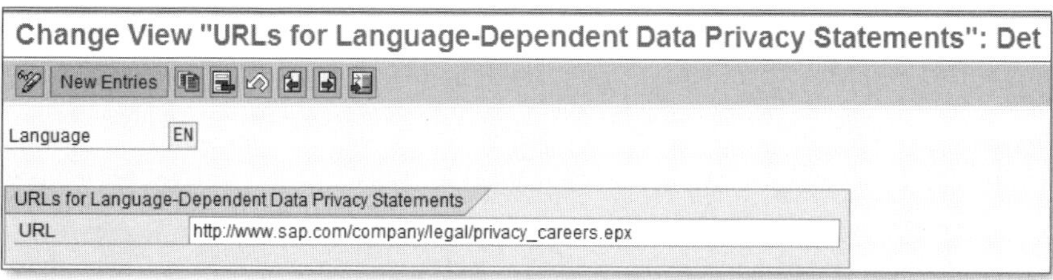

Figure 5.3 IMG Customizing Screen to Configure the URL for the Data Privacy Statement

After the candidate has read and accepted the data privacy statement, he can click on the Register button to accept his entries and register in the talent warehouse. Once registered in the talent warehouse, the candidate will receive an acknowledgment that the registration has been received and he can access the applicant cockpit to create and maintain the candidate profile, search for jobs, or send applications for requisitions. In the next section, we will explain the applicant cockpit in detail and the different functionalities available.

5.1.3 Applicant Cockpit

After the candidate has registered in the talent warehouse, he can log in using the newly created user and password. You can work with your web developer to design and customize the landing page to brand it appropriately.

You can design the landing page to explain your organization's recruiting process and direct candidates to the appropriate channels. For example, in your landing page, you can create links for alumni, veterans, new graduates, and so on. Your landing page can provide an introduction to your organization and describe why it is a great place to work.

Figure 5.4 shows the screen to log in to the applicant cockpit. In the login screen you can check the Accessibility option. Using this option, you can provide accessibility assistance to partially disabled individuals.

Figure 5.4 Candidate Log-In Screen

Candidates can use the login screen to change their passwords or request a new password if they have forgotten. SAP E-Recruiting provides standard delivered workflows that facilitate these functionalities. Refer to Section 5.10, Workflows, for more details on the SAP standard delivered workflows.

> **Note**
>
> In some countries, it is mandatory to provide accessibility assistance to partially sighted users to use software and other IT applications. One of the ways assistance can be provided is to have content on the portal read aloud using an external interface.

In the applicant cockpit (see Figure 5.5), the candidate can perform the following activities:

- **Delete registration**
  The candidate can delete his registration in the talent warehouse by clicking on the link Delete Registration. Once the candidate has deleted his registration, he can no longer log in to the talent warehouse, and all of his data including the candidate profile is deleted. The candidate receives a correspondence from the SAP E-Recruiting application confirming the deletion.

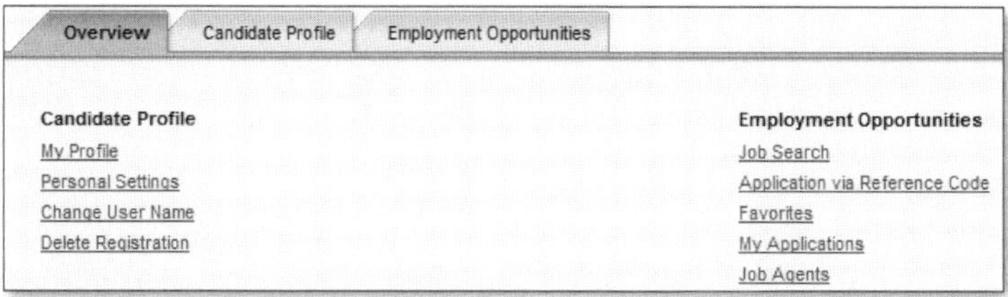

Figure 5.5 Applicant Cockpit

> **Tip**
>
> If the candidate is no longer available in the job market, he can lock his profile rather than deleting his registration. When the profile is locked, the candidate data is no longer visible to the recruiters. When a candidate deletes his registration, she has to reregister to gain access to the talent warehouse.

As shown in Figure 5.6, it is best practice for the candidate to lock his profile rather than deleting the registration.

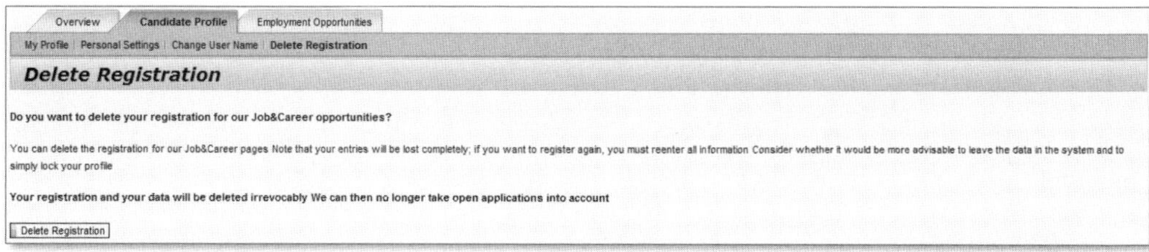

Figure 5.6 Delete Registration

The candidate can also perform the following activities in the applicant cockpit:

- **Change user name**
  The candidate can change the user name required to log in to the SAP E-Recruiting application by clicking on the link Change User Name. The candidate enters the new user name and clicks on the Save button to accept the entries. Next time the candidate logs in to the talent warehouse, he must use the new user name.
- **Customize personal settings**
  Within personal settings, the candidate can select the language in which he prefers to receive candidate correspondence from the SAP E-Recruiting application.
- **Search for job openings**
  The candidate can review current job opportunities at the company.

- **Apply to a requisition using its reference code**
  The candidate can apply to a job posting using a reference code (we describe reference codes later in this chapter).
- **Create favorites**
  The favorites are all of the job openings that the candidate bookmarks as interesting during search. SAP E-Recruiting moves the bookmarked job openings into a separate folder.
- **My applications**
  This link displays all of the applications for which the candidate has applied. He can also check the status of the applications or withdraw or delete them. The candidate can resubmit an application for the withdrawn or deleted applications.
- **Job agents**
  The candidate can create job agents. We will explain more about job agents later in the chapter.

In the applicant cockpit, the candidate can click on the My Profile link to create a profile. External candidates can use the candidate profile to store their resumes, communication data, and job preferences.

In the Candidate Profile screen (see Figure 5.7), you can see the "bread crumbs" (or Floor Plan Manager) on top of the screen that guide the candidate through the process of creating a profile.

Note

If your organization has implemented a resume parsing tool, the candidate can upload his resume and click on the resume parsing utility to parse the resume and fill the data in the candidate profile. Currently, there is no standard delivery of resume parsing within SAP E-Recruiting. However, several vendors offer resume parsing tools that you can integrate with the SAP E-Recruiting application. We will discuss more about resume parsing tools in Chapter 9, Vendor Services.

The following data needs to be filled to complete the candidate profile.

- **Personal Data**
  In the Personal Data section of the candidate profile, the data that was entered during registering in the talent warehouse is automatically displayed. This include details such as the candidate's first name, last name, and email address.
- **Education/Training**
  To add education and training experience and qualifications, the candidate can click on the Add button.

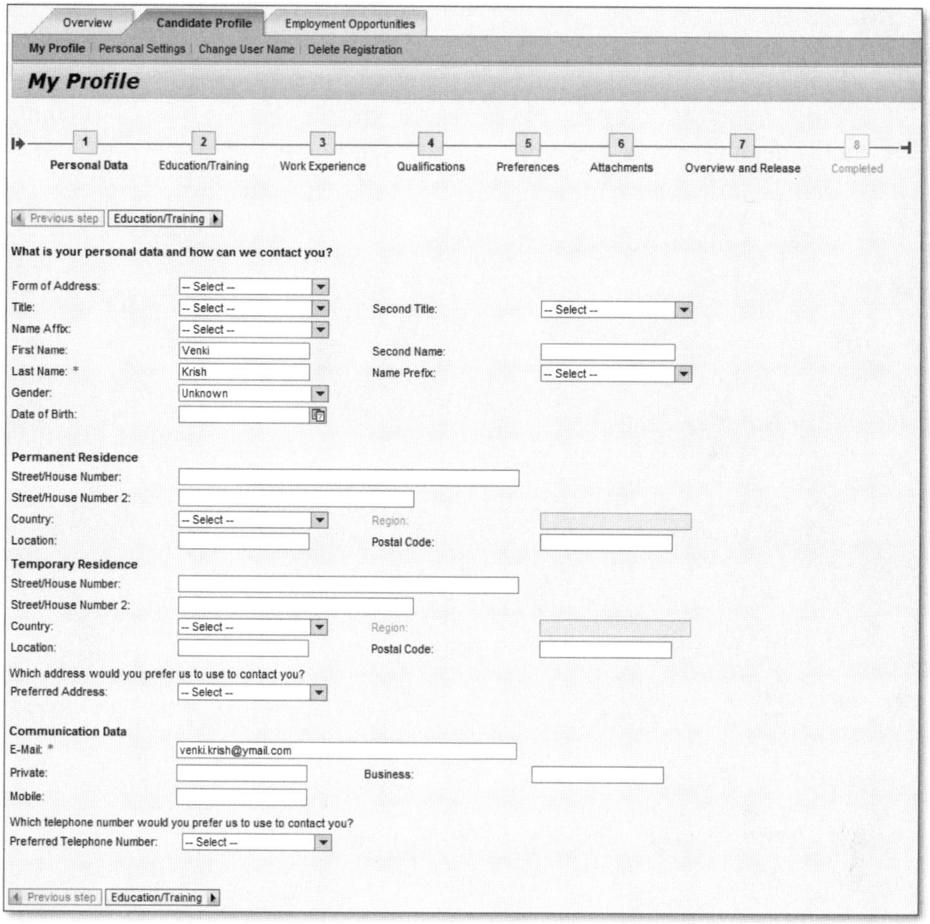

Figure 5.7 Candidate Profile Interface

- **Work Experience**
  To add details about the candidate's work experience, the candidate can click on the Add button.
- **Qualifications**
  In the qualifications section, qualifications are displayed as individual tabs. The candidate can choose his qualifications and assign a proficiency to each of these.
- **Preferences**
  In the preferences section, the candidate can enter preferences such as the interest group, the desired work location, the hierarchy level, and the functional area in which he is interested.

- **Attachments**
  Any additional details the candidate would like to add to the candidate profile can be uploaded as attachments (see Figure 5.8). These attachments can supplement the information given in the candidate profile. Example documents include reference letters, training certificates, and licenses.

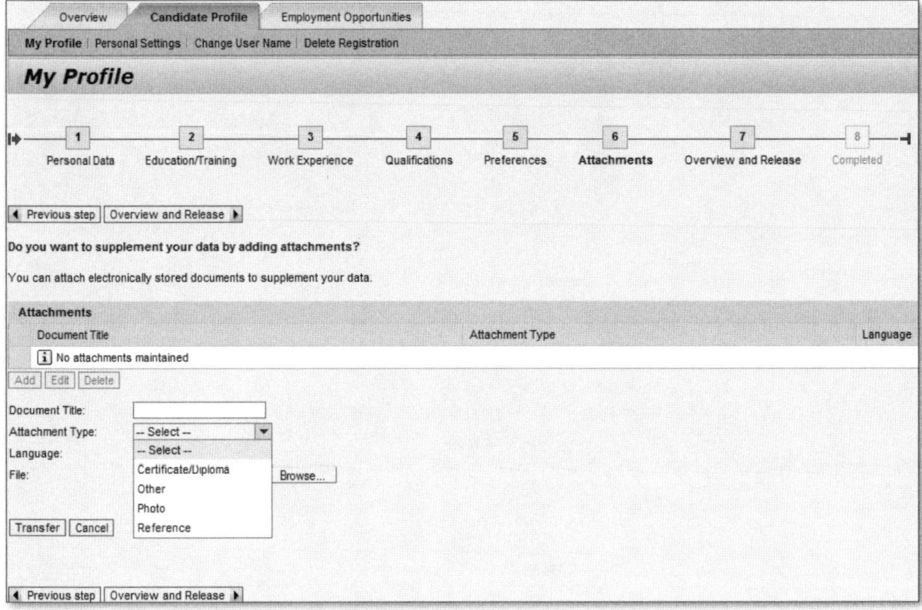

Figure 5.8 Attachments in the Candidate Profile Interface

- **Overview and Release**
  The overview and release section displays the data overview of the candidate profile. This screen also requires the candidate to approve the profile for release. If the candidate is not interested in releasing his profile, he can lock it.

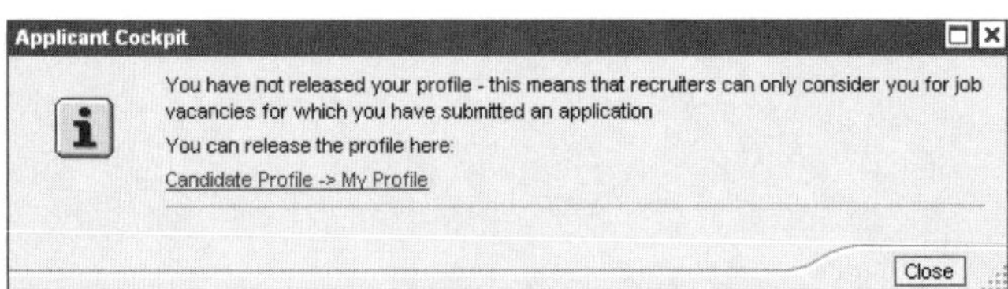

Figure 5.9 Candidate Profile Release

If the candidate does not release his profile, the next time the candidate logs in to the talent warehouse, he will see a dialog box (see Figure 5.9) reminding him to release the profile. When released, the profile becomes visible to the recruiters when they perform a search in the talent warehouse. If the recruiter feels the candidate is qualified, the recruiter can assign the candidate to the requisition. After the candidate has completed entering the data, he can click on the Complete button and accept his entries. All fields that are marked with an asterisk (*) are mandatory.

We have discussed the functions available for an external candidate. Let's now discuss the same for the internal candidate.

5.1.4 Internal Candidates

As shown in Figure 5.10, internal candidates do not have access to delete their registrations or to change their user names. This is because of the integration between your SAP ERP HCM and SAP E-Recruiting systems. Internal candidate access their functionality from within your SAP Portal.

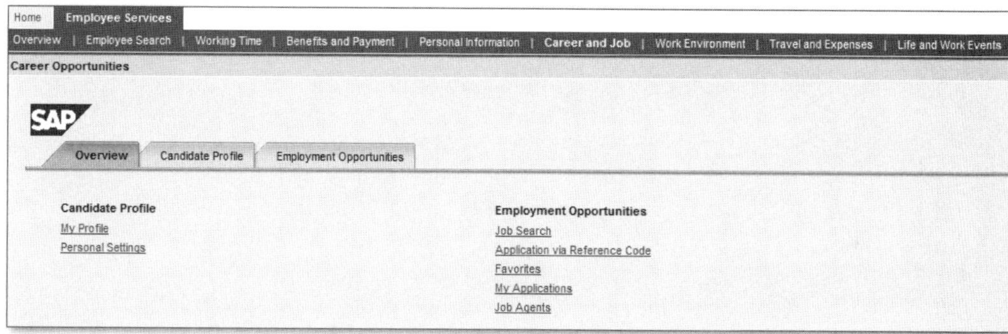

Figure 5.10 Applicant Cockpit for Internal Candidates

Within the SAP Portal, internal candidates can perform the following functions:

- Create and maintain profiles
- Search for job openings
- Apply to a requisition via a reference code
- Create favorites
- Obtain an overview of all applications
- Create job agents and receive notifications of job openings that suit interest and experience

Now that we have an understanding of the functions available to internal and external candidates, we will discuss application management and applicant tracking. In the next section, we will see how candidates can apply to a requisition, how a recruiter can enter an application on behalf of the candidate, and how a recruiter can manually assign a candidate to a requisition. We will also explain about application groups and how to collect unsolicited applications in SAP E-Recruiting.

5.2 Application Management

In this section, we will explain the processing of applications by the recruiter and support team. A recruiter can receive an application by any of the following means:

- A candidate applies to a requisition by using the reference code in the job posting.
- A candidate sends a paper application by mail or emails an application. The recruiter enters the candidate application by using the functionality Create Internal Application/Create External Application in the recruiter dashboard. Later, the recruiter can assign the candidate to other requisitions if the candidate is suitable.
- The recruiter can assign a candidate to the favorites list in a requisition.
- The recruiter can receive unsolicited an application from the candidate.

5.2.1 Job Search

From the applicant cockpit, the candidate can do a job search by clicking on the link Job Search. In the Job Search screen (see Figure 5.11), the candidate can enter the search criteria and click on the Start button to execute the search based on the entered search criteria.

In the Job Search screen, the candidate can save the search criteria by clicking on the Save Search Query button. The next time the candidate has to search for the job posting, he can select the query from the dropdown list Search Query. The candidate can also delete the saved query by clicking on the Delete Search Query button.

Overview | Candidate Profile | Employment Opportunities

Job Search | Application via Reference Code | Favorites | My Applications | Job Agents

Job Search

Are you looking for a new challenge?

We have lots of different jobs on offer - come and have a look at our employment opportunities!

You can restrict the search result by specifying search criteria

Notes on Search

Start | Reset | Save Search Query | Delete Search Query | Save as Job Agent

You can save your search criteria for later reuse

Search Query: -- No search query saved --

Full Text Search

Keywords:

Search Method: With at least one of the words

Search Criteria for Employment Opportunities

Functional Area: Consulting, Controlling / Accounting / Financials, Customer Service, Facilities Management

Hierarchy Level: Apprentice/Student / Trainee, Entry Level (Less than 5 Years Work Experience), Executive, Professional I (move than 5 Years work experience)

Country: Argentina, Canada, Germany, Switzerland

Contract Type: Internship, Regular, Temporary, Union

Education Level: Associate's degree, Bachelor's degree, High school diploma, Master degree

Search Method

(•) All search criteria must be filled

( ) At least one search criterion must be filled

General Search Settings

Start | Reset | Save Search Query | Delete Search Query | Save as Job Agent

Figure 5.11 Job Search Criteria

In the Job Search screen, the candidate can click on the link Notes on Search (see Figure 5.12). The Notes on Search screen provides more details about the Job Search screen, the various fields, and the search criteria. Candidates benefit greatly from understanding how the query works.

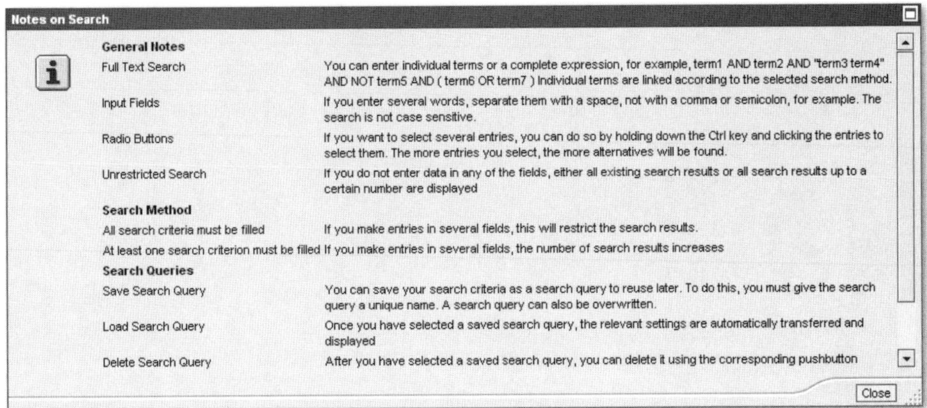

Figure 5.12 Notes on Job Search

Based on the criteria entered in the Job Search screen, the job search results are displayed in a new screen (see Figure 5.13). In the displayed results, every job posting has the reference code displayed in the corresponding Reference Code column. The candidate can click on the job posting and get more details about it. The candidate can highlight the job posting and click on the Add Favorite button to add the job posting to his favorites list. A message saying "Job posting <title of the job posting> was added to your favorites" is displayed at the top of the screen. If a job posting is added to the favorites list, the Favorite column of the particular job posting is checked.

If the candidate wants to apply to a job posting, he can click on the Apply button, which takes her to the application wizard. We will discuss the application wizard in a later section.

5.2.2 Favorites

From the applicant cockpit, the candidate can click on the Favorites link, to display all of the job postings he has added to the favorites list (see Figure 5.14). If the candidate wants to apply to a job posting, he can select the job posting and click on the Apply button, which takes him to the application wizard.

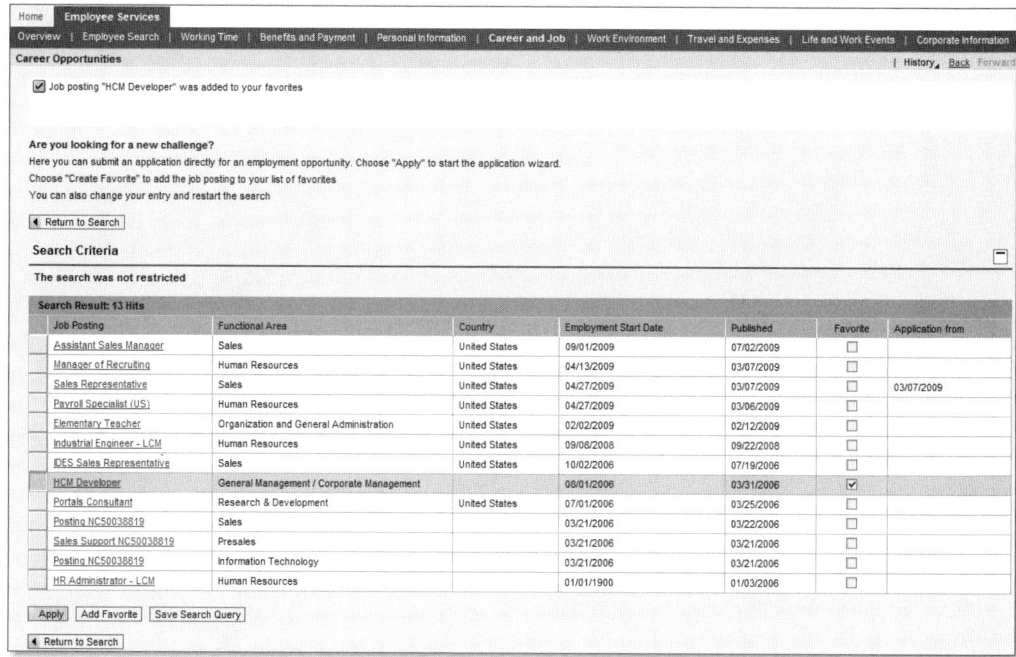

Job Posting	Functional Area	Country	Employment Start Date	Published	Favorite	Application from
Assistant Sales Manager	Sales	United States	09/01/2009	07/02/2009	☐	
Manager of Recruiting	Human Resources	United States	04/13/2009	03/07/2009	☐	
Sales Representative	Sales	United States	04/27/2009	03/07/2009	☐	03/07/2009
Payroll Specialist (US)	Human Resources	United States	04/27/2009	03/06/2009	☐	
Elementary Teacher	Organization and General Administration	United States	02/02/2009	02/12/2009	☐	
Industrial Engineer - LCM	Human Resources	United States	09/08/2008	09/22/2008	☐	
IDES Sales Representative	Sales	United States	10/02/2006	07/19/2006	☐	
HCM Developer	General Management / Corporate Management		08/01/2006	03/31/2006	☑	
Portals Consultant	Research & Development	United States	07/01/2006	03/25/2006	☐	
Posting NC50038819	Sales		03/21/2006	03/22/2006	☐	
Sales Support NC50038819	Presales		03/21/2006	03/21/2006	☐	
Posting NC50038819	Information Technology		03/21/2006	03/21/2006	☐	
HR Administrator - LCM	Human Resources		01/01/1900	01/03/2006	☐	

Figure 5.13 Job Search Results

Overview | Candidate Profile | Employment Opportunities

Job Search | Application via Reference Code | Favorites | My Applications | Job Agents

Favorites

Do you want to apply for one of the bookmarked job postings?

On this page, you can see all the employment opportunities you bookmarked as interesting during the search.

Favorites

Functional Area	Job Posting	Published	Country	Application from
Consulting	Portals Consultant	03/25/2006	United States	
Software Development	HCM Developer	03/31/2006		
Human Resources	Payroll Specialist (US)	03/06/2009	United States	

Apply | Delete

Figure 5.14 Favorites List

To delete a job posting from the favorites list (see Figure 5.15), the candidate can select the job posting and click on the Delete button. A message saying "Job posting <title of the job posting> was removed from your list of favorites" is displayed in the interface.

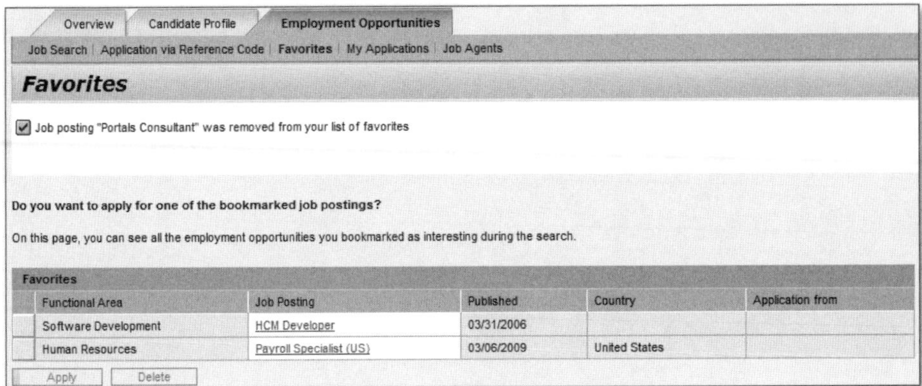

Figure 5.15 Delete Favorites

Let's now discuss applying to a job posting via a reference code.

5.2.3 Application via Reference Code

Both internal and external candidates can apply to a job posting directly by using its reference code. The system generates the reference code for a job posting and publishes it along with the job posting. We discussed job posting reference codes in Section 4.4.9 of Chapter 4, Requisition Management.

From the applicant cockpit, the candidate can click on the link Application via Reference Code. In the Quick Search screen (see Figure 5.16), the candidate can enter the reference code of the job posting in which he is interested. When the candidate clicks on the Start Search button, it displays the relevant job posting in the Search Result. The candidate can click on the job posting link to review and get more details about the job posting.

While reviewing the job posting, the candidate can click on the Apply button displayed in the job posting if he wants to apply to the job posting (see Figure 5.17). This takes the candidate to the application wizard. In the Quick Search screen (see Figure 5.16 again), the candidate can also apply to a job posting by clicking on the Apply button. This takes the candidate directly to the application wizard. If the candidate had already started the application process but did not complete it, the text in the button will read Continue Application, and the candidate will be able to continue where he left off.

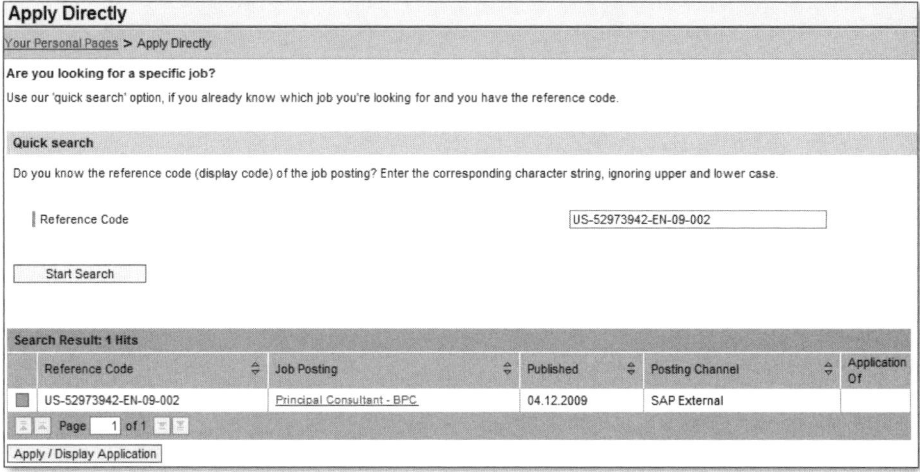

Figure 5.16 Apply to a Requisition via Reference Code

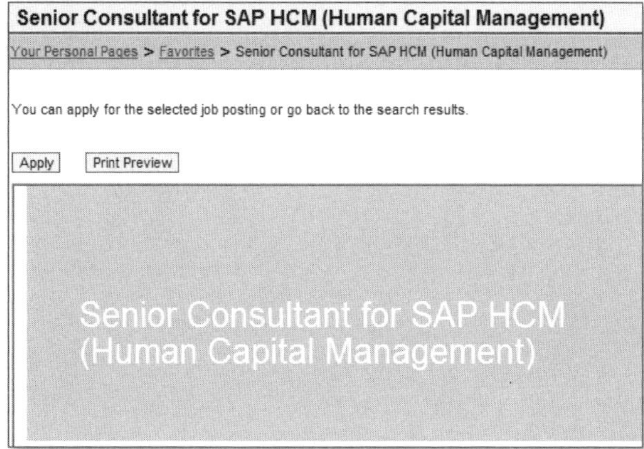

Figure 5.17 Apply to the Job Posting from the Job Posting Details Screen

5.2.4 Application Wizard

Both registered and unregistered candidates can use the application wizard to apply to job postings.

In the application wizard (see Figure 5.18), you can see "bread crumbs" (Floor Plan Manager) that guide the candidate to enter the required information during the application process.

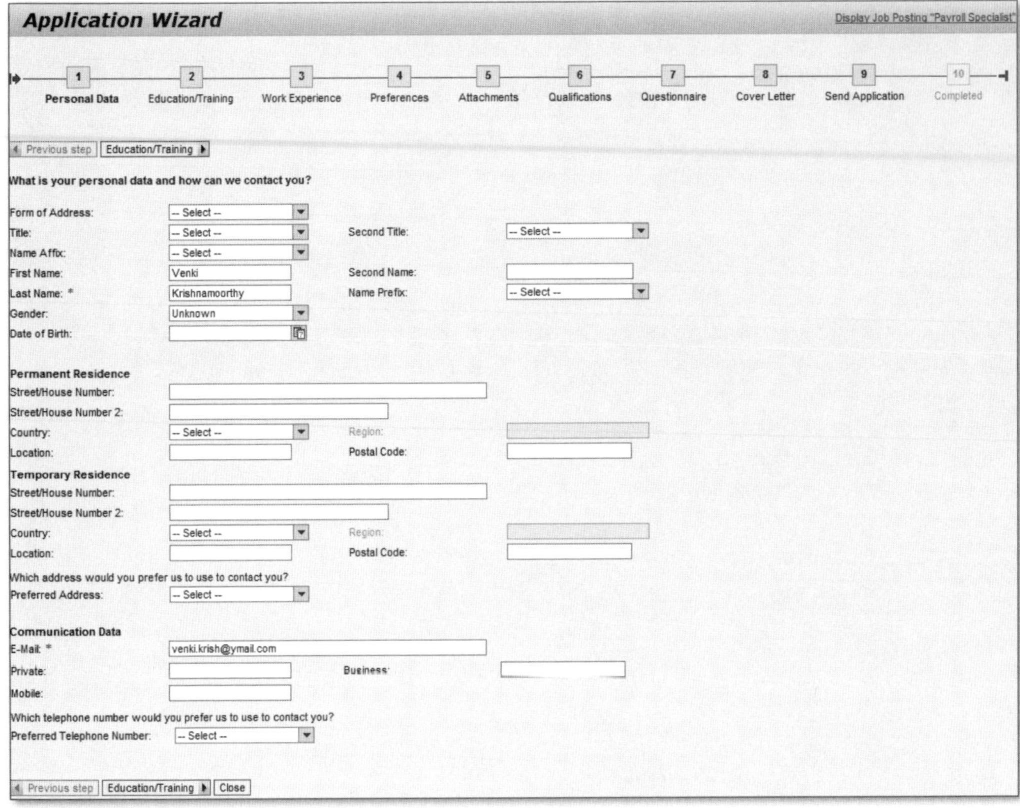

Figure 5.18 Application Wizard

When an unregistered candidate applies to a job posting, the candidate is asked to enter a first name, last name, and email address (see Figure 5.19). The SAP E-Recruiting system automatically generates a user name and password for the candidate and emails this information back to the candidate. Prompting an unregistered external candidate to enter the basic data is a suggested best practice because if the unregistered candidate returns again to complete the application on a future visit, he can use the system-generated username and password to log back in.

On a later visit at login, the system asks the candidate to enter a new password because the old password is system generated. Also, at any time, the candidate can change the user name and password on the candidate page. It is much easier for a candidate to remember a user-generated user name and password than a system-generated user name. Therefore, it is best practice for candidates to register in the talent warehouse prior to applying to a job posting. Also, if the candidate is already registered in the talent warehouse, much of the data required in the application wizard is entered by the system. The fields that are marked with an asterisk (*) are mandatory and have to be completed by the candidate.

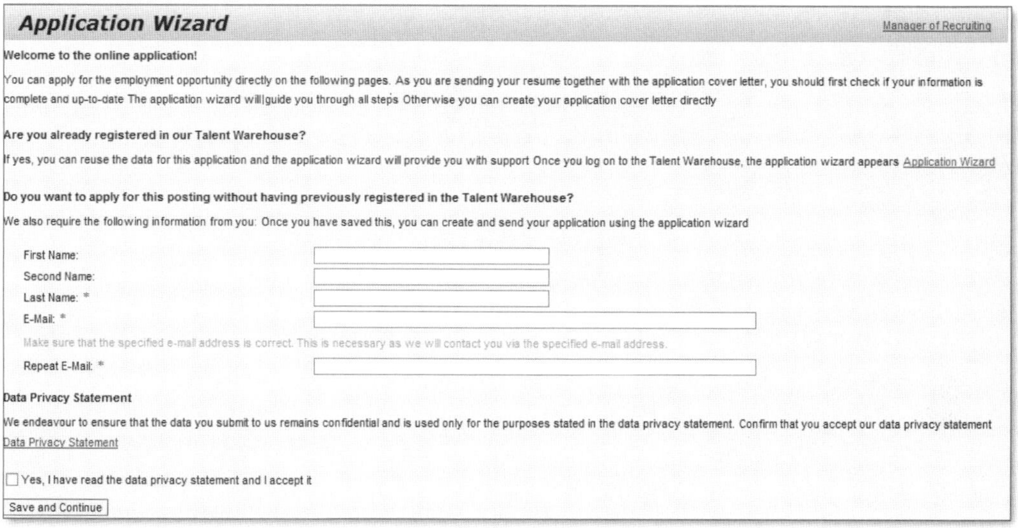

Application Wizard Manager of Recruiting

Welcome to the online application!

You can apply for the employment opportunity directly on the following pages. As you are sending your resume together with the application cover letter, you should first check if your information is complete and up-to-date The application wizard will guide you through all steps Otherwise you can create your application cover letter directly

Are you already registered in our Talent Warehouse?

If yes, you can reuse the data for this application and the application wizard will provide you with support Once you log on to the Talent Warehouse, the application wizard appears Application Wizard

Do you want to apply for this posting without having previously registered in the Talent Warehouse?

We also require the following information from you: Once you have saved this, you can create and send your application using the application wizard

First Name:
Second Name:
Last Name: *
E-Mail: *
Make sure that the specified e-mail address is correct. This is necessary as we will contact you via the specified e-mail address.
Repeat E-Mail: *

Data Privacy Statement

We endeavour to ensure that the data you submit to us remains confidential and is used only for the purposes stated in the data privacy statement. Confirm that you accept our data privacy statement Data Privacy Statement

☐ Yes, I have read the data privacy statement and I accept it

Save and Continue

Figure 5.19 Application Wizard for Unregistered Candidate

In the Attachment tab of the application wizard, candidates can upload cover letters, resumes, reference letters, and any additional documentation they want to share with the recruiting team.

Note

SAP E-Recruiting has no standard delivered functionality to validate if the resume is attached and uploaded into the system. If this is a business requirement, you need to implement a custom BAdI to do so.

Prior to the candidate submitting the application, your company may want to collect information such as the application source. You can customize the application source categories from which you would like the candidate to choose. You perform this customizing activity in the IMG under the menu path SAP E-Recruiting • Applicant Tracking • Define Application Source Types and Assign Note Texts to Them.

In this customizing activity (see Figure 5.20), you create the application source categories the candidate can choose from when filling the data for the source type. When creating the source category, you can also enter the Online Text Repository (OTR) text for each source category. This OTR text can be displayed for each source category in the application wizard user interface. It is a prerequisite that the OTR texts stored in this customizing activity be available in the OTR.

Change View "Application Source Types": Overview

New Entries

Application Source Types

Type	Name	OTR Source Category
1	Employee Referral	PAOC_RCF_UI/EMPLOYEE_REFERRAL_TEXT
2	Third-Party Provider	PAOC_RCF_UI/3RDPARTY_TEXT
5	Job Board	SOTR_VOCABULARY_BASIC/DESCRIPTION
6	Agencies	SOTR_VOCABULARY_BASIC/DESCRIPTION

Figure 5.20 Application Source Categories

After performing the customizing activity Define Application Source Types and Assign Note Texts to Them, you can customize application sources for each of the source categories (see Figure 5.21). This provides the candidate with selection options for the selected source category. You perform this customizing activity in the IMG under the menu path E-RECRUITING • APPLICANT TRACKING • DEFINE APPLICATION SOURCES. You create the application source by assigning a unique ID and description of the source and assigning a source category.

Change View "Application Sources": Overview

New Entries

Application Sources

Source	Name	Type	Name
1	Employee Referral	1	Employee Referral
2	Agency 001 for E-recruiting	2	Third-Party Provider
5	America's Job Bank	5	Job Board
6	Monster	5	Job Board
7	Staffing Services	6	Agencies
90	Agency 002 for E-recruiting	2	Third-Party Provider
91	Executive Search Firm	2	Third-Party Provider

Figure 5.21 Application Sources

Note

Collecting application source information from the candidate is a suggested best practice. This information helps the recruiting team determine which application sources generate the most applications and which application sources provide the most hires. If your organization uses several job boards for publishing job postings, you will want to know which Internet job board is most effective. One of the sources for gathering that information is the candidate.

After the candidate has completed entering the data, he can click on the Submit button and submit the application for the job posting. On receipt of the application, the system sends a candidate acknowledgment email to the candidate. If the candidate does not provide an email address, the acknowledgment activity can be disabled. You can customize the contents of the candidate simple correspondence to meet business requirements. Refer to Chapter 4, Requisition Management, Section 4.6.3, Activity Management, for more details about Changeable Letter sections.

You need to perform the following IMG activities to complete the configuration for the application process.

- **Customize the application wizard**
  You can customize the application wizard to meet your business requirements. For example, you can add tabs . To perform the customizing steps, in the IMG follow the menu path SAP E-RECRUITING • TECHNICAL SETTINGS • USER INTERFACES • CANDIDATE • FLEXIBILIZATION.
- **BAdI: Specify Application Configuration for Application Wizard**
  In this customizing step, you can use an implementation of BAdI HRRCF00_DETERMINE_APPL_CONFIG to hide or display certain fields in the application wizard interface.
- **BAdI: Specify Application Configuration for Start Page**
  In certain scenarios, candidates can arrive at the application wizard indirectly, for example, by clicking on a link in the candidate correspondence. In this customizing step, you use the BAdI HRRCF00_DET_APPL_CONFIG_STARTP to store the application configuration for the start page to call the application wizard indirectly.
- **Display an overview page**
  To do this, you need to set the parameter SP_OVERVIEW_TAB = "X" in the customizing activity Assign Values to Interface Parameters (Web Dynpro ABAP). The menu path for this customizing activity is SAP E-RECRUITING • TECHNICAL SETTINGS • USER INTERFACES • CANDIDATE • BACKEND CANDIDATE • ASSIGN VALUES TO INTERFACE PARAMETERS (WEB DYNPRO ABAP).
- **Create Structuring Elements for First Level**
  In this customizing activity, you create the structuring elements for the first navigation level.
- **Create Structuring Elements for Second Level**
  Create the structuring elements for the second navigation level.

- **Define Start Pages**
  You can customize the standard delivered start page or create variants of the same start page. If you are creating new entries in this customizing activity, you must have created the OTR texts in the SAP E-Recruiting system. (You can use the newly created OTR texts to label the navigation level and the structuring elements.)

You should perform the following activities to configure the roadmap pattern:

- **Create Roadmap Steps**
  In this customizing step, you create the roadmap steps, which you can use to customize the roadmap pattern.
- **Create Roadmap Pattern**
  In this activity, you can customize the SAP standard delivered roadmap to suit your business requirements. To customize a roadmap pattern, create a variant of the SAP standard delivered roadmap and assign the roadmap steps to that pattern in the order you wish to display them.

In this section, we explained how registered and unregistered candidates use the application wizard to apply to job postings. Next, we will explain how the recruiter enters applications for internal and external candidates.

5.3 Entry of Applications by the Recruiter

The processes by which the recruiter enters applications differs for internal and external candidates.

5.3.1 Entry of Application for an Internal Candidate

When the recruiter receives an application from an internal candidate (employee) by email or mail, he can create an application manually.

From the Recruiter Work Center, the recruiter clicks on the link Create Internal Application service under Manual Application Management. In the Create Internal Application screen (see Figure 5.22), the recruiter enters the details of the application such as the reference code of the job posting and the internal candidate's personnel number. The recruiter can upload paper applications as attachments into the system. After the recruiter has completed entering the data, he clicks on the Save button to save the entries. As part of the save process, the system checks whether an application already exists for the same reference code. If an application already exists for the same reference code, an error message is displayed in a dialog box.

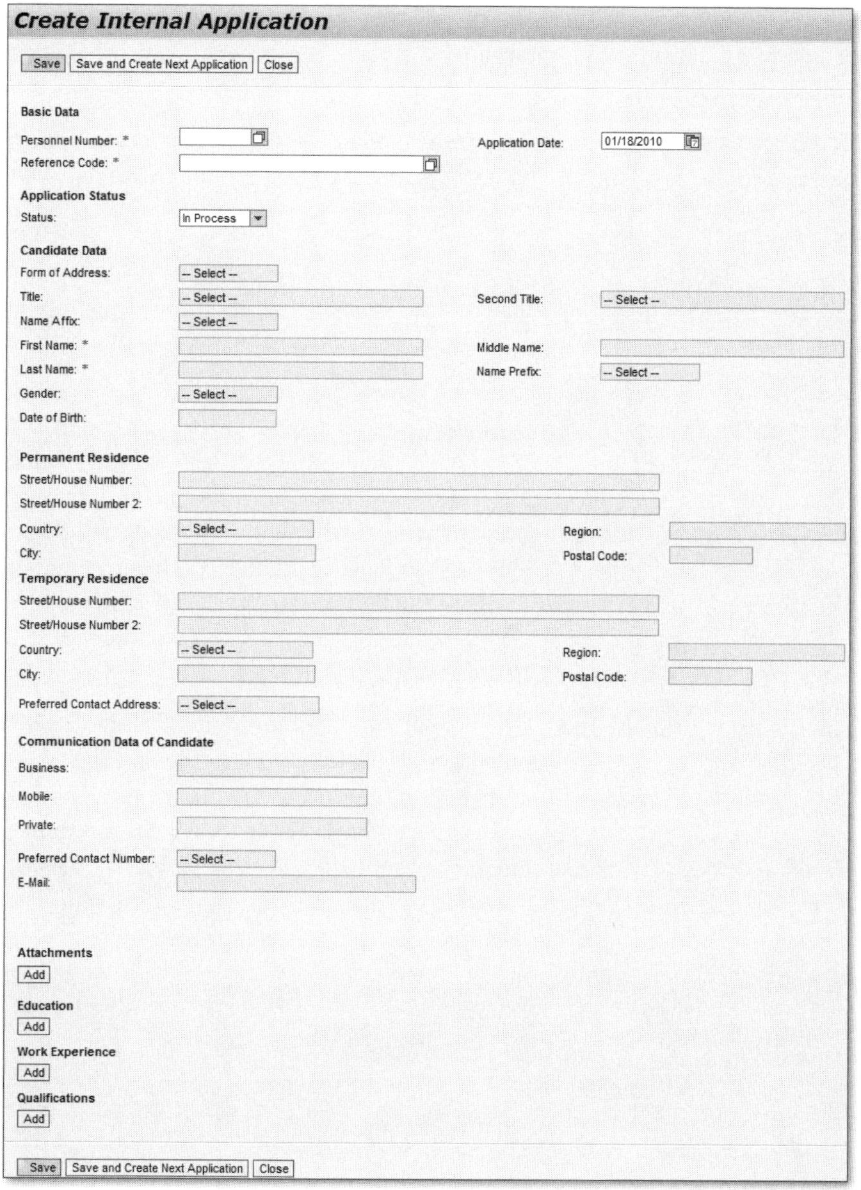

Figure 5.22 Create Application for Internal Candidate

The recruiter can then change the reference code (if the recruiter entered a wrong reference code) or reply back to the internal candidate informing him that an online application already exists for him. The recruiter can also provide a status update of the application at this time, if desired. If no application exists for the reference code, the application entered by the recruiter is saved, and the system sends a candidate acknowledgment.

The internal candidate's application is now available for review by the support team assigned to the requisition. The statuses of the candidacy and the application will be In Process.

5.3.2 Entry of Application for an External Candidate

When the recruiter receives an application from an external candidate by email or by mail, he may need to create an application for the candidate manually.

When the recruiter enters the application for the external candidate, you can implement BAdI HRRCF00_GET_DUPL_EXT_CAND (Determine External Candidates that Match a Search Pattern) to determine if the applicant data is unique and prevent duplicate entries. In the custom implementation, you can define the criteria to be used to check duplicate entries. When this BAdI is implemented, the system performs the check and displays a listing of potential duplicate entries. The menu path for this customizing activity is SAP E-RECRUITING • APPLICANT TRACKING • BADI: DETERMINE EXTERNAL CANDIDATES THAT MATCH A SEARCH PATTERN.

If this BAdI is not implemented, the system executes the default class CL_FB_HRRCF00_GET_DUPL_EXT_CAN assigned to the BAdI to determine that the applicant data is unique. The pattern that is used to determine the unique entry is first name, last name, and email address. In the standard delivered system, no implementation is activated, and the system executes the default class CL_FB_HRRCF00_GET_DUPL_EXT_CAN to check and determine that the applicant's data is unique in the talent pool. It is a suggested best practice that you define and activate your own implementation.

Note

Based on your business requirements, you can add more search pattern to the BAdI HRRCF00_GET_DUPL_EXT_CAND to determine the uniqueness of the candidate. For example, the applicant's zip code can be a valid search pattern.

To create an application for an external candidate in the Recruiter Work Center, the recruiter clicks on the link Create External Application under Manual Application Management. In the Create External Application screen (see Figure 5.23), the recruiter enters the details of the application such as the reference code of the job posting.

Create External Application

Save | Save and Create Next Application | Close

Basic Data

Application Date: 01/18/2010

Application for: * Reference Code / Application Group -- Select --

Application Status

Status: In Process

Candidate Data

Form of Address: -- Select --

Title: -- Select -- Second Title: -- Select --

Name Affix: -- Select --

First Name: * Middle Name:

Last Name: * Name Prefix: -- Select --

Gender: -- Select --

Date of Birth:

Permanent Residence

Street/House Number:

Street/House Number 2:

Country: -- Select -- Region:

City: Postal Code:

Temporary Residence

Street/House Number:

Street/House Number 2:

Country: -- Select -- Region:

City: Postal Code:

Preferred Contact Address: -- Select --

Communication Data of Candidate

Business:

Mobile:

Private:

Preferred Contact Number: -- Select --

E-Mail:

Additional Candidate Data

Preferred Language: -- Select -- Interest Group: -- Select --

Application Source Details

Application Source Type: -- Select -- Application Source:

Other Information:

Attachments

Add

Education

Add

Work Experience

Add

Qualifications

Add

Save | Save and Create Next Application | Close

Figure 5.23 Create Application for an External Candidate

SAP E-Recruiting enhancement pack 4 includes a standard delivered role, SAP_RCF_DATA_TYPIST_ERC_CI_2, for data entry clerks. The data entry clerk is responsible for entering applications received from internal and external candidates. The access type DUPL_CHECK is assigned to the data entry clerk in the standard delivery. This access type enables the SAP E-Recruiting system to check if the candidate is registered in the talent warehouse. If the candidate is registered in the talent warehouse, the application can be assigned to the candidate.

If the application from the external candidate does not contain the reference code, the recruiter can assign the external candidate to an application group. When the candidate is assigned to a particular application group, the SAP E-Recruiting system assigns the reference code of that application group to the candidate application. We will discuss more about application groups in the next section.

Note

If a candidate is already assigned to an application group, we recommend that you assign the candidate *again* to another application group. If you again receive an unsolicited application from the same candidate, perform a search to see if the candidate is assigned to an application group. If the candidate is already assigned, make a note in the candidate profile, saying you have received another application from the candidate. You can also use this as an opportunity to invite the candidate to register in the talent warehouse.

Other application activities available to the recruiter include:

- Uploading the paper applications as attachments into the SAP E-Recruiting system.
- Entering details of the application source. If an employee receives an application as a referral or if an external candidate gives an employee's name as the source of the application, the recruiter can note these details.
- Recording the name of the agency as the source if the application was received from a third party or a recruiting agency. (If the external candidate application is entered by an agency, the agency must be created in the SAP ERP HCM system as a business partner. We will discuss more about maintaining agencies when we discuss the role of the recruiting administrator in Chapter 6.)

After the recruiter has completed entering the data, he clicks on the Save button to save the entries. If a data entry clerk changes a reference code in an application at any time, the system automatically creates a new application object and sets the status of the original application to Rejected during the save process. The standard delivered workflow Correct Data Entry Error (abbreviation: ERCAdjEntry) is available to process this change. In the standard delivery, the linkage between the trigger event ERRONEOUSENTRY and the workflow is not activated. In customizing, this event linkage needs to be activated so you can use this functionality.

If the candidate does not exist in the talent warehouse, the system creates a new candidate object, and the status is set to Blocked. When the candidate status is Blocked, the candidate profile is not included when a search is conducted in the talent warehouse.

Once the entries are saved, the system sends the candidate a candidate acknowledgment. The system creates a candidacy object and an application object with the statuses of In Process. The application of the external candidate is now available for review by the support team assigned to the requisition.

Creating applications is an important task for a recruiter. If your recruiting team does not have a data entry clerk, recruiters themselves can be assigned to the SAP standard delivered role data entry clerk to perform these duties. This enables the recruiters to use the standard functionality of the data entry clerk offered in SAP E-Recruiting.

Often, recruiting teams receive unsolicited applications or applications through a reference code. In SAP E-Recruiting, you can group unsolicited applications under application groups. In the next section, we will explain application groups and how they can be integrated into your recruiting process.

5.4 Application Groups

The recruiting administrator typically creates application groups, which are a special type of requisition used to group unsolicited applications (see Figure 5.24). Only external candidates are assigned to application groups.

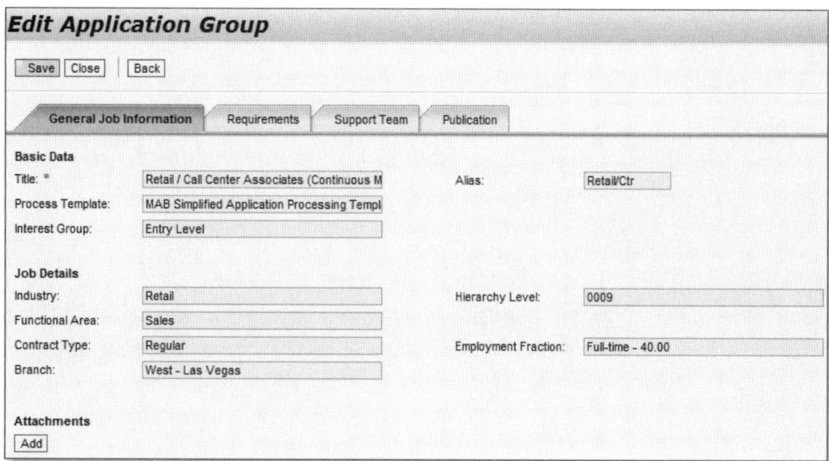

Figure 5.24 Edit an Application Group

Data stored within an application group includes:

- **Name of the application group**
  The name of the application group is published and is visible to the candidates.
- **Alias for the application group**
  The recruiter uses the alias to sort the applications. In the Applications Overview screen, a new tab page is created for each application group. The title of the tab page corresponds to the alias of the application group.
- **Interest group**
  A category chosen by the candidate, which is used by recruiter to message future job opportunities within that given category. For example, a category group could be Technical Operations. A recruiter could then broadcast specific messages to all candidates having that interest group.
- **Job requirements**
  Statements that describe the duties and responsibilities of a position in a company.
- **Education requirements**
  Statements that describe the educational level/skill needed for a position in a company.
- **Attachments**
  Candidates can upload attachments that might be required for processing the application.
- **Publication**
  In the publication section, a reference code is given that the candidates use when they send their applications.
- **Process templates**
  You can create process templates specifically to meet the recruiting requirements of an application group.
- **Support team**
  Only members of the support team have access to the assigned application group.

When the application group is set to Released status, the SAP E-Recruiting system generates a URL with the link to the application wizard. This URL can be published in your company's careers website. Candidates can click on this link to send their applications, which are then received and assigned to the corresponding application group.

Note

One of the areas where application groups can be effectively implemented is for college and new-graduate hiring. Organizations that hire new graduates or college students for internships often receive a huge volume of applications. Without a proper recruiting strategy, the recruiting team might not process these applications. When an application group is created, the support team can use the process template to prequalify the candidates, rank them, and assess their qualifications.

You can also create application groups to receive unsolicited applications from experienced candidates. When a candidate does a job search and does not find a suitable vacancy, he could be encouraged to send his application to the application group. The recruiter or a member of the support team can then follow up on the application.

Application groups provide an efficient way to process unsolicited applications. By creating application groups and integrating them into your recruiting strategy, you will be able to manage and process unsolicited applications efficiently. In the next section, we will discuss three important functionalities in SAP E-Recruiting candidate services: Hot Jobs, Tell-a-Friend, and Job Agents.

5.5 Candidate Services

Candidate services, such as Hot Jobs, Tell-a-Friend and Job Agents, offer important capabilities for your recruitment strategy. Let's discuss Hot Jobs first.

5.5.1 Hot Jobs

The Hot Jobs identifier identifies publications that have a critical importance to the organization. In the SAP E-Recruiting system, publications that are identified as Hot Jobs are processed in the same fashion as other job publications. You can use the Hot Jobs identifier to get candidates' attention when they are searching for suitable job opportunities.

Often, recruiters are asked to work on requisitions that are identified as having a high priority. Obviously, these are vacancies that need to be filled as soon as possible. These positions — if kept vacant too long — might adversely affect the projects or the organization with which the position is associated. The publications of such vacancies can be identified as Hot Jobs.

On the careers page, the candidate cannot use "Hot Jobs" as a search criteria; hence, the candidate *cannot search only for Hot Jobs.* Instead, the Hot Jobs identifier can be displayed in the following scenarios:

- On the careers page, the Hot Jobs identifier can be displayed in publications the recruiter identifies as Hot Jobs.
- Within the results listing, when the candidate does a job search, the hot jobs identifier can be displayed in publications that the recruiter identifies as Hot Jobs.

To make the Hot Job identifier visible to the candidate in the search results or in the job listing, you must assign the attribute VISIBLE to the context HOT_JOB in the component controller of the HRRCF_C_SEARCH_UI Web Dynpro component.

To create a URL of the Hot Jobs publication, you can execute function module ERC_HOTJOB_URLS, which returns the GUID of the posting instance, the URL, the title, and the language of the posting. The URL can then be displayed as a link on the careers page of your organization's website. The candidate can click on the link and view the job posting to get more details about the job.

Hot Jobs identifiers are an effective way of informing candidates about job postings that have a high priority in your organization. It is important that Hot Job identifiers are used only for job postings that have to be filled as soon as possible. Recruiters can reach out to candidates and seek referrals to the Hot Job postings as well.

In the next section, we will discuss Job Agents — another popular candidate service. We will explain how you can create job agents and the customizing activities involved.

5.5.2 Job Agents

Candidates can create job agents so they can be notified about postings that meet certain criteria. Candidates are notified via email when a suitable criteria is met. Both internal and external candidates can create job agents. In their settings, candidates can also define the frequency (monthly, weekly, daily, and so on) of updates for each job agent.

In the Applicant Cockpit, the candidate can click on the link Job Agents. The Job Agents screen (see Figure 5.25) displays all of the job agents the candidate has created. To create a new Job Agent in the Job Search screen, the candidate needs to define the search criteria.

Figure 5.25 Job Agents Interface

After entering the search criteria for the job agent, the candidate clicks on the Save button to save the entered data. The Save as Job Agent dialog box (see Figure 5.26) is displayed. In the dialog box, the candidate needs to specify the name of the job agent, the frequency for the job agent, and the active indicator.

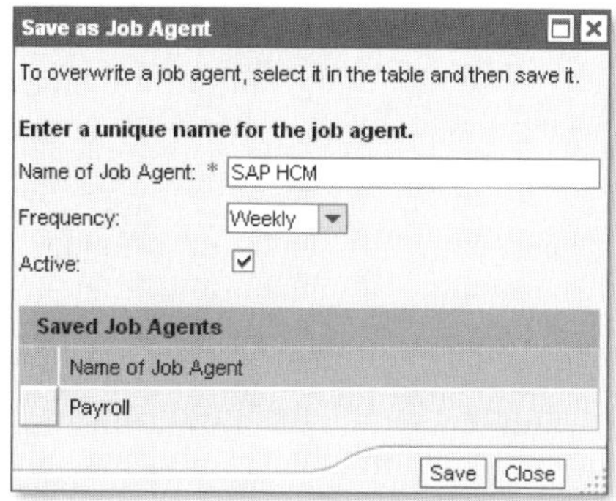

Figure 5.26 Save as Job Agent

The Job Agent has two standard delivered statuses:

- Active
- Inactive

The job agent needs to be in Active status for the system to execute it. The SAP E-Recruiting system runs the Job Agent at the defined frequency and notifies the candidate of publications that match the criteria. If the candidate wants to make changes to the Job Agent, he can click on the Edit button and edit the job agent at any time.

Note

Please note that the job agent service is only available if the candidate user interface is set up in Web Dynpro for ABAP (WD4A).

You have to complete a few customizing activities prior to job agents being made available to your internal and external candidates. You can perform these customizing activities in the IMG under the menu path SAP E-RECRUITING • TALENT WAREHOUSE • CANDIDATE • CANDIDATE SERVICES • JOB AGENT.

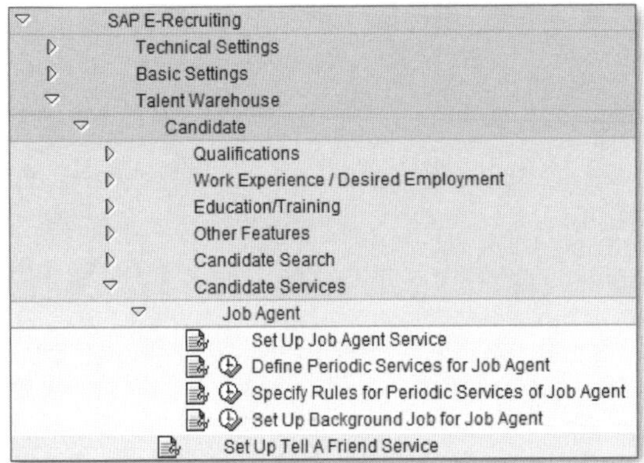

Figure 5.27 Customizing Steps for Job Agents

You must execute the following four customizing steps (see Figure 5.27) to set up Job Agents:

- **Set Up Job Agent Service**
  To set up the Job Agent service, you need to create a service user by following the IMG menu path SAP E-RECRUITING • TECHNICAL SETTINGS • USER INTERFACES • CANDIDATE • BACKEND CANDIDATE • CREATE SPECIAL USERS FOR BACKEND SYSTEM (WEB DYNPRO ABAP). After creating the service user, you must perform the customizing activity Assign Values to Interface Parameters (Web Dynpro ABAP). In this customizing activity, you assign the service user to parameter SERVICE_USER. Here you can also assign the SMARTFORM template to the parameter JA_SMARTFORM_NAME. This form is used to communicate the publications that match the search criteria defined in the job agent service to the candidate. The SAP standard delivered template is HRRCF_JOB_AGENT. The menu path to assign values to both the parameters is SAP E-RECRUITING • TECHNICAL SETTINGS • USER INTERFACES • CANDIDATE • BACKEND CANDIDATE • ASSIGN VALUES TO INTERFACE PARAMETERS (WEB DYNPRO ABAP). If you want to customize the form con-

tent for the job agent service, copy the SAP standard delivered template HRRCF_JOB_AGENT and enhance as necessary.

- **Define Periodic Services for Job Agent**
  In this customizing activity, you define the services that the system runs periodically for the job agent service. For each service, you define a class, which carries the execution instructions for that service. The SAP standard delivered periodic service is JOB_AGENT. Any class that you assign to the service must implement the IF_HRRCF_AGENT_SERVICE interface.
- **Specify Rules for Periodic Services of Job Agent**
  This customizing activity defines the rules for the periodic service that you defined earlier. The SAP standard delivered rules for the JOB_AGENT periodic service are:
  - **MAX_JOB_AGENTS**
    This defines the maximum number of job agents a candidate can create.
  - **MAX_POSTINGS**
    This defines the maximum number of postings that can be contained in a job agent.
- **Set Up Background Job for Job Agent**
  In this customizing activity, you set up the background job for the JOB_AGENT service that you created earlier. You must have performed the customizing activity Activate Periodic Services as a prerequisite for this activity.

Note

The job agent is the periodic service running with the periodic service RCF_AGENT_SERVICES. It is a best practice to execute this report as a daily periodical job.

Candidates can create job agents to be notified of new publications that match predefined search criteria. This is an efficient way of staying aware of job postings rather than visiting the careers page frequently and running the job search.

Another functionality popular within candidate services is Tell-A-Friend.

5.5.3 Tell-A-Friend

When a candidate performs a job search, he may find a posting that might be of interest to one his friends. He can select that posting and click on the Tell-a-Friend button. The Tell-a-Friend dialog box is displayed (see Figure 5.28). In the dialog box, the candidate can enter the friend's name, email address, and a short message.

The candidate is required to enter his name also. The candidate then clicks on the Send button to send the publication to his friend.

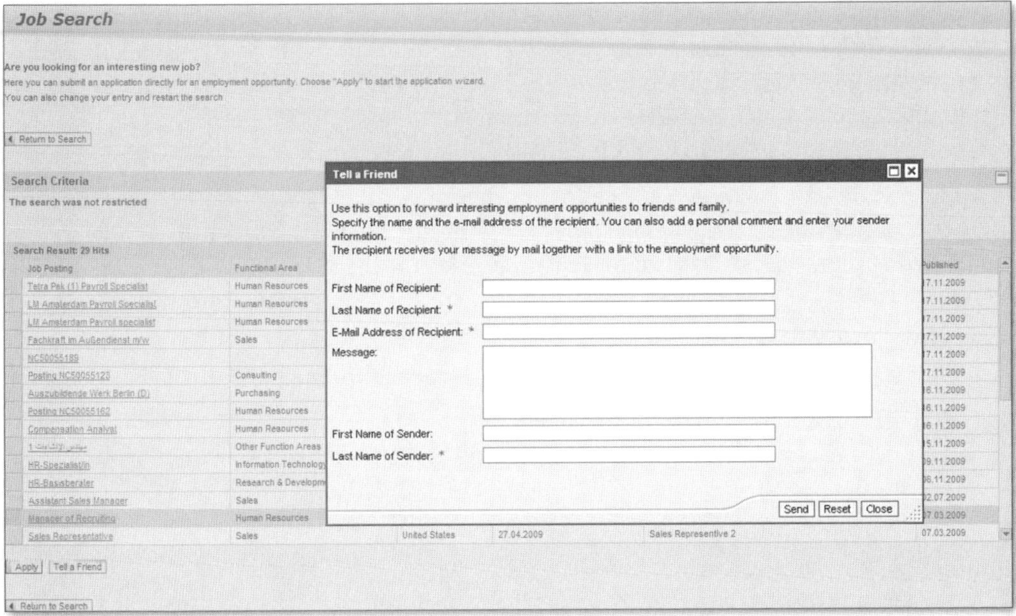

Figure 5.28 Tell-a-Friend

The recipient receives the notification with the short message and link to the publication. The recipient can click on the link to review the job posting details and click on the Apply button if he wants to apply to the job posting.

The customizing activities for the Tell-A-Friend service are similar to those for the job agents service. To set up the Tell-a-Friend service, you need to create a service user by following the menu path SAP E-Recruiting • Technical Settings • User Interfaces • Candidate • Backend Candidate • Create Special Users for Backend System (Web Dynpro ABAP).

After you have created the service user, perform the customizing activity Assign Values to Interface Parameters (Web Dynpro ABAP). In this customizing activity, the service user is assigned to the parameter SERVICE_USER. Here, you also assign the SMARTFORM template to the parameter TF_SMARTFORM_NAME. This form template is used for the Tell-a-Friend service. The SAP standard delivered template is HRRCF_TELL_A_FRIEND_RAW. The menu path to assign values to both the parameters is SAP E-Recruiting • Technical Settings • User Interfaces • Candidate • Backend Candidate • Assign Values to Interface Parameters (Web Dynpro ABAP).

In this section, we reviewed the various candidate services available in SAP E-Recruiting and the customizing steps required for implementation. Next, we will discuss applicant tracking.

5.6 Applicant Tracking

In this section, we will discuss the various activities involved in the recruiting process from an applicant tracking perspective. For example, we will see how to use the process templates assigned to the requisition and how to create the activities for the candidate's assignment to requisitions, application groups, or talent groups. We will also discuss how to search for suitable candidates in the talent pool, how to send questionnaires to the candidates, the importance of ranking candidates and candidacies, how to review the candidate profile to check for suitability, and how to create notes in the candidate profile.

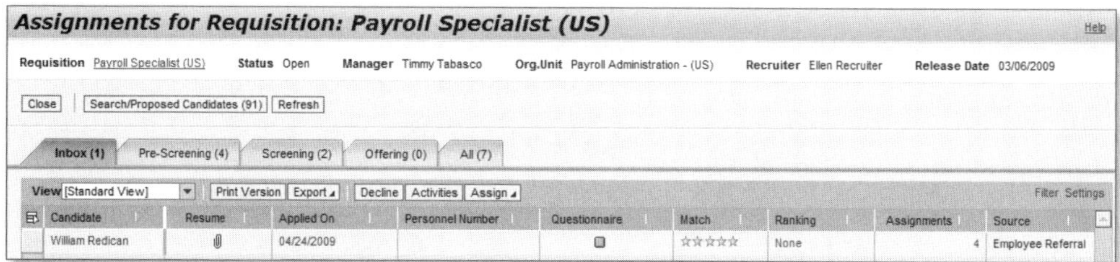

Figure 5.29 Assignments for Requisition Screen

From the recruiter work center, the recruiter can click on an open query for requisitions. In the requisitions listing, the recruiter sees a list of all requisitions that are currently open and the number of candidates in the different stages of the recruiting process. Select the requisition for which you want to start the applicant tracking process. Then click on any column displaying the number of candidates in the different stages of the recruiting process. This displays the Assignments for Requisition screen (see Figure 5.29), where the various stages of the recruiting process are displayed on tabs. The tabs also display the number of candidates in each process.

> **Note**
>
> There are two main prerequisites for applicant tracking: (1) The process template needs to be assigned to the requisition, and (2) activities and customizing steps for activity management have been completed.
>
> You can refer to Chapter 4, Section 4.6 for more details about process templates and activity management.

When you click on the Assign button in the Assignments for Requisition screen (see Figure 5.30), you can assign the candidate to another requisition, assign the candidate to a talent group, or move the candidate to another stage in the recruiting process.

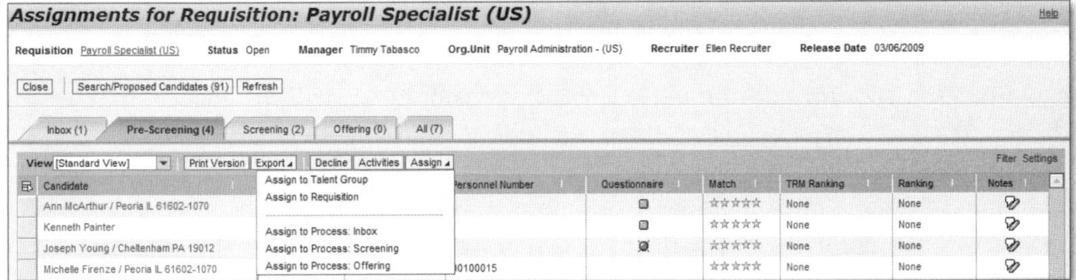

Figure 5.30 Assigning a Candidacy

In the Assignments for Requisition screen, you can click on the Search/Proposed Candidates button and search for candidates in the talent pool. In the Candidate Search dialog box (see Figure 5.31), you can enter the search criteria by clicking on the link Display Search Criteria. SAP E-Recruiting executes the search and displays the candidates that match the criteria. If you do not define a search query, the candidates are displayed based on the criteria defined in the requisition.

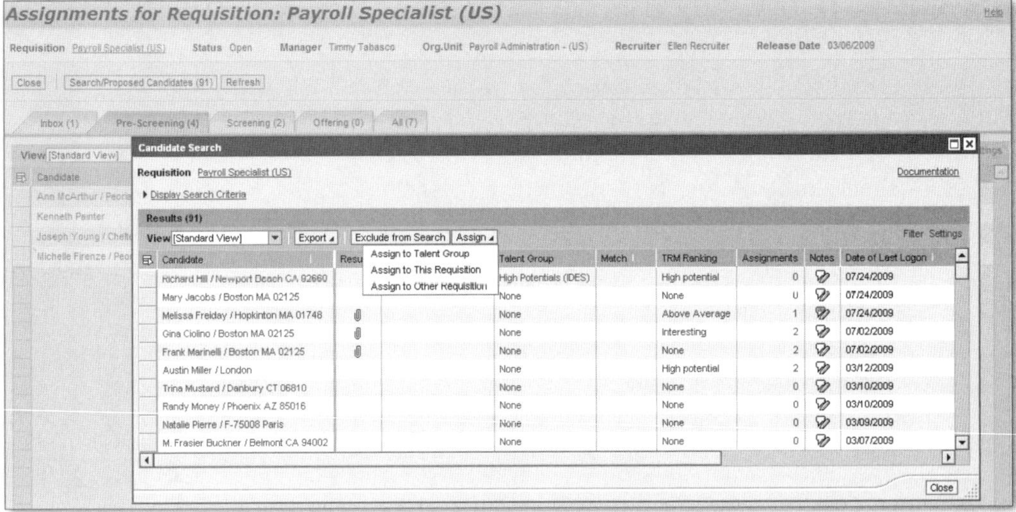

Figure 5.31 Candidate Search

You can select candidates and assign them to the requisition you are currently working on, assign the candidate to a talent group, or assign the candidate to any other requisition for which you feel the candidate is a fit.

In the Assignments for Requisition screen, you can click on the candidate's name and display the candidate profile (see Figure 5.32). The candidate profile provides details about the candidate including a data overview tab displaying the data the candidate filled in while registering in the talent warehouse. The Activities tab gives the list of activities, the activity status, and the requisition for which these activities were executed.

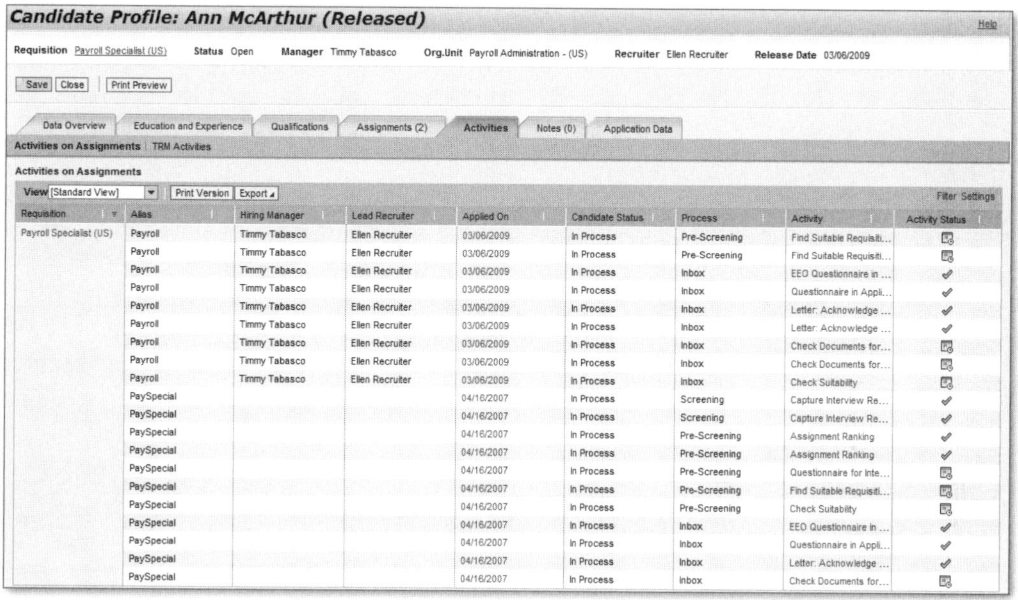

Figure 5.32 Activities Tab on the Candidate Profile

> **Note**
>
> If you display the candidate profile for an internal candidate, you cannot edit or make any changes to the personal data or to the communication data. This data is migrated from the SAP ERP HCM system, and edits can be made only there.

The Application Data tab in the candidate profile is displayed only if the candidate profile is called from the Assignments for Requisition or Application Groups screens. The tab page is displayed only if an assignment to a requisition or to an application groups exists.

In the Assignments for Requisition screen, the questionnaire column displays the ranking of the candidacy based on the candidate's response to the questionnaire attached to the particular requisition. A green traffic light means the candidate has responded to the questions, and a red traffic light means either there is a negative feedback or the candidate has not yet completed the questionnaire. When you click on the Traffic Light icon, the questionnaire and the candidate's responses are displayed.

5.6.1 Creating Activities for a Requisition

Activities are the individual steps that are executed to process a candidate's assignment to a requisition, to an application group, or to the candidacy application. In Chapter 4, we discussed activity management and the customizing steps required to create such activities and assign them to the appropriate HR objects. In this section, we will explain how to create activities for a candidate.

You can create activities for:

- A single candidate (single processing)
- Multiple candidates (multi processing)

Let's first discuss how to create activities for a single candidate. In the required process step of the Assignments for Requisition screen (see Figure 5.29), select a candidate and click on the Activities button. A dialog box (see Figure 5.33) with the list of all activities assigned to the process template is displayed by default.

If an activity is already created in the Activities dialog box, Edit and Delete icons are shown. The status column displays the status of the activity — either Planned or Completed.

> **Note**
>
> For correspondence activities, the Create Activity dialog box has two radio buttons: Deactivated and Activated. If you select the Activated radio button, the activity can be sent to the candidate or candidacy as a letter or as an email.

In the Activities dialog box, clicking on the All Activities radio button allows you to display all activities that are customized and available.

In the Activities dialog box (see Figure 5.33), double-click on the activity that you want to create. Depending on the activity type, in the Create Activity dialog box (see Figure 5.34), the status is set to Planned by default. You can enter notes, add attachments, and set a date by which this activity needs to be completed. After you have entered the required data, click on the OK button to save your entries.

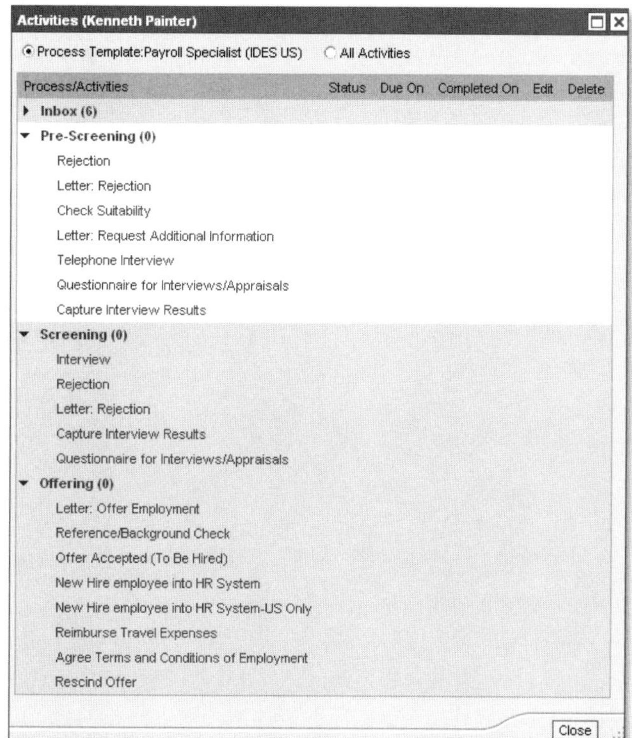

Figure 5.33 Activities for a Candidate

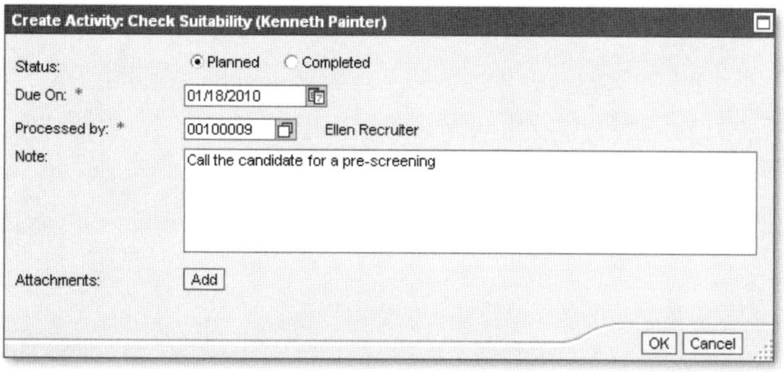

Create Activity: Check Suitability (Kenneth Painter)

Status: Planned Completed

Due On: * 01/18/2010

Processed by: * 00100009 Ellen Recruiter

Note: Call the candidate for a pre-screening

Attachments: Add

OK Cancel

Figure 5.34 Create an Activity Dialog

Depending on the activity type, after you have completed the activity, you need to set the status to Completed. You can create another activity for that activity type, set the status to Completed, and enter your notes. The Activities dialog box (see Figure 5.35) for the candidate is updated accordingly; for that activity type, two activities are displayed – one planned and one completed. Alternatively, you can edit the same activity that you created earlier and set its status to Completed.

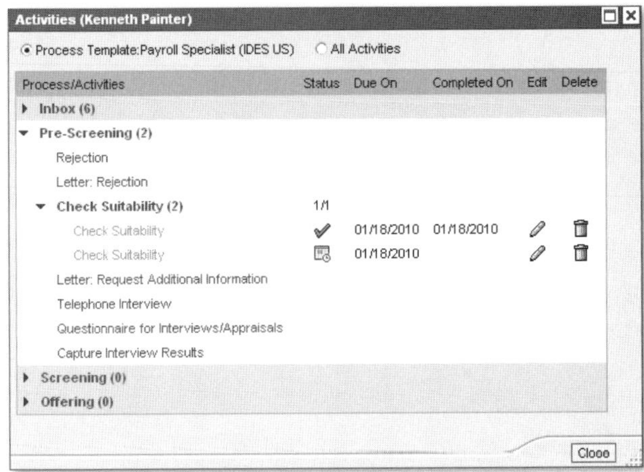

Figure 5.35 Completed Activity

For processing multiple candidates, you can select the candidates for whom you need to create the activities and then click on the Activities button to display the Activities dialog box (see Figure 5.36).

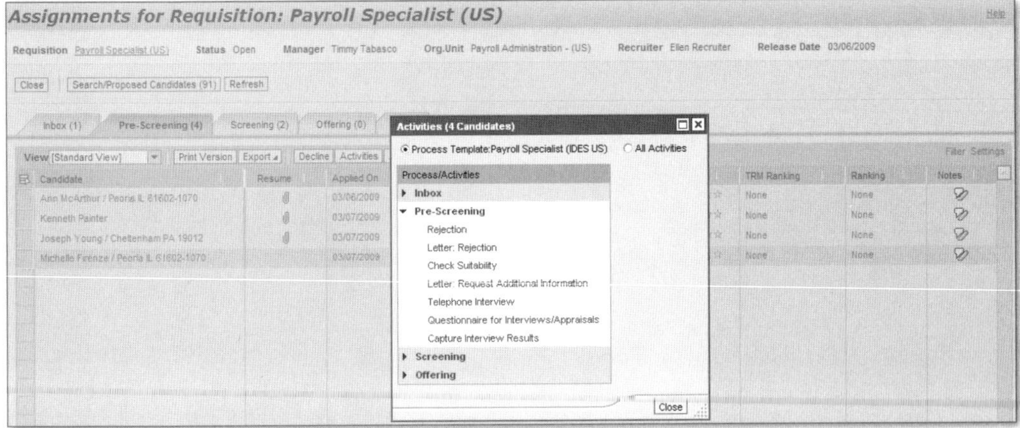

Figure 5.36 Multi-Processing of Activities

The dialog box displays all of the activities you can create for the selected candidacies. You then select the appropriate activity type and create the activity. In the Create Activity dialog box, enter the required data and click on the OK button to accept the entries.

> **Tip**
>
> In the Assignments for Requisition screen, you can customize to display some of these activities as buttons in the tab page of the respective process. For more details refer Section 3.4.2, Customizing Activities, in Chapter 3, SAP E-Recruiting Basics.

5.6.2 Sending Questionnaires to a Candidate

Questionnaires are an important activity in the recruiting process. Hiring managers and recruiters use questionnaires to qualify candidates. It is a best practice to attach job-related questionnaires to which the candidates need to respond to the application wizard. You can use the responses to these questionnaires to prequalify candidates. Often, recruiters and hiring managers need to send additional questionnaires to candidates to further qualify them. The recruiter can create an activity to send these questionnaires to the candidates.

Before completing the activity Send Questionnaire to a Candidate or a Candidacy, ensure that you have completed the customizing steps required to create the questionnaire and assigned the process templates. For more details refer to Chapter 4, Requisition Management, Section 4.5, Questions and Questionnaire Management.

In the Assignments for Requisition screen, select the candidate and click on the Activities button. In the Activities dialog box, select the questionnaire activity types.

In the Create Activity dialog box (see Figure 5.37), you can enter the required data and create the activity. You do not have to use the questionnaire attached to the process template.

If you need to use a different questionnaire, you search for and assign a different questionnaire to the activity. In the Activities dialog box, click on the Edit button (Pencil icon) displayed after the questionnaire field. A Questionnaire Search dialog box is displayed (see Figure 5.38). In the Questionnaire Search interface, you can search for and assign the questionnaire to the activity. Click on the OK button to accept the assigned questionnaire and to create the activity.

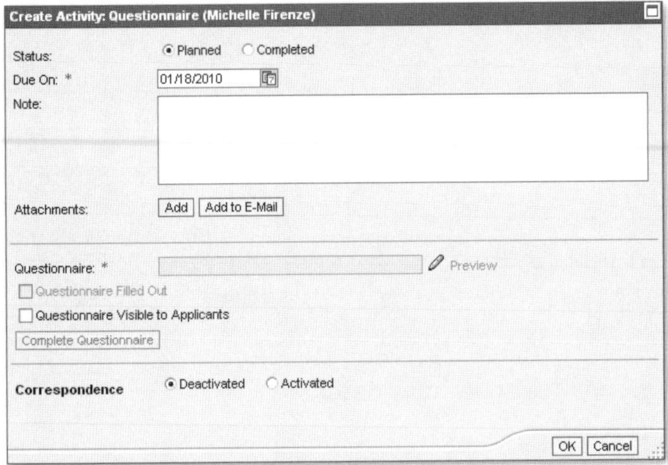

Figure 5.37 Create Activity: Questionnaire

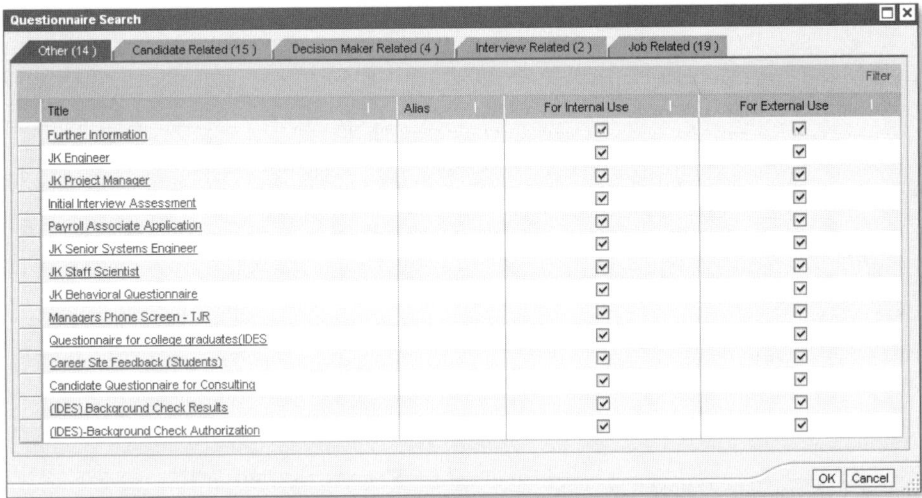

Figure 5.38 Questionnaire Search

In the Create Activity: Questionnaire dialog box (see Figure 5.37), selecting the Questionnaire Visible to Applicants checkbox allows the completed and saved questionnaire to be visible to the candidate in the application overview.

When you click on the Complete Questionnaire button, the assigned questionnaire will be displayed. If required, the recruiter or the hiring manager can complete the questionnaire on the candidate's behalf.

In this section, we reviewed how to create activities for the candidate. In the next section, we will dive into Talent Relationship Management (TRM). We will explain what TRM means and how to develop the right talent relationship with your candidates.

5.7 Talent Relationship Management (TRM)

The goal of talent relationship management is to encourage and foster recruiters to develop long-term relationships with candidates. In concept, TRM is similar to Customer Relationship Management (CRM) in that your candidates are treated like your customers. You can conduct TRM activities on any candidate registered in the talent pool of the talent warehouse.

Using TRM, recruiters build relationships with their candidates. These relationships help candidates gain a better understanding of the organization and the opportunities that exist within it. Similarly, the relationship with the candidate provides an opportunity for the recruiter to recruit a talented candidate and seek referrals from the candidate.

Tip

In Appendix A, we have included the *HR Expert* article "Talent Groups in SAP E-Recruitment Target the Right Candidate," which was published in the July 2009 issue. This article provides a good overview of talent groups and the talent services that SAP E-Recruiting offers.

In this next section, we will discuss talent groups, the talent services that can be offered to candidates in these talent groups, and the customizing steps required for TRM.

5.7.1 Talent Groups

Talent groups are the segmentation of the talent pool. You can segment the talent pool based on several criteria and on the business requirements of your organization. For example, you can segment the talent pool based on experience. For example, all candidates with executive experience can be segmented into one talent group. Similarly, educational degree (such as PhDs, MBAs, etc.) can be a criteria to create a new talent group.

Talent groups are dynamic and you can create and delete them to meet your current recruiting strategy. When you delete a talent group, all of the candidates belonging to it are moved back to the talent warehouse or can be assigned to another talent group. A recruiting administrator creates and maintains talent groups (see Figure 5.39).

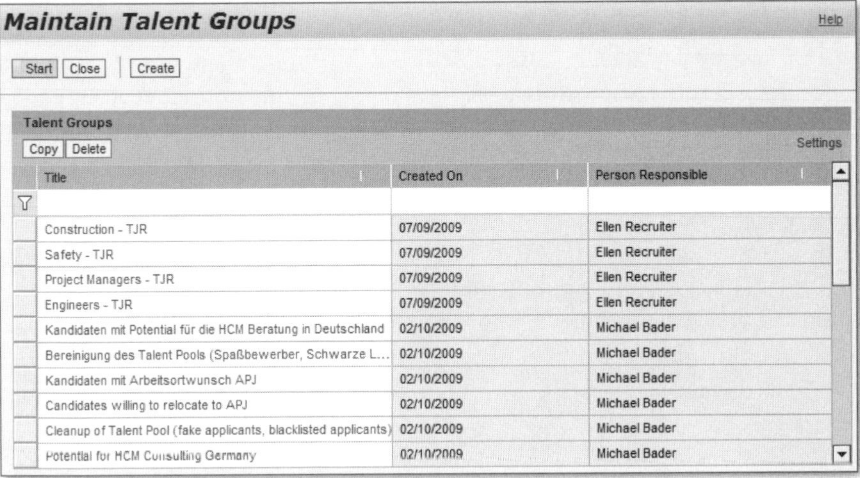

Figure 5.39 Maintaining Talent Groups

> **Tip**
>
> When you delete a talent group, you are not deleting the candidates belonging to that talent group. The candidates continue to exist in the talent warehouse; you are only deleting a particular segmentation of the talent pool.

A recruiter should manually assign candidates to a talent group. A candidate can be assigned to one or more talent groups. To create a talent group, click on the Create button in the Maintain Talent Groups screen (shown in Figure 5.39).

In the Create Talent Group screen (see Figure 5.40), you enter the title of the talent group and a short description. In the Person Responsible field, the system, by default, enters the name of the recruiting administrator. In the Support Team tab, you can add individual members or a support group for the support team. By default, the system always adds the person responsible for the talent group as a member of the support team. You need to be a member of the support team to gain access to the talent group or to assign candidates to the talent group. In the Attachments tab, you can upload documents as attachments. These attachments can provide further details about the talent group or can include the possible talent services that can be offered to this talent group. The Data Overview tab provides a summary of the data that you have entered on the talent group. Click on the Save button to save your entries and to complete the creation of the talent group.

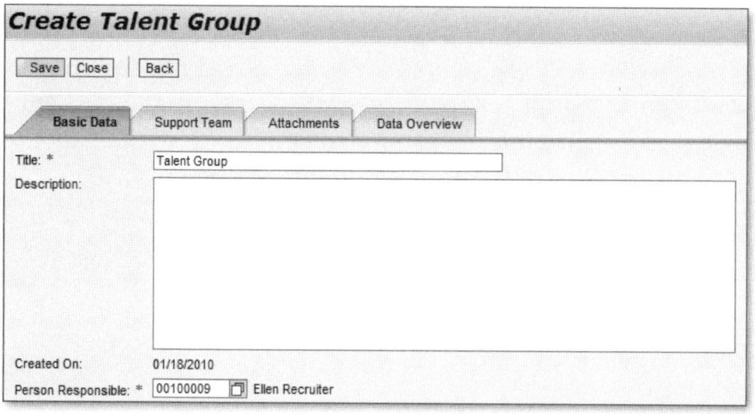

Figure 5.40 Create Talent Group

> **Tip**
>
> You can also create a talent group by a copy method. In the Maintain Talent Groups screen, select the talent group that you want to use as a template and click on the Copy button. In the Copy Talent Groups screen, enter a new title for the talent group and the required data.

To Edit a talent group, select the talent group that you want to edit and click on the Start button. The Edit Talent Groups screen is displayed. You can make the required changes to the talent group, and then click on the Save button to accept your changes.

5.7.2 Talent Services

Talent services are functionalities provided to the talent pool. When you provide excellent talent services to candidates, you are executing an effective TRM. In SAP E-Recruiting, you can customize talent services to meet the specific needs of the talent groups. For example, if your organization is planning a job fair for new college graduates, it is not good practice to send the invitation to all candidates in the talent pool. A candidate in the Executives talent pool will most likely not be interested in attending the job fair for new graduates.

Similarly, if your organization has a newsletter for alumni, it is not good practice to send it to all candidates in the talent pool. If you have a talent pool for ex-colleagues of your organization who may be interested in returning to the organization if a suitable opportunity arises, you can create a candidate correspondence inviting the alumni in the talent pool to register so they can begin to receive the newsletter.

You should customize talent services to meet the interests and requirements of the talent pool. By customizing the talent services, recruiters can provide better services to candidates. This enables the recruiter to build better long-term relationships with candidates. For example, if you are planning a webinar to explain why your organization is a great place to work, this talent service may be of interest to all of the talent groups. For such talent services, you can send the invitation to all talent groups.

5.7.3 Activity Management in TRM

Earlier in the chapter, we explained activity management for candidates assigned to a requisition or to an application group. Similarly, in SAP E-Recruiting, there are TRM-related activities that can be created for candidates. To process a TRM-related activity, a candidate need not be assigned to a requisition or to an application group. All recruiters can create and view TRM-related activities.

In this section, we will explore activity management for TRM. The prerequisite to creating activities for TRM is that you must have completed the customizing steps shown in the IMG under the menu path SAP E-RECRUITING • APPLICANT TRACKING • ACTIVITIES. For more details, refer to Chapter 4, Requisition Management, section 4.6, Process Templates and Activity Types.

Assign a Candidate to a Talent Group

You can assign a candidate to a talent group in several ways. In this section, we will explain two ways to assign a candidate to a talent group.

Candidate Search

To assign a candidate to a talent group, you can search for candidates in the talent pool whom you want to assign to a talent group. To conduct a candidate search, go to the Recruiter Work Center in the Services group of the Work Overview. The Candidate Search is under the Candidates section.

In the Candidate Search screen, enter the search criteria and click on the Search button. The search results are displayed at the bottom of the screen. In the results listing, select the candidate you want to assign to a talent group and click on the Assign button. Two options are displayed: Assign to Talent Group and Assign to Requisition. Select Assign to Talent Group.

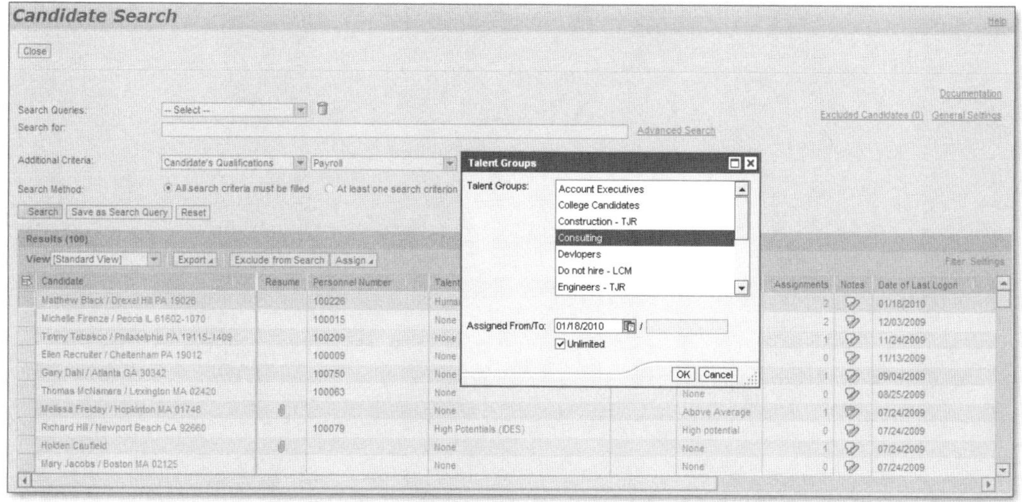

Figure 5.41 Assign Candidate to a Talent Group

This displays the Talent Groups dialog box (see Figure 5.41). Select the talent group to which you want to assign the candidate and click on the OK button to confirm your assignment.

You can also assign a candidate to a talent group from the candidate profile. In the Data Overview tab of the Candidate Profile, click on the link displayed near the Talent Groups in the Profile Summary section.

> **Note**
>
> If the candidate is not assigned to any talent group, the link is displayed as None. If the candidate is assigned to a single talent group, the name of the group is displayed. If the candidate is assigned to multiple talent groups, the number of assignments is displayed as a link.

The Talent Groups dialog box is displayed. It shows all of the talent groups to which the candidate is currently assigned. In the Talent Groups dialog box, click on the Assign to Other Talent Groups button. The Assign Talent Group dialog box (see Figure 5.42) is displayed, which shows all of the talent groups to which you are currently assigned as a support team member.

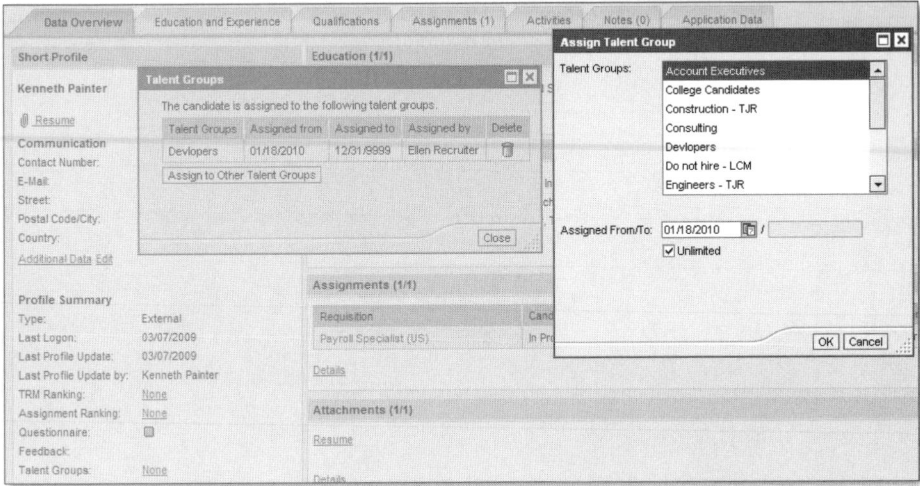

Figure 5.42 Assign a Candidate to a Talent Group from the Candidate Profile

Candidate Profile Screen

In the Assign Talent Group dialog box, unselect the Unlimited checkbox if you want to make the assignment for a limited time only. This enables the To field of the Assigned From/To fields. In the To field, enter the end date of the assignment. By default, all assignments to a talent group are for an unlimited period of time (to 12/31/9999); the assignments are valid as long the talent groups are valid and exist in the system. After you complete the assignments, click on the Save button to save your entries.

> **Tip**
>
> If you want to delete the candidate's assignment to a talent group in the Talent Groups dialog box, click on the Trash Can icon that is displayed next to the talent group.

Creating Activities for TRM

Using the Candidate Search service, you can search for the candidate for whom you want to create TRM activities. To do this, first click on the Activities tab in the Candidate Profile screen. In the Activities interface, select the TRM Activities option. When you click on the Create Activity button, the Activities dialog box (see Figure 5.43) is displayed. The Activities dialog box displays the processes assigned to TRM and the activity types assigned to the respective processes.

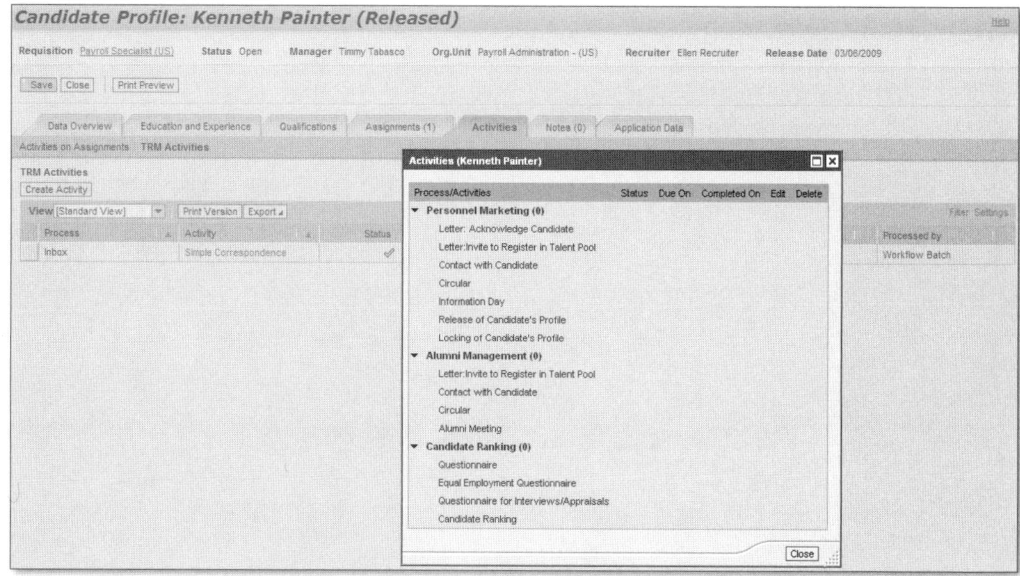

Figure 5.43 Activities for Talent Relationship Management (TRM)

In the Activities dialog box, click on the process and the activity type that you want to create. In the Create Activity dialog box, enter the required data and click on the OK button to accept your entries. SAP E-Recruiting adds the activity to the list of TRM activities. TRM-related activities can be maintained for a candidate only from the Candidate profile. After you select Send E-Mail or Print Letter for all Simple Correspondence activity types, the activity type is set to Completed status when you click on the OK button.

TRM Ranking

Recruiters use the TRM ranking functionality to categorize candidates in the talent pool. Recruiters rank candidates to determine their suitability for a vacancy. The ranking and the notes a recruiter enters can be viewed by other recruiters in the organization. A candidate can be ranked differently by different recruiters in the organization. Therefore, a recruiter can view his own TRM rankings of a candidate and the rankings provided by other recruiters. SAP E-Recruiting also provides an average of all of the rankings assigned to a candidate.

To assign a TRM ranking to the candidate, click on the link displayed next to the TRM Ranking field in the Data Overview tab of the Candidate Profile. In the Create Activity: Candidate Ranking dialog box (see Figure 5.44), select the ranking you want to assign to the candidate. You can also enter your assessment as a note in the dialog box. Click on the OK button to accept your entries. Based on the latest TRM ranking assigned to the candidate, the SAP E-Recruiting system calculates the average of the assigned TRM rankings once again.

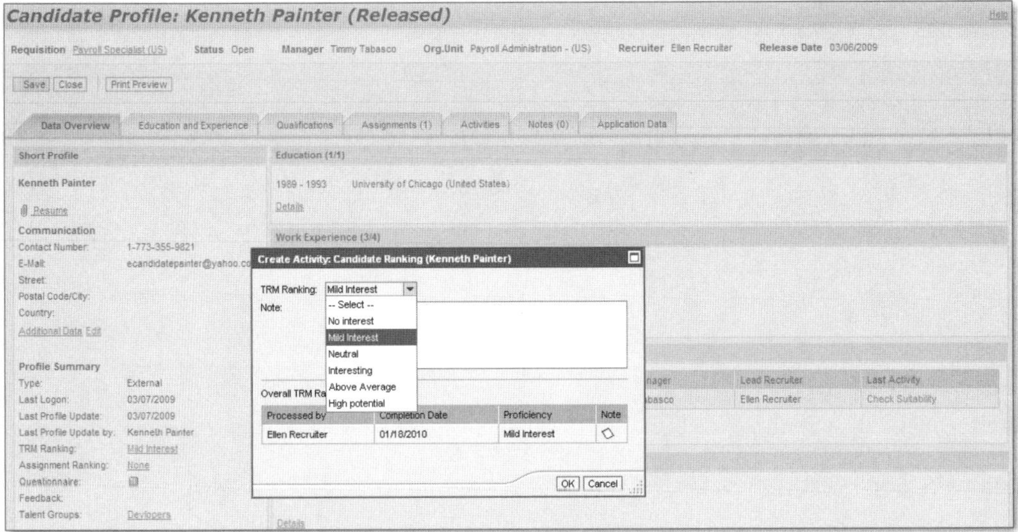

Figure 5.44 Candidate Ranking

TRM ranking can also be performed as a TRM activity. In the Candidate Profile screen, click on the Activities tab and select the TRM Activities option. When you click on the Create Activity button, the Activities dialog box is displayed. In the Activities dialog box, select the Classification process and the Candidate Ranking activity type to create the TRM ranking.

If you have previously assigned a TRM ranking to a candidate, your latest entry will overwrite any previous ranking. The Create Activity: Candidate Ranking dialog box displays the TRM rankings assigned to this candidate by the different recruiters in the organization. In the Assignments for Requisition screen, your TRM ranking is displayed in the Own TRM Ranking column. The average of the TRM rankings is displayed in the TRM Ranking column.

Note

The TRM ranking is assigned by the recruiters for TRM activity only and has no impact on the candidate's application or assignment to a requisition.

Customizing Steps for TRM Ranking

To perform TRM Ranking, you need to complete the following customizing steps.

- **Define Scales for Ranking and Reporting**
  In this customizing activity, you configure the quality scales that are used in SAP E-Recruiting. The scales are used in TRM ranking to rate candidacy assignments to requisitions and specify weightings for search and match criteria. After you have defined the scales, you should assign proficiencies to the scale in the IMG under the menu path SAP E-RECRUITING • APPLICANT TRACKING • DEFINE SCALES FOR RANKING AND REPORTING.
- **Assign Scales to Scale Types**
  In this customizing activity, you assign scales that you defined in the Define Scales for Ranking and Reporting activity to the scale type Candidate Classification. You can perform this customizing in the IMG under the menu path SAP E-RECRUITING • APPLICANT TRACKING • ASSIGN SCALES TO SCALE TYPES.

Deleting External Candidates

To delete external candidates, you can create a new talent group and assign all external candidates that you want to delete from the talent pool to the new talent group. From the IMG, run the report Program for Deleting External Candidates to delete the external candidates assigned to this talent group. To be able to use this talent group, you should be assigned as a member of the support team. The menu path for this customizing step is SAP E-RECRUITING • TOOLS • DELETE EXTERNAL CANDIDATES.

When you click on the process step Delete External Candidates, the selection screen for the report Program for Deleting External Candidates is displayed (see Figure 5.45). In the Talent Group field, enter the talent group ID.

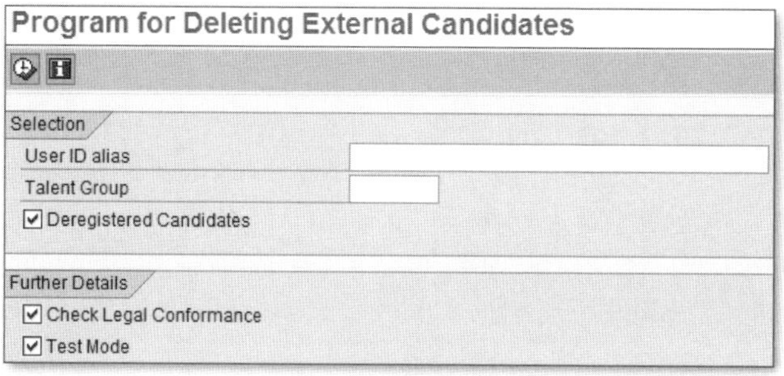

Program for Deleting External Candidates

Selection

User ID alias

Talent Group

☑ Deregistered Candidates

Further Details

☑ Check Legal Conformance

☑ Test Mode

Figure 5.45 Delete External Candidates

5.8 Ranking

SAP E-Recruiting provides the functionality to rank candidates and candidacies. Ranking helps recruiters and support teams assess the suitability of the candidate and the candidacy for a job vacancy. Other recruiters can view all rankings and notes entered by a recruiter. SAP E-Recruiting calculates the average of the different rankings entered by the different recruiters for a candidate.

You can rank a candidate in the Assignments for Requisition screen or create a ranking via an activity in the Candidate Profile screen. As a prerequisite to performing the rankings, you must complete the following customizing steps:

- Define Scales for Ranking and Reporting
- Assign Scales to Scale Types

As shown in Figure 5.46, in the Assign Scales to Scale Types customizing activity, you assign scales that you customized in the Define Scales for Ranking and Reporting activity to the scale types Assignment Ranking, Candidate Classification, and Weighting for Search & Match.

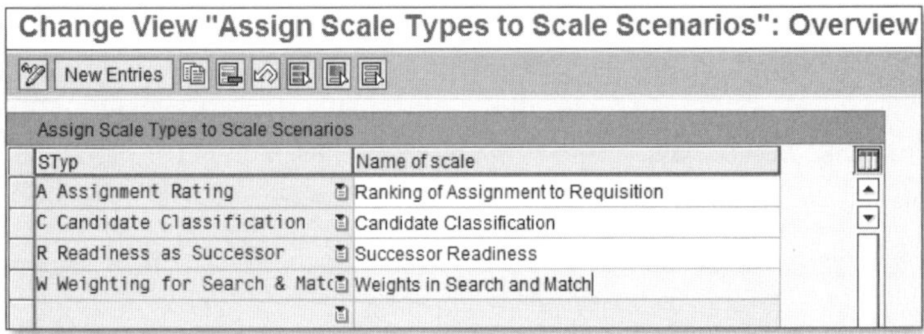

Change View "Assign Scale Types to Scale Scenarios": Overview

Assign Scale Types to Scale Scenarios

STyp	Name of scale
A Assignment Rating	Ranking of Assignment to Requisition
C Candidate Classification	Candidate Classification
R Readiness as Successor	Successor Readiness
W Weighting for Search & Matc	Weights in Search and Match

Figure 5.46 Assign Scale Types

The ranking functionalities available in SAP E-Recruiting are as follows:

- **Assignment ranking**
  During assignment ranking, the recruiter ranks the suitability of the candidate assignment to a requisition or to an application group. The other recruiters can view the ranking and the notes entered by the recruiter. The support team of a requisition can also enter the Assignment ranking of a candidate for that particular requisition. In the Assignments for Requisitions screen, the ranking entered by the recruiter is displayed in the Ranking columns. Based on the rankings entered by the recruiters, the SAP E-Recruiting application calculates the average of the rankings. This value is displayed in the Ranking column.

- **TRM Ranking**
  We discussed TRM ranking in Section 5.7.3, Activity Management in TRM.
- **Questionnaire ranking** (Response of the candidate and the evaluation by the hiring manager)
  The questionnaire ranking is used to automatically rank the candidate's responses to the questionnaire attached to a requisition. The questionnaire ranking is determined by comparing the candidate's responses to the questions in the questionnaire to the required responses entered by the recruiter while creating the questionnaire. The results of automatic ranking are displayed as a Traffic Light icon in the Questionnaire column in the Assignments for Requisition screen. If the questionnaire contains feedback by the managers and other support team members regarding the candidacy assignment to the requisition, this is displayed in the Feedback column of the Assignments for Requisition screen.

Note

To include a questionnaire in the questionnaire ranking, you must first complete the customizing step Assign Categories to Activity Steps. Refer to Section 4.6.3, Activity Management, in Chapter 4 for more details on the customizing step.

The questionnaire can be filled by the candidate or by the recruiter on behalf of the candidate. The questionnaire ranking is not used to rank TRM-related questionnaires. When you click on the Traffic Light icon, the questionnaire and the candidate's responses are displayed in a dialog box. The marks assigned to the candidate's responses to the individual questions are also displayed.

- A green traffic light means the candidate has completed the assigned questionnaire and has received positive feedback. Often, the response to a mandatory question gets high ranking.
- A red traffic light means the candidate has failed in his responses to the questionnaire. In most instances, this means the response to a mandatory question did not match the required response established by the recruiter.
- A yellow traffic light means the candidate has not yet completed the questionnaire.

If a candidate responds to multiple questionnaires for the requisition, the SAP E-Recruiting system uses the following process to display the icon:

- If a questionnaire has the value Passed and any remaining questionnaire has the value Not Equal to Failed, then a green traffic light icon is displayed.
- If a questionnaire has the value Failed, then a red traffic light icon is displayed.

- If a questionnaire has the value Not Equal to Failed and any remaining questionnaire has the value Not Completed, then a yellow traffic light is displayed.

Match with Search Criteria as Percentage

In SAP E-Recruiting, the match with search criteria functionality is used to compare the candidate with the search criteria entered in the reference search query for the requisition. The result displays how much the candidate or candidacy profile matches the search criteria. The output is displayed as icons in the Match column of the Assignments for Requisition screen. If a search reference query is not available, the SAP E-Recruiting system uses the data stored in the requisition to perform the comparison.

You need to execute several customizing activities to configure this functionality.

In the Enter Comparison Fields customizing activity, you can modify the match fields that are used in comparing the reference search criteria with the candidate or candidacy profile. An SAP standard delivered table (see Figure 5.47) exists for setting up the match criteria.

Change View "Set Up Matching Fields for Automatic Search and Ranking":

New Entries

Set Up Matching Fields for Automatic Search and Ranking

CompID of Callin...	Templ.	Element	Information Category	Field
cdcysrch	2	CAND_EDU_DEGREE_LEVEL_LISTBOX	REQUISITION_REQUIRED_EDUCATION	GREE_LEVEL
cdcysrch	2	CAND_EDU_EDU_FIELD_LISTBOX	REQUISITION_REQUIRED_EDUCATION	EDUCATION_FIELD
cdcysrch	2	CAND_EDU_EDU_TYPE_LISTBOX	REQUISITION_REQUIRED_EDUCATION	EDUCATION_TYPE
cdcysrch	3	DES_JOB_COUNTRY_LISTBOX	REQUISITION_JOB_INFORMATION	COUNTRY
cdcysrch	3	DES_JOB_FUNC_AREA_LISTBOX	REQUISITION_JOB_INFORMATION	FUNCTIONAL_AREA
cdcysrch	3	DES_JOB_HIER_LEVEL_LISTBOX	REQUISITION_JOB_INFORMATION	HIERARCHY_LEVEL
cdcysrch	8	CANDIDATE_QUALI_WITH_PROF	REQUISITION_REQUIRED_QUALIFICATION	
cdcysrch	10	WORK_EXP_COUNTRY_LISTBOX	REQUISITION_JOB_INFORMATION	COUNTRY
cdcysrch	10	WORK_EXP_FUNC_AREA_LISTBOX	REQUISITION_JOB_INFORMATION	FUNCTIONAL_AREA
cdcysrch	10	WORK_EXP_HIER_LEVEL_LISTBOX	REQUISITION_JOB_INFORMATION	HIERARCHY_LEVEL
cdcysrch	60	CAND_INFO_TARGET_GROUP_LIBO	REQUISITION_INFORMATION	TGROUP
cdcysrchscp	2	CAND_EDU_DEGREE_LEVEL_LISTBOX	REQUISITION_REQUIRED_EDUCATION	DEGREE_LEVEL
cdcysrchscp	2	CAND_EDU_EDU_FIELD_LISTBOX	REQUISITION_REQUIRED_EDUCATION	EDUCATION_FIELD
cdcysrchscp	2	CAND_EDU_EDU_TYPE_LISTBOX	REQUISITION_REQUIRED_EDUCATION	EDUCATION_TYPE
cdcysrchscp	3	DES_JOB_COUNTRY_LISTBOX	REQUISITION_JOB_INFORMATION	COUNTRY
cdcysrchscp	3	DES_JOB_FUNC_AREA_LISTBOX	REQUISITION_JOB_INFORMATION	FUNCTIONAL_AREA
cdcysrchscp	3	DES_JOB_HIER_LEVEL_LISTBOX	REQUISITION_JOB_INFORMATION	HIERARCHY_LEVEL
cdcysrchscp	8	CANDIDATE_QUALI_WITH_PROF	REQUISITION_REQUIRED_QUALIFICATION	
cdcysrchscp	10	WORK_EXP_COUNTRY_LISTBOX	REQUISITION_JOB_INFORMATION	COUNTRY
cdcysrchscp	10	WORK_EXP_FUNC_AREA_LISTBOX	REQUISITION_JOB_INFORMATION	FUNCTIONAL_AREA
cdcysrchscp	10	WORK_EXP_HIER_LEVEL_LISTBOX	REQUISITION_JOB_INFORMATION	HIERARCHY_LEVEL
cdcysrchscp	60	CAND_INFO_TARGET_GROUP_LIBO	REQUISITION_INFORMATION	TGROUP

Figure 5.47 Enter Comparison Fields

In this customizing activity, you can modify and override these settings. Prior to performing the customizing activity, you must customize the search templates. (We will discuss more about Search Templates in Chapter 7, Search.) The menu path for this customizing activity is IMG • SAP E-RECRUITING • REQUISITION MANAGEMENT • POSTING SEARCH • SEARCH TEMPLATES • ENTER COMPARISON FIELDS.

In the Define Graphic Representations of Search Results customizing activity, you can customize how the SAP E-Recruiting application displays the match results of the comparison. The results are displayed as different numbers of icons that represent how closely the results match the search criteria in terms of percentage.

In this customizing activity (see Figure 5.48), you can define up to five icons. For each icon, you can define the range of the percentages that represents the match. The menu path for the customizing activity in the IMG is SAP E-RECRUITING • REQUISITION MANAGEMENT • POSTING SEARCH • DEFINE GRAPHIC REPRESENTATION OF SEARCH RESULTS.

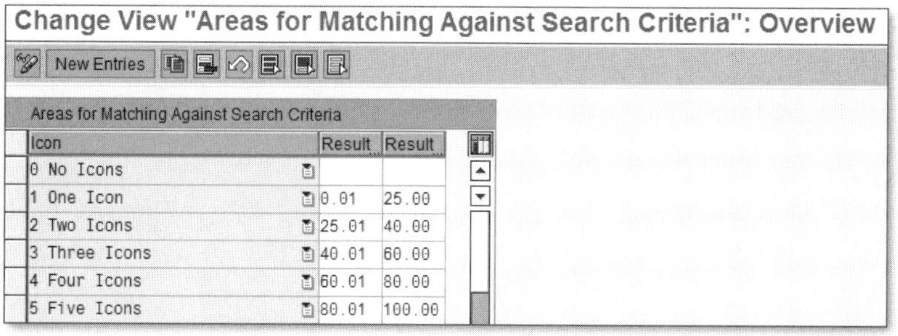

Change View "Areas for Matching Against Search Criteria": Overview

New Entries

Areas for Matching Against Search Criteria

Icon	Result	Result
0 No Icons		
1 One Icon	0.01	25.00
2 Two Icons	25.01	40.00
3 Three Icons	40.01	60.00
4 Four Icons	60.01	80.00
5 Five Icons	80.01	100.00

Figure 5.48 Customizing Activity for Graphic Representation

Note

In the Assignments for Requisition screen, you can use the match with Search Criteria as Percentage ranking functionality to search and create a list of proposed candidates for a requisition. Candidates who are already proposed for the requisition are not displayed in the search result. Also, the results list does not display any candidates who were excluded from the search.

When the recruiter is doing a candidate search for assignment to a requisition or a talent group, the recruiter can exclude candidates from the search. You can customize the reasons for excluding the candidate from the search in the IMG under the menu path SAP E-RECRUITING • TALENT WAREHOUSE • CANDIDATE • CANDIDATE SEARCH • SPECIFY REASONS FOR EXCLUSION OF CANDIDATES.

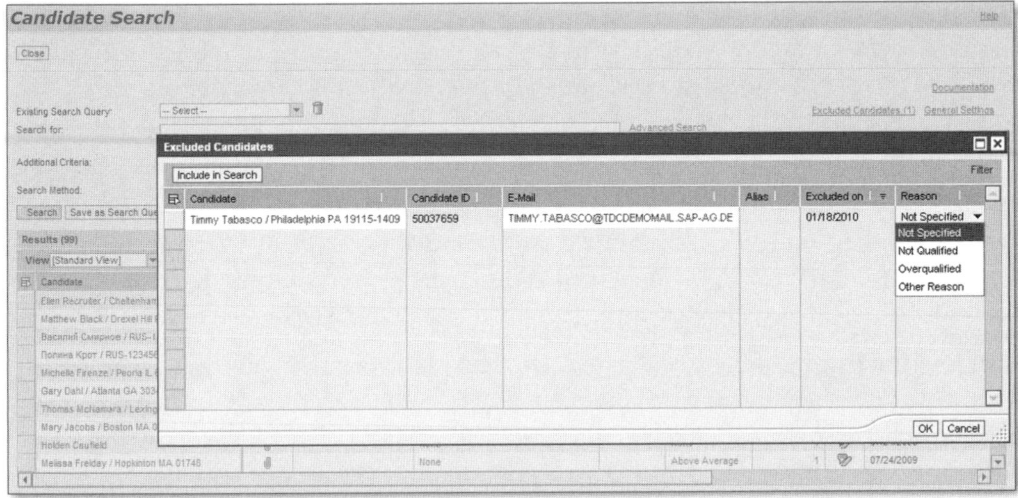

Figure 5.49 Specify Reasons for Candidate Exclusion

To specify a reason to exclude a candidate from the search, click on the Display Search Criteria link in the Candidate Search screen. Then click on the Excluded Candidates link. This displays the Excluded Candidates interface (see Figure 5.49), where you can specify the reasons for exclusion.

In this section, we explored the various ranking functionalities available in SAP E-Recruiting. Ranking helps recruiters and the support team efficiently source candidates suitable for a requisition. The support team of a requisition can create notes about the candidate that other recruiter can view. SAP E-Recruiting creates an average of the rankings, which is displayed in the Assignments for Requisition.

In the next section, we will discuss customizing the talent warehouse. In SAP E-Recruiting you can customize the talent warehouse to meet your business requirements.

5.9 Customizing the Talent Warehouse

The talent warehouse is the storage location for all candidates in SAP E-Recruiting. It is in this database where information on the candidates is stored along with references such as qualifications, work experience, education, and training.

You perform the customizing steps for the talent warehouse in the IMG (see Figure 5.50) by following the menu path SAP E-Recruiting • Talent Warehouse • Candidate.

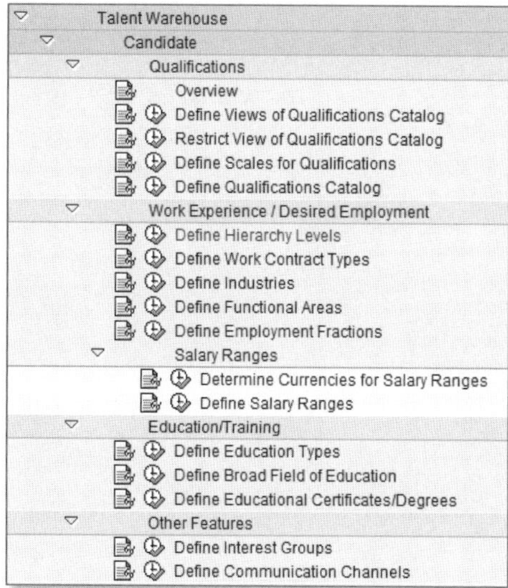

Figure 5.50 Customizing the Talent Warehouse

Now we will discuss the various customizing steps and the configuration settings that are required.

Qualifications

Qualifications form a big part of talent management in SAP E-Recruiting. Qualifications can be included in candidates' resumes and can be stored on the candidate profile. They can be placed as requirements on requisitions. If you are using the qualifications catalog in your SAP ERP HCM system, you can integrate it with the SAP E-Recruiting system by following the customizing steps discussed in Chapter 3, SAP E-Recruiting Basics, Section 3.6.2 Technical Settings. Refer here for more details about integrating the SAP ERP HCM qualifications catalog with the SAP E-Recruiting application. Also, SAP Note 677924 provides details on the qualifications catalog distribution between the SAP ERP HCM and SAP E-Recruiting systems.

The following two IMG activities form an important step in defining the qualifications available to internal and external candidates within the SAP E-Recruiting application.

- **Define Views of Qualifications Catalog**
  In this customizing step, you create a view of the SAP ERP HCM qualifications catalog for the SAP E-Recruiting application. The SAP standard delivered view is SAP_ERECRUITING.

- **Restrict View of Qualifications Catalog**
  In this customizing step (see Figure 5.51), you specify which qualification groups in the SAP ERP HCM qualifications catalog is assigned to the SAP E-Recruiting view that you defined in the prior step. By assigning the qualifications groups to the view, you restrict which qualifications groups are visible in the SAP E-Recruiting application.

Change View "View of Qualifications Catalog": Overview

New Entries

View of Qualifications Catalog

Quali Catalog View	Quali Catalog View	OT	ObjectID
SAP_ERECRUITING	SAP E-Recruiting	QK	50012824
SAP_ERECRUITING	SAP E-Recruiting	QK	50015797
SAP_ERECRUITING	SAP E-Recruiting	QK	50015804
SAP_ERECRUITING	SAP E-Recruiting	QK	50016331
SAP_ERECRUITING	SAP E-Recruiting	QK	50016335
SAP_ERECRUITING	SAP E-Recruiting	QK	50016336
SAP_ERECRUITING	SAP E-Recruiting	QK	50016699
SAP_ERECRUITING	SAP E-Recruiting	QK	50016700
SAP_ERECRUITING	SAP E-Recruiting	QK	50016719
SAP_ERECRUITING	SAP E-Recruiting	QK	50017200
SAP_ERECRUITING	SAP E-Recruiting	QK	50017202
SAP_ERECRUITING	SAP E-Recruiting	QK	50034151
SAP_ERECRUITING	SAP E-Recruiting	QK	50034152
SAP_ERECRUITING	SAP E-Recruiting	QK	50034153
Z_QUAL_VIEW	Customer Specific View	QK	50012750
Z_QUAL_VIEW	Customer Specific View	QK	50016322

Figure 5.51 Restricting View of the Qualifications Catalog for SAP E-Recruiting

If you are not using any qualification groups from your SAP ERP HCM qualifications catalog, then you need to complete the following customizing steps:

- **Define Scales for Qualifications**
  In this customizing step, you define the scales and the proficiencies that you use in the qualifications in the SAP E-Recruiting application.
- **Define Qualifications Catalog**
  In this customizing step, you define the qualifications and the qualifications groups for the qualifications catalog. The Define Scales for Qualifications step is a prerequisite for this customizing step.

Tip

We recommend that the qualifications catalog be customized and maintained in the SAP ERP HCM system. If the qualifications catalog is maintained in the SAP E-Recruiting application, there is a possibility that the qualifications catalog in SAP E-Recruiting might eventually become out of sync with the qualifications catalog in the SAP ERP HCM system.

For Work Experience/Desired Employment, you need to perform the following IMG steps:

- **Define Hierarchy Levels**
  Define the hierarchy levels that exist in your organization, for example, apprentice, senior professional (more than 10 years work experience), and top management/executive.
- **Define Work Contract Types**
  Define the different types of work contracts that exist in your organization, for example, regular, part-time, and temporary.
- **Define Industries**
  Define the industries in which your organization is currently doing business. The industries you customize in this activity can also reflect the industries in which the candidate needs to have experience, for example, retail, real estate, and technology.
- **Define Functional Areas**
  Define the different functional areas in your organization, for example, human resources, sales, and research and development.
- **Define Employment Fractions**
  Define the minimum number of working hours for the different employment fractions, for example, full-time and part-time.

For Salary Ranges, you need to perform the following IMG steps:

- **Determine Currencies for Salary Ranges**
  Define the currencies that are used in the salary ranges. You can also define if the currency is a reference currency.
- **Define Salary Ranges**
  Define the currency and the salary ranges. You can customize multiple salary ranges for a particular currency, depending on the requisition requirements. You must customize Determine Currencies for Salary Ranges prior to customizing Define Salary Ranges.

For Education/Training, you need to perform the following IMG steps:

- **Define Education Types**
  Define the education types that the candidate can use when creating the candidate profile. The recruiter and the support team can use these education types as search criteria while searching the talent pool for suitable candidates. Possible education types are high school, university, and so on.

- **Define Broad Field of Education**
  Define the fields of education the candidate can use when creating the candidate profile. The recruiter and the support team can use these fields of education as search criteria while searching the talent pool for suitable candidates. Possible fields of education are law, economics, computer science, and engineering.
- **Define Educational Certificates/Degrees**
  Define the educational certificates and degrees the candidate can use when creating the candidate profile. The recruiter and the support team can use these as search criteria when searching the talent pool for suitable candidates. Possible educational certificates and degrees are diploma, master's, and PhD.

To enable other features in the talent warehouse, perform the following IMG steps:

- **Define Interest Groups**
  Define the interest groups that can be used to categorize candidates. While creating the candidate profile, a candidate can assign himself to an interest group. While creating a requisition, the recruiter can state the interest group that will be suitable for the particular requisition. Possible interest groups are entry level, apprentice, and specialist.

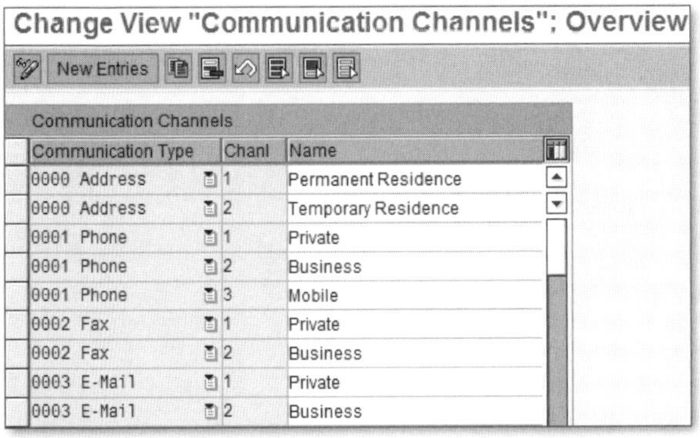

Change View "Communication Channels": Overview

New Entries

Communication Channels

Communication Type	Chanl	Name
0000 Address	1	Permanent Residence
0000 Address	2	Temporary Residence
0001 Phone	1	Private
0001 Phone	2	Business
0001 Phone	3	Mobile
0002 Fax	1	Private
0002 Fax	2	Business
0003 E-Mail	1	Private
0003 E-Mail	2	Business

Figure 5.52 Customize Communications Channels

- **Define Communication Channels**
  The recruiter can use the data entered in the communication channels to communicate with the candidate. In this customizing step (see Figure 5.52), you define the different channels that can be used to communicate with the candidate. Possible communication channels are phone (home), phone (mobile), and Email (private).

In enhancement pack 4, the following tables are maintained for both SAP E-Recruiting and the talent management specialist in SAP Succession Planning.

- Industries
- Functional areas
- Contract types
- Hierarchy levels
- Education types
- Broad field of education
- Educational certificates and degrees

Therefore, the entries in SAP E-Recruiting and Talent Management should be identical or you will likely encounter errors when the information is brought from SAP E-Recruiting into the Talent Management infoptype (used in SAP Succession Planning) should you ever integrate the two applications.

In the next section, we will give an overview of the workflow templates that support candidate management in SAP E-Recruiting.

5.10 Workflows

Workflows are an important component of SAP E-Recruiting. When workflows are activated, you can use them to send simple correspondence to candidates. In SAP E-Recruiting, the following workflow templates are standard delivered:

- **Create object:**
  - Workflow template – 51900008
  - Abbreviation – ERCObjCreate
  - Triggering event – The CREATED event for the objects Candidate (ERC_CAND), Candidacy (ERC_CDCY), Application (ERC_APPL), Requisition (ERC_REQUI), and Job Posting (ERC_POST)
- **Create activity:**
  - Workflow template – 51900011
  - Abbreviation – ERCActCrea_2
  - Triggering event – The ACTIVITYCREATED event for the object type ERC_ACTIV (SAP E-Recruiting activities)
- **Delete candidate registration:**
  - Workflow template – 51900006
  - Abbreviation – ERCCandDerig

  - Triggering event – The CANDIDATE-DEREGISTER event for the object Candidate (ERC_CAND)
- **Assign new password:**
  - Workflow template – 51900003
  - Abbreviation – ERCSendPwd
  - Triggering event – The NEWPASSWORDREQUESTED event for the object Candidate (ERC_CAND)
- **Status change:**
  - Workflow template – 51900010
  - Abbreviation – ERCStatChg_2
  - Triggering event – The STATUSCHANGED event for the objects Candidate (ERC_CAND), Candidacy (ERC_CDCY), Application (ERC_APPL), Requisition (ERC_REQUI), and Job Posting (ERC_POST)
- **Correct data entry error:**
  - Workflow template – 51800042
  - Abbreviation – ERCAdjEntry
  - Triggering event – The ERRONEOUSENTRY event for the object type ERC_OBJECT (General object type in SAP E-Recruiting)

If any changes are needed to the SAP-provided workflow, copy these workflow templates into your customer namespace and work with a workflow resource to enhance the custom workflow. For more details on the SAP E-Recruiting data model and the objects in SAP E-Recruiting, you can refer to Chapter 3, SAP E-Recruiting Basics, Section 3.3 SAP E-Recruiting Data Model.

5.11 Summary

In this chapter, we explored Candidate Management within the SAP E-Recruiting system. Talent Relationship Management and Talent Services are important concepts in SAP E-Recruiting and are effective tools in Candidate Management. Whereas customers' candidate registration requirements differ, we strongly urge that candidates be registered in the talent warehouse prior to applying to a requisition.

In the next chapter, we will explain about the role of the recruiting administrator and the administrative functions that a recruiting administrator is responsible for.

In SAP E-Recruiting, recruitment administrators are responsible for several important functions such as maintaining support groups, talent groups, requisitions, and process templates. In enhancement pack 4, the Recruiting Administrator functionality is delivered via a standard role. In this chapter, we will explain the role of the Recruiting Administrator, the different functions he is responsible for, and the best practices that can be followed.

6 Administration

In SAP E-Recruiting, the main role of the Recruiting Administrator is to support the recruiting activities and the support team. The Recruiting Administrator has access to the services that the recruiting and support team access regularly. Recruiting administrators are responsible for the following administrative activities:

- **User management**
  - Maintain internal users
  - Delete registrations
  - Delete external candidates
  - Maintain support groups
  - Adjust support teams
- **Central system administration**
  - Maintain companies and branches
  - Maintain agencies
  - Requisition management
  - Maintain process templates
- **Transaction data management**
  - Maintain talent groups
  - Maintain application groups
  - Access audit trails

In this chapter, we will explain in detail each of these functionalities.

To deploy the Recruiting Administrator role (technical name: SAP_RCF_REC_ADMIN_ERC_CI_2), you need to implement the business package for Recruiting Administrator 1.40 (or BP for Recruiting Administrator 1.41, depending on the support pack).

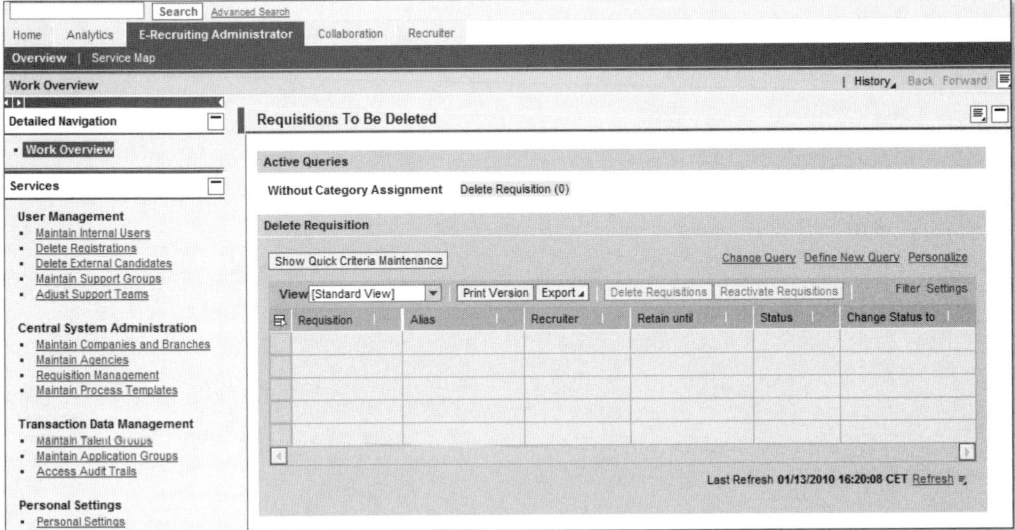

Figure 6.1 User Interface for Recruiting Administrator in enhancement pack 4

In enhancement pack 4, the interface for the Recruiting Administrator is delivered in Web Dynpro for ABAP (WD4A). The user needs to be assigned the role of the Recruiting Administrator in the SAP Portal to see the available functionalities (see Figure 6.1).

In the Recruiting Administrator user interface, the user can click on the link Personalize to Personalize the Work Overview interface.

In the Personalization interface (see Figure 6.2), the user can select queries from the Available Queries list and add them to the Active Queries list. The user can also select which query should be the default. In addition, the user can click on the Layout tab and select if the Work Overview needs to be displayed as Tabstrip or as Links.

Next, we will explain user management services and how to create and maintain different services.

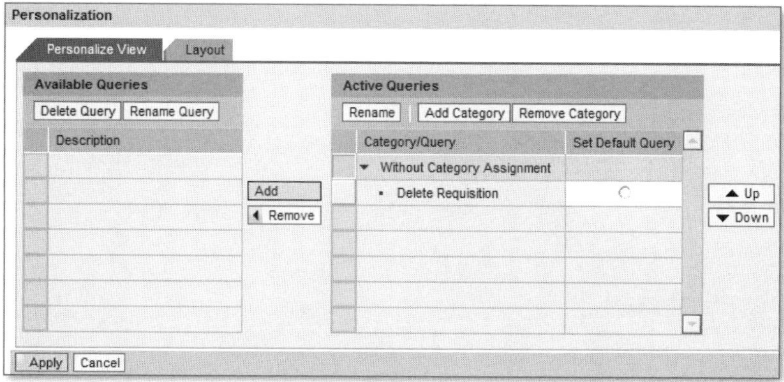

Figure 6.2 Work Overview Personalization

6.1 User Management Services

6.1.1 Maintain Internal Users

The Recruiting Administrator uses the service Maintain Internal Users to create and maintain internal users in SAP E-Recruiting. To access this service in the Recruiting Administrator interface, click on the Maintain Internal Users link under User Management in the Services area.

To create a new internal user in the Maintain Users interface, click on the Create button. In the Create Users interface (see Figure 6.3), enter the following basic data required to create the internal user:

- User Name
- Personnel Number
- First Name
- Last Name
- Email
- Role

The role contains the user authorizations required in SAP E-Recruiting. The default value for the role is Candidate (Internal), and every internal user is assigned the role Candidate (Internal). Click on the Save button to accept your entries.

Create Users

Save Close Back

User Name: *

Personnel Number: *

First Name: *

Last Name: *

E-Mail: *

Role: Candidate (internal)

Administrator
Assistant Manager
Candidate (internal)
Data Entry Clerk
Decision Maker
Director of Staffing
HR Admin
Interview Committee
Manager
Recruiter

Figure 6.3 Create Users

To edit or make changes to the internal users data in the Maintain Users interface (see Figure 6.4), enter the User Name or the Personnel Number of the internal user and click on the Start button to display the Edit User interface. The details of the internal user are displayed in the Edit User interface. You can make any necessary changes and click on the Save button to accept your changes.

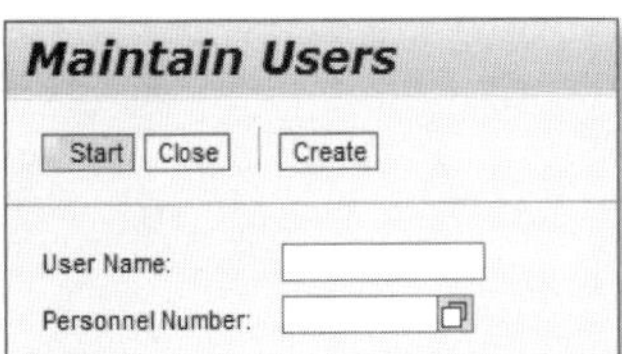

Figure 6.4 Maintain Users

> **Note**
>
> If you implement SAP E-Recruiting in an integrated environment, you should maintain the internal users in the SAP ERP HCM system using Transaction code SU01. We recommend that you remove the service Maintain Internal Users from the work area of the Recruiting Administrator interface if you are running an integrated scenario.

6.1.2 Delete Registrations

The Recruiting Administrator uses the service Delete Registrations to delete the registrations of external candidates when necessary. To access this service in the

Recruiting Administrator interface, click on the Delete Registrations link under User Management in the Services area.

In the Delete Registration interface (see Figure 6.5), enter the selection criteria and click on the Search button. The search results are displayed in the free listing below the selection criteria. In the results, select the candidate you want to delete and click on the Delete Registration button.

Delete Registration

Close

Selection Criteria

Last Name:	young*
First Name:	
E-Mail Address:	
Maximum Number of Hits:	100

Search Reset

Result: 2 Hits

Delete Registration Settings

Candidate	E-Mail	Alias	Last Logon
Megan Young / Clevelan...			
Joseph Young / Chelten...	ecandidateyoung@yahoo.com	JYOUNG	03/07/2009

Figure 6.5 Delete Registration

You can click on the Reset button to clear the selection criteria and reset the Delete Registration interface.

In the free listing that displays the results of the search criteria, you can click on the Settings link and personalize the columns to be displayed, the sorted column, the display features, and so on (see Figure 6.6).

Settings

Column Selection | Sort | Filter | Display

Table

Displayed Rows:	-1
Displayed Columns:	All 8
Table Design:	Standard
Grid Lines:	All

OK Cancel Apply

Figure 6.6 Settings for Delete Registration Interface

> **Note**
>
> If you have customized the legal periods, SAP E-Recruiting system will take the legal periods into account prior to deleting the candidate registrations. Refer to Chapter 3, SAP E-Recruiting Basics, for more details about storing legal periods.

When the external candidate registrations are deleted, the SAP E-Recruiting system performs the following actions:

- The candidate is locked and can no longer log in to the SAP E-Recruiting system. (If the candidate wants to access the system again, he has to reregister.)
- All assignments to the talent groups or application groups are deleted.
- All applications and candidacies with the status Draft are deleted.
- The candidate's applications and the candidacies are withdrawn.

6.1.3 Delete External Candidates

The Recruiting Administrator can use the service Delete External Candidates to delete external candidates from the talent pool. To access this service in the Recruiting Administrator interface, click on the Delete External Candidates link under User Management in the Services area.

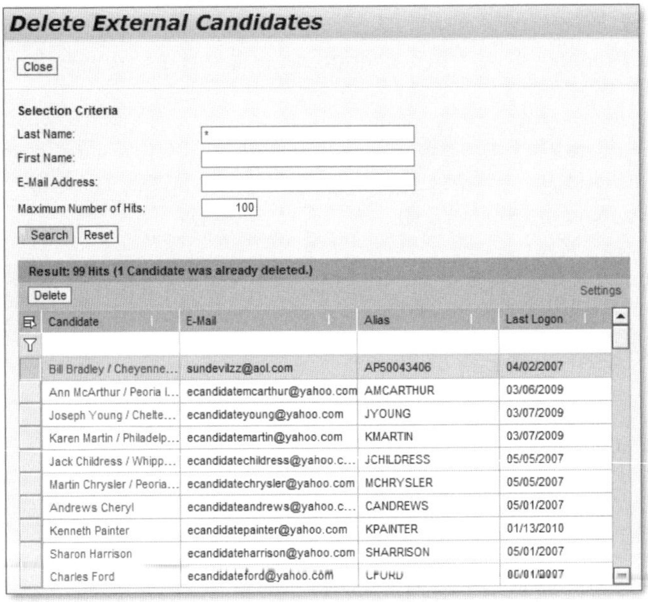

Delete External Candidates

Close

Selection Criteria

Last Name: *

First Name:

E-Mail Address:

Maximum Number of Hits: 100

Search Reset

Result: 99 Hits (1 Candidate was already deleted.)

Delete Settings

Candidate	E-Mail	Alias	Last Logon
Bill Bradley / Cheyenne...	sundevilzz@aol.com	AP50043406	04/02/2007
Ann McArthur / Peoria I...	ecandidatemcarthur@yahoo.com	AMCARTHUR	03/06/2009
Joseph Young / Chelte...	ecandidateyoung@yahoo.com	JYOUNG	03/07/2009
Karen Martin / Philadelp...	ecandidatemartin@yahoo.com	KMARTIN	03/07/2009
Jack Childress / Whipp...	ecandidatechildress@yahoo.c...	JCHILDRESS	05/05/2007
Martin Chrysler / Peoria...	ecandidatechrysler@yahoo.com	MCHRYSLER	05/05/2007
Andrews Cheryl	ecandidateandrews@yahoo.c...	CANDREWS	05/01/2007
Kenneth Painter	ecandidatepainter@yahoo.com	KPAINTER	01/13/2010
Sharon Harrison	ecandidateharrison@yahoo.com	SHARRISON	05/01/2007
Charles Ford	ecandidateford@yahoo.com	CFORD	05/01/2007

Figure 6.7 Delete External Candidates

In the Delete External Candidates interface (see Figure 6.7), enter the selection criteria and click on the Search button. The search results are displayed in the free listing below the selection criteria. In the results, select the candidate you want to delete and click on the Delete button.

You can click on the Reset button, to clear the selection criteria and reset the Delete External Candidate interface.

In the free listing that displays the results of the search criteria, you can enter the filter criteria (see Figure 6.8) and click on the Filter button to further restrict the results.

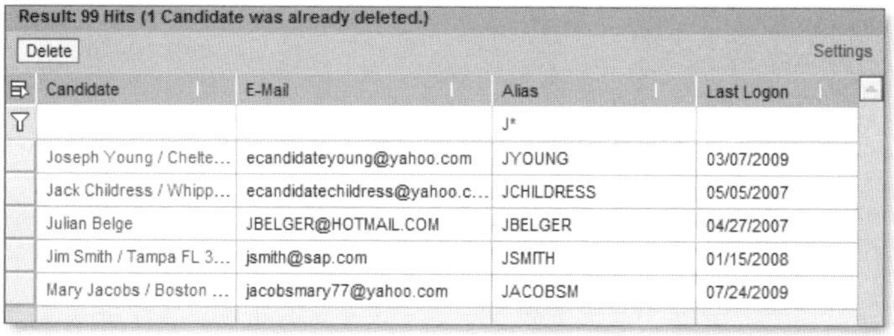

Result: 99 Hits (1 Candidate was already deleted.)

Delete | Settings

Candidate	E-Mail	Alias	Last Logon
		J*	
Joseph Young / Chelte...	ecandidateyoung@yahoo.com	JYOUNG	03/07/2009
Jack Childress / Whipp...	ecandidatechildress@yahoo.c...	JCHILDRESS	05/05/2007
Julian Belge	JBELGER@HOTMAIL.COM	JBELGER	04/27/2007
Jim Smith / Tampa FL 3...	jsmith@sap.com	JSMITH	01/15/2008
Mary Jacobs / Boston ...	jacobsmary77@yahoo.com	JACOBSM	07/24/2009

Figure 6.8 Filter Results

You can click on the Close button to exit the Delete External Candidates interface.

6.1.4 Create and Maintain Support Groups

The Recruiting Administrator can use the service Maintain Support Groups, to create and maintain support groups. To access this service in the Recruiting Administrator interface, click on the Maintain Support Groups link under User Management in the Services area.

Support groups (object type NG) consists of a group of people who can be assigned to the support team as a group. Support groups are assigned to the support team for a requisition, talent group, application, application group, or agency. By assigning a support group to a support team, the recruiter can assign all of the members in a single step. Any changes made to the support group affect all requisitions, talent groups, applications, application groups, and agencies where the support group is assigned to the support team.

The Recruiting Administrator creates and maintains support groups. They can be formed for a specific requisition or for any recruiting requirement.

To create a support group in the Maintain Support Groups interface, click on the Create button. In the Create Support Group interface (see Figure 6.9), enter the basic data required to create the support group. If you create a support group to assign to an agency, you must assign Data Entry Clerk to the Group Role field.

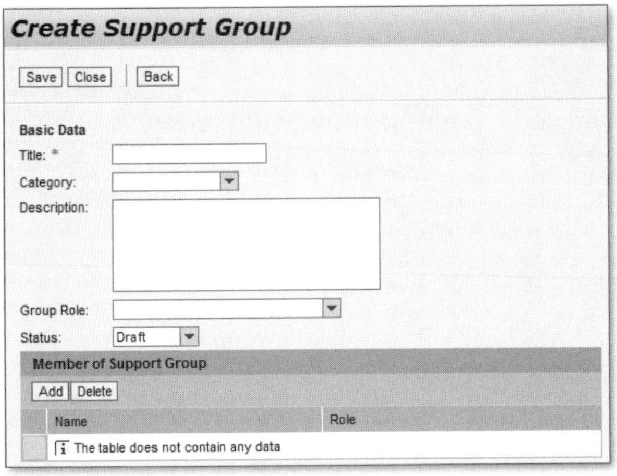

Figure 6.9 Create Support Group

As a prerequisite to creating support groups, you must complete customizing the Category values in the IMG. The menu path for this customizing activity is SAP E-RECRUITING • TECHNICAL SETTINGS • USER ADMINISTRATION • DEFINE CATEGORIES FOR GROUPINGS.

You can customize the roles that are displayed in the dropdown list when you click on the Group Role field (see Figure 6.10). You perform this customization in the IMG under the menu path SAP E-RECRUITING • TECHNICAL SETTINGS • USER ADMINISTRATION • ROLES IN E-RECRUITING • DEFINE ROLES IN E-RECRUITING.

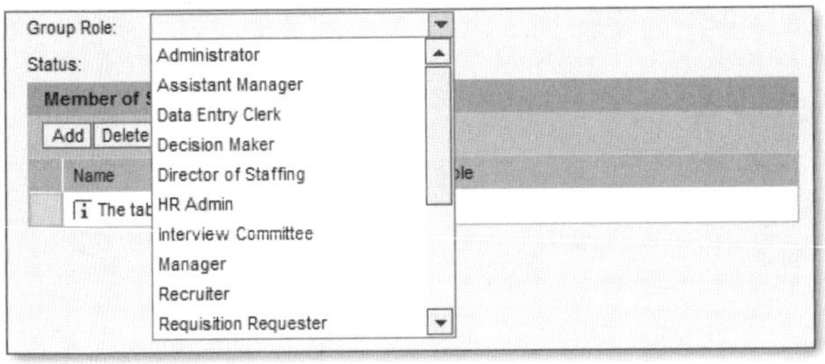

Figure 6.10 Roles Available in Support Groups

After you have entered the basic data for the support group, you can assign members to the support group by clicking on the Add button in the Member of Support Group section. You can enter the name of the support group member in the Name column or press F4 to display the Personal Value list.

In the Full Name: Personal Value List dialog box, click on the More Values... link to display the Full Name: General Value List dialog box (see Figure 6.11). Here, you can enter the search criteria and search for employees who can be added to the support group. After you assign the members to the support group, you can assign roles to the members.

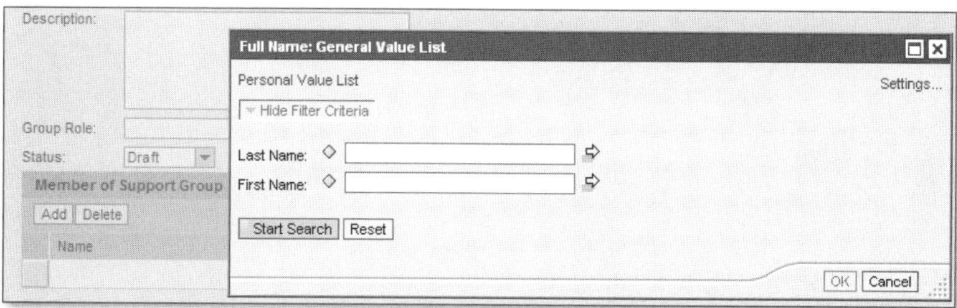

Figure 6.11 Adding a Member to a Support Group

Assign the status Released to the support group and click on the Save button to accept your entries.

You can create a new support group by using an existing support group as a template. In the Maintain Support Groups interface, enter the search criteria and click on the Search button. The support groups that match the search criteria are displayed as a free listing (see Figure 6.12). To create a new support group by the Copy Method, select the support group that you want to use as a template and click on the Copy button. Rename the support group, edit the data, and click on the Save button to accept your entries.

To edit a support group in the Maintain Support Groups interface, enter the search criteria. The support groups that match the search criteria are displayed as a free listing. Select the support group that you want to edit and click on the Start button.

To delete a support group, select the support group that you want to delete and click on the Delete button. The SAP E-Recruiting system checks if the support group is currently assigned and issues a hard error if it is not. Support Groups that are assigned to agencies cannot be deleted.

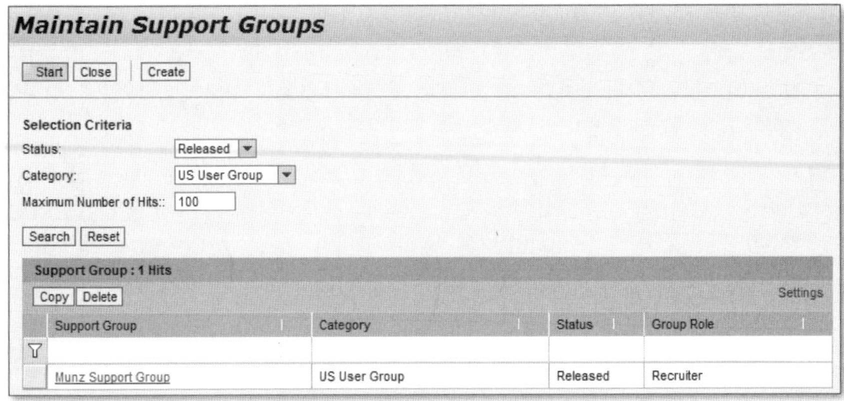

Figure 6.12 Create a Support Group by the Copy Method

If the support group is in Released status, the recruiter can assign it to support teams. If the support group has the group role Data Entry Clerk, it can be assigned to agencies.

6.1.5 Adjust Support Teams

In SAP E-Recruiting, a support team is assigned to requisitions, application groups, and talent groups. The support team is responsible for processing the applications assigned to the requisitions or to the application groups. The Recruiting Administrator uses the service Adjust Support Team to adjust support teams. To access this service in the Recruiting Administrator interface, click on the Adjust Support Teams link under User Management in the Services area.

In the Adjust Support Teams main interface (see Figure 6.13), enter the search criteria and click on the Search button. The support teams that match the criteria are displayed in the free listing. Select the support team you want to maintain and click on the Start button.

In the Adjust Support Teams interface (see Figure 6.14), enter the personnel number of the employee you want to add or delete from the support team. If you do not know the personnel number, press F4 to display the Personnel Number: Personnel Value List dialog box. In the dialog box, click on More Values..., and you can do a free search.

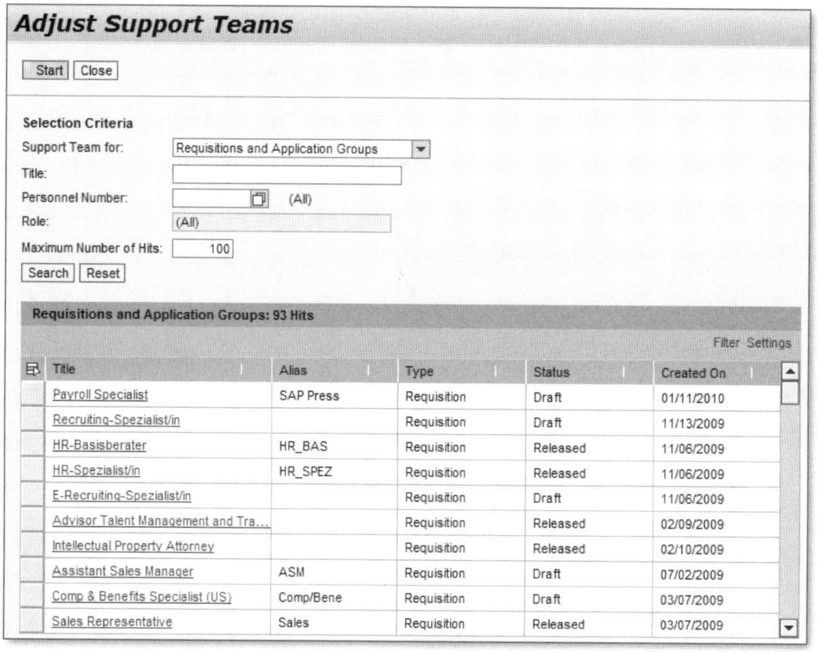

Figure 6.13 Adjust Support Teams – Main Interface

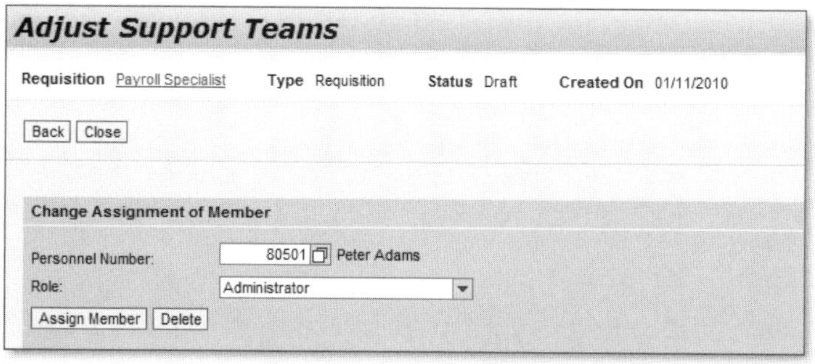

Figure 6.14 Adjust Support Teams

After you have entered the employee personnel number, select the role you want to assign to the employee. The default value displayed in the Role field is All. After you have assigned the role to the employee, the buttons Assign Member and Delete are enabled.

If you want to assign the employee to the support team, click on the Assign Member button. If you want to delete the employee from the support team, click on the Delete button.

After an employee is assigned to the support team, the employee has access to all of the requisitions, application groups, and talent groups that are assigned to the support team. If an employee is deleted from a support team, the employee no longer has access to the requisitions, application groups, and talent groups that are assigned to the support team.

6.2 Central System Administration

The recruiting administrator also has important capabilities with central system administration functions, such as maintaining companies and branches, maintaining agencies, and maintaining requisitions including their process templates. We will cover these topics next.

6.2.1 Maintain Companies and Branches

The Recruiting Administrator can use the service Maintain Companies and Branches to create, maintain, and delete companies and branches in the SAP E-Recruiting system. To access this service in the Recruiting Administrator interface, click on the Maintain Companies and Branches link under Central System Administration in the Services area.

The Maintain Companies and Branches interface (see Figure 6.15) displays all of the companies that are created in the SAP E-Recruiting system and the branches that belong to the selected company.

To create a new company, click on the Add button in the Companies listing. The Add Company dialog box is displayed. Enter the Company ID and the Company Name and click on the OK button to accept your entries. To edit a company name, select the company and click on the Edit button. In the Edit Company dialog box, edit the company name and click on the OK button to accept your entries. After you have created the company or made edits to the company, click on the Save button to accept and save your entries.

To create branches for a company in the company listing, select the company for which you want to create the branches. In the branches listing, click on the Add button. In the Add Branches dialog box, enter the data and click on the OK button to accept your entries. Click on the Save button to save your entries. When you click on the Save button, the system automatically generates the Branch's ID. Then edit the branch, select it, and click on the Edit button. In the Edit branch dialog box, make the required edits and click on the OK button. After you have completed editing the branch data, click on the Save button to save your changes.

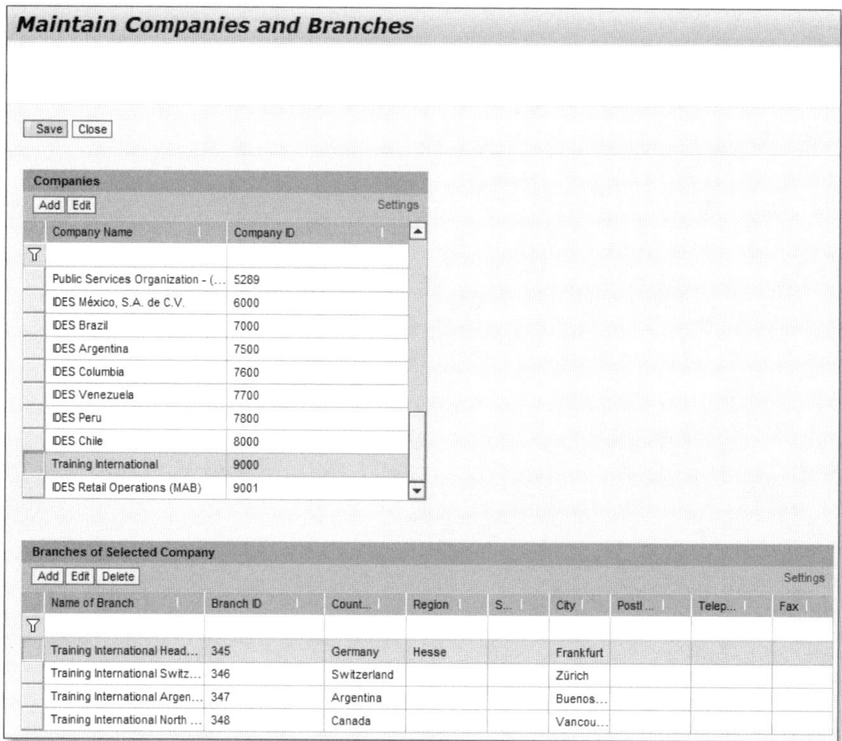

Figure 6.15 Maintain Branches

To delete a branch, select it and click on the Delete button. The Delete Branch dialog box (see Figure 6.16) is displayed. Select Yes if you want to delete the branch. Click on the Save button to accept the deletion.

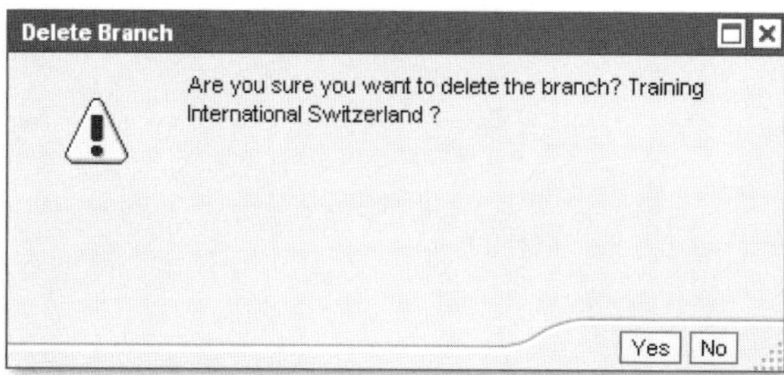

Figure 6.16 Delete Branch Pop-Up Confirmation

6.2.2 Maintain Agencies

Recruiting administrators can also maintain agency data for any third-party providers that submit or enter applications in the SAP E-Recruiting system. Administrators can use the service Maintain Agencies to create, maintain, and delete agencies in the SAP E-Recruiting system. To access this service in the Recruiting Administrator interface, click on the Maintain Agencies link under Central System Administration in the Services area.

You need to meet the following prerequisites prior to creating a new agency:

- In the SAP IMG, you should have completed the customizing activity Define Application Sources to define the third-party providers for whom you want to define agencies.
- You should have created the support group that you want to assign to the agencies. The support group should have Data Entry Clerk assigned to the group role.

In the Maintain Agencies interface, click on the Add button to create a new agency. In the Add Agency dialog box (see Figure 6.17), enter the basic data required to create a new agency. In the User section, select a User or a Support Group for the agency.

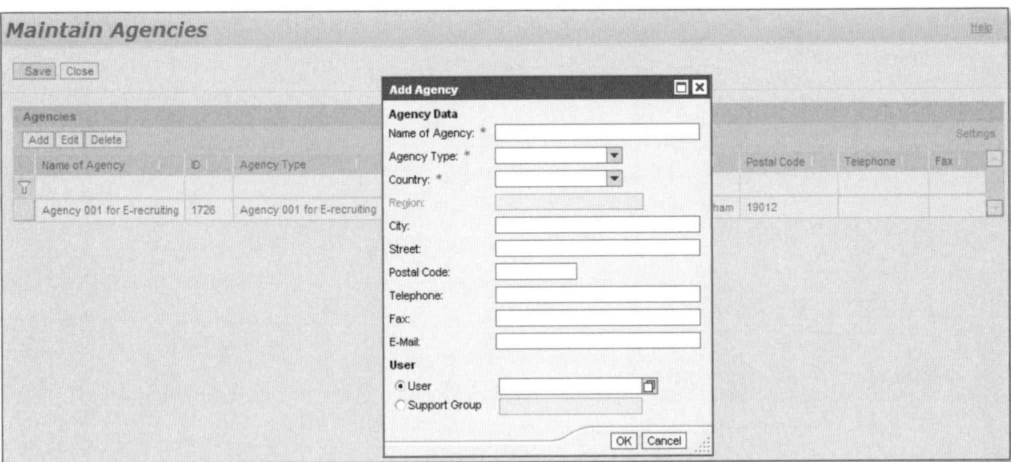

Figure 6.17 Add Agency

Note

When the users assigned to an agency enter applications, the SAP E-Recruiting system automatically creates a link with the agency and assigns the agency as the application source.

When a recruiter enters the application on behalf of the agency, the recruiter can choose third-party providers as the application source type and choose an agency as the application source.

After you have entered the basic data for the agency, click on the OK button to accept your entries. Click on the Save button to save your entries. The newly created agency is displayed in the free listing. SAP E-Recruiting automatically creates a Business Partner (object type BP) for the agency you created.

To edit an agency, select the agency displayed in the free listing and click on the Edit button. Make the required changes, click on the OK button to accept your changes, and click on the Save button to save your changes. To delete an agency, select the agency displayed in the free listing and click on the Delete button. The system displays a dialog box to confirm that you want to delete the agency. Select Yes and click on the Save button to save the deletion.

6.2.3 Requisition Management

The Recruiting Administrator can use the service Requisition Management to delete requisitions, reactivate requisitions that were marked To Be Deleted by accident, and to extend the storage of requisitions in the system. To access this service in the Recruiting Administrator interface, click on the Requisition Management link under Central System Administration in the Services area.

- **Extending the retention period**
  You might have a legal requirement to extend the time limit for retaining the data of a requisition.

In the Requisition Administration interface (see Figure 6.18), enter the selection criteria and click on the Search button. The requisitions that match the selection criteria are displayed in the free listing. Select the requisition whose retention period you want to extend. In the Extended Storage Until column, enter or overwrite the date up to which the data is to be retained. Click on the Save button to save your entries.

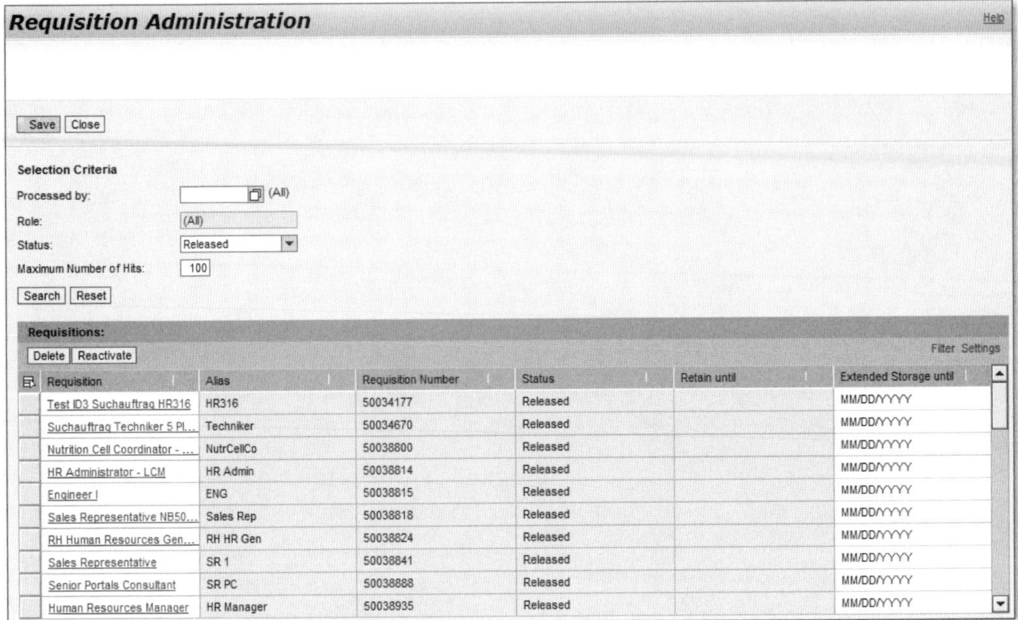

Figure 6.18 Requisition Administration

SAP E-Recruiting uses the date entered in the Extended Storage Until column to determine the period to retain the requisition data. The requisition and the associated data must remain in the SAP E-Recruiting system at least until the retention date.

Note

Only requisitions with the status To Be Deleted can be permanently deleted.

- **Deleting or reactivating a requisition**
  To permanently delete a requisition and its data in the Requisition Administration interface, enter the status To Be Deleted and specify additional selection criteria (if required). Click on the Search button. The requisitions that match the selection criteria are displayed in the free listing. Select the requisition that you want to delete and click on the Delete button.

If you set the status of a requisition to To Be Deleted by mistake, you can reset the status to the requisition's last valid status by clicking on the Reactivate button. Click on the Save button to save your actions.

6.2.4 Maintain Process Templates

The Recruiting Administrator can use the service Maintain Process Templates to create, maintain, and delete process templates in the SAP E-Recruiting system. To access this service in the Recruiting Administrator interface, click on the Maintain Process Templates link under Central System Administration in the Services area.

We explained Process Templates in Chapter 4, Requisition Management. For more details about process templates and how to create, maintain, and delete them, refer to Section 4.6, Process Templates and Activity Types.

In the Maintain Process Template interface, click on the Create button. In the Create Process Template interface, enter the basic data and select the processes you want to include in the process template.

When you select a process, a free listing is displayed at the bottom of the screen. Click on the Add button to add activity types to the process. The Add Activity dialog box with the list of activity types that can be assigned to the particular process is displayed (see Figure 6.19). Select the activity types you want to include and click on the OK button to accept your selections. Click on the Save button to save your entries.

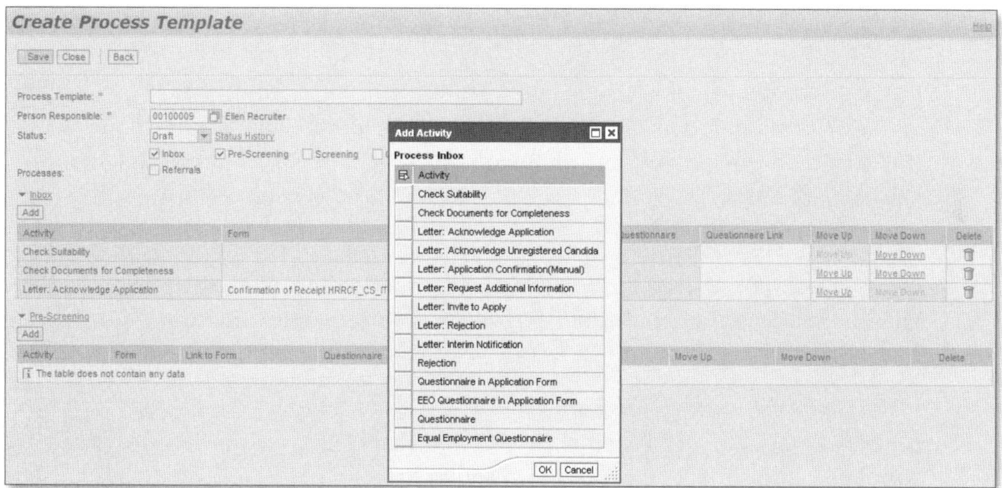

Figure 6.19 Create Process Template

When you have completed creating the process template, you must assign it with a status of Released to make it available for assignment to requisitions.

In the Add Activity dialog box, you can select multiple activity types at once by holding down the [Ctrl] key and selecting the activity types in the dialog box. The selected activity types are highlighted. After you have made the multiple selections and if you want to deselect an activity type, continue to hold down the Ctrl key and click on the activity type you want to deselect. The deselected activity type is no longer highlighted.

You can create a new process template by the copy method. Select the process template you want to copy and click on the Copy button. In the Copy Process Template interface, rename the Process template, add additional data that might be required, and click on the Save button to save your entries.

To delete a process template, select the process template you want to delete and click on the Delete button. A process template can only be deleted if it is in Draft status.

6.3 Transaction Data Management

Recruiting Administrators also have transaction data management responsibilities. The next section discusses the functionalities available within the recruiter work center.

6.3.1 Maintain Talent Groups

In SAP E-Recruiting, you can use talent groups to structure the talent pool and group candidates in the talent pool. The Recruiting Administrator can use the service Maintain Talent Groups to create and maintain talent groups. To access this service in the Recruiting Administrator interface, click on the Maintain Talent Groups link under Transaction Data Management in the Services area.

In the Maintain Talent Groups interface, click on the Create button to create a new talent group. In the Create Talent Group interface, enter the data in the Basic Data tab. The Person Responsible field defaults to the name of the recruiting administrator; you can change the Person Responsible to suit your requirements.

In the Support Team tab, click on the Add Member button to add a member to the support team. In the Add Member dialog box (see Figure 6.20), enter the Personnel Number of the employee you want to add to the support team. You can also assign a role to the employee in the support team. Click on the Add Support Group button to assign a support group to the support team. The members included in the support team can use the talent group for talent relationship management activities and for assigning candidates to the talent group. Please note that it is a prerequisite to have already created a Support Group to assign it to a talent group

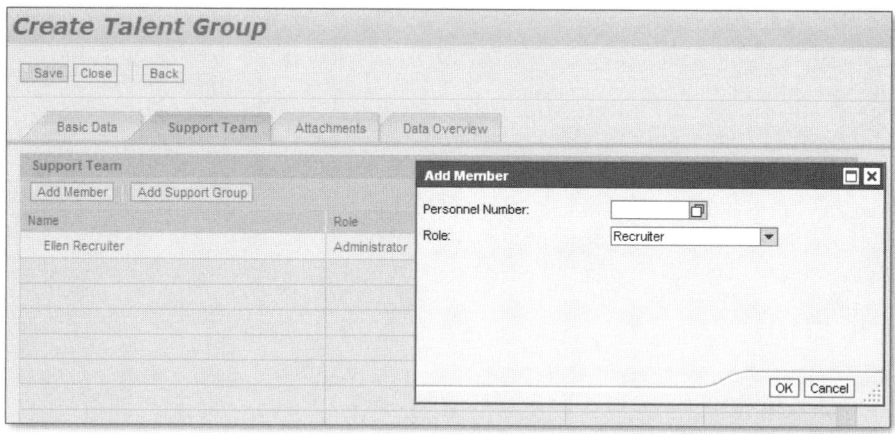

Figure 6.20 Create Talent Group – Add Member Pop-up

In the Attachments tab, you can upload attachments that provide more details about the talent group or any details that might be helpful to the support team. The Data Overview tab provides an overview of the data you entered for the talent group. Click on the Save button to save your entries and to create the talent group.

You can also create a talent group by the copy method. In the Maintain Talent Groups interface, select the talent group in the free listing that you want to use as a template. Click on the Copy button. In the Copy Talent Groups: Talent Group interface, rename the talent group and add or edit any data that might be required. Click on the Save button to save your entries.

To edit a talent group in the Maintain Talent Groups interface, select the talent group you want to edit and click on the Start button.

To delete a talent group in the Maintain Talent Groups interface, select the talent group you want to delete and click on the Delete button. When you delete the talent group, all candidates that were assigned to it are updated in the talent pool and are available to be assigned to other talent groups. If the candidates are assigned to other talent groups (one or multiple talent groups), they continue to be assigned to those talent groups.

6.3.2 Maintain Application Groups

When interested candidates do not find suitable job openings that match their experience or qualifications, they can send in unsolicited applications. In SAP E-Recruiting, you can use application groups to group unsolicited applications. The

Recruiting Administrator can use the service Maintain Application Groups to create and maintain application groups. To access this service in the Recruiting Administrator interface, click on the Maintain Application Groups link under Transaction Data Management in the Services area.

Note

We explained about application groups in Chapter 5, Candidate Management. For more details about application groups and the data structure, refer to Section 5.4, Application Groups.

In the Maintain Application Groups interface, click on the Create button to create a new application group. In the Create Application Group interface, enter the basic data and job details in the General Job Information tab.

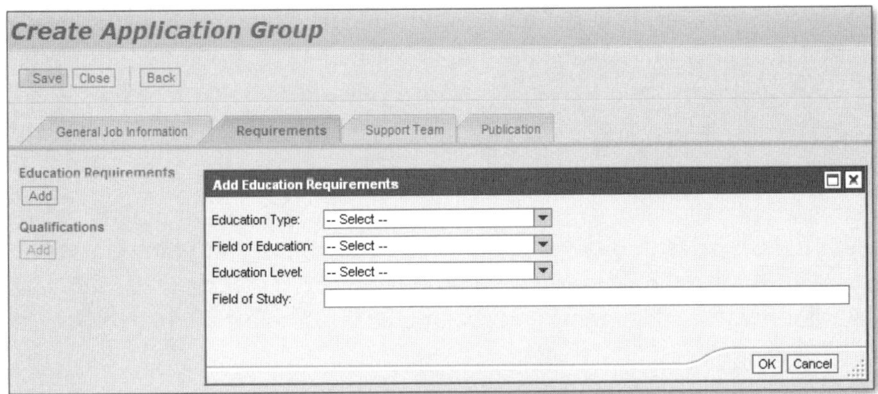

Figure 6.21 Create Application Group – Add Education Requirements Pop-up

In the Requirements tab (see Figure 6.21), add the education requirements and the qualifications for the application group. In the Support Team tab, add a member to the support team or add a support group to the support team.

It is important to enter a meaningful title and alias for the application group. Candidates use this title when they send in their applications. If you do not enter an alias for the application group, the SAP E-Recruiting system assigns a default alias. The data entry clerk or the recruiter assigned to enter unsolicited paper applications of external candidates uses this title to assign the candidate applications to the application group.

In the Applications Overview screen, a new tab page is created for each application group. The title of the tab page corresponds to the alias of the application group.

In the Publication tab, enter a reference code for the application group. If you have completed entering the data, change the status to Released. An Application group can be published only if a reference code is assigned to it and the status is set to Released.

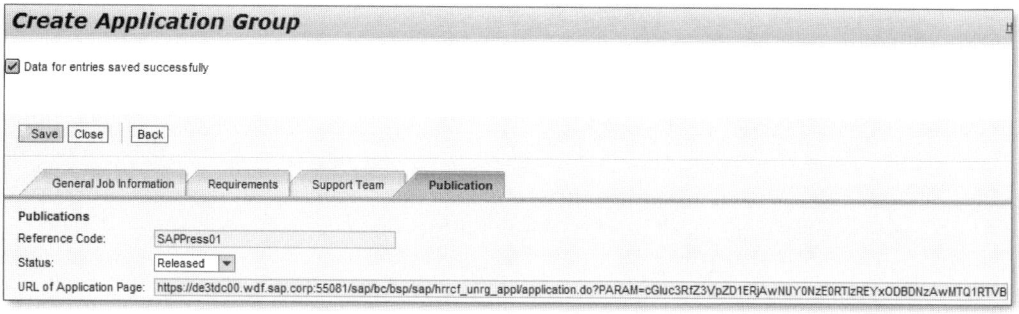

Figure 6.22 URL of Application Page

Click on the Save button to save your entries. The SAP E-Recruiting system automatically creates a URL (see Figure 6.22) that can be linked to your career website, and interested candidates can click on the URL to submit applications.

In your organization, you can create multiple application groups with different education and qualification requirements. The data entry clerk responsible for entering external candidate applications can group the unsolicited applications into different application groups based on the candidate qualifications and experience. Once an application group is set to Released status, you cannot make any edits to the *basic data* of the application group. So, if you want to make any changes to the basic data, you need to replace the application group.

You can also create an application group by the copy method. In the Maintain Application Groups interface, enter the selection criteria and click on the Search button. The results that match the selection criteria are displayed in the free listing. Select the application group you want to use as a template and click on the Copy button. In the Copy Application Group interface, rename the application group. Add or edit the basic data, the requirements data, and the support team. In the Publication tab, enter the reference code, change the status to Released, and click on the Save button to save your entries.

To edit an application group, in the Maintain Application Groups interface, enter the selection criteria and click on the Search button. The results that match the selection criteria are displayed in the free listing. Select the application group you want to edit and click on the Start button. After you have completed the changes, click on the Save button to accept and save your changes.

> **Note**
>
> After you have created an application group (the status can be Draft or Released), you can set it to Withdrawn status. Once you have set an application group to Withdrawn status, it cannot be used again.

To delete an application group in the Maintain Application Groups interface, enter the selection criteria and click on the Search button. The results that match the selection criteria are displayed in the free listing. Select the application group you want to delete and click on the Delete button.

6.3.3 Access Audit Trails

In SAP E-Recruiting, you can access audit trails for candidates and for search query logs.

SAP E-Recruiting automatically retains snapshots of the candidate profile during the recruiting process. You do not need to perform any customizing activity. SAP E-Recruiting facilitates retaining snapshots of the candidate profile using workflow. The snapshot retained contains the candidate profile that is available in the system at that point in time.

In SAP E-Recruiting, an audit trail is recorded when:

- The status of a candidacy application is changed to In Process, Rejected, or To Be Hired.
- A qualifying event activity is created for a candidacy.

Using the audit trail, you can view a candidate's snapshot and determine what data was used to make a decision on an application or on a candidate assignment.

For search query logs, you can activate the SAP standard delivered BAdI HRRCF00_QUERY_LOG to log search queries for specified requisitions. You can customize the BAdI to meet your business requirements. The menu path for the customizing activity is SAP E-Recruiting • Basic Settings • BAdI: Log Search Query.

When the BAdI is activated, the following information is saved:

- Requisition title
- Requisition number
- Date the search query was executed

- User name of the user who executed the search
- Full name of the user who executed the search
- Number of candidates assigned to the requisition based on the search query
- Candidates who were assigned to the requisition based on the search query
- Search query that was executed

This log is maintained in the SAP E-Recruiting system until the requisition is deleted. You can display the log by executing the report Display Search Query Log for Requisitions by following the menu path SAP E-RECRUITING • TOOLS • DISPLAY SEARCH QUERY LOG FOR REQUISITIONS.

To access the service Access Audit Trails in the Recruiting Administrator interface, click on the Access Audit Trails link under Transaction Data Management in the Services area.

In the Access Audit Trail interface (see Figure 6.23), enter the selection criteria and click on the Search button. The results that match the selection criteria are displayed in the free listing. If an audit trail exists for the candidate (candidate profile or search query assignment), these are displayed as links in the columns Access Audit Trails for Profiles and Access Audit Trails for Assignments of Candidates from Search Results.

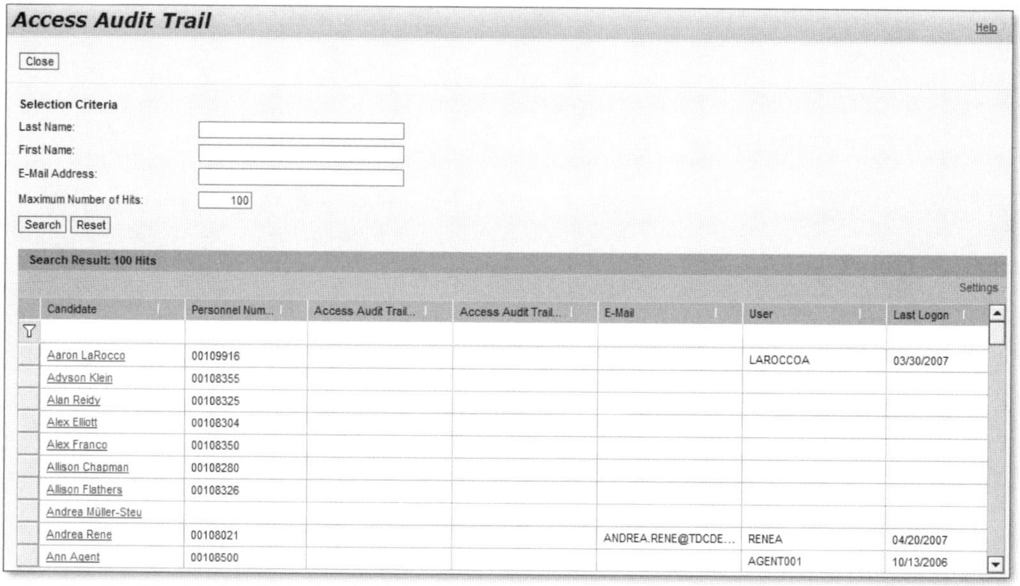

Access Audit Trail

Help

Close

Selection Criteria

Last Name:

First Name:

E-Mail Address:

Maximum Number of Hits: 100

Search | Reset

Search Result: 100 Hits

Settings

Candidate	Personnel Num...	Access Audit Trail...	Access Audit Trail...	E-Mail	User	Last Logon
Aaron LaRocco	00109916				LAROCCOA	03/30/2007
Advson Klein	00108355					
Alan Reidy	00108325					
Alex Elliott	00108304					
Alex Franco	00108350					
Allison Chapman	00108280					
Allison Flathers	00108326					
Andrea Müller-Steu						
Andrea Rene	00108021			ANDREA.RENE@TDCDE...	RENEA	04/20/2007
Ann Agent	00108500				AGENT001	10/13/2006

Figure 6.23 Access Audit Trail

Double-click on the link to display a list of the audit trails and the different versions. Click on the version you want to review, and the data overview is displayed.

6.4 Personal Settings

The recruiting administrator can also use the service Personal Settings to personalize the services and how data should be displayed. To access this service in the Recruiting Administrator interface, click on the Personal Settings link under Personal Settings in the Services area.

In the Personal Settings interface (see Figure 6.24), make the necessary settings and click on the Save button to save your entries. You have to log off and back on again into the system to see these changes.

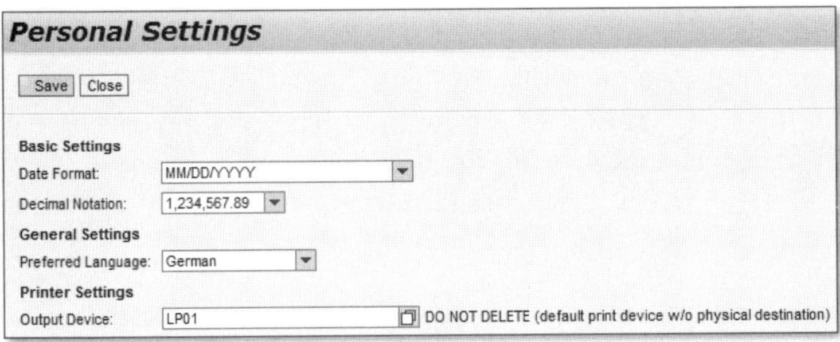

Figure 6.24 Personal Settings

6.5 Summary

In this chapter, we reviewed the various services that are available for recruiting administrators. With enhancement pack 4, the recruiting administrator role is more robust and is integrated more tightly into the portal via a standard delivered role. You will want to identify who on your team will perform the role of recruiting administrator once the system goes live. This person will need to understand the operational nuances of the business and know how to use the system efficiently.

In the next chapter, we will explain TREX and Search Engine Services (SES). TREX is the SAP-delivered search engine used in SAP E-Recruiting. Proper configuration of TREX is essential for an effective and successful implementation of SAP E-Recruiting.

Searching capability within SAP E-Recruiting is one of the most important features of the solution. With SAP now using the Search Engine Service (SES) as an interface between SAP E-Recruiting and the Search and Classification search engine (TREX), you can perform more robust searching, as well as filtering and ranking. In this chapter, we will discuss searching within the SAP E-Recruiting system.

7 Search

Perhaps no other subject is as important within the recruitment function as searching. All end users of the SAP E-Recruiting application need a robust searching mechanism at their disposal. Recruiters, for example, need to be able to search the talent warehouse to see good matches for talent needs quickly. Both internal and external candidates also need searching for available job postings. Without a dependable and robust platform on which to search applications, job seekers, and requisitions, the recruitment function would not be able to accomplish its objectives.

In this chapter, we will cover the basics of search. Due to its technical nature, we will not cover searching in great depth. You should work alongside a Basis resource to implement the search configuration needed for your SAP E-Recruiting system.

7.1 Background

The SAP E-Recruiting system uses SAP's search engine Search and Classification (TREX) for searching. This functionality allows users to search for objects such as candidates, requisitions, candidacies, and job postings. For all objects searched, the related data must first be indexed. The process of indexing the data is different for structured and unstructured data.

7.1.1 Structured Data

SAP E-Recruiting uses the Search Engine Service (SES) as an interface to TREX. The search engine service enables you to search for business objects using the TREX search engine technology. All structured data for an E-Recruiting object (e.g., requisition) is saved in the corresponding SAP E-Recruiting infotypes. For you to be able to search for this structured data, an SES business object must exist for the SAP E-Recruiting object type (See Table 7.1). The SES business object forwards the data to the SES. SES uses the TREX ABAP client to access the TREX functions, replicates the data in the TREX system, and supports TREX when creating indices for each SES business object and for each relationship between the SES business objects.

Business Object	Object Type	Notes
ERC_CAND	NA	Candidate
ERC_CDCY	NE	Candidacy
ERC_REQ	NB	Requisition
INT_POER	NC	Internal job posting
EXT_POST	NC	External job posting
AES_DOC	Dependent on category group	Relevant for the different categories of the documents from appraisal, evaluation, and survey (AES), such as performance management forms and questionnaires

Table 7.1 SES Business Objects

Please note that in addition to the indices for each SES business object, TREX creates the required indices for the relationships between the SES business objects and the relevant index information.

7.1.2 Unstructured Data

The system saves unstructured data such as reports and certificates in a content repository. The unstructured data is managed by the so-called Knowledge Provider (KPro). KPro triggers the indexing process for the unstructured data and supports the creation of an index for the unstructured data in the TREX system.

Note

If you have activated the business function HCM_ERC_CI_3 and you use Search and Classification (TREX) with version 7.10.18.1 or higher, the unstructured data is indexed together with the structured data. This means that the attachments of an object are now part of the object's search profile and therefore the KPro index is obsolete and SAP E-Recruiting uses *only* SES for indexing and searching. For more information, you can reference SAP Note 1301016 (BF HCM_ERC_CI_3 active: Use of Search with SES), SAP Note 1098046 (BF HCM_ERC_SES_1: Enhancements of the Search Functions), and SAP Note 1292143 (BF HCM_ERC_CI_2 active: Using the Search with SES.)

For general troubleshooting for TREX, you can reference composite SAP Note 817145 (Composite SAP note/overview: TREX troubleshooting).

For general FAQs on SES, you can reference SAP Note 1345777 (FAQs Search Engine Service (SES)).

Let's now talk more about communication between SAP E-Recruiting and TREX.

7.2 Communication Between SAP E-Recruiting and TREX

SAP E-Recruiting and Search and Classification (TREX) communicate via the Knowledge Provider (KPro) and the Search Engine Service (SES). Figure 7.1 displays the relationships between the two graphically.

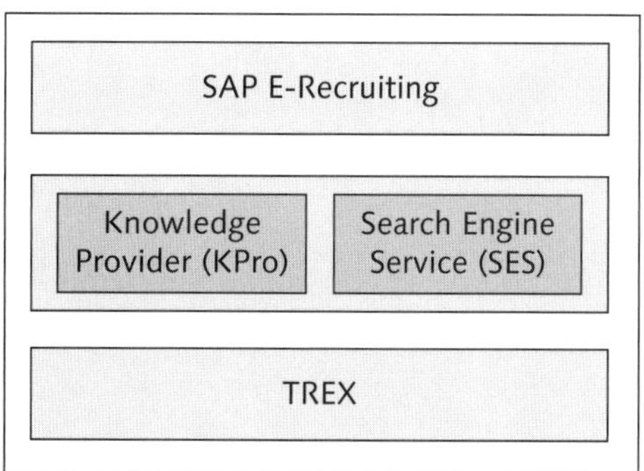

Figure 7.1 Communication Between SAP E-Recruiting and TREX

After creating a special user (of type communication) that has the SAP role SAP_RCF_CONTENT_SERVER (or similar), you must set up access to the contentserver service of the SAP E-Recruiting system. This enables users to access documents from document area HR_KW (Document Storage for HR Objects). You can perform this configuration under the IMG path SAP E-RECRUITING • TECHNICAL SETTINGS • SEARCH ENGINE • ACTIVATE INDEXING. Chapter 10, Authorization Management, discusses this more.

7.2.1 Document Storage

Documents within SAP E-Recruiting are stored and managed in SAP's Knowledge Provider (KPro) service. KPro is a service of the Web Application Server (WAS) that provides interfaces for accessing the search engine TREX. Because multiple applications can use KPro, SAP E-Recruiting documents must be distinguishable from the documents of other applications. This is achieved using so-called *document areas*. SAP E-Recruiting uses the document area HR_KW.

In the configuration, you must activate the document area HR_KW (Document Storage for HR Objects) for indexing purposes. Indexing is required to enable the engine to search the search profiles. To activate indexing, select the Indexing Release checkbox for the HR_KW document area. You can access this in the IMG under the menu path SAP E-RECRUITING • TECHNICAL SETTINGS • SEARCH ENGINE • ACTIVATE INDEXING. Figure 7.2 shows table view V_SDOKIDSP where this configuration occurs.

In addition to being assigned to the document area HR_KW, documents are assigned to a document class. The document class specifies the type of information contained in a document. All applications (including SAP E-Recruiting) that use an HR object as a key attribute use the document class HR_DOC.

The KPro monitoring utility can track the health of your search engine. Be sure to select document class HR_DOC when reviewing results. You can access the utility by executing Transaction SKPR07 or through the IMG under the menu path SAP E-RECRUITING • TECHNICAL SETTINGS • SEARCH ENGINE • CHECK SETTINGS. Figure 7.3 displays the main console of the monitoring tool.

Next, let's discus search profiles and search profile types.

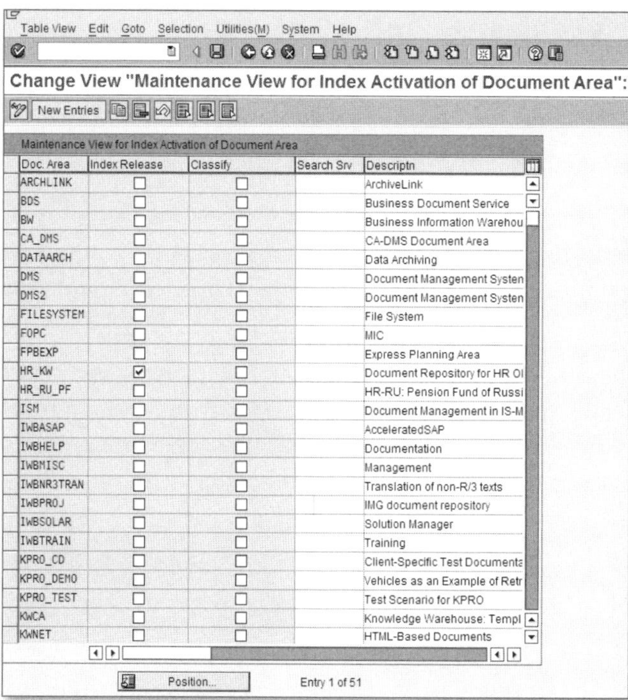

Figure 7.2 Activating the Index for Document Area HR_KW

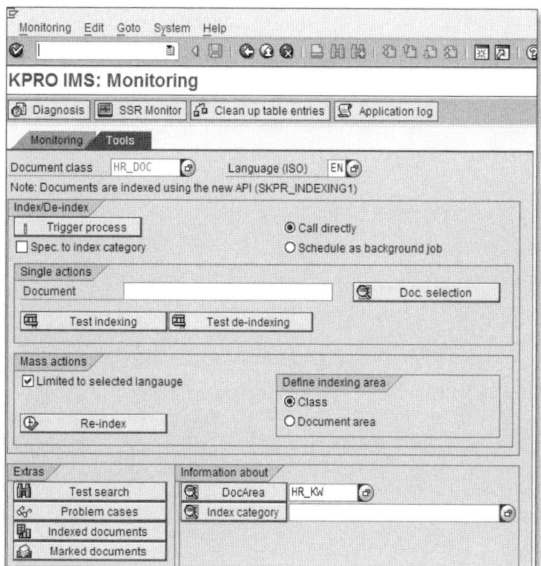

Figure 7.3 KPro Monitoring of Document Class HR_DOC

7.3 Search Profiles and Search Profile Types

Two sources contain relevant information within the search framework in SAP E-Recruiting — the attributes and relations indexed via SES and attachments. Attachments are unstructured data such as a resume or a candidate's reference.

A search profile represents a structured set of diverse object data that enables you to find objects in SAP E-Recruiting, such as candidates, requisitions, or job postings. This implies that each object has a search profile whose attributes are indexed via SES and that is assigned to a search profile type.

Search profile types map the different object types in SAP E-Recruiting and serve as templates for creating search profiles. All search profiles that are derived from one search profile type have the same attribute structure. A specific builder class is assigned to each search profile type. This is used to index the attributes of this search profile type.

You assign fields of an information category to a search profile type to define the structure of the search profile of a given search profile type or to specify which data of an object in SAP E-Recruiting can be found.

An information category is used for grouping fields belonging to a specific infotype or business partner. Each information category is assigned a structure, a content extraction class, and an object type. The structure indicates which fields are available in the information category. The object type assignment plays a role when defining search template elements and when assigning information category fields to a search profile type. When a search profile of a given search profile type is generated or updated, the content extraction class uses the builder class to fill the fields with data of the objects assigned.

Figure 7.4 shows how all of these concepts relate to each other. Both the search profiles and search templates are configured in the IMG path SAP E-RECRUITING • RECRUITMENT • TALENT WAREHOUSE • CANDIDATE • CANDIDATE SEARCH.

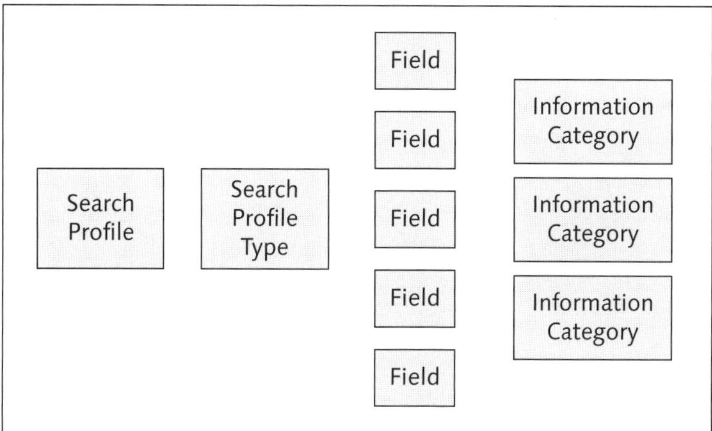

Figure 7.4 Search Profile, Search Profile Type, Fields, and Information Categories

7.4 Summary

We reviewed the search capabilities available within SAP E-Recruiting. SAP's search engine TREX — and the SES interface — enables recruiters, candidates, and so on to search for data stored in SAP E-Recruiting such as candidates, requisitions, candidacies, and job postings.

In the next chapter, we discuss the important topic of integration.

Integration is one of SAP's hallmarks. Key touch points across applications and platforms allow data and processes to harmonize and become more efficient. SAP provides critical areas for integrating functionalities into its SAP E-Recruiting platform. This chapter explores the integration components relevant for SAP E-Recruiting and highlights interest areas specific to making the recruiting and on-boarding processes more robust.

8 Integration Components

Tight integration is one of SAP's most powerful offerings. Within SAP E-Recruiting, many key integration opportunities are available. Integration within SAP E-Recruiting allows recruitment processes to become better synchronized and data to be better utilized for employees, managers, HR, and HR recruitment professionals. In this chapter, we discuss integration on several levels. We first tackle one of the most important integration topics — instance strategy, or how best to architect and integrate the SAP ERP HCM and SAP E-Recruiting systems. This discussion will include the options available and details of the inbound and outbound processing of data between systems. We will then discuss integration of specific applications, such as Organizational Management and Qualification Management. We will discuss integration at a platform level as well, including functionalities available in Employee and Manager Self-Service.

Let's kick off our integration discussion at a macro level.

8.1 Overview

Figure 8.1 shows a diagram depicting the various integration components for SAP E-Recruiting. From an application perspective, the following SAP ERP HCM applications are available for integration with SAP-Recruiting:

- Personnel Administration (PA)
- Organizational Management (OM)
- Qualifications Catalog

- User Management
- Business Partner

From a platform perspective, the following delivery channels are supported:

- Employee and Manager Self-Service via the SAP NetWeaver Portal
- Careers website (i.e., website for external job seekers)
- Business Intelligence via SAP NetWeaver Business Warehouse

These platforms are represented on the left and right in the diagram.

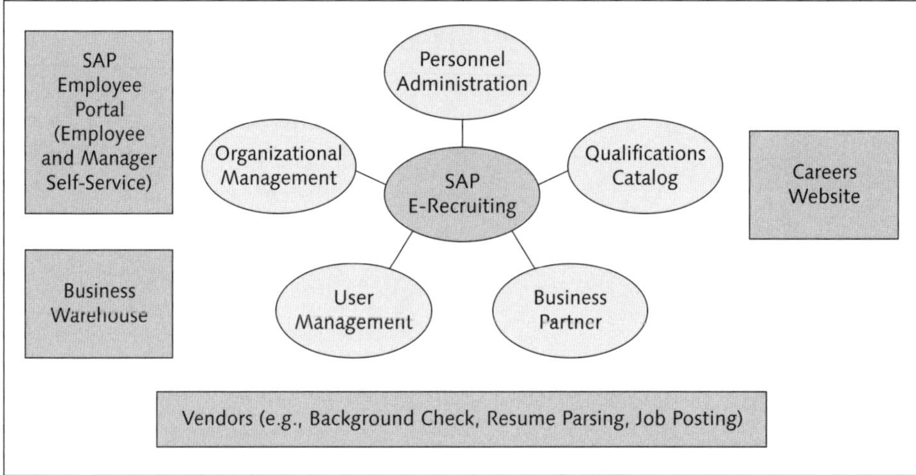

Figure 8.1 Integration Components of E-Recruiting

Vendor integration is also a key part of the recruiting end-to-end solution. Vendors providing services such as background checking, drug testing, resume parsing, and job board posting are often critical success factors for many implementations. We will discuss these vendor-specific services in the next chapter — Chapter 9, Vendor Services.

For now, let's review a critical integration consideration with respect to architecture. This decision will influence how your data is processed in the system.

8.2 Landscape and Data Integration

One of the most important integration decisions has a profound impact on the architect of your HR system landscape. The decision to deploy SAP E-Recruiting via a one- or two-instance model is a critical decision for the architecture of the solution. It also has profound impacts on how and when data is processed.

Figure 8.2 shows the one-instance model, whereby both the SAP ERP HCM and SAP E-Recruiting systems are housed within the same SAP system instance (i.e., in the same box). In this scenario, SAP NetWeaver components are implemented to support both the SAP ERP HCM and SAP E-Recruiting applications.

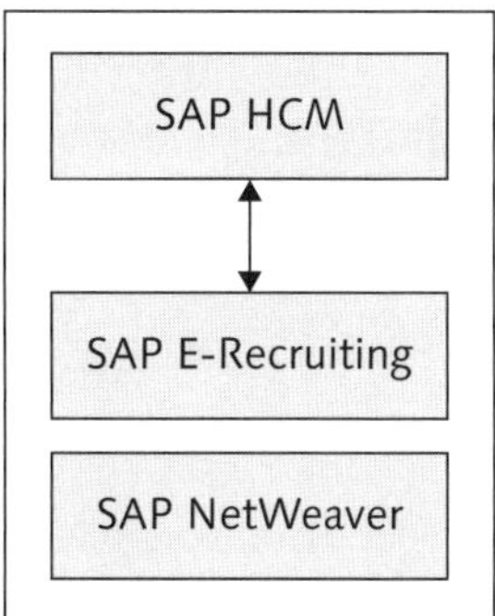

Figure 8.2 SAP E-Recruiting and SAP ERP HCM on the Same Instance

Figure 8.3 shows the two-instance (or stand-alone) model, whereby the SAP ERP HCM and SAP E-Recruiting systems are housed in two separate instances of the SAP system (i.e., in different boxes). Both are supported by the SAP NetWeaver stack — but on different instances of the SAP system.

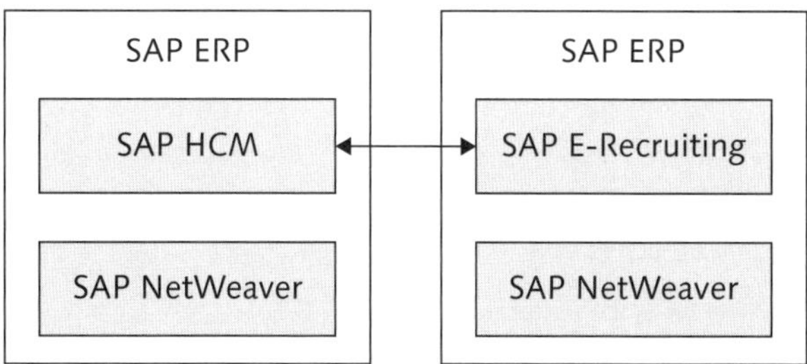

Figure 8.3 SAP E-Recruiting and SAP ERP HCM on Separate Instances

Although both scenarios are possible, we will assume a two-instance (stand-alone) approach in this chapter because the vast majority of implementations are deployed in this fashion. It is also our strong recommendation, based on experience, that you deploy with this architecture because several security and system performance risks are associated with the one-instance model. We will discuss this in further detail in our chapter on lessons learned, Chapter 12. For more information on a one-instance setup, you can reference SAP Note 997181 – ERP integration SAP E-Recruiting 600 and SAP ERP.

Assuming a stand-alone implementation of SAP E-Recruiting, let's first discuss the inbound processing of data.

8.2.1 Inbound Processing via ALE

The two-instance, or stand-alone, model relies heavily on the application link enabling (ALE) process to keep master data in sync between the SAP ERP HCM system and the SAP E-Recruiting system. Via the standard program RHALEINI (Transaction code PFAL), personnel and organizational information from the SAP ERP HCM is distributed to the SAP E-Recruiting system using iDocs (see Figure 8.4).

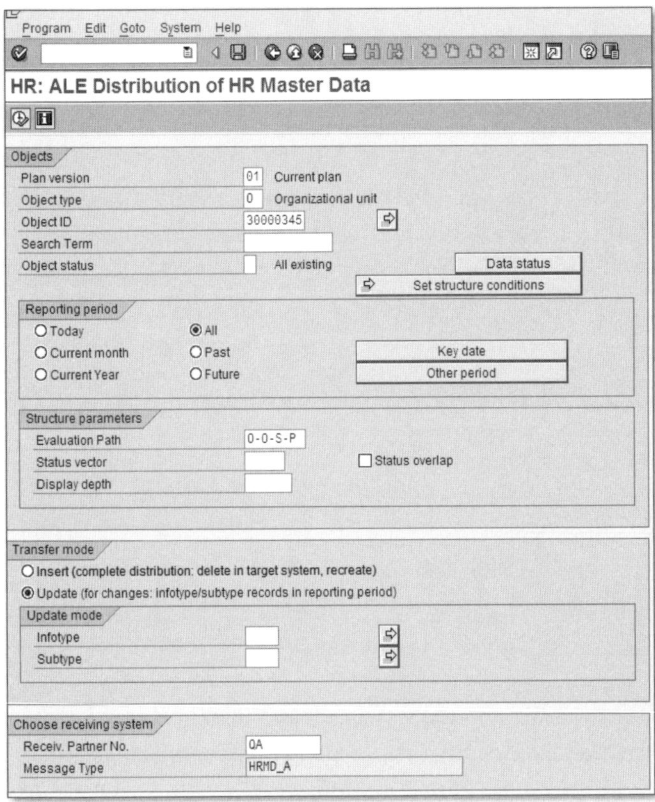

Figure 8.4 Transaction PFAL (ALE Distribution of HR Master Data)

With this program, the following objects are typically sent from SAP ERP HCM:

- Personnel number (P)
- Organizational unit (O)
- Position (S)
- Job (C)
- Qualification (Q)

After the initial loading of these objects into the SAP E-Recruiting system during cutover, you must work with your Basis team to establish so-called change pointers to capture all of the delta changes needed (e.g., new hires, changes in positions, etc.). The distribution can then be set up to only send delta updates to the SAP E-Recruiting system. Typically, several delta runs are established nightly (or more frequently) when the SAP ERP HCM system is not heavily used. The SAP E-Recruiting system receives the iDocs sent via the ALE process and processes them according to instructions from the distribution model and logic contained within several BAdIs (discussed later). Again, this distribution model must be completed in concert with a Basis resource via Transaction SALE.

When the iDocs are processed successfully, several objects are created and/or updated in the target system (i.e., the SAP E-Recruiting system). Figure 8.5 shows a relational data model including the linkages between the objects. In SAP E-Recruiting, a central person object (CP) is a critical component to the integration because it ties everything together. All candidates — whether external or internal — obtain a central person object. In addition, all candidates obtain a user (US) and business partner (BP) number. Only internal candidates have a personnel number (P) and position (S) — for good reason. The central person (CP) is linked to the candidate object (NA). All of these connections are created and kept in sync via the ALE communication mechanism established and reviewed previously.

To facilitate the creation and update of these objects in the SAP E-Recruiting system, several BAdIs are critical for the inbound processing logic. As of with enhancement pack 4, BAdI HRALE00SPLIT_INBOUND allows for inbound data to be manipulated for proper update within the SAP E-Recruiting system. Using the method POST_PROCESS_IDOC, the system is able to analyze and interpret any new and updated data received from the inbound iDOC. In EP4, the method DO_ALE_POST_PROCESSING of the class CL_HRRCF_ALE_EE_INBOUND is where much of the update resides. Up to enhancement pack 3, method HRRCF_CAND_FROM_EE_ALE of the class CL_HRRCF_EMPLOYEE_INBOUND was used for this updating logic. In enhancement pack 4, standard implementation HRRCF00_INBD_NEWMOD of BAdI HRALE00INBOUND_IDOC is used to assign the positions to the central persons (instead of keeping the positions linked to the personnel number). Up until release enhancement pack 3, standard implementation HRRCF00_DELETE_SPREL was used for this purpose.

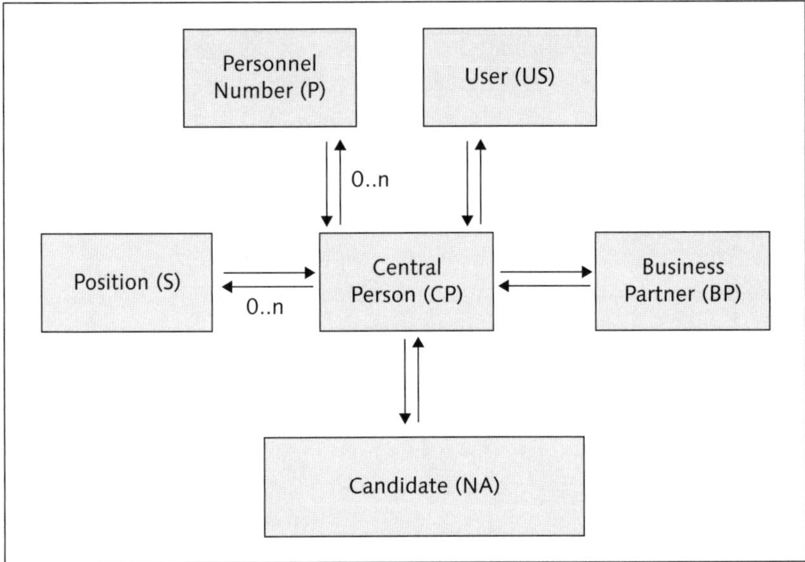

Figure 8.5 Objects Created in SAP E-Recruiting via ALE Integration

You can find information on these BAdIs (and general documentation of integration scenarios) in the IMG under the menu path SAP E-Recruiting • Technical Settings • SAP ERP Central Component (ECC) Integration.

Note

As of enhancement pack 4, the inbound ALE processing for SAP E-Recruiting has changed to accommodate concurrent employment scenarios (for customers who have implemented them).

In addition to the ALE setup mentioned previously, important customizing switches are needed within system table T77S0 for integration to work. Table 8.1 shows each of these switches, including a description of the capability.

Group	Semantic Abbreviation	Value	Description
HRALX	HRAC	X	Activates HR integration
HRALX	OBPON	ON	Activates O-BP integration
HRALX	PBPHR	ON	Distributes employees from connected HR system
HRALX	USRAC	X	Creates relationship to user
RECFA	HRRCF	Logical system; not required when using XI technology for the data transfer, but required for integration in organizational management	Logical system of the coupled HR system
RECFA	RECCE	Specifies whether concurrent employment (CE) is active in the SAP E-Recruiting system	Concurrent employment is active in the SAP E-Recruiting system (parameter is relevant as of Release 604)
RECFA	DTCBA	Logical system (required on the HR system side); not required when using XI technology for data transfer	RFC connection to the SAP E-Recruiting system

Table 8.1 System Table T77S0 Parameters for Integration Settings

In summary, SAP provides a robust solution for creating and updating data within the SAP E-Recruiting system based on changes occurring in SAP ERP HCM. Using standard ALE functionality, iDocs are sent from the source system (SAP ERP HCM) to the target system (SAP E-Recruiting) on a set batch schedule established based on business need (typically every day at minimum). On the SAP E-Recruiting side, the data is parsed, and necessary updates are made via the logic housed within the specific BAdI implementations mentioned previously. This keeps employee and organizational information in sync between the two systems and maintains data integrity.

In addition to the inbound integration, there is also an important outbound integration component — data transfer. The data transfer of candidate data back to the SAP ERP HCM system is a critical piece of the process because it completes the end-to-end process by facilitating the on-boarding process, which we'll talk about now.

8.2.2 Outbound Data Transfer

Data transfer is one of the more mission-critical pieces of the solution because it closes the loop on the process. Gaining process efficiencies from the data transfer activity (and follow-up processes) is an important step in achieving the return on investment (ROI) sought from your recruitment implementation. Enabling data transfer to occur allows important indicative data on candidates to be sent to the HR system.

There are two ways of integrating the data transfer scenario:

- Data transfer via remote function call (RFC)
- Data transfer via SAP Exchange Infrastructure (XI)

With data transfer via RFC, candidate information is sent via a remote function call from the SAP E-Recruiting system to your SAP ERP HCM system. To set up the RFC connection, follow the IMG path SAP E-Recruiting • Recruitment • Applicant Tracking • Activities • Set Up Data Transfer for New Employees • Set Up RFC Connection. This should be performed by a Basis professional in your organization. If the RFC method is selected, you must ensure that the logical system of your SAP ERP HCM system is specific in table T77S0, group RECFA, semantic abbreviation HRRFC. You can perform the IMG activity under the IMG path SAP E-Recruiting • Recruitment • Applicant Tracking • Activities • Set Up Data Transfer for New Employees • Set Up System Parameters.

From Transaction PA48 (Figure 8.6), you can perform a hiring (or promotion/transfer/lateral) action, and the candidate is hired as an employee. This action is essentially just the normal HR action that prepopulates the information from storage table T752F. The normal processing of infotypes is performed via the infogroup and infogroup modifier configuration. At the end of the action, a call is made to function module HR_RCF_ASSIGN_EE_TO_CANDIDATE. This function informs the SAP E-Recruiting system that the candidate now has a personnel number. As a result, the system creates the CP to P relationship, linking the personnel number to the candidate. The candidate remains an external candidate until the ALE inbound processing discussed previously is performed.

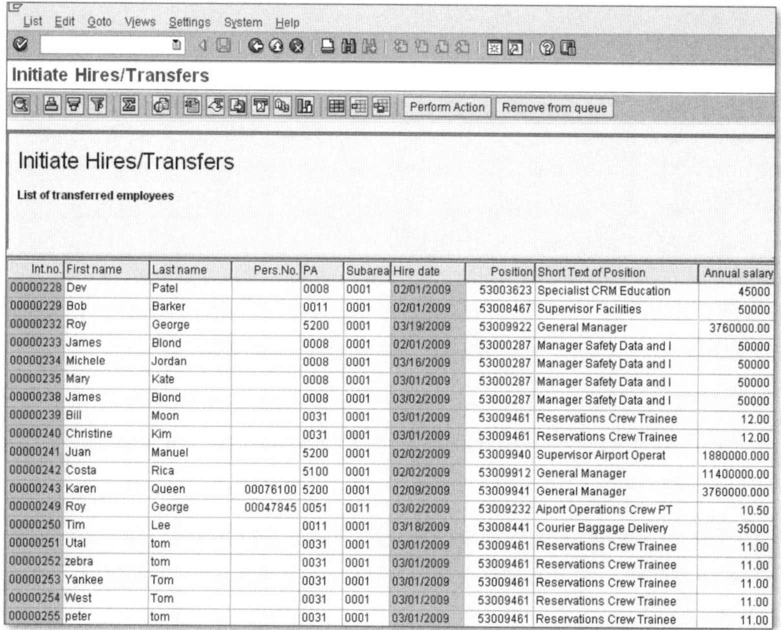

Int.no.	First name	Last name	Pers.No.	PA	Subarea	Hire date	Position	Short Text of Position	Annual salary
00000228	Dev	Patel		0008	0001	02/01/2009	53003623	Specialist CRM Education	45000
00000229	Bob	Barker		0011	0001	02/01/2009	53008467	Supervisor Facilities	50000
00000232	Roy	George		5200	0001	03/19/2009	53009922	General Manager	3760000.00
00000233	James	Blond		0008	0001	02/01/2009	53000287	Manager Safety Data and I	50000
00000234	Michele	Jordan		0008	0001	03/16/2009	53000287	Manager Safety Data and I	50000
00000235	Mary	Kate		0008	0001	03/01/2009	53000287	Manager Safety Data and I	50000
00000238	James	Blond		0008	0001	03/02/2009	53000287	Manager Safety Data and I	50000
00000239	Bill	Moon		0031	0001	03/01/2009	53009461	Reservations Crew Trainee	12.00
00000240	Christine	Kim		0031	0001	03/01/2009	53009461	Reservations Crew Trainee	12.00
00000241	Juan	Manuel		5200	0001	02/02/2009	53009940	Supervisor Airport Operat	1880000.000
00000242	Costa	Rica		5100	0001	02/02/2009	53009912	General Manager	11400000.00
00000243	Karen	Queen	00076100	5200	0001	02/09/2009	53009941	General Manager	3760000.000
00000249	Roy	George	00047845	0051	0011	03/02/2009	53009232	Aiport Operations Crew PT	10.50
00000250	Tim	Lee		0011	0001	03/18/2009	53008441	Courier Baggage Delivery	35000
00000251	Utal	tom		0031	0001	03/01/2009	53009461	Reservations Crew Trainee	11.00
00000252	zebra	tom		0031	0001	03/01/2009	53009461	Reservations Crew Trainee	11.00
00000253	Yankee	Tom		0031	0001	03/01/2009	53009461	Reservations Crew Trainee	11.00
00000254	West	Tom		0031	0001	03/01/2009	53009461	Reservations Crew Trainee	11.00
00000255	peter	tom		0031	0001	03/01/2009	53009461	Reservations Crew Trainee	11.00

Figure 8.6 Transaction PA48

The other option is data transfer via SAP XI, although more is involved in its initial setup and ongoing operation. In this scenario, the SAP XI server receives a message from the SAP E-Recruiting system, and a work item is created for an HR administrator to process. Once the employee is hired successfully (and an SAP XI message is sent back to the SAP E-Recruiting system), the system calls the same function module HR_RCF_ASSIGN_EE_TO_CANDIDATE to sync up the CP and P relationship. Again, the ALE process must run to perform the rest of the processing.

Using the data transfer via SAP XI method, you must ensure that several items are activated, implemented, or configured:

- Ensure that the switch is activated for SAP XI in table T77S0, group RECFA, semantic abbreviation HRXI. You can perform the IMG activity under following IMG path SAP E-Recruiting • Recruitment • Applicant Tracking • Activities • Set Up Data Transfer for New Employees • Set Up System Parameters.
- Download and import the SAP XI content to support the HCM Processes and Forms solution. You can see the latest available content on the Software Developer Network (SDN) site at *http://www.sdn.sap.com/irj/sdn/netweaver*. To use the SAP XI content, you must import it into the Integration Repository. SAP Note 836200 contains important information on this download and import process.

The SAP XI scenarios used need to be configured, so having an SAP XI expert on your team would be a great benefit to the project.

- Define, activate, and schedule the periodic service HIRE_REQUEST_VIA_XI. This is defined in the customizing activities SAP E-RECRUITING • TECHNICAL SETTINGS • PERIODIC SERVICES • DEFINE PERIODIC SERVICES and SAP E-RECRUITING • TECHNICAL SETTINGS • PERIODIC SERVICES • ACTIVATE PERIODIC SERVICES. This enables the service class CL_HRRCF_HIRE_REQUEST_XI.
- Review workflow templates WS17900415 and WS17900015 and associated tasks. These are the workflows that are instantiated when the inbound communication is received by the XI message and processing is started.

In either the RFC or SAP XI data transfer scenario, candidate data can be sent in real time from the SAP E-Recruiting system to the SAP ERP HCM system. Depending on your existing business (and existing technical landscape and capabilities), your approach may differ. For example, if you have not yet implemented HCM Processes and Forms and do not have SAP XI set up, it may be best to use the RFC method until the other technologies are implemented and/or configured. Most customers have implemented data transfer through RFC (or an enhanced version), but as the HCM Processes and Forms technology becomes more prevalent with SAP customers, this may change over time.

Another important aspect of data integration at the employee level that concerns status updates (such as terminations and rehires) need to be considered. We will discuss this next.

8.2.3 Status Updates

The proper handling of employee status updates is another important part of keeping in sync the data in the SAP ERP HCM and SAP E-Recruiting systems. Some possible status update scenarios include when an employee is terminated, rehired, or goes on leave of absence. Also, the handling of future dated actions is needed.

To synchronize these employee events, periodic service PROCESS_CAND_STATUS_CHANGE is available. Using this periodic service, an indicator based on the employee's employment status (field STAT2 on infotype 0000) is stored in table T77RCF_P_STAT. If an employee is planning a retirement in the future, the E-Recruiting system updates the indicator table T77RCF_P_STAT based on that future-dated status change. The periodic service via class CL_HRRCF_UPDATE_P_

STAT sweeps this table and takes the appropriate actions (e.g., update the user master record with the appropriate authorizations).

Note

If you use concurrent employment, all of an employee's personnel numbers must be inactive for SAP E-Recruiting to recognize that the employee is an inactive employee.

We have now seen the mechanism that SAP uses to process status changes. Let's discuss further integration considerations, specifically, those concerning organizational management objects.

8.2.4 Integration with Organizational Management

Organizational management (OM) is typically a popular area for integration within SAP ERP HCM, and SAP E-Recruiting is no different. SAP has provided the capability to select which organizational management objects (and relationships) should be available for synchronization between SAP ERP HCM and SAP E-Recruiting. Extractors collect this data into so-called integration units. You can integrate these integration units and synchronize only the data you need based on your business requirements.

You can also define your own integration units and fill them using extractors. (If custom integration units are used, you should work within the customer namespace and begin with the number 9. Custom extractors may be needed for any custom objects and relationships sent to the SAP E-Recruiting system.) The menu path for customizing integration units in the IMG is SAP E-Recruiting • Technical Settings • SAP ERP Central Component (ECC) Integration • Set Up Integration with SAP Organizational Management. Figure 8.7 shows this configuration. The Integrated checkbox must be selected for the integration units to flow over. Notice that all extractor classes start with the prefix CL_HRRCF_OIX_*.

Qualifications are an important part of talent management strategy. They provide a linkage between many areas of talent management including recruiting, succession planning, and performance management. With SAP E-Recruiting, you can choose to integrate qualifications from the SAP ERP HCM system (from its qualification catalog) or manage them separately.

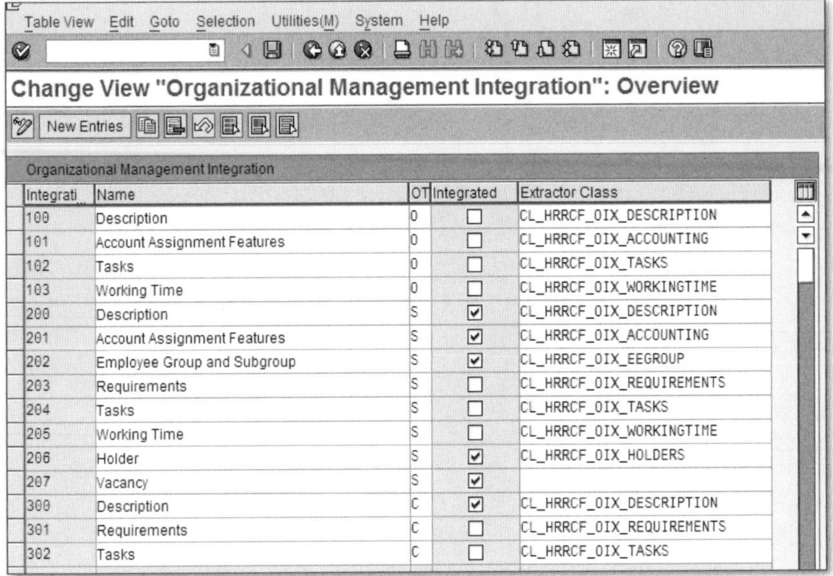

Integrati...	Name	OT	Integrated	Extractor Class
100	Description	O	☐	CL_HRRCF_OIX_DESCRIPTION
101	Account Assignment Features	O	☐	CL_HRRCF_OIX_ACCOUNTING
102	Tasks	O	☐	CL_HRRCF_OIX_TASKS
103	Working Time	O	☐	CL_HRRCF_OIX_WORKINGTIME
200	Description	S	☑	CL_HRRCF_OIX_DESCRIPTION
201	Account Assignment Features	S	☑	CL_HRRCF_OIX_ACCOUNTING
202	Employee Group and Subgroup	S	☑	CL_HRRCF_OIX_EEGROUP
203	Requirements	S	☐	CL_HRRCF_OIX_REQUIREMENTS
204	Tasks	S	☐	CL_HRRCF_OIX_TASKS
205	Working Time	S	☐	CL_HRRCF_OIX_WORKINGTIME
206	Holder	S	☑	CL_HRRCF_OIX_HOLDERS
207	Vacancy	S	☑	
300	Description	C	☑	CL_HRRCF_OIX_DESCRIPTION
301	Requirements	C	☐	CL_HRRCF_OIX_REQUIREMENTS
302	Tasks	C	☐	CL_HRRCF_OIX_TASKS

Figure 8.7 Organizational Management Integration

Depending on whether you decide to integrate (or "distribute") qualifications, you must make various settings in the configuration. In table T77SO, group RECFA, semantic abbreviation HRQUA, you determine how qualifications can be maintained in SAP E-Recruiting and how they are to be used for recruitment purposes. You can perform the IMG activity under the IMG path SAP E-RECRUITING • TECHNICAL SETTINGS • SET UP SYSTEM PARAMETERS.

- If you set RECFA HRQUA to blank, qualifications for internal candidates can be maintained in the SAP E-Recruiting system. This only includes the qualification groups from the SAP qualifications catalog that are assigned to the SAP_ERECRUITING view for SAP E-Recruiting. A prerequisite for this qualification is that employees from your HR system are *not* distributed in the SAP E-Recruiting system.
- If you set RECFA HRQUA to X, qualifications for internal candidates cannot be maintained in the SAP E-Recruiting system. The distributed qualifications are all included for recruitment and succession planning purposes. A prerequisite for this is that qualifications for employees from the HR system are distributed in the SAP E-Recruiting system. It is possible to distribute qualifications only they are synchronized between Organizational Management and SAP E-Recruiting. To do this, you must integrate integration units 203 and 301 via the IMG

menu path SAP E-RECRUITING • TECHNICAL SETTINGS • SAP ERP CENTRAL COMPONENT (ECC) INTEGRATION • SET UP INTEGRATION WITH SAP ORGANIZATIONAL MANAGEMENT.

- If you set RECFA HRQUA to EREC_VIEW, qualifications for internal candidates cannot be maintained in the SAP E-Recruiting system. Only the distributed qualifications that are assigned to the SAP_ERECRUITING view for SAP E-Recruiting are included for recruitment purposes. (A prerequisite is that the qualifications for employees from the HR system are distributed in the SAP E-Recruiting system.)

Note

Regardless of the setup of this switch, qualifications for external candidates can always be maintained in the SAP E-Recruiting system. This only includes the qualification groups from the SAP qualifications catalog (Transaction OOQA) that are assigned to the SAP_ERECRUITING view for SAP E-Recruiting. You set up this view using the IMG menu path SAP E-RECRUITING • RECRUITMENT • TALENT WAREHOUSE • CANDIDATE • QUALIFICATIONS • RESTRICT VIEW OF QUALIFICATIONS CATALOG.

If you decide to distribute qualifications, you must sync the qualification catalog using the ALE distribution Transaction PFAL described earlier in the chapter. Use evaluation path QUALCATA. The top node qualification group (QK) should be identified as the root object for transfer. This ensures that all qualifications that roll up to that qualification group are included in the iDOC that is distributed to the SAP E-Recruiting system.

Let's now discuss some other areas of integration.

8.2.5 Other Integration Areas

Other important areas of integration include user management and business partners. We will discuss user management — the creation, maintenance, and provisioning of users and roles — in detail in Chapter 10, Authorization Management. We will discuss user administration topics including service users, reference users, and roles in that chapter.

The business partner (BP) object exists in the system for many different purposes outside of HR. Within SAP E-Recruiting, the business partner object is used to represent a variety of different actors in the process including:

- Employees (internal candidates)
- Outside job seekers (external candidates)

- Company branches
- Vendors

You must configure the business partner number ranges must be configured in the IMG under the menu path SAP E-RECRUITING • TECHNICAL SETTINGS • SAP BUSINESS PARTNER • DEFINE NUMBER RANGES. In this activity, you specify the number ranges needed. The business partner number range must also be grouped and identified as external or internal. For SAP E-Recruiting, the Business Partner object should be an internal number range. You perform this configuration in the IMG under the menu path SAP E-RECRUITING • TECHNICAL SETTINGS • SAP BUSINESS PARTNER • DEFINE GROUPINGS AND ASSIGN NUMBER RANGES.

Now, let's discuss integration from a platform perspective.

8.3 Platform Integration

Understanding how the SAP E-Recruiting solution is implemented across delivery environments is an integral part of any team's success. It is important to understand that, although you may have a stand-alone model for your SAP E-Recruiting architecture, this does not mean the process will be disjointed. In fact, SAP provides several robust mediums, including SAP NetWeaver Portal, SAP NetWeaver Business Warehouse, and your external careers website, to provide a mechanism with which to deliver the recruitment functionality.

The first area of platform integration we will discuss is Employee and Manager Self-Service.

8.3.1 Employee and Manager Self-Service

Employee Self-Service (ESS) and Manager Self-Service (MSS) provide a service delivery channel for employees and managers to participate in recruitment processes via the SAP NetWeaver Portal. The Employee Self-Service Business Package 1.41 contains several prepackaged iViews ready for deployment into your SAP NetWeaver Portal. The workset contained in this business packaged is called Career and Job. Within this workset, employees can use the functionality to:

- Maintain their candidate profiles
- Display an overview of the data in the candidate profiles
- Release candidate profiles
- Apply directly to a job posting

- Search for suitable jobs
- Display a list of job postings that they have stored as favorites
- Send applications
- Store personal settings

The technical name of the employee workset is *com.sap.pct.erp.ess.area_career_job*. All iViews within this workset are dependent on Home Page Framework (HPF) configuration. The following services are available in the configuration for the HPF:

- EMPLOYEE_CANDIDATE_APPLICATIONS_SERVICE
- EMPLOYEE_CANDIDATE_DATA_OVERVIEW
- EMPLOYEE_CANDIDATE_DIRECT_APPL_SERVICE
- EMPLOYEE_CANDIDATE_FAVORITES_SERVICE
- EMPLOYEE_CANDIDATE_PERSONAL_SETTINGS
- EMPLOYEE_CANDIDATE_PROFILE_RELEASE
- EMPLOYEE_CANDIDATE_PROFILE_SERVICE
- EMPLOYEE_CANDIDATE_SEARCH_JOBS_SERVICE.

Note

For more information on Home Page Framework and Employee and Manager Self-Service in general, please reference the SAP PRESS book *Implementing Employee and Manager Self-Services in SAP ERP HCM* written by Jeremy Masters and Christos Kotsakis.

Besides employees, managers can also engage in several recruitment activities. SAP provides many standard self-service applications for managers. The following services are available for managers in the latest Manager Self-Service Business Package (SAP ERP 1.41):

- **Process browser**
  Provides an overview of all of the requisition requests that the manager initiates.
- **Requisition monitor**
  Provides an overview of all requisitions that have been initiated through requisition requests, that are edited as a substitute, or that were assigned to the manager by a recruiter.

- **Questionnaires**
  View and edit questionnaires. A manager can use these questionnaires to provide recruiters with feedback about candidates.
- **Candidacy assessment**
  Assess candidates with regard to a requisition.
- **Candidate assessment**
  Assess candidates with regard to the talent pool.
- **Create requisition request**
  Create, edit, and send a requisition request to a higher-level manager for approval.
- **Maintain substitute**
  Maintain substitutes that can assume tasks for planned or unplanned absences. Depending on the substitution type selected, these substitutes can create new requisition requests or assess candidates. The manager can add new substitutes and edit or delete existing substitutes.

Please see Chapter 4, Requisition Management, for a more detailed explanation of Manager Self-Service activities. The new services provided for managers allow for a more robust platform of service delivery for the SAP E-Recruiting solution.

Let's now turn to integration considerations for those using SAP NetWeaver Business Warehouse.

8.3.2 SAP NetWeaver Business Warehouse

The functionality available within SAP NetWeaver Business Warehouse can provide robust analytical capabilities for managers, HR professionals, and executives. Available SAP NetWeaver Business Warehouse (also called Business Intelligence) content can provide recruiting managers with robust reporting and statistics, including the following standard queries:

- Requisition status changes
- Requisitions created
- Number of open requisitions
- Time-to-fill
- Offer versus acceptance rate
- Interview versus offer rate

- Application submittal versus offers
- Application source
- Candidate's qualifications
- Application submittal versus offers
- Offer versus acceptance rate

The delivery of these queries is achieved through the SAP NetWeaver Portal. Managers can log onto the portal and obtain business warehouse content. We will discuss more about SAP NetWeaver Business Warehouse and its capability within SAP E-Recruiting in Chapter 11, Reporting.

Let's now talk about the delivery channel for external job seekers — via your company's external careers website.

8.3.3 Careers Website

Most companies post job opportunities on their corporate website. For most corporations, a careers section on the website is a common place to advertise exciting careers for outside job seekers.

One of the most challenging parts of implementing SAP E-Recruiting for your external careers website may be branding the site. Most organizations take branding very seriously. Deviation from the company's look and feel and user experience is typically not accepted by communications and e-business teams who have worked hard to maintain the company brand on the website.

Whether you are implementing the Business Server Page (BSP) or Web Dynpro for ABAP version of the candidate interface, you need to invest time and resources on its look and feel to match (or match as closely as possible) your company's external website. You may need to match the style sheets from your website to more accurately reflect font, style, and colors. Although this is possible with the right technical expertise, it is more difficult to change the navigation and taxonomy from the standard SAP delivery. If you are looking to do so, you need to invest the proper development resources in the project and understand what it means from a support perspective after implementation. Do not underestimate the project resources needed to perform these enhancements.

To conclude this chapter, let's briefly discuss vendor services.

8.4 Vendor Integration

Integration with third-party vendors provides another opportunity to take advantage of the SAP platform. The selection of and relationship to these vendors can be one of the more important parts of the implementation because the success of the project is dependent on the competency level of the vendors and their ongoing ability to deliver their services efficiently and cost-effectively. The following four vendor types are typically integrated with SAP E-Recruiting:

- Background checks
- Drug testing
- Resume parsing
- Job board posting

We consider the integration with these vendors a critical success factor for any implementation. To that end, we have dedicated the next chapter, Chapter 10, to vendor services.

8.5 Summary

We reviewed many integration components of SAP E-Recruiting in this chapter. We also reviewed landscape options (one-instance versus standalone) and the importance of the ALE process to distribute objects from SAP ERP HCM to the E-Recruiting system. And, we looked at other important integration components including organizational management and qualifications. In the next chapter, we will turn our focus to vendor products and the integration considerations inherent to them.

Integrating services such as resume parsing, drug testing, and background checks into SAP E-Recruiting offers important functionalities and recruitment implementations. In this chapter, we will explain these vendor services and how their integration can be configured and implemented in SAP E-Recruiting. We will also explain the best practices involved in implementing these services and highlight new features available in enhancement package 4.

9 Vendor Services

Many SAP E-Recruiting customers have to conduct background checks and drug tests prior to hiring a candidate. In some countries, it is a legal requirement that the candidate be able to pass a background check and drug test prior to on-boarding. If the candidate fails the drug test or the background check, the organization can rescind or withdraw the offer (even after it is made).

SAP E-Recruiting can interact with vendors who provide these services — both synchronously and asynchronously. The recruiter can initiate a background check and drug test for the candidate by sending a request to the vendor from the SAP E-Recruiting system. On completion of the tests, the vendors can send the results to the SAP E-Recruiting system, which notifies the recruiter.

> **Note**
>
> Asynchronous communication is when a system can communicate and/or send details to another system without expecting an immediate response.
>
> Synchronous communication is when a system can communicate and/or send details to another and expect a response immediately.

Many customers also offer resume parsing either as a third-party add-on or as a vendor service to ease the creation and entry of candidate profiles. Resume parsing is not always an accurate technology and sometimes requires human intervention and validation to check the accuracy of the parsed resume.

Please note that it is not a prerequisite to configure a background check, drug test, or resume parsing services for a successful SAP E-Recruiting go-live. A recruiter can still initiate the drug test or background check for a candidate outside the SAP E-Recruiting system and record the results in the candidate profile.

If your organization does not have business or legal requirements to conduct background checks and/or drug tests on the candidate, you need not initiate these services. Resume parsing is a part of many implementations but is theoretically "nice-to-have" because candidates can update their information from their resumes manually on the candidate profile in the system.

Let's explain each of these services in detail along with the customizing steps required for the configuration. We will start with resume parsing.

9.1 Resume Parsing

In SAP E-Recruiting you can offer the candidate resume parsing during candidate registration and creation of the candidate profile. Unregistered candidates can use resume parsing during application process.

The resume parsing tool parses the candidate resume and automatically fills the data in the candidate profile interface. The resume parsing tool extracts data from a number of file formats and outputs the data in HR-XML, HTML, or text and stores the resume in the original format in which it was received.

Resume parsing is a very attractive tool to offer to candidates. It greatly reduces the time required to create the candidate profile and enhances the candidate experience.

Note

Talent Technology (*www.talenttech.com*) is one of SAP's certified providers of resume parsing. Their product, Resume Mirror, complies with OFCCP (OFCCP is relevant for United States only) and data privacy laws. Resume Mirror can handle multiple resume attachments, extract resumes from over 85 file formats, and provide built-in antivirus and reporting capabilities.

If your resume parsing tool is integrated into SAP E-Recruiting, the candidate uploads the resume into the SAP E-Recruiting user interface (see Figure 9.1), and the resume parsing engine parses the candidate's resume and fills the candidate's profile with the data extracted from the resume. In enhancement package 4, the recruiter can parse the candidate's (internal or external) resume by using the resume parsing engine integrated into SAP E-Recruiting or by sending the resume to an external vendor who provides resume parsing services.

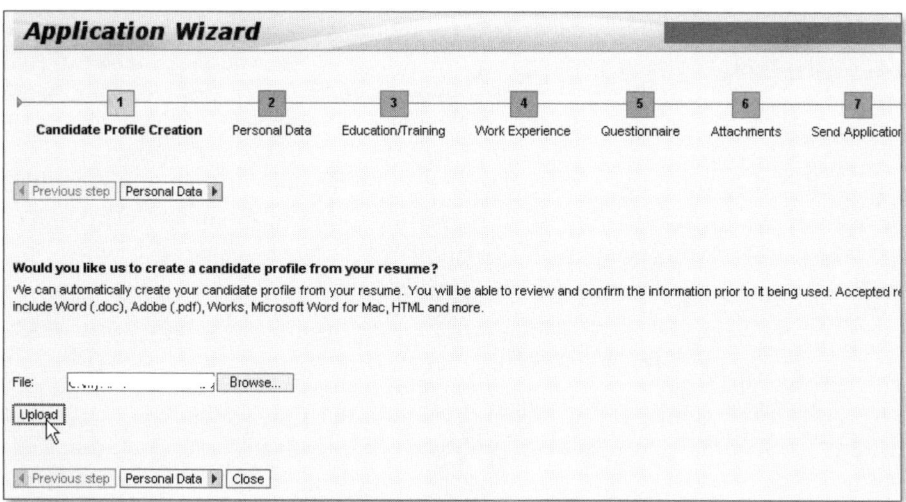

Figure 9.1 Resume Parsing – Candidate Interface

If your organization uses an external vendor to provide resume parsing, communication in real time (*synchronous communication*) is possible. SAP E-Recruiting sends the resume to be parsed to the vendor as an attachment. The vendor parses the resume and sends the parsed data to the SAP E-Recruiting system. The SAP E-Recruiting system creates the required objects and saves the formatted resume. The resume parsing engine should be integrated into SAP E-Recruiting for resume parsing to be available to the candidates. If the resume parsing engine is not integrated into the SAP E-Recruiting system, your organization should retain a resume parsing vendor for the recruiter to be able to send candidates' resume for parsing. When the resume parsing vendor sends back the resume after parsing, you can determine in what format the parsed resume needs to be presented to the candidate. This presentation of the parsed resume in a certain format (PDF, for example) is called a *formatted resume*.

So let's discuss the configuration necessary to provide resume parsing in your SAP E-Recruiting system.

9.1.1 Customizing Steps

To be able to perform resume parsing in SAP E-Recruiting and display the required fields in the candidate interface, you must complete several activities in the IMG. The menu path for customizing is SAP E-Recruiting • Technical Settings • User Interfaces • Administrator and Recruiter • General Settings • Assign Values to Interface Parameters. The interface parameter USE_RSP should have a value X. This displays the resume parsing fields in the candidate interface (both external and internal). If the parameter USE_RSP has no value, the resume parsing fields are hidden.

You can also customize the settings to display the original resume or the formatted resume. To display the formatted resume, the interface parameter DISPLAY_RESUME should have a value of F. The standard-delivered value is X, which displays the original resume. The menu path for customizing is SAP E-Recruiting • Technical Settings • User Interfaces • Administrator and Recruiter • General Settings • Assign Values to Interface Parameters.

If you are using a third-party vendor for resume parsing, you need to maintain a business partner role (BP) and business partner information for the vendor. Execute this customizing activity by following the menu path SAP E-Recruiting • Technical Settings • SAP Business Partner • Define Business Partner Role for Vendors.

If resume parsing is integrated into the system and you want candidates to maintain their resumes via resume parsing only, you set the parameter FILTER_CAND_ORIG_RSM to X. This means candidates cannot upload resumes as attachments; the Resume attachment type is not available for selection. The menu path for this customizing activity is SAP E-Recruiting • Technical Settings • User Interfaces • Candidate • Backend Candidate • Assign Values to Interface Parameters (WebDynpro ABAP).

If you want to provide functionality for unregistered candidates to parse their resumes via the application wizard, you must set parameter RSP_IN_UNREG_AWZD to X. For this customizing activity, follow the menu path SAP E-Recruiting • Technical Settings • User Interfaces • Candidate • Backend Candidate • Assign Values to Interface Parameters (WebDynpro ABAP).

If resume parsing is integrated in the SAP E-Recruiting system, you must perform the customizing step where the resume parsing interface is integrated into the candidate's start page (second-level navigation). The menu path for this customizing activity is SAP E-Recruiting • Technical Settings • User Interfaces • Candidate • Flexibilization • Back End • Start Pages • Create Structuring Elements for Second Level.

You can implement a custom BAdI implementation to confirm that the parsed resume is not a duplicate. The SAP-delivered BAdI HRRCF00_GET_DUPL_EXT_CAND prevents multiple candidates being created for the same person. You can customize the delivered BAdI to include time logic and implement an extended duplicate check. If the time parameter is set to 30 days, the BAdI checks Infotype 5102 (Candidate Information) to determine the date on which the candidate profile was last changed. If nobody has changed the candidate profile in the past 30 days, the system does not consider the parsed resume to be a duplicate. This is an example implementation, and other logic can be instituted with a custom implementation of the BAdI based on your business requirements.

SAP E-Recruiting stores the parsed resumes in cluster tables. The system deletes the resume from the cluster tables after the recruiter reviews the resume and accepts or declines it.

9.1.2 Review Parsed Resumes

In the Recruiter Work Center, the recruiter can click on the link Parsed Resumes To Review (see Figure 9.2) to review the parsed resumes sent by the vendor. In this step, the recruiter can accept or decline the parsed resumes. The recruiter can review the parsed resumes he receives for both his requisitions and application groups. In the detail screen (not shown), the recruiter can also modify the data populated by the resume parsing. Decline and accept actions are available for mass processing as well.

Active Queries

Requisitions	My Open Requisitions (5)	Open Team Requisitions (19)	Open Application Groups (0)	My Draft Requisitions (1)	All Requisitions (27)
Postings	My Expiring Postings (0)	Expiring Team Postings (0)			
My Tasks	Open Background Checks (0)	Parsed Resumes To Review (0)			

Figure 9.2 Delivered Queries

Note

Review SAP Note 1122135, which describes how to implement resume parsing in SAP E-Recruiting. This SAP Note describes the customizing steps you need to complete and the flexibilization you need to perform in the candidate start page to implement a resume parsing solution.

For registered candidates, resume parsing greatly reduces the time required to complete the candidate profile. For unregistered candidates, it reduces the time required to submit applications. In the next section, we will talk about another critical vendor service within the recruiting process — background checks. We will discuss options for how to best integrate SAP E-Recruiting with vendors who provide this service.

9.2 Background Checks

With SAP E-Recruiting, you can integrate your system with third-party vendors who provide background checks. By integrating SAP E-Recruiting with these vendors, background check data related to the candidate can be prepopulated in the vendor system. This provides the benefit of data accuracy and minimizes errors of dual entry. The recruiter or the HR personnel who initiated the background checks can request a status update during the processing and receive the results on completion of the background checks.

HireRight (*www.hireright.com*) is an SAP-authorized vendor that provides background checks and drug tests. When you integrate HireRight with your SAP E-Recruiting system, you can also implement single sign-on (SSO) into the HireRight system, if desired. The HireRight system is service-oriented architecture (SOA)-based and HR-XML compliant.

Let's review the processing steps involved in a typical background check.

9.2.1 Processing Steps

Within the Recruiter Work Center in the Requisitions – My Open Requisitions free list display, click on the Offering column of the requisition for the candidate for whom you want to initiate the background check.

In the Assignments for Requisition interface, select the candidate for whom you want to initiate the background check. Click on the Activities button and select the Reference/Background Check activity (see Figure 9.3). In the Create Activity dialog box, complete the details about the activity and click on the OK button to accept your entries. This executes the workflow to initiate the background check for the candidate.

As of in enhancement pack 4, there is a standard-delivered Open Background Checks query is available within the Recruiter Work Center. This query displays all candidates for whom a background check is initiated and for whom the final result is not assigned. Using this query, the recruiter can check on the status. On receipt of the results from the vendor, the recruiter can select Final Result and enter any required notes for the candidate. If the final status is assigned for the candidate, the activity is set to Completed status.

As mentioned, HireRight is one of the integration vendors available for background checks. In the HireRight interface (see Figure 9.4), select the package and any add-on service that might be offered.

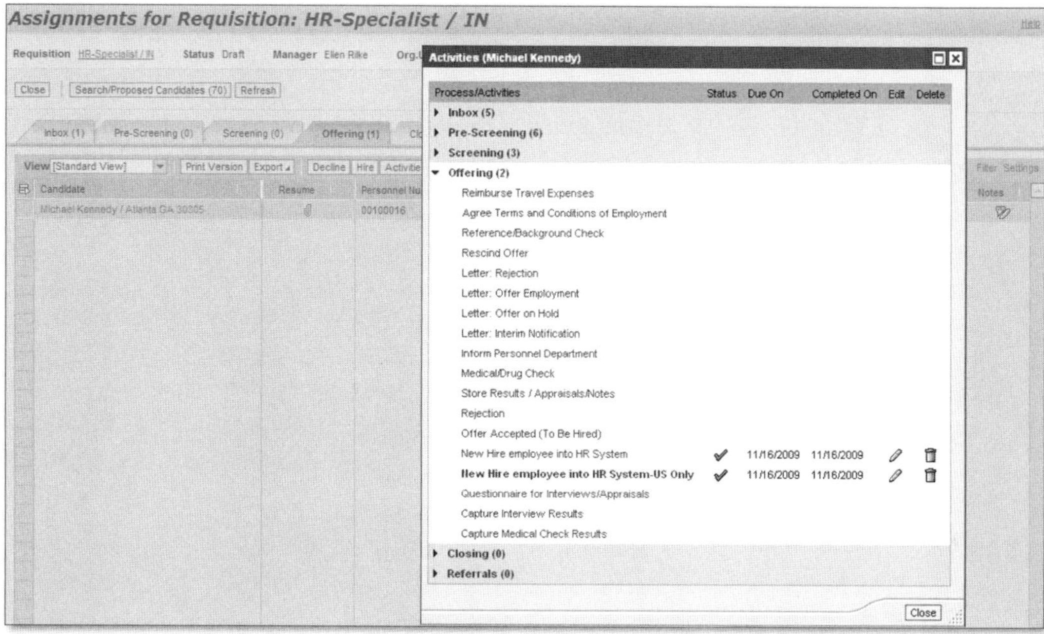

Figure 9.3 Create Background Check Activity

HireRight
Save Form | Save Form & Exit | Contact Us Print Cancel & Discard

1 DEFINE REQUEST
Select Package & Add-ons
2 COMPLETE FORMS
Select Form Completion Option
Provide Applicant Information
Education & Training
Self-Reported Convictions
Court Records Search Settings
3 COMPLETE REQUEST
Review Request
Submit

Background Request — Select Package & Add-on Services
Packages
Select Package * Basic Details
Order Details
Package Details
Criminal Felony & Misdemeanor
SSN Trace (1)
Education Report (1)
You can now include Add-on services from the list below.
As you add services, they will appear here.
Once you are finished adding services, click Next.
Please select Add-on services
Civil Records
Civil Upper & Lower
Civil Upper
Civil Lower

Figure 9.4 HireRight Interface

The recruiter can complete a form that is prepopulated with the candidate data from the SAP E-Recruiting system. Alternatively, the recruiter can send an email to the candidate inviting him to log in to the HireRight system and complete the forms (see Figure 9.5). Once the forms are completed and the order is submitted, HireRight initiates the process to start the background check on the candidate.

Figure 9.5 Invite Candidate to Complete Background Check Forms

At any time during the process, the recruiter or the HR employer who initiated the background check can log in to the HireRight system and get status updates about the background checks they have initiated for the candidate. A recruiter can also initiate background checks for multiple candidates (but only in an asynchronous mode). The background check package should be sent to the same vendor, and the candidates should be applying to the same requisition.

So, let's review the configuration activities necessary to integrate with a background check vendor.

9.2.2 Customizing Steps

The vendor providing the background check service needs to be maintained as a Business Partner in the SAP E-Recruiting system. The menu path for this customizing activity is SAP E-Recruiting • Technical Settings • SAP Business Partner • Define Business Partner Role for Vendors.

Another consideration for your implementation is what to do with duplicate activities during the background check process. You can leverage the standard delivered BAdI Enhancement for Background Check Duplicate Check to define what is to be considered as a duplicate. Most likely, there are situations when a recruiter has to reorder background checks for a candidate. In such circumstances, you can allow duplicates, but duplicates are allowed only for the same background vendor and package combination.

Note

In enhancement pack 3, you can initiate the activities Background Check Order, Background Check Order Status, and Background Check View in synchronous mode.

In enhancement pack 4, you can still initiate the activities Background Check Order, Background Check Order Status, and Background Check View synchronously, but the Background Check Order and Background Check Order Status activities can be initiated *asynchronously*. This means you can initiate the background check with the vendor in both a synchronous and asynchronous mode.

Integrating a background check vendor service to SAP E-Recruiting greatly reduces the time required to initiate the check. Integrating a drug test vendor service to SAP E-Recruiting is very similar. In the next section, we will explain how to integrate such a vendor.

9.3 Drug Testing

In SAP E-Recruiting, you can integrate with third-party vendors who provide drug testing. By integrating SAP E-Recruiting with these vendors, you can prepopulate drug test data related to the candidate in the vendor system. As with background checks, the benefit is improved data accuracy. The recruiter or the HR employee who initiated the drug tests can request a status update at any time during the process and receive results on completion of the drug tests.

9.3.1 Processing Steps

Within the Recruiter Work Center in the Requisitions – My Open Requisitions free list display, click on the Offering column of the particular requisition for the candidate wish want to initiate the drug test. In the Assignments for Requisition interface, select the candidate for whom you want to initiate the drug test. Click on the Activities button and select the Medical/Drug Check activity.

In the Create Activity dialog box, populate the details about the activity and click on the OK button to accept your entries (see Figure 9.6). This executes the workflow to initiate the medical or drug check for the candidate.

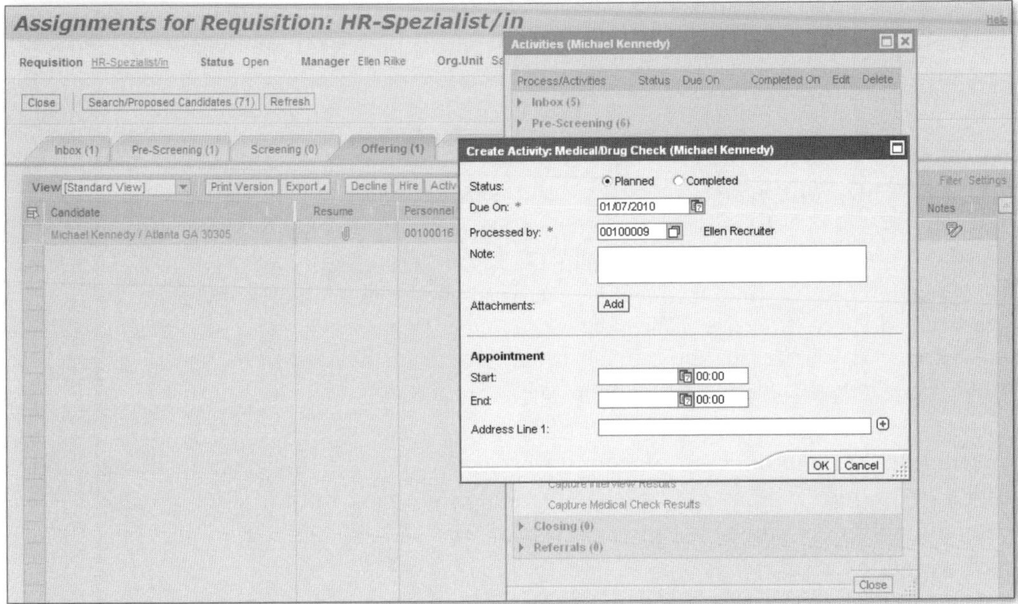

Figure 9.6 Create Drug Test Activity

If you are implementing HireRight or another vendor's product to provide drug testing services, you should be able to select the package and any add-on service within the vendor system. The recruiter can complete the form that is prepopulated with the candidate data from the SAP E-Recruiting system. Alternatively, the recruiter can send an email to the candidate inviting him to log into the vendor system and complete the form. Once the forms are completed and the order is submitted, the vendor initiates the process to start the drug test on the candidate. As with the background checks, the recruiter or HR personnel who initiated the drug test can log into the vendor system to obtain updates about which drug checks have been initiated for the candidate.

9.3.2 Customizing Steps

You need to maintain the vendor providing drug testing needs as a business partner in the SAP E-Recruiting system by following the menu path SAP E-RECRUITING • TECHNICAL SETTINGS • SAP BUSINESS PARTNER • DEFINE BUSINESS PARTNER ROLE FOR

VENDORS. If you are using the same vendor to provide background checks and drug tests, then you need to create the business partner role only once.

In SAP E-Recruiting, you can integrate with vendors who can distribute your job postings to one or more Internet job boards. Retaining and using a single vendor for job posting distribution greatly reduces the recruiter's workload. Some vendors also negotiate (the fees and costs per job posting) with the Internet job boards — even on your behalf. In the next section, we will explain on how to integrate with a vendor who provides such services.

9.4 Job Posting Service

Many organizations allow recruiters to make job postings in multiple job boards. For cost efficiency, some organizations distribute the job boards among the recruiting team. Creating job postings for multiple job boards adds to the recruiter's workload. Some vendors provide services to distribute job postings to the various Internet job boards. The process to integrate a job posting distribution vendor service with SAP E-Recruiting is very similar to integrating SAP E-Recruiting with an Internet job board. One of the vendors who provides a job posting distribution service is JobViper (*www.JobViper.com*). You have to negotiate the services contract directly with JobViper. In your country, there might be other vendors who provide similar types of job posting distribution services.

9.4.1 Processing Steps

If you are using JobViper as the job posting distribution vendor, in SAP E-Recruiting, you can select JobViper as a publication channel. After you have created the requisition in the system, you can select JobViper as an external publication channel (see Figure 9.7) on the Job Postings tab of the Published Job Postings section. You should have completed the customizing steps in the IMG in order to create JobViper as an external publishing channel. (For details on creating a publication channel for your job posting and other customizing steps, refer to Section 4.4.9, Publications, in Chapter 4, Requisition Management). Depending on your customizing requirements, additional processing steps may be involved.

Implementing a job posting distribution service is beneficial if you have a high volume of job postings on multiple job boards. Some vendors even offer analytics to show you which job boards are more effective for various types of job requirements.

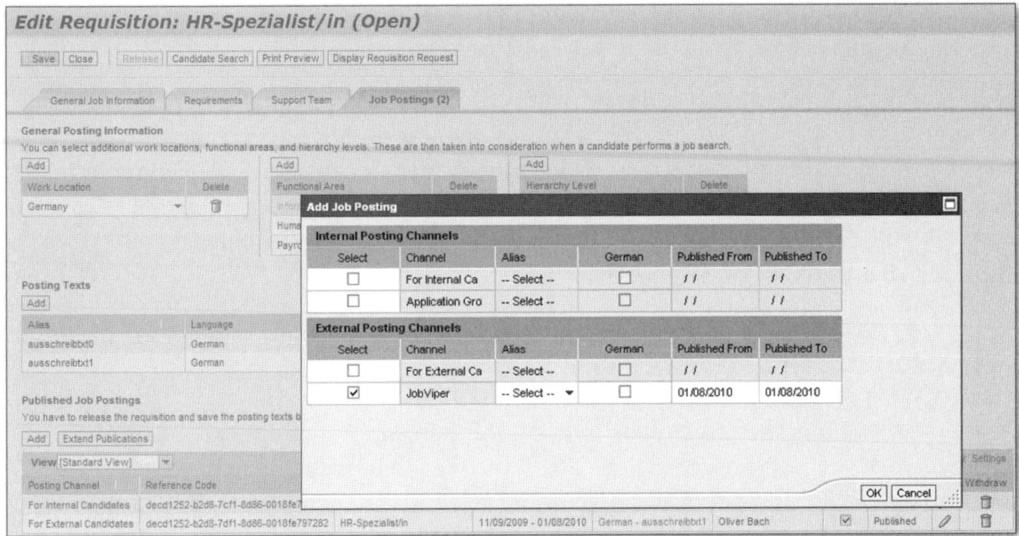

Figure 9.7 Creating JobViper as an External Posting Channel

9.5 Summary

In this chapter we reviewed the vendor services that you can integrate into SAP E-Recruiting. As we mentioned earlier, implementing and integrating these services is not required for a successful SAP E-Recruiting go-live. Services such as drug testing or background checks might not be mandatory in your country. Also, you can choose to have these services processed without any platform integration and recorded manually by the recruiter in the system.

In the next chapter, we will discuss authorization management including the standard delivered roles available in SAP E-Recruiting and the customizing settings required.

Authorization management within SAP E-Recruiting offers enhanced capabilities for securing confidential data for employees and job seekers. A recruiting system holds some of the most private information (gender, ethnicity, age, etc.), so it is critical to build the appropriate controls around it. In this chapter, we discuss SAP authorizations, standard roles, and how to most effectively secure the system.

10 Authorization Management

Authorization management is a critical component of the SAP E-Recruiting solution because personally identifiable information (PII) such as address, gender, and ethnicity is stored in the system. Security breaches in your recruitment database can have severe legal consequences. Due to the nature of SAP E-Recruiting, the system is more susceptible because it is exposed to users outside your corporate firewall (i.e., registered and unregistered external candidates). Without a doubt, it is evident that defining proper authorizations to the system users of SAP E-Recruiting is a critical success factor.

In addition to reviewing the authorizations available, we will also discuss the standard delivered backend roles that SAP provides. As with other standard roles, copies of these standard roles should be made to your customer namespace and edited based on your business requirements. We will inventory each role and highlight its usage.

Let's first discuss user administration, where we will focus on the various user types available in the system.

10.1 User Administration

One of the most unique aspects of the SAP E-Recruiting application is its authorization concept. Although it leverages all standard functionality, it is one of the only SAP ERP HCM applications that uses several different types of users in its design. In SAP E-Recruiting, it is necessary to specify different security policies for different types of users. This is due to the large user base of the system; some users require anonymous access from the outside (e.g., unregistered external candidates) to search open job postings on the careers website, whereas other users (e.g., managers, recruiters, internal candidates, registered external candidates) require specific authorizations. Also, some users who perform daily tasks (e.g., recruiters, data entry clerks, etc.) should be required to change their passwords on a regular basis, while other system users (such as those created to run background processing jobs) should not be required to.

Five user types are utilized within the SAP E-Recruiting system:

- Dialog user
- System user (for workflow background tasks)
- Reference user
- Service user
- Communication user

We will discuss each user type, beginning with the most popular user type — the dialog user.

10.1.1 Dialog Users

As of EP4, SAP comes delivered with 14 standard roles, covered in Section 10.3 of this chapter. Each of these standard roles is intended for one and only one user type. Most users of the SAP E-Recruiting system are of dialog type because explicit authorizations are known and provisioned (e.g., for internal candidates and registered external candidates). All roles should be copied into your customer namespace and changed according to your specifications. Role configuration is performed in Transaction PFCG (Role Maintenance). You can also access it through the IMG under the menu path SAP E-Recruiting • Technical Settings • User Administration • Create User Profiles. Figure 10.1 shows the IMG node structure where all user management activities can be accessed.

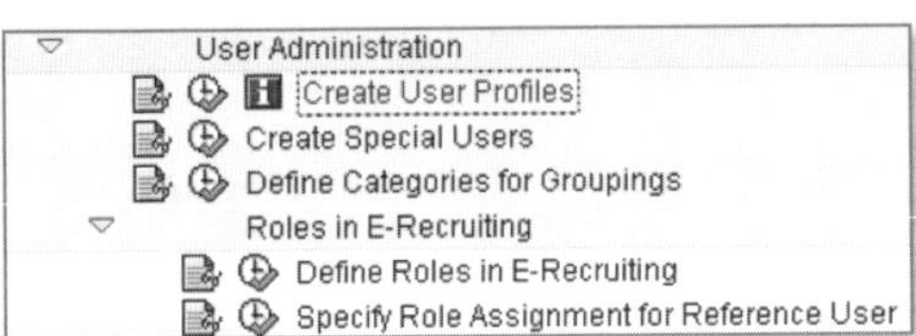

Figure 10.1 User Administration IMG Activities

Dialog users enable the typical employee and outside job seeker to access the system. Dialog users are linked to a reference user (discussed later). This linkage is first made during the user provisioning process (or, more specifically, from logic within the BAdI implementation part of the ALE distribution from SAP ERP HCM to SAP E-Recruiting).

Let's discuss the system user necessary for workflow.

10.1.2 System User (for Workflow)

To be able to use workflow functions, you must create a system user (such as WF-BATCH) in the system. You need to create a candidate for this user. To do so, run program RCF_CREATE_USER. Create an e-mail address at the same time with this report. Then update the printer and authorization profile, in particular the authorization to change the status of E-Recruiting objects (P_RCF_STAT). Typically, WF-BATCH is given the SAP_ALL profile, or something close to it, so that authorization is never an issue for workflow updates.

Next comes the reference user and its importance within the SAP E-Recruiting system.

10.1.3 Reference Users

With a reference user, you create users to simplify authorization maintenance. As part of the initial setup, you assign different roles to each reference user. If you then assign a reference user to a dialog user, that dialog user inherits all of the reference user's role attributes and authorization profiles.

Figure 10.2 shows dialog user ZNILSON in Transaction SU01 (User Maintenance). On the Roles tab, reference user RCF_CAND_INT is identified in the field Reference User for Additional Rights. This means the user ZNILSON will inherent all of the authorizations granted to the RCF_CAND_INT reference user. This makes the maintenance in SAP E-Recruiting a lot simpler because one change in RCF_CAND_INT will permeate to all users with that reference user linked.

The same is done with many other reference users. As shown in Table 10.1, SAP recommends creating the following reference users and associating them to the provided backend roles (or a copy of them).

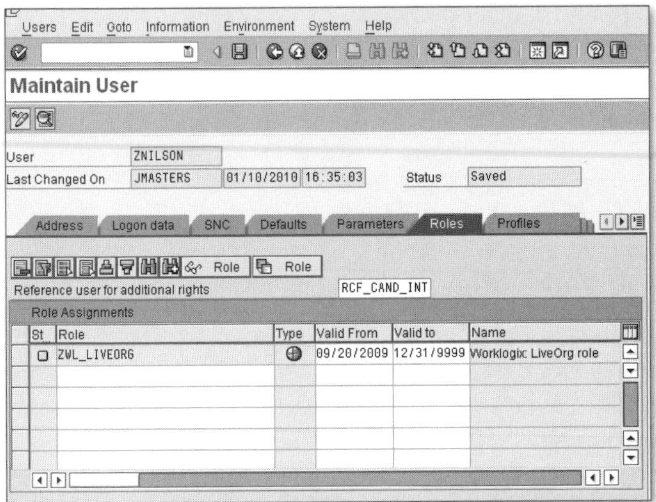

Figure 10.2 Dialog User ZNILSON Linked to Reference User RCF_CAND_INT (Internal Candidate)

Reference User	Reference User Description	Standard SAP Role
RCF_CAND_INT	Candidate (internal)	SAP_RCF_INT_CANDIDATE_CLIENT
RCF_MANAGER	Manager	SAP_RCF_MANAGER
RCF_MGRASS	Manager's assistant	SAP_RCF_MANAGER_ASSISTANT
RCF_CAND_EXT	Candidate (external)	SAP_RCF_EXT_CANDIDATE_CLIENT
RCF_RECRUIT	Recruiter	SAP_RCF_RECRUITER_ERC_CI_2
RCF_DATA_TYP	Data entry clerk	SAP_RCF_DATA_TYPIST_ERC_CI_2
RCF_REQUEST	Requester	SAP_RCF_REQUISITION_REQUESTER
RCF_DECISION	Decision maker	SAP_RCF_DECISION_MAKER
RCF_RES_REC	Restricted recruiter	SAP_RCF_RES_RECRUITER_ERC_CI_2

Table 10.1 SAP Recommendations for Reference Users with Associated Standard Roles

These reference users should be created in your SAP E-Recruiting system using the standard Transaction SU01 (Maintain Users). You can also create them in the IMG under the menu path SAP E-RECRUITING • TECHNICAL SETTINGS • USER ADMINISTRATION • CREATE SPECIAL USERS.

In addition to these reference users, you need service users.

10.1.4 Service Users

Because some scenarios (e.g., registration, job postings, direct application) need to be accessible to unregistered users, you must assign a service user to certain services so that the unregistered user can be authorized to use them. One of the following service users must be set up (depending on which candidate interface you implement):

- **Unregistered candidate (using the Web Dynpro interface)**
  Suggested reference user RCF_WD_SERV with standard role SAP_RCF_UNREG_CANDIDATE_CLIENT
- **Unregistered candidate (using the BSP interface)**
  Suggested reference user RCF_UNREGSER with standard role SAP_RCF_UNREGISTERED_CANDIDATE

The last user type to discuss is the communication user.

10.1.5 Communication User

You need to create a communication user to support the searching of documents in the database. A content server user (suggested reference user RCF_CONT_SER with standard role SAP_RCF_CONTENT_SERVER) needs to be created during initial setup. After creating this user, you must perform additional configuration to enable access to the content server service in the system that permits users to access documents in document area HR_KW (Document Storage for HR Objects). Attachments, search profiles, and other documents are stored in this repository.

You can access this customizing activity in the IMG under the menu path SAP E-RECRUITING • TECHNICAL SETTINGS • SEARCH ENGINE • SET UP ACCESS TO DOCUMENTS. This is Transaction SICF, which is used for activating and configuring various SAP services. Figure 10.3 shows communications user RCF_CONTENT, which could have standard role SAP_RCF_CONTENT_SERVER (or a copy within your customer namespace).

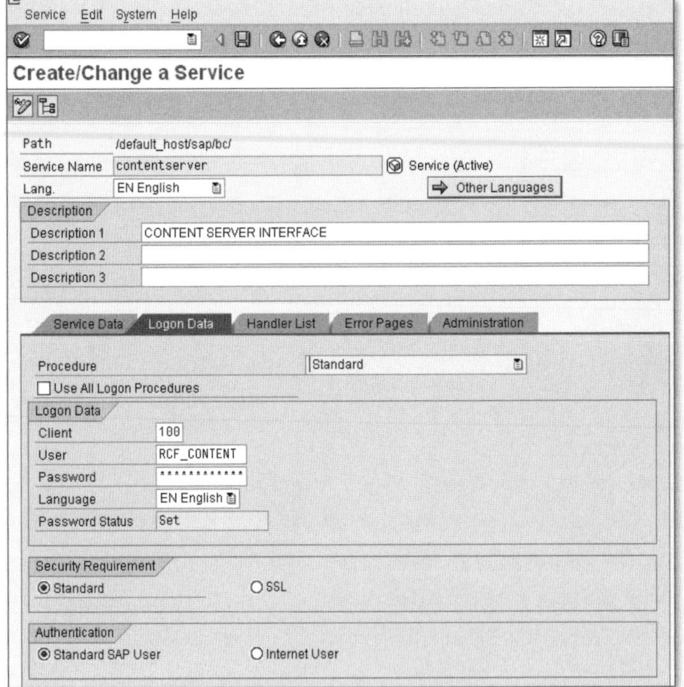

Figure 10.3 Setup of Content Server Service in SICF

This concludes the discussion of the various user types and the setups needed for each, so let's explore some of the most important authorization objects required in SAP E-Recruiting.

10.2 Authorizations Used within SAP E-Recruiting

Table 10.2 contains a lists of the most important authorization objects used within SAP E-Recruiting. Each authorization object is listed with its primary use. All of these authorizations (except PLOG, P_HAP_DOC, and perhaps CA-POWL) will be new to your security team because they are specific to SAP E-Recruiting. All authorizations starting in P_RCF* are reserved for SAP E-Recruiting.

Authorization Object(s)	Use
P_RCF_WDUI	Specifies which Web Dynpro for ABAP applications a user can access
P_RCF_APPL	Specifies which BSP application(s) a user can access
P_RCF_VIEW	Specifies which data overviews a user can access
P_RCF_POOL	Specifies which type of direct access a user can have to candidates in the talent pool
P_RCF_STAT	Specifies authorization for status changes to SAP E-Recruiting objects
P_RCF_ACT	Specifies the level of access a user can have to activities in each process
P_HAP_DOC	Specifies authorizations needed for questionnaires and questions
PLOG	Specifies which Organizational Management or Personnel Development objects can be accessed
CA_POWL	Specifies authorizations needed for the Personal Object Worklist (POWL).

Table 10.2 Common Authorization Objects Used within SAP E-Recruiting

10.2.1 P_RCF_WDUI

Authorization object P_RCF_WDUI provides access to Web Dynpro for ABAP applications. It does not indicate what the users can do once they access the application; it only says if they have permission to initially reach the application. Please note that this authorization is only available through the activation of Business Function HCM_ERC_CI_2 (HCM, SAP E-Recruiting 2), which is part of enhancement pack 4.

The following authorization field comprises the P_RCF_WDUI authorization object:

Name of Web Dynpro Application (RCF_WDUI)
Determines which Web Dynpro Application the user has access to.

10.2.2 P_RCF_APPL

Authorization object P_RCF_APPL provides access to BSP applications. It does not indicate what the users can do once they access the application; it simply says if they have permission to reach the application.

The following authorization field comprises the P_RCF_APPL authorization object:

Application in E-Recruiting (RCF_APPL)
Determines to which BSP applications the user should have access. Possible applications include AGENCY_MNT, APPL_GRP_MNT, BRANCH, CANDIDATE_DELETE, CANDIDATE_DEREGISTER, and CAND_SRCH_AUDIT_TRAIL. These are the BSP versions of each application. If you are implementing the Web Dynpro for ABAP version, you need to identify that application in the P_RFC_WDUI authorization object instead.

Note

Authorization object P_RCF_WDUI contains all Web Dynpro applications the user is authorized to execute in SAP E-Recruiting. The authorization objects that were valid up to enhancement pack 3 (P_RCF_APPL [logical applications based on BSP] and P_RCF_WL [accessing worklists]) are obsolete for these roles after you activate the new business function form, SAP E-Recruiting enhancement pack 2. For the candidate roles for which the BSP applications continue to be supported, the authorization object P_RCF_APPL is still relevant. For more information, please reference SAP Note 1241014, which contains important enhancement pack 4 release notes including impacts to security roles and design.

10.2.3 P_RCF_VIEW

Authorization object P_RCF_VIEW provides the user visibility to one or more data overviews.

The following authorization field comprises the P_RCF_VIEW authorization object.

Data Overview (RCF_VIEW)
Determines which data overviews a user can access.

The following data overviews are available for display: Activity (ACT_DOVR), Application (APPL_DOVR), Candidate (CAND_DOVR), Candidacy (CDCY_DOVR), Equal Employment Information (EEO), Publication (PINST_PBL), Requisition/Posting (REQ_DOVR), Support Group (SGR_DOVR), and Talent Group (TG_DOVR).

10.2.4 P_RCF_POOL

Authorization object P_RCF_POOL determines which type of direct access users can have to their candidates in the talent pool.

The following authorization field comprises the P_RCF_POOL authorization object:

Permitted Type of Access to Talent (RCF_POOL)
Determines which type of direct access a user can have to candidates in the talent pool.

Available authorizations include Maintenance of Candidate Data (CAND_MAINT), Status-Independent Access to Candidates (DIRECT_ACC), and Recognition of Multiple Applicants (DUPL_CHECK).

10.2.5 P_RCF_STAT

Authorization object P_RCF_STAT provides authorization for status changes to SAP E-Recruiting objects (e.g., candidates, applications, candidacies).

The following authorization fields comprise the P_RCF_STAT authorization object. Each field is described separately and highlighted with important information on usage.

Object Type (OTYPE)
Determines which objects the user can access.

Relevant objects for SAP E-Recruiting include NA (Candidate), NB (Requisition), NC (Job Posting), ND (Application), NE (Candidacy), NF (Talent Group), and NG (Support Group). Also, VA (template) and VB (criterion group) are needed for visibility to questionnaires and questions.

Generic Object Status (RCF_STATUS)
Determines which statuses the user can access for each object.

10.2.6 P_RCF_ACT

Authorization object P_RCF_ACT provides authorization to activities within each process. For each activity, you can define create, change, and/or delete access.

The following authorization fields comprise the P_RCF_ACT authorization object. Each field is described separately and highlighted with important information on usage.

- *Activity* (ACTVT)
  Determines what operations (or activities) a user can perform on an appraisal form. Available options are 02 (Change), 03 (Display), and 06 (Delete).

- *Process* (RCF_A_PROC)
  Determines which process the user can access. Processes within SAP E-Recruiting are defined in your configuration.
- *Activity Type* (RCF_A_TYPE)
  Determines which activities the user can access. Like processes, activities within SAP E-Recruiting are defined in your configuration.

10.2.7 PLOG

Authorization object PLOG provides access to organizational management (OM) and personnel development (PD) objects, infotypes, and relationships.

The following authorization fields comprise the PLOG authorization object. Each field is described separately and highlighted with important information on usage.

- *Infotype* (INFOTYP)
  Determines to which infotypes a user has access. The group of Infotypes 1000 (Object), 1001 (Relationships), and 1002 (Description) contain the core infotypes of any OM or PD object. Without read authorization to these infotypes, no OM or PD information can be read from the SAP system.
- *Planning Status* (ISTAT)
  Determines to which planning statuses a user has access. The vast majority of objects are set in status 1 (active).

Object Type (OTYPE)
Determines to which object types a user has access. Objects commonly found in SAP E-Recruiting include S (positions), O (organizational units), NA (candidate), NB (requisition), NC (job posting), ND (application), NE (candidacy), NF (talent group), NG (support group), VA (appraisal template), and VB (criteria group).

Plan Version (PLVAR)
Determines to which plan versions a user has access. Plan version 01 (Active plan) is the default plan version for most objects and should be the only plan version used. Avoid using other plan versions. You should never use plan versions ** and .:.

Function Code (PPFCODE)
Determines what permissions the user has —read, write, delete, and so on — for the object. Most likely, you will use one or more of the following function codes in your implementation: AEND (Change), DEL (Delete), DISP (Display), and INSE (Insert).

Subtype (SUBTYP)
Determines to which subtypes a user has access. Values for subtype go hand-in-hand with those infotypes identified in your infotype authorization field (INFOTYP), discussed earlier. Subtypes in PLOG only refer to subtypes within Organizational Management and Personnel Development.

10.2.8 P_HAP_DOC

P_HAP_DOC is an authorization object within the Objective Setting and Appraisals functionality (i.e., employee performance management). Within the E-Recruiting application, questions and questionnaires are stored as templates, so this authorization object must be included into the appropriate roles.

The following authorization fields comprise the P_HAP_DOC authorization object:

- *Activity* (ACTVT)
  Determines what operations (or activities) a user can perform on an appraisal form. Available options are 02 (Change), 03 (Display), and 06 (Delete). Note that there is no Create activity. Without change authorization, an administrator is unable to create a questionnaire.
- *Appraisal Category ID* (HAP_CAT)
  Determines to which catalog ID a user has access. The appraisal category ID is the eight-digit ID category defined in your configuration. In addition to Transaction PHAP_CATALOG, you can also view your categories via Transaction OOHAP_CATEGORY.
- *Appraisal Category Group ID* (HAP_CAT_G)
  Determines to which catalog group ID a user has access. The appraisal category group ID is the eight-digit ID category group defined in your configuration. In addition to Transaction PHAP_CATALOG, you can also view your category groups via Transaction OOHAP_CAT_GROUP. The standard SAP system out-of-the-box delivers category groups 1 (Personnel Appraisals), 10 (Learning Solution), and 100 (E-Recruiting).
- *Appraisal Template ID* (HAP_TEMPL)
  Determines to which appraisal template ID a user has access. The appraisal template is the eight-digit ID defined in your configuration.
- *Plan Version* (PLVAR)
  Determines to which plan versions a user has access. Plan version 01 (Active plan) is the default plan version and should be the only plan version used in

your process. Avoid using other plan versions. Again, do not use plan versions ** and .: under any circumstances.

- *Authorization Profile* (PROFL)
  Identifies the authorization profile to be used (this is optional). If your organization uses structural authorizations, you can integrate an authorization profile directly in P_HAP_DOC through this authorization field. You can use any profile defined in table T77PR. Structural profiles are built and maintained in Transaction OOSB.

Additional authorizations are needed when using a candidate scenario where the frontend and backend are on different systems. Table 10.3 shows these additional authorizations.

Authorization Object	Use
S_RFC	Authorization object for RFC access
S_RFCALC	Authorization check for RFC users (for example, Trusted System)
S_ICF	Authorization checks for using services in the Internet Communication Framework (SICF), for calling remote function modules using an RFC destination (SM59), and for configuring proxy settings (SICF)

Table 10.3 Additional Authorization Objects Used in Some SAP E-Recruiting Scenarios

Authorizations are also needed to access the business partner functions associated with SAP E-Recruiting. Several authorizations have to be incorporated into your security roles. You need the authorization objects listed in Table 10.4.

Authorization Object(s)	Description
B_BUPA_ATT	Business Partner: Authorization types
B_BUPA_FDG	Business Partner: Field groups
B_BUPA_GRP	Business Partner: Authorization groups
B_BUPA_RLT	Business Partner: BP roles

Table 10.4 Additional Authorization Objects Required for Business Partner Access

This concludes our review of the most common authorizations used within SAP E-Recruiting. Now, let's turn our attention to the SAP standard roles available within the system.

10.3 Standard Roles Available in SAP E-Recruiting

In the standard system, SAP delivers many backend security roles for SAP E-Recruiting that can be copied to your customer namespace and altered according to your specific security requirements via Transaction PFCG (Role Maintenance). Depending on your security practices, you may or may not use composite roles within your functionality. Table 10.5 lists the standard SAP-delivered roles related to SAP E-Recruiting with a short description of their access levels.

SAP Standard Role	Typical Actor Assigned	Description
SAP_RCF_REC_ADMIN_ERC_CI_2 (new as of EP4)	Administrator	Administrator-level access
SAP_RCF_DATA_TYPIST_ERC_CI_2 (new as of EP4)	Data entry clerk	Access for minimum data entry for incoming paper applications
SAP_RCF_RECRUITER_ERC_CI_2 (new as of enhancement pack 4)	Recruiter	Access to the following data: all candidate data for candidates in the talent pool, all publications, all requisitions, all applications, and all data for the selection processes. The role also contains the authorization for minimum data entry for incoming paper applications.
SAP_RCF_RES_RECRUITER_ERC_CI_2 (new as of enhancement pack 4)	Restricted recruiter	Restricted access to the following data: candidate data for candidates in the talent pool, publications, requisitions, applications, and data for the selection processes
SAP_RCF_MANAGER	Manager	Access from the Portal (via Manager Self-Service). The manager wants to fill the vacant jobs in his area. To do this, the manager creates requisitions with the status In Process that are then processed further by recruiters. Access to the following data: candidate data: The manager can see only the candidate data that is assigned to requisitions for which the manager is responsible. Requisition data and data for selection processes: The manager can only see data for which he is responsible.

Table 10.5 SAP Standard-Delivered Roles for SAP E-Recruiting

SAP Standard Role	Typical Actor Assigned	Description
SAP_RCF_MANAGER	Manager	The role also contains the authorization to respond to questionnaires about candidates that are assigned to the relevant requisitions.
SAP_RFC_MANAGER_SERVICE	Service user	Access to request a requisition from the HR system. The service user to which this role is assigned must exist in the SAP E-Recruiting system.
SAP_RCF_UNREG_CANDIDATE_CLIENT	Unregistered candidate (client)	Contains necessary authorizations for unregistered candidates/service users that are required on the frontend system when using a separated system (frontend and backend on different systems). If you execute unregistered scenarios directly on the backend system, you must also assign this role to the service user in the backend system.
SAP_RCF_UNREG_CANDIDATE_SERVER	Unregistered candidate (server)	Provides necessary authorizations for an unregistered candidate/service user in SAP E-Recruiting that are required on the backend system when using a separated system (frontend and backend on different systems).
SAP_RCF_UNREGISTERED_CANDIDATE	(Unregistered) candidate/service user	Provides necessary authorizations for an unregistered candidate/service user in SAP E-Recruiting that are required when using the frontend and backend on one system
SAP_RCF_EXT_CANDIDATE_CLIENT	External candidate (client)	Contains necessary authorizations for external candidates that are required on the frontend system when using a separated system (frontend and backend on different systems).
SAP_RCF_EXT_CANDIDATE_SERVER	External candidate (server)	Provides the necessary authorizations for an external candidate in SAP E-Recruiting that are required on the backend system when using a separated system (frontend and backend on different systems).
SAP_RCF_EXTERNAL_CANDIDATE	External candidate	Provides display-only access to view job postings that have been published via publications using the external posting channels.

Table 10.5 SAP Standard-Delivered Roles for SAP E-Recruiting (Cont.)

SAP Standard Role	Typical Actor Assigned	Description
SAP_RCF_INT_ CANDIDATE_CLIENT	Internal candidate (client)	Contains the necessary authorizations for internal candidates that are required on the frontend system when using a separated system (frontend and backend on different systems). If you allow internal candidates direct access to the backend system, you must also assign this role to the reference user for internal candidates in the backend system.
SAP_RCF_INT_ CANDIDATE_SERVER	Internal candidate (server)	Provides necessary authorizations for an internal candidate in SAP E-Recruiting that are required on the backend system when using a separated system (frontend and backend on different systems).
SAP_RCF_INTERNAL_ CANDIDATE	Internal candidate	Provides display-only access to view job postings that have been published via publications using the internal posting channels. The role does not have access to the following data: requisition data, posting data, application data, and data for the selection process.

Table 10.5 SAP Standard-Delivered Roles for SAP E-Recruiting (Cont.)

Please note that all roles starting with the prefix SAP_RCF_* have been reserved for SAP E-Recruiting. As previously mentioned, it is important that all roles are copied into your customer namespace before being incorporated into your existing security model and composites.

This concludes our review of the standard SAP roles available within the SAP E-Recruiting system.

10.4 Summary

We covered a wide range of authorization topics in this chapter including user administration, SAP E-Recruiting authorization objects, and the standard roles available within SAP E-Recruiting. Like other applications within SAP ERP HCM, the SAP E-Recruiting system offers a robust security framework. Concepts such as user types (e.g., service, communications, dialog, and system) are critical to understand in your implementation. The authorization objects available in the solution provide sufficient controls to prevent issues with segregation of duties and security breaches.

In the next chapter, we will discuss the reporting functionality available within the SAP E-Recruiting system including standard queries, backend reports, and business warehouse capabilities.

SAP E-Recruiting provides critical reporting and analytical data to help managers, recruiters, and executive leaders make better hiring decisions. Tools such as SAP query and SAP NetWeaver Business Warehouse provide important capability to retrieve real-time or near real-time data from end users. In this chapter, we discuss the reporting components within SAP E-Recruiting.

11 Reporting

SAP provides reporting capabilities for recruitment professionals and managers involved in the process. Several reports are available for recruitment teams to execute, review, and support key processes such as requisition management, candidate management, application management, and activity management. Along with some available backend reports, standard SAP query functionality is available within SAP E-Recruiting. In addition to the standard queries provided, you can create custom queries with a functional resource via the query builder. Lastly, standard Business Intelligence (BI) content is available within SAP NetWeaver Business Warehouse. Please note that this last option is only available to customers who own and have implemented the SAP NetWeaver Business Warehouse platform.

Note

For more information on reporting capabilities within SAP E-Recruiting (and HCM in general), you can reference the SAP PRESS book *HR Reporting with SAP* by Hans-Jürgen Figaj, Richard Haßmann, and Anja Junold.

In this chapter, we will cover the reporting tools that SAP provides within SAP E-Recruiting, beginning with some standard backend reporting and then the SAP query and SAP NetWeaver Business Warehouse capabilities.

11.1 Backend (ABAP) Reports

In this section, we review two backend (ABAP) reports that are available within SAP E-Recruiting. Table 11.1 lists these standard reports with their program names.

Report	Program Name
Display Search Query Log for Requisitions	RCF_SEARCH_VARIANT_LOG
Generate All Relevant URLs	RCF_GENERATE_URLS

Table 11.1 Two Important SAP E-Recruiting Backend Reports

11.1.1 Display Search Query Log for Requisitions

The Search Query Log for Requisitions report is used to display search queries that were performed during the processing of certain requisitions. In addition to search queries, the report also displays the candidates that were selected from the search result and assigned to the requisition.

The report can be accessed via Transaction OO_HRRCF_VIEW_SRVLOG or via the SAP Easy Access menu by following the path SAP E-Recruiting • Tools • Display Search Query Log for Requisitions. Figure 11.1 shows the selection screen of the query.

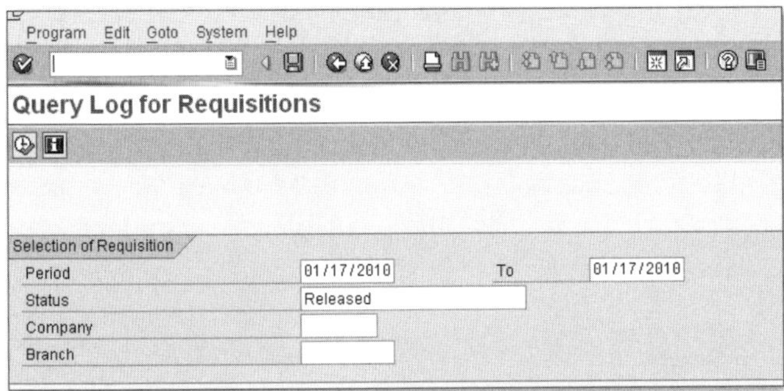

Figure 11.1 Selection Screen for the Query Log for Requisitions

In the selection screen, the following parameters are available to the user:

- Period (from and to)
- Requisition Status (Draft, Released, Closed, To Be Deleted, On Hold)
- Company
- Branch

The requisitions that are recorded depend on the implementation of business add-in HRRCF00_QUERY_LOG. You can activate the standard logging via the IMG under the menu path SAP E-Recruiting • Basic Settings • BAdI: Log Search Query.

The report's output contains important fields for audit purposes including requisition ID, requisition title, creation date/time, username, and assignments. For more on record keeping and reporting, see SAP Note 929247, which discusses OFCCP regulations regarding record keeping of information related to recruiting in the United States.

11.1.2 Generate All Relevant URLs

The report Generate All Relevant URLs provides the project team with a quick way of determining the URLs of the BSP start applications. You can specify HTTP versus HTTPS, the preferred language, and the context. Figure 11.2 shows the output of the report.

List Edit Goto Settings System Help

E-Recruiting: Generate All Relevant URLs

Name of BSP Application	Name	Ap Cl.	URL
Call Internal Start Page	Employee	I	http://pl1pa152.corio.com:8000/sap/bc/bsp/sap/hrrcf_start_int?sap-client=100&sap-language=EN&rcfSpId=0001
Call External Start Page	External Candidate	E	http://pl1pa152.corio.com:8000/sap/bc/bsp/sap/hrrcf_start_ext?sap-client=100&sap-language=EN&rcfSpId=0002
Call Internal Start Page	Recruiter	I	http://pl1pa152.corio.com:8000/sap/bc/bsp/sap/hrrcf_start_int?sap-client=100&sap-language=EN&rcfSpId=0003
Call Internal Start Page	Administrator	I	http://pl1pa152.corio.com:8000/sap/bc/bsp/sap/hrrcf_start_int?sap-client=100&sap-language=EN&rcfSpId=0004
Call Internal Start Page	Requesting Person	I	http://pl1pa152.corio.com:8000/sap/bc/bsp/sap/hrrcf_start_int?sap-client=100&sap-language=EN&rcfSpId=0005
Call Internal Start Page	Succession Planner	I	http://pl1pa152.corio.com:8000/sap/bc/bsp/sap/hrrcf_start_int?sap-client=100&sap-language=EN&rcfSpId=0006
HRRCF_AGENCY	Maintain Agencies	I	http://pl1pa152.corio.com:8000/sap/bc/bsp/sap/hrrcf_start_int?sap-client=100&sap-language=EN&rcfLogAppl=AGENCY_MNT
HRRCF_AGENCY	Maintain Agencies	E	http://pl1pa152.corio.com:8000/sap/bc/bsp/sap/hrrcf_start_ext?sap-client=100&sap-language=EN&rcfLogAppl=AGENCY_MNT
HRRCF_APPL_HIST	List of Applications (Candidate)	I	http://pl1pa152.corio.com:8000/sap/bc/bsp/sap/hrrcf_start_int?sap-client=100&sap-language=EN&rcfLogAppl=APPLICATIONS
HRRCF_APPL_HIST	List of Applications (Candidate)	E	http://pl1pa152.corio.com:8000/sap/bc/bsp/sap/hrrcf_start_ext?sap-client=100&sap-language=EN&rcfLogAppl=APPLICATIONS
HRRCF_APPLY	Apply Direct	I	http://pl1pa152.corio.com:8000/sap/bc/bsp/sap/hrrcf_start_int?sap-client=100&sap-language=EN&rcfLogAppl=APPLY_DIRECTLY
HRRCF_APPLY	Apply Direct	E	http://pl1pa152.corio.com:8000/sap/bc/bsp/sap/hrrcf_start_ext?sap-client=100&sap-language=EN&rcfLogAppl=APPLY_DIRECTLY
HRRCF_APPL_GRPL	Maintain Application Groups	I	http://pl1pa152.corio.com:8000/sap/bc/bsp/sap/hrrcf_start_int?sap-client=100&sap-language=EN&rcfLogAppl=APPL_GRP_MNT
HRRCF_APPL_NEW	List of Applications (Recruiter)	I	http://pl1pa152.corio.com:8000/sap/bc/bsp/sap/hrrcf_start_int?sap-client=100&sap-language=EN&rcfLogAppl=APPL_NEW
HRRCF_APPL_NEW	List of Applications (Recruiter)	I	http://pl1pa152.corio.com:8000/sap/bc/bsp/sap/hrrcf_start_int?sap-client=100&sap-language=EN&rcfLogAppl=APPL_OLD
HRRCF_WITEM_LST	Approvals	I	http://pl1pa152.corio.com:8000/sap/bc/bsp/sap/hrrcf_start_int?sap-client=100&sap-language=EN&rcfLogAppl=APPROVALS
HRRCF_WITEM_LST	Approvals	I	http://pl1pa152.corio.com:8000/sap/bc/bsp/sap/hrrcf_start_int?sap-client=100&sap-language=EN&rcfLogAppl=APPROVALS_SUCC_PLNG
HRRCF_APP_E_EXT	Application Entry (External)	I	http://pl1pa152.corio.com:8000/sap/bc/bsp/sap/hrrcf_start_int?sap-client=100&sap-language=EN&rcfLogAppl=APP_E_EXT
HRRCF_APP_E_INT	Application Entry (Internal)	I	http://pl1pa152.corio.com:8000/sap/bc/bsp/sap/hrrcf_start_int?sap-client=100&sap-language=EN&rcfLogAppl=APP_E_INT
HRRCF_BRNCH_LST	Maintain Branches	I	http://pl1pa152.corio.com:8000/sap/bc/bsp/sap/hrrcf_start_int?sap-client=100&sap-language=EN&rcfLogAppl=BRANCH
HRRCF_CAND_DEL	Delete External Candidates	I	http://pl1pa152.corio.com:8000/sap/bc/bsp/sap/hrrcf_start_int?sap-client=100&sap-language=EN&rcfLogAppl=CANDIDATE_DELETE
HRRCF_CAND_DER	Deregister External Candidates	I	http://pl1pa152.corio.com:8000/sap/bc/bsp/sap/hrrcf_start_int?sap-client=100&sap-language=EN&rcfLogAppl=CANDIDATE_DEREGISTER
HRRCF_CAND_SRCH	Candidate Overview	I	http://pl1pa152.corio.com:8000/sap/bc/bsp/sap/hrrcf_start_int?sap-client=100&sap-language=EN&rcfLogAppl=CAND_SRCH
HRRCF_CAND_SRCH	Candidate Information (Audit Trail)	I	http://pl1pa152.corio.com:8000/sap/bc/bsp/sap/hrrcf_start_int?sap-client=100&sap-language=EN&rcfLogAppl=CAND_SRCH_AUDIT_TRAIL
HRRCF_CAND_SRCH	Candidate Info (Audit Trail Assignments)	I	http://pl1pa152.corio.com:8000/sap/bc/bsp/sap/hrrcf_start_int?sap-client=100&sap-language=EN&rcfLogAppl=CAND_SRCH_AUDIT_TRAILCDCY
HRRCF_PERS_SETT	Change User Name	E	http://pl1pa152.corio.com:8000/sap/bc/bsp/sap/hrrcf_start_ext?sap-client=100&sap-language=EN&rcfLogAppl=CHANGE_ALIAS
HRRCF_PROFILE	Change Interest Group	E	http://pl1pa152.corio.com:8000/sap/bc/bsp/sap/hrrcf_start_ext?sap-client=100&sap-language=EN&rcfLogAppl=CHANGE_INTEREST_GROUP
HRRCF_COMPANY	Maintain Company List	I	http://pl1pa152.corio.com:8000/sap/bc/bsp/sap/hrrcf_start_int?sap-client=100&sap-language=EN&rcfLogAppl=COMPANY
HRRCF_CONT_DATA	Communication Data	E	http://pl1pa152.corio.com:8000/sap/bc/bsp/sap/hrrcf_start_ext?sap-client=100&sap-language=EN&rcfLogAppl=CONTACT_DATA
HRRCF_MPROC_COR	Correspondence	I	http://pl1pa152.corio.com:8000/sap/bc/bsp/sap/hrrcf_start_int?sap-client=100&sap-language=EN&rcfLogAppl=CORRESPONDENCE
HRRCF_DASHBOARD	Dashboard	I	http://pl1pa152.corio.com:8000/sap/bc/bsp/sap/hrrcf_start_int?sap-client=100&sap-language=EN&rcfLogAppl=DASHBOARD
HRRCF_PROFILE	Data Overview: Candidate	I	http://pl1pa152.corio.com:8000/sap/bc/bsp/sap/hrrcf_start_int?sap-client=100&sap-language=EN&rcfLogAppl=DATAOVERVIEW_CAND
HRRCF_PROFILE	Data Overview: Candidate	E	http://pl1pa152.corio.com:8000/sap/bc/bsp/sap/hrrcf_start_ext?sap-client=100&sap-language=EN&rcfLogAppl=DATAOVERVIEW_CAND
HRRCF_TPI_SHTL	Decision List (Manager Involvement)	I	http://pl1pa152.corio.com:8000/sap/bc/bsp/sap/hrrcf_start_int?sap-client=100&sap-language=EN&rcfLogAppl=DECL_TPI
HRRCF_CAND_DRG	Deregistration	E	http://pl1pa152.corio.com:8000/sap/bc/bsp/sap/hrrcf_start_ext?sap-client=100&sap-language=EN&rcfLogAppl=DEREGISTRATION
HRRCF_QA_TPLBLD	EEO Questionnaires	I	http://pl1pa152.corio.com:8000/sap/bc/bsp/sap/hrrcf_start_int?sap-client=100&sap-language=EN&rcfLogAppl=EEO_QUESTIONNAIRES
HRRCF_QA_QSTBLD	EEO Questions	I	http://pl1pa152.corio.com:8000/sap/bc/bsp/sap/hrrcf_start_int?sap-client=100&sap-language=EN&rcfLogAppl=EEO_QUESTIONS
HRRCF_REG_SRCH	Favorites	I	http://pl1pa152.corio.com:8000/sap/bc/bsp/sap/hrrcf_start_int?sap-client=100&sap-language=EN&rcfLogAppl=FAVORITES

Figure 11.2 Output of the Generate BSP URLs Report

The next type of reporting possible within SAP E-Recruiting is via the SAP query tool.

11.2 SAP Query

SAP's query tool enables users to create queries using a flexible, robust user interface. Frequently used queries can be saved and executed at a later time. The SAP query is good for straightforward reports. Although more complex logic can be included within the tool (by adding additional custom fields), it's best to use the query tool for what it is best at: quickly and easily extracting information. You can achieve more complex reporting through custom ABAP reports.

The query has several components. All pieces are important to understanding the full breadth of functionality available with query functionality, including:

- **Transaction**
  The transaction shortcut to the query tool with the default user group
- **User group**
  The functional grouping of infosets, also serving as a point of access control
- **Infoset**
  The group of infotypes available for inclusion within a query
- **Query**
  The report that is created by the end user, which can be saved for later use

There is also a section within the IMG on Reporting for SAP E-Recruiting. Figure 11.3 shows the IMG activities, some of which are discussed next.

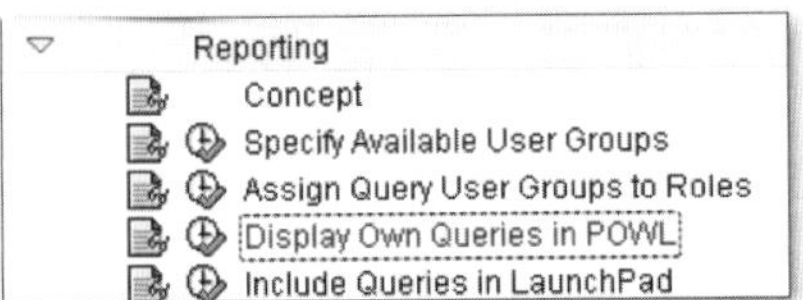

Figure 11.3 Reporting Section within the IMG for SAP E-Recruiting

Let's discuss how we can first access the query tool.

11.2.1 Transaction

Queries can also be accessed via Transaction SQ01 (via the SAP Easy Access screen by following the menu path Human Resources • Information System • Reporting Tools • SAP Query). If you use Transaction SQ01 transaction, you must first check to see whether you are in the right query area and infoset. Figure 11.4 shows Transaction SQ01 with user group ERC_RECR selected.

Let's discuss the user group and its relevance within the query functionality.

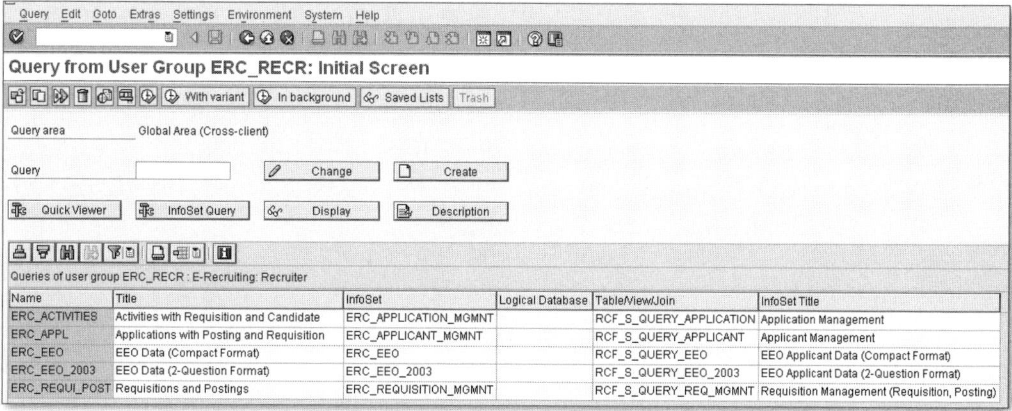

Figure 11.4 List of Standard Queries within User Group ERC_RECR from Transaction SQ01

11.2.2 User Group

Within SAP E-Recruiting, you can define which user groups should be available. If you want to limit the queries that a user can call using SAP E-Recruiting, you must enter the appropriate user groups in table V_77RCF_EREC_UGR. If you do not select any user groups in this table, all user groups that exist in the system are available in SAP E-Recruiting. You can configure this table in the IMG under the menu path SAP E-Recruiting • Technical Settings • Reporting • Specify Available User Groups. Figure 11.5 shows the table configuration with entry ERC_RECR in work area G.

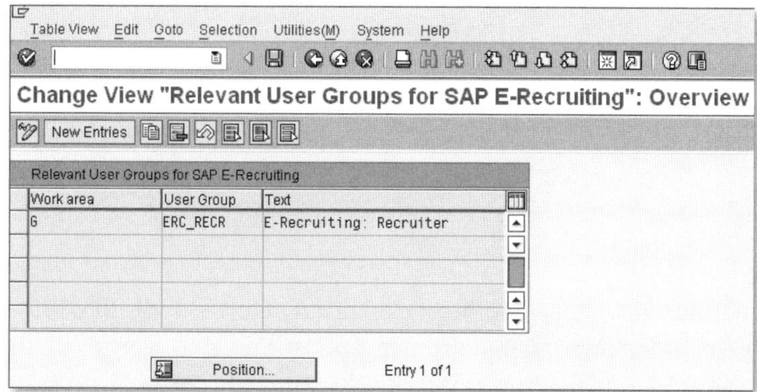

Figure 11.5 Relevant User Groups within SAP E-Recruiting

The next step, to assign users to a particular user group, occurs at the user level. To do this, you must assign the user group to the relevant role in the Personalization tab page of the role within Transaction PFCG (Role Maintenance) (see Figure 11.6). Users assigned to the role can then run queries for that user group. Please note that only one user group can be assigned to a role. You can follow the menu path SAP E-Recruiting • Technical Settings • Reporting • Assign Query User Groups to Roles or execute Transaction PFCG directly.

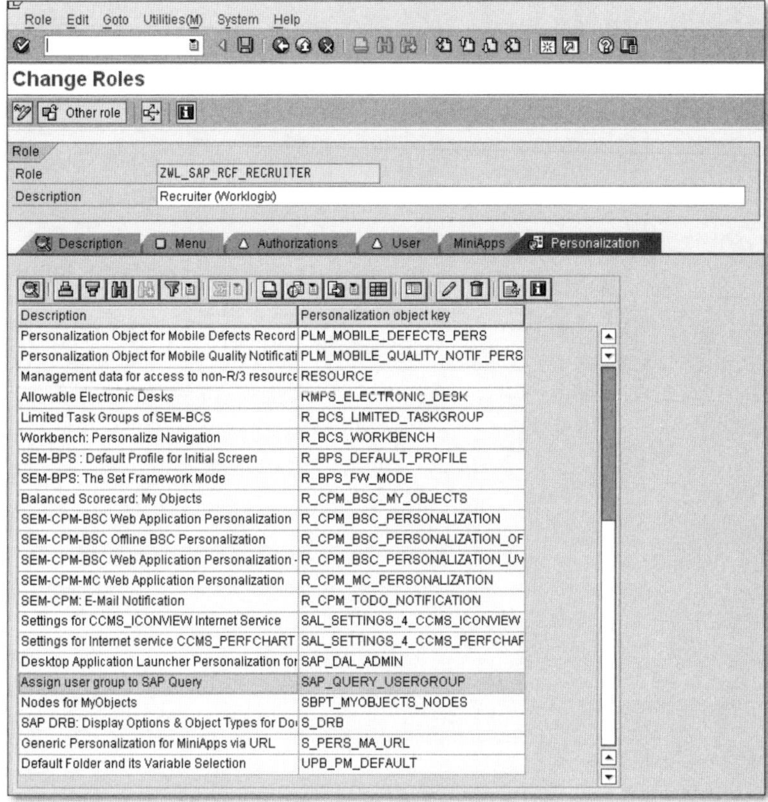

Figure 11.6 Personalization of User Group for E-Recruiting

In the system, the queries are displayed in the personalized object worklist (POWL). However, if you develop your own custom queries, you will need to register them in the POWL from the IMG under the menu path SAP E-Recruiting • Technical Settings • Reporting • Display Own Queries in POWL. Figure 11.7 shows the selection screen of the registration transaction.

Program Edit Goto System Help

Register InfoSet Query @ POWL

Namespace	/ERC/
Parent Application ID	
Usergroup	ERC_RECR
InfoSet Query ID	ERC_EEO_COMPAC

☐ Create transport request

Figure 11.7 Registering Your Own Query for the POWL

To register your own query, you must provide at least your customer namespace, user group, and infoset query ID. Optionally, you can select Create Transport Request if you want to move the query to another environment via a transport.

After adding any custom queries to the POWL, you need to include the new query in the standard Recruiter LaunchPad. You can find the configuration under the IMG menu path SAP E-Recruiting • Technical Settings • Reporting • Include Queries in LaunchPad. Figure 11.8 shows the configuration of the LaunchPad.

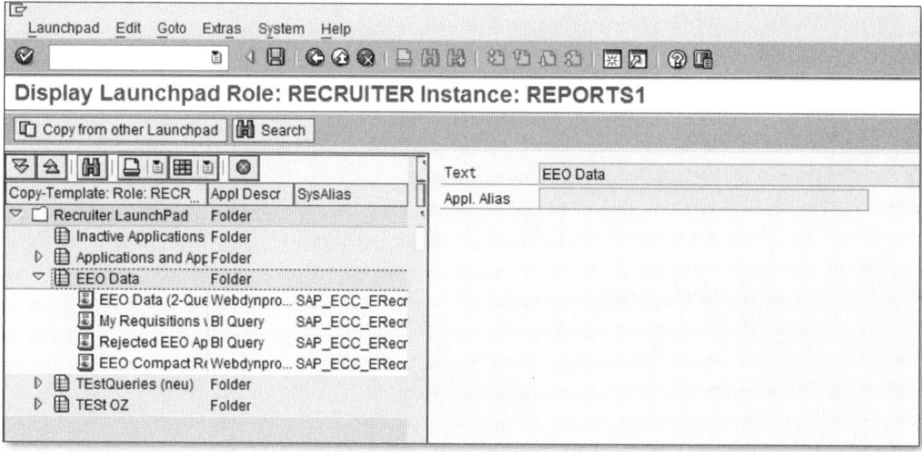

Figure 11.8 Configuration of the Recruiting LaunchPad

The LaunchPad is available to recruiters within their recruiter portal page. Figure 11.9 shows the recruiter portal page after clicking on the Change LaunchPad button. This dialog box allows the recruiter to add or remove queries available for that user in the system.

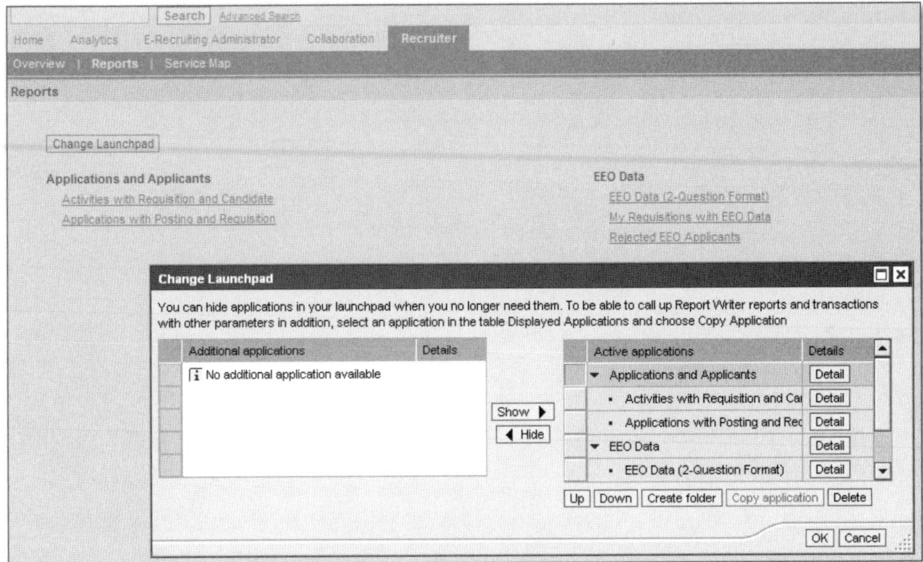

Figure 11.9 LaunchPad Options within the Recruiter Reports Portal Page

Let's now discuss infosets, which form the critical piece of query.

11.2.3 Infosets

Infosets allow you to group and relate objects and infotypes together. This allows the system to organize and group infotypes with a similar functional purpose. SAP provides a number of standard delivered infosets for SAP E-Recruiting. These infosets can be copied into your customer namespace and enhanced according to your business requirements. The following standard infosets are available:

- ERC_REQUISITION_MGMNT (Requisition)
- ERC_APPLICANT_MGMNT (Applicant)
- ERC_APPLICATION_MGMNT (Application)
- ERC_EEO (EEO Applicant Data (Compact Format))
- ERC_EEO_2003 (EEO Applicant Data (2-Question Format))

All infosets use a program for data retrieval (e.g., Infoset ERC_APPLICATION_MGMNT uses report RSAQDVP_TEMPLATE for its data collection). Figure 11.10 shows the data available within Infoset ERC_REQUISITION_MGMNT.

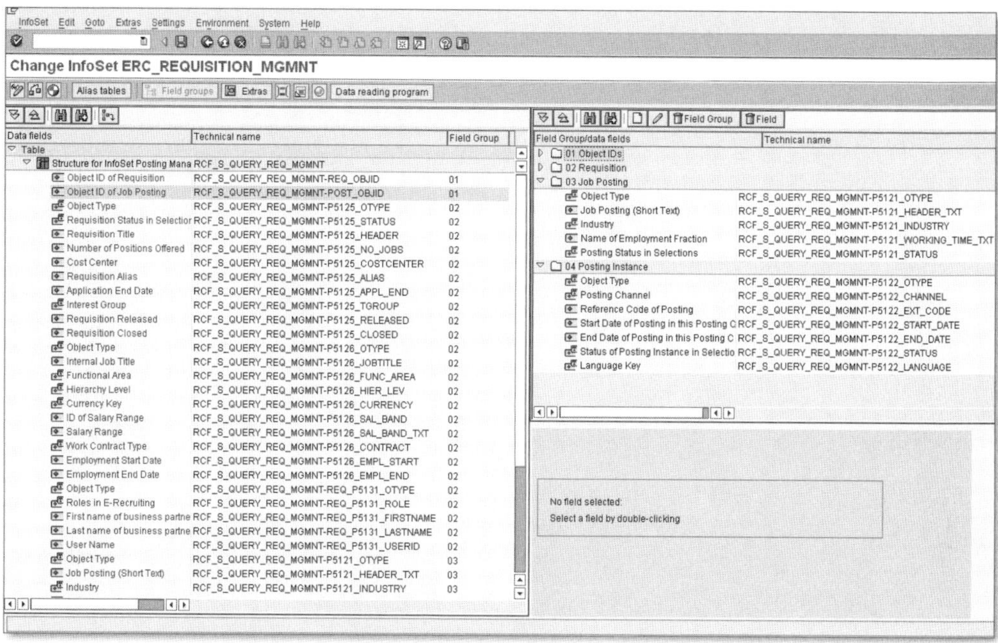

Figure 11.10 Standard Infoset ERC_REQUISITION_MGMNT

Infoset ERC_REQUISITION_MGMNT (Requisition Management) pulls data from the requisition object (Infotypes 5125, 5126, and 5131), the job posting object (Infotype 5121), and the posting channel (Infotype 5122).

Infosets form the foundation for queries, which we will discuss next.

11.2.4 Queries

Queries allow end users to create quick reports based on infotype data defined within an infoset. When creating a query, you specify the selection screen and output. The following queries are available for the recruiter via the portal:

- Applications with Posting and Requisition
- Activities with Requisition and Candidate
- EEO Data (2-Question Format)

The Applications with Posting and Requisition query (shown in Figure 11.11) displays the applications available in the system along with their posting and requisition details. Output fields include candidate name, job posting, reference code, and requisition alias. The query is rendered via the POWL (personal object worklist) functionality.

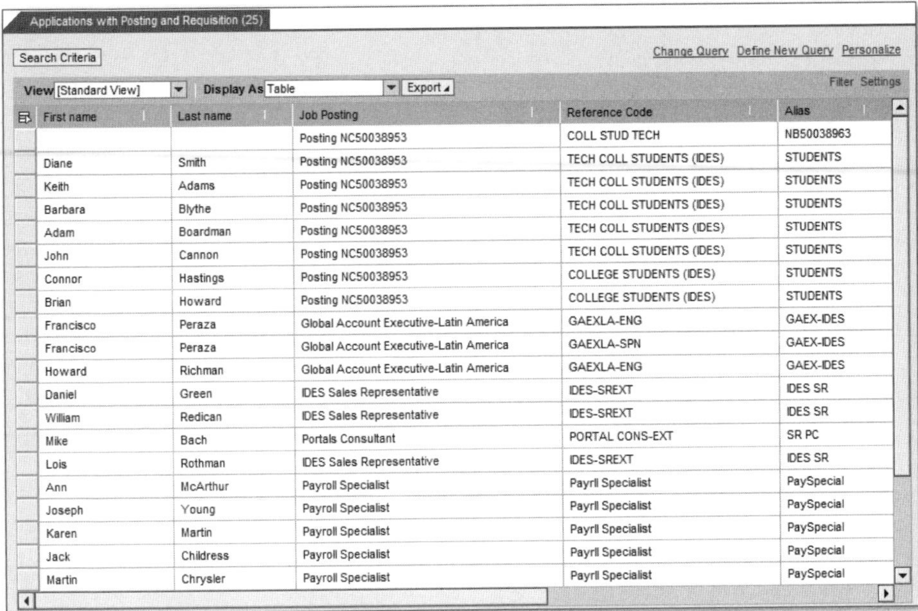
Applications with Posting and Requisition (25)

Search Criteria — Change Query Define New Query Personalize

View [Standard View] Display As Table Export — Filter Settings

First name	Last name	Job Posting	Reference Code	Alias
		Posting NC50038953	COLL STUD TECH	NB50038963
Diane	Smith	Posting NC50038953	TECH COLL STUDENTS (IDES)	STUDENTS
Keith	Adams	Posting NC50038953	TECH COLL STUDENTS (IDES)	STUDENTS
Barbara	Blythe	Posting NC50038953	TECH COLL STUDENTS (IDES)	STUDENTS
Adam	Boardman	Posting NC50038953	TECH COLL STUDENTS (IDES)	STUDENTS
John	Cannon	Posting NC50038953	TECH COLL STUDENTS (IDES)	STUDENTS
Connor	Hastings	Posting NC50038953	COLLEGE STUDENTS (IDES)	STUDENTS
Brian	Howard	Posting NC50038953	COLLEGE STUDENTS (IDES)	STUDENTS
Francisco	Peraza	Global Account Executive-Latin America	GAEXLA-ENG	GAEX-IDES
Francisco	Peraza	Global Account Executive-Latin America	GAEXLA-SPN	GAEX-IDES
Howard	Richman	Global Account Executive-Latin America	GAEXLA-ENG	GAEX-IDES
Daniel	Green	IDES Sales Representative	IDES-SREXT	IDES SR
William	Redican	IDES Sales Representative	IDES-SREXT	IDES SR
Mike	Bach	Portals Consultant	PORTAL CONS-EXT	SR PC
Lois	Rothman	IDES Sales Representative	IDES-SREXT	IDES SR
Ann	McArthur	Payroll Specialist	Payrll Specialist	PaySpecial
Joseph	Young	Payroll Specialist	Payrll Specialist	PaySpecial
Karen	Martin	Payroll Specialist	Payrll Specialist	PaySpecial
Jack	Childress	Payroll Specialist	Payrll Specialist	PaySpecial
Martin	Chrysler	Payroll Specialist	Payrll Specialist	PaySpecial

Figure 11.11 Standard Query Applications with Posting and Requisition

The Activities with Requisition and Candidate query (shown in Figure 11.12) displays the activities together with the associated requisition and candidate. Again, this query is rendered based on the POWL framework.

Activities with Requisition and Candidate (2)

Search Criteria — Change Query Define New Query Personalize

View [Standard View] Display As Table Export — Filter Settings

Date of Application Activity	Date of Candidacy Activity	Candidate First Name	Candidate Last Name	Alias
03/31/2006	03/31/2006	Diane	Smith	STUDENTS
03/31/2006	03/31/2006	Diane	Smith	STUDENTS

Figure 11.12 Standard Query Activities with Requisition and Candidate

The EEO Data (in 2-Question Format) query (shown in Figure 11.13) is another standard report and is specific for the United States. EEO (Equal Employment Opportunity) is the agency of the United States government that enforces federal employment discrimination laws. Output includes candidate name, ethnic origin, and gender.

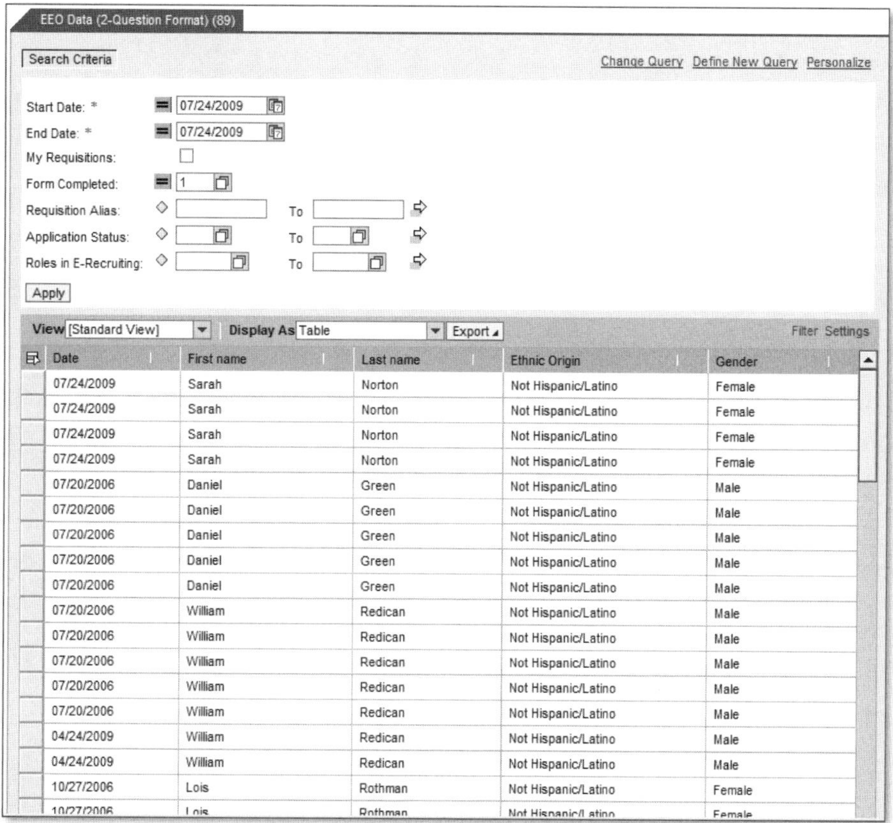

Figure 11.13 Standard Query EEO Data (in 2-Question Format)

Note

Two additional queries related to EEO — My Requisitions with EEO Data and All Rejected EEO Applicants — are also included in the LaunchPad but with one important distinction: these queries use the data source from SAP NetWeaver Business Warehouse.

Let's now review the functionality within SAP NetWeaver Business Warehouse and what standard queries are available for SAP E-Recruiting.

11.3 Business Warehouse

If your company owns SAP NetWeaver Business Warehouse, you can perform more robust analytical reporting on applicant, candidate, and requisition data. There are 11 recruitment-related standard queries available within SAP NetWeaver 7.0 BW content. These queries can also be used as a baseline for any customer-specific reports you will need to create in SAP NetWeaver Business Warehouse. We will discuss the standard content available below by query.

11.3.1 BI Content Available

The BI content available in SAP E-Recruiting is pertinent for recruiters and recruiting leaders. Eleven out-of-the-box queries are available for such analytics. Listed below are the standard queries available with a short description.

- **Requisition Status Changes**
  This query displays the number of requisitions by a given status and status reason. You can specify a time period when you start the query. Recruiters need to be able to keep track of the different statuses of requisitions at various times to be able to handle problems and identify opportunities in the recruiting process.
- **Requisitions Created**
  This query displays the number of requisitions that were created in a given time period. You can display queries by recruiter, by organizational unit, or based on other selection criteria. This enables you to identify the workload of your recruitment department and, if necessary, to make changes. The values for status and status reason correspond to the values that are valid on the date the query is called.
- **Number of Open Requisitions**
  This query enables you to gain an overview of the requisitions whose status is currently released and thus identify the workload in the individual areas. You can break down the structure displayed by organizational unit or recruiter. The query displays the number of requisitions that currently have the status Released.

- **Time-to-Fill**
  This query displays the number of days between the date the requisition was created and the date the candidate accepted the offer of employment (status of assignment: To Be Hired). When you start the query, you can restrict the display to requisitions that were created in a specific time period. The selection of time-dependent data is restricted to the date on which the query is started.
- **Offer vs Acceptance Rate**
  This query displays the ratio of accepted and rejected offers of employment to the total number of offers made. You can restrict the number of requisitions to requisitions that were created in a specific time period.
- **Interview vs Offer Rate**
  This query reports on the number of activities of the type First Interview and Offer for the candidate assignments. These are displayed in relation to one another, which enables you to report on how many interviews are necessary to achieve an offer of employment. You can restrict the number of requisitions to requisitions that were created in a specific time period. The number of interviews per offer of employment can be a reliable indicator of how effective your candidate selection process is.
- **Application Submittal vs Offers**
  This query counts the number of applications submitted per requisition and the number of activities of the type Job Offer. The values are displayed as a ratio of one another. You can restrict the data displayed by specifying a validity period.
- **Application Sourcing**
  This query identifies which of the application channels you use are the most effective. The query displays the number of applications for each application source type and application source. The query also displays the number of interviews, offers, and acceptances. You can restrict the number of requisitions to those created in a specific time period.
- **Candidate's Qualifications**
  This query displays the candidate's qualifications in the talent pool with proficiency details. You can expand the hierarchy tree display down to the level of the candidate's individual qualifications. One key figure displays the number of qualifications; another key figure displays the number of candidates with a given qualification.
- **Application Submittal vs Offers (SAP Analytics)**
  This query shows the number of applications, the number of offers, and the offers per application submittal for the current year.

- **Offer vs Acceptance Rate (SAP Analytics)**
  This query shows the number of applications and job offers and the related proportion of hirings and rejections.

11.3.2 Manager Self-Service Dashboards

In addition to the recruiter reports available within SAP NetWeaver Business Warehouse, several Manager Self-Service options are available via Business Objects. Using this functionality, you can create several dashboards for presentation to managers. Figure 11.14 displays a recruitment dashboard showing an Applicant Overview. Some metrics pictured here include applicants by requisition, applicants by gender, and applicant EEO information.

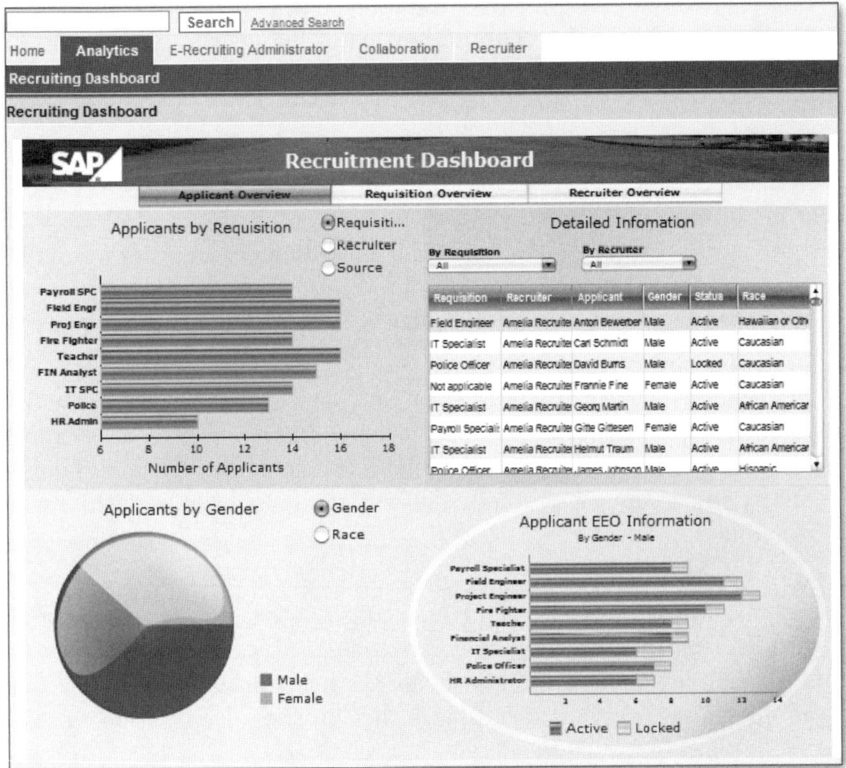

Figure 11.14 Recruitment Dashboard – Applicant Overview

Figure 11.15 displays a recruitment dashboard showing a Requisition Overview. Some metrics pictured here include cost by requisition, number of open requisitions, number of interviews and offers, and number of job openings.

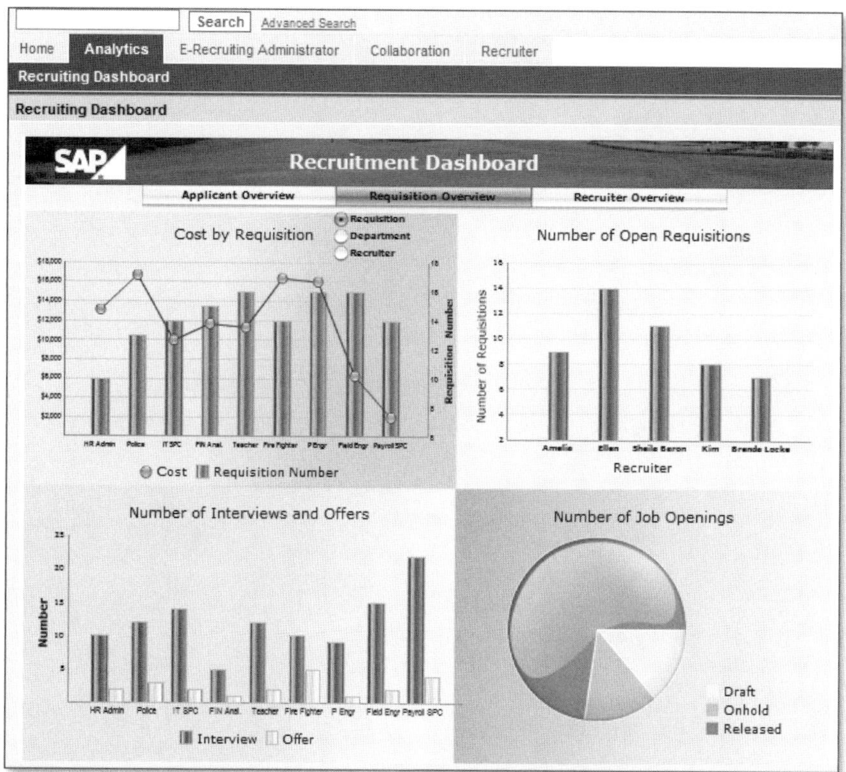

Figure 11.15 Recruitment Dashboard – Requisition Overview

Figure 11.16 displays a recruitment dashboard showing a Recruiter Overview. Some metrics pictured here include time to hire and number of open requisitions.

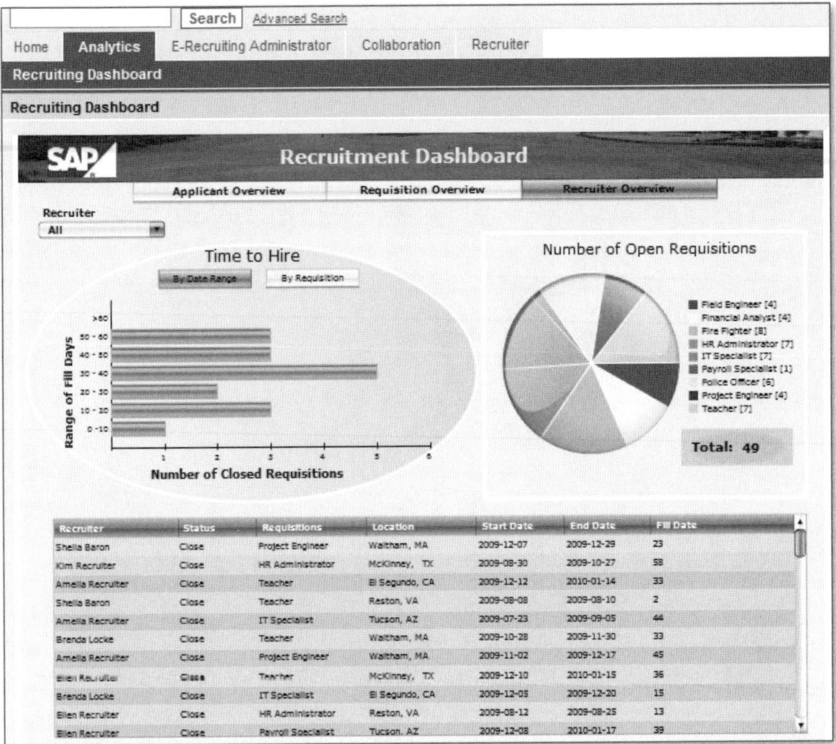

Figure 11.16 Recruitment Dashboard – Recruiter Overview

This concludes the list of queries and MSS dashboards available using the SAP NetWeaver Business Warehouse.

11.4 Summary

In this chapter, we reviewed the reporting components available within the SAP E-Recruiting system. As with other areas within SAP ERP HCM, the SAP E-Recruiting functionality offers some standard ABAP reporting via the SAP backend system, SAP query capabilities with delivered user groups, infosets, and queries, as well as BI and Business Objects content via SAP NetWeaver Business Warehouse.

In the next chapter, we will review some lessons learned from our experiences implementing SAP E-Recruiting.

If you approach things the way you have always approached them, you will always end up with the same results.

12 Lessons Learned

This chapter presents a summary of the lessons learned from various projects that have implemented SAP E-Recruitment either independently or as part of a larger SAP HR implementation. We have selected lessons learned that apply across more than one implementation. Although not all project circumstances are the same, we can draw many parallels from one engagement to the next.

We have organized the lessons learned by topic. The following topics are covered:

- Recruitment process and system design
- Change management
- Social media and mobile platforms
- System implementation

This should not be seen as a comprehensive list of "gotchas." The lessons learned should be understood and related in the context of your own implementation. Depending on your organization's size, culture, and global reach, some lessons learned will mean more to you than others.

12.1 Recruitment Process and System Design

Recruiting the right talent is not a magical process where people appear, sign up on the career site, and get hired. It is a critical aspect of the organization and requires the process to be integrated with other talent management initiatives, planned accordingly, and executed strategically.

12.1.1 Recruitment Management Process

Design Your Solution Based on Your Needs and Not as a Replacement of Your Current Recruiting System.

Many organizations that are implementing SAP E-Recruiting are replacing an existing solution. We have found that approaching your implementation design with the existing solution as the reference point can lead to a poor implementation. This occurs because each system tends to have a different approach for dealing with activities and has a different solution for managing the recruitment process. Try to approach your SAP E-Recruiting implementation as a new application and approach your blueprint by defining a suitable process and current requirements.

We also highly recommend that you have a sandbox implementation available during the blueprint phase. This approach allows the project team and business stakeholders to preview functionality as decisions are made about process and system design.

Level set the Team on the Dynamic Nature of the Recruitment Process.

The processes related to recruiting are very dynamic and can present a challenge to team members that are accustomed to thinking of HR processes, which are usually sequential in nature.

Consider dedicating a portion of the blueprinting session to the day in the life of a recruiter. This will help the team understand how the system needs to accommodate a recruitment process.

Automate and Integrate the Recruitment Process with the Headcount Review and Approval Process.

Initiating the recruiting process requires a high level of integration, and the process needs to be fairly simple for managers to initiate the request for a position to be filled.

Consider introducing a form for managers to complete when requesting a position to be filled and allow the form to route through the proper approval process and administrative process, such as compensation and organization management, before the recruitment process is started. We have found that organizations that use a position request form initiated by managers and/or human resources dramatically streamline the process and reduce the amount of time needed to get a position posted while providing a greater level of visibility to changes in headcount.

The process of recruiting for candidates is further improved if the forms are routed to teams such as compensation, which can ensure that the right range of compensation is used to target potential candidates and that the underlying master data is set up correctly for the position.

Leverage Organizational Management to Manage Budgeted Headcount.

Understanding the cost of your potential workforce (approved headcount that has yet to be hired) is very difficult, considering that many organizations cannot adequately report current headcount numbers. One option that has been successful is the use of positions to represent headcount and approved headcount to be hired. We have found that using a combination of vacant positions and position status can be effective in managing approved headcount. Once new headcount is approved, the representative positions are created or existing position status is set to denote that the position can be filled as of a certain date.

Using positions to represent current headcount and potential headcount can be very effective. The approach also streamlines the requisition process because the position has already been created, represents the correct job, and has the correct compensation range.

Identify and Manage Specific Jobs Differently to Maximize the Recruitment Process.

Most organizations consist of several jobs that make up a major part of the workforce. This is typical and along with the percentage of turnover can represent challenges when recruiting for these positions. You will want to highlight these jobs during blueprinting and determine if the same process applies or if these positions need to be addressed differently.

We have found that organizations can dramatically improve the way they source candidates, perform evaluations, and reduce the cost per hire if they address process differences and methodology for these key jobs.

Leverage Job-Specific Questionnaires and Automated Ranking to Improve the Selection Process.

Some jobs can receive many applicants, making the selection process longer and possibly resulting in recruiters overlooking the right candidates. One approach that works well is to leverage the questionnaire functionality provided by SAP E-Recruiting and tailor the questionnaire to the job. Doing this allows you to ask specific questions that can eliminate candidates that are not qualified and allow you to leverage the automated ranking process, which ranks the candidates, making it easier to target the right candidates.

This is especially useful for large pools of applicants, but as with any selection methodology, ensure that you involve your legal department so that the process can be reviewed along with any questions and information provided to potential candidates.

Leverage the Qualifications Catalog to Enhance the Candidate Screening Process.

SAP offers a powerful solution for tracking required qualifications against a position and/or job. Once qualifications are tied to a position and/or job, they can be used to evaluate a position holder, a potential application, or an internal employee to see how they stack up against the requirements.

This can be an effective way to filter candidates. You can ask potential candidates to complete questionnaires with targeted questions and couple the questionnaires with qualifications that can drive a higher level of granularity.

Leverage the Talent Warehouse to Build Long-lasting Relationships with Potential Employees.

Some jobs require that companies go beyond traditional approaches of posting a job and selecting candidates. Consider the power of tapping into previous employees, vendors, and partners. Also consider the benefits of building relationships with potential employees that are in the same or a complimentary industry. Managing the relationship with key resources can increase the chances of hiring them into your company and can drive your competitive advantage.

Talent Relationship Management (TRM) can provide you with deep pools of candidates that are highly qualified, segmented into categories that address key requirements, and easy to target with opportunities that arise in your organization.

SAP provides the Talent Warehouse, which is the foundation for Talent Relationship Management. Both internal and external candidates can provide their skills, interests, and information about the type of jobs they seek. With TRM you can create talent groups, search for candidates in the pool, and target specific candidates for jobs and questionnaires about jobs.

TRM can provide significant benefits to organizations seeking to find, recruit, and hire the best talent along with gaining a competitive advantage over their competitors.

12.2 Change Management

12.2.1 Adoption and Productivity

Conduct Usability Labs as Early as Possible with a Representative Set of Users.

Having the best user experience possible and an intuitive flow for accessing forms, applying for jobs, and managing candidates helps achieve your business objectives and avoids the introduction of a solution that does not cater to its audience and results in poor adoption.

During the realization phase of the project, find times in the schedule where the application is close to working as expected and create a user group that can test the application. Have individual sessions where you provide the users with a scenario and ask them to complete that part of the process. Do not provide any instructions on how to complete the process or task and observe where they get stuck. If the user is at a dead end and can no longer navigate, ask him to explain what does not make sense on the screen and what he would expect to continue.

Once all of the users have completed the usability lab, collect the results and isolate the common issues. It is best to address these issues before rolling out the process to get the maximum acceptance and adoption of the new solution.

Plan for Productivity Loss During the Conversion Process, Especially if Two Systems Will be Used in Parallel.

The new system will be very different for the staffing department and will more than likely introduce some productivity challenges early on in the introduction. We have found that training super users can greatly reduce the impact of the new system.

Where we typically see a larger issue is when two systems are run in parallel. You may decide to cut over to the new system gradually, once all of the job postings have been closed in the other system. This poses challenges for the staffing department, because they have to deal with some requisitions being created in the new system and others being closed in the old system.

Having two systems can also cause issues for managers, because they may have to continue to check the old system for some requisitions and follow the new process if they create new requisitions. Careful planning is required when rolling out the new recruiting system with targeted communications for each use group.

12.2.2 Communication

Limit the Number of Automated Emails that the System Generates.

Automated communications can sound like a great idea during blueprinting, but we advise that email automation be kept to a minimum. Emails work well to kick off the process but can become overwhelming if they are used to notify employees and managers of every change in the state of a requisition.

At the end of the blueprinting phase, it is important to review the various notifications and communications that potential employees and managers will receive to ensure that they will not be overwhelmed. Look at alternatives such as portal work items and notifications in the Universal Worklist.

12.2.3 Stakeholder Management

Form a steering committee to review project progress and resolve project-level issues, and advise on any outstanding issues. Typically, the committee consists of senior-level management and other key stakeholders in the process. The project sponsor or his representative is usually on the committee as well.

The steering committee also can exist after go-live by advising on more operational issues or future enhancements and projects.

Review any Changes in Processes with Affected Business Units and Functions.

Nothing should be done in a vacuum, especially when it impacts a critical process for the organization. Redesigning forms should prompt review from other areas in the company, such as legal and marketing, that may have dependencies or comments about the how the form will impact the company.

We have seen organizations complete blueprint and delay the project because they could not get the required signoffs when other functions did not agree with the redesigned process, forms, or language used.

Additionally, the legal and compliance teams should have a representative on the project. It is better to get them involved early because they may be able to identify issues within the process and impose requirements that must be met before going live.

Understand the Dynamics of Different Business Units and Functions within the Organization when Finalizing the Process.

During the blueprint phase, it is not valid to assume that a process timeline will be applicable to every department in the organization. Certain jobs require additional screening by several people in the department, additional face-to-face interviews, and behavioral tests.

It is critical to identify these areas or departments early in the blueprinting phase so that the system can be designed accordingly or a compromise in the process can occur.

We have found that certain industries have specific jobs that have a dedicated process due to the specialization and the exception cases involved. The key here is to have stakeholders that represent this department. For example, in the airline industry, you would have a stakeholder that was responsible for the process of hiring pilots. The involvement of these stakeholders greatly reduces the risk of project delays and helps finalize the processes required for these specialized jobs.

12.3 System Implementation

12.3.1 SAP E-Recruiting Integration and Interfacing

Decide How to Support SAP E-Recruiting Integration early in the Project.

SAP E-Recruitment can be integrated with SAP ERP using two methods. The first is a stand-alone scenario that has the SAP E-Recruiting instance installed and managed separately from SAP ERP. The second is an integrated scenario that has SAP E-Recruiting sharing the same system and client as SAP ERP.

It is very important to consider which scenario will best support your requirements and the effects it has on the implementation. The integrated scenario requires the use of various data elements to be linked, and this may not be suitable or might complicate your implementation.

Many implementations have opted for the stand-alone scenario because of the implementation considerations such as exposure to the Internet, master data requirements, and time to implementation, but this depends on your unique requirements. SAP recommends that companies implement a stand-alone instance using ALE to transfer the data between SAP ERP and SAP E-Recruiting.

Plan Carefully for the Transition From Your Current System to SAP E-Recruiting.

Recruiting data can be complex, and it is costly to convert from one system to another. Data conversion can be further complicated depending on the location and type of the source system.

Many organizations that are implementing SAP E-Recruitment choose to not convert existing data or limit it to portions of data. This approach reduces project costs and overall project risk but requires careful planning to retire the legacy system.

You need to pay careful attention to the following issues:

- Both systems need to be run in parallel until none of the positions and candidate are in progress in the legacy system.
- Ensure that all new requisitions are created in the new system.
- Clear communications must be sent out to managers regarding the process between the legacy and new system.
- Provide instructions to potential candidates that they may need to recreate their online profile if they need to review and apply for jobs. It is a good idea to explain that a new system has been implemented.
- Allow access to the legacy system for a period of time that is suffecient for recruters to find legacy data and candidates.
- Consider the need for running reports or extracting data that can be referenced once the legacy system has been retired.

Define a Strategy for Interfacing with External Job Boards and Get the Interface Requirements Early in the Project.

It has never been easier to accomplish tasks and advertise posted jobs than with the current proliferation of vendors and job boards. You can quickly automate processes to do background checks with external vendors and post your jobs to various job boards that can deliver a wealth of qualified candidates. However, it is typical to underestimate the complexity of connecting to the various vendors given the different interface specifications and requirements.

We have found that it is best to identify as early as possible which vendors will be part of the process, what activities will trigger the exchange of data, and what the interface requirements will be.

Once this information is consolidated, the technical team should define a strategy for implementing these interfaces with the necessary technology selections, interface monitoring, and approach for testing interfaces with the various vendors.

12.3.2 Security

Put Controls in Place to Safeguard Information During Implementation and Production.

Do not underestimate the effort of defining and managing security during the implementation. Depending on your requirements, you may need to convert existing and past candidate profiles. This data is highly sensitive and should not be used during development or testing. Use only sample data when testing and assign specific users access when you need to load the data during the cutover.

Limit the number of HR users that have access to the data once the system is in production. Only key HR users should be able to see confidential data.

12.3.3 Workflow

Carefully Review and Adapt the Standard Workflows to Meet Your Specific Requirements.

SAP E-Recruiting offers a range of workflows from assigning a new password to a candidate that has forgotten his password to approval of requisitions and job postings. These workflow templates can be used as they are supplied, but you will want to review them and ensure that the activities they create or statuses they change match your processes.

We highly recommend that you have a resource who is skilled in workflow review the standard workflows during the blueprinting session.

12.3.4 Access to Forms and Navigation

Apply Your Website Branding Throughout the Application for a Seamless Experience.

Depending on your portal configuration, the page that contains a form may have other elements such as menus and/or iViews constraining the real estate. When you position a form in the portal, it should occupy as much of the screen real estate as possible to support the adding of additional reviewers and objectives.

Try to avoid popping up the form as a new screen (pop-up window) because of issues with browser pop-up blocking and poor user experience. Warning and error messages should be presented in areas visible to the end user.

Adapt and Brand all SMARTFORMS to Extend the Company Image to Candidates.

SAP E-Recruiting offers various SMARTFORMS that are used for job posting and correspondence with candidates. You will want to adapt these forms so that they meet your requirements and are branded with the specific company information (such as logo, company address, etc.).

Consider these forms as part of your overall branding and user experience because they equally represent the company image and affect the user experience.

Leverage the New ABAP Web Dynpro Interfaces.

As of SAP E-Recruiting 600 SP08, SAP has provided an alternative to some of the BSP functionality by delivering the user interfaces using the new Web Dynpro technology. These interfaces offer a richer user experience and should be more suitable for your implementation.

If you are considering doing extensive customizations to the look and feel, functionality, and integration, we suggest that you consider staying with the BSP technology. The BSP technology provides for a simpler customization path and allows your development team to leverage Javascript for deeper integration.

If you plan to stay closer to standard and only plan to do simple customizations, we strongly suggest that you migrate to the new Web Dynpro applications, because they will be enhanced in the future and will offer more functionality over time.

The following functionality has been ported to Web Dynpro:

- Storage of data in Talent Warehouse
- Online application of registered candidate
- Application with reference code (registered candidate)
- Online application of unregistered candidate
- Application with reference code (unregistered candidate)

Other functionality using the new Web Dynpro technology may be available in the version that you are using. Please refer to the documentation specific to your version.

Test your Applicant Flow with Multiple Browsers.

Your company standards don't apply to the Internet. Whereas your company can set standards that mandate the use of a particular browser, those standards don't apply on the Internet. Additionally, with trends to allow employees access from home, it becomes critical to test the various popular browsers during the development and quality assurance phases of the project.

We have seen many companies set the standard to Internet Explorer 6.x and at the same time push the functionality to the Internet. This support of many browsers has caused IT departments many issues when other browsers such as Internet Explorer 8, Google Chrome, and Firefox are used.

Any changes to the standard BSP or Web Dynpro applications should be adequately tested using all of the popular browsers to ensure that your company can reach and support the widest pool of resources possible.

Sizing Your System Appropriately Prevents Issues With Performance and Unavailability of Your Recruitment System.

Depending on the size of a company, market conditions, agreements with third-party vendors, and the number of jobs posted, your company might receive a high number of job searches. Handling the load with your systems is critical for many users including recruiters, who are also conducting searches for candidates and content such as resumes.

We recommend that you implement a stand-alone instance for SAP E-Recruiting and adequately performance-test your system before going live. Base your performance tests on peak load of Internet users conducting searches, maintaining profiles, and completing applications as well as recruiters performing key tasks.

12.4 Social Media and Mobile Platforms

Social media and mobile platforms have changed the face of networking over the past few years. With the advent of sites such as Facebook, LinkedIn, and Plaxo, companies find themselves trying to tap into the hidden potential behind the changes in our interaction and online use of these platforms.

Today social media and social networking sites account for over 130 million active users, who post personal information and subscribe to topics and groups that interest them.

Currently, recruiters use these sites to target potential candidates or find out information about candidates that have applied for a job. This approach can be hit or miss, but for the most part offers a quick way to target candidates with the right skills and use their digital footprint as another reference.

Many recruiters are now starting to look at ways to further leverage these sites for attracting talent and getting more qualified candidates while at the same time reducing hiring costs. There are several ways to achieve results in this space, and you will want to make sure that you review your online strategy to see how you can use this additional channel to enhance your recruiting strategy.

We suggest that you look at Ernst and Young as an example. They have been wildly successful, attracting over 36,000 fans to their career section, which they created on Facebook in January 2007. You can access the E&Y career section by using the following URL: *http://www.facebook.com/ernstandyoungcareers*.

12.5 Summary

Lessons learned in SAP implementations are invaluable to delivering a usable solution that achieves the intended objectives and business results. We encourage you to use these lessons learned and connect with other companies that have implemented SAP E-Recruitment to exchange ideas and experiences.

Knowing where to look for answers is perhaps one of the single most important skills of a project team. Resourcefulness is crucial in implementations such as SAP E-Recruiting. This chapter inventories important resources available to assist you before, during, and after your implementation.

13 Resources

This chapter describes recommended websites, information repositories, and user communities that may help you gain a better understanding of the SAP E-Recruiting application. This chapter consists of a thorough inventory of resources you can leverage before, during, and after your implementation.

13.1 Solution Documentation on SAP Service Marketplace

Solution documentation for SAP E-Recruiting is available on the SAP Service Marketplace website for registered users. For those that do not have a Service Marketplace username and password, speak to one of your project leaders and/or Basis resources about how to obtain a username and password for the Service Marketplace. A lot of good solution documentation for SAP E-Recruiting is available in the Media Library sections of the Service Marketplace (Figure 13.1).

To peruse and download product documentation in the Media Library, do the following:

1. Go to *http://service.sap.com/erp-hcm* in your web browser. Log in with your Service Marketplace username and password.
2. On the left navigation panel, under SAP ERP • SAP ERP Human Capital Management • Talent Management • Recruiting, click on Media Library for access to documents such as:

- Collaterals such as solution brochures
- Customer success stories
- Demos using SAP Tutor software

- Detailed documentation such as configuration, infotypes, and topics such as ranking, workflow, applicant tracking, and requisition management
- Detailed and brief overview presentations on functionality
- Presentations on talent groups, job board integration, and data retention tools

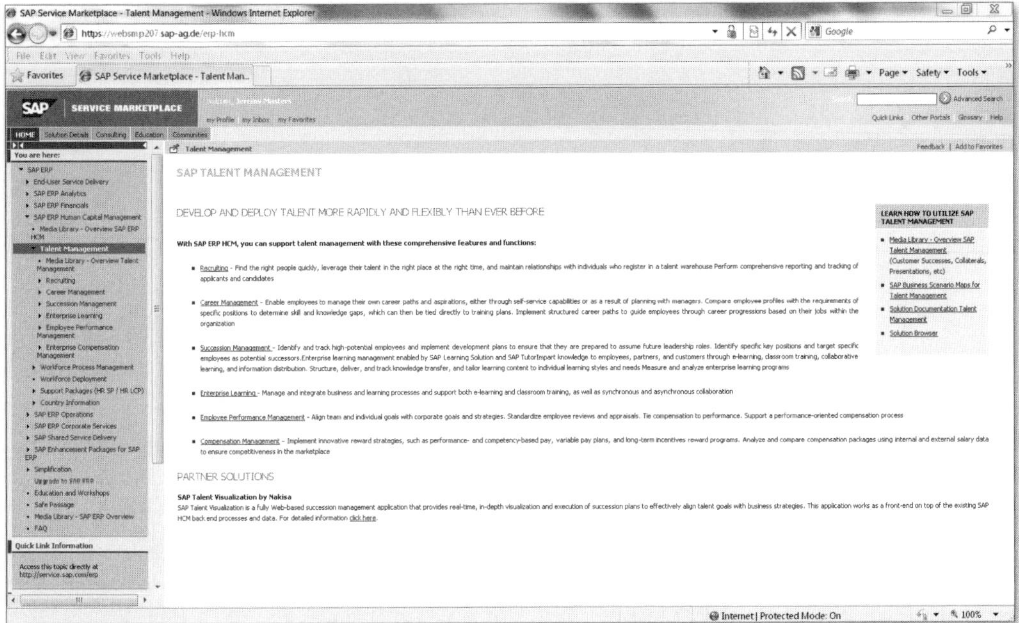

Figure 13.1 Talent Management Homepage within SAP Service Marketplace

We recommend that you bookmark this site and refer to it regularly because SAP posts useful documentation within the Service Marketplace.

13.2 SAP Online Help

SAP's online help is often overlooked as a great resource for documentation. It is always helpful to ground yourself with the standard documentation from SAP. SAP posts the latest revised help documentation online on this site. To read the documentation on SAP's help website, do the following:

1. Go to *http://help.sap.com* in your web browser.
2. On the SAP Solutions tab, click on SAP ERP.

3. Open the documentation by clicking on the available language you prefer. (The latest documentation as of this book's release is ERP Central Component 6.0, SP16, available in English and German.) If you are on an enhancement package, click on the link underneath SAP ERP Central Component called SAP ERP Enhancement Packages and navigate based on your package level.
4. Another window will launch with the SAP Library. Click on SAP ERP Central Component in the left navigation panel.
5. Expand the Human Resources folder in the left navigation panel.
6. Expand the Talent Management folder in the left navigation panel.
7. Click on the folder SAP E-Recruiting (PA-ER) in the left navigation panel.

The help is organized into the following high-level topics:

- Candidate
- Recruiter
- Administrator
- Master data for SAP E-Recruiting
- Shared topics

For information on SAP E-Recruiting security, reference the information within the SAP E-Recruiting Security Guide in the SAP Library under SAP ERP SECURITY GUIDE • SAP ERP CENTRAL COMPONENT SECURITY GUIDE • HUMAN CAPITAL MANAGEMENT • SAP E-RECRUITING.

For information about BI content for SAP E-Recruiting, reference the information within the SAP NetWeaver Library under BI CONTENT • HUMAN RESOURCES • SAP E-RECRUITING.

For information about portal content for SAP E-Recruiting, reference the information within the SAP Library under SAP ERP CROSS-APPLICATION FUNCTIONS • ROLES • BUSINESS PACKAGES (PORTAL-CONTENT) • BUSINESS PACKAGE FOR RECRUITER 1.41 and BUSINESS PACKAGE FOR RECRUITING ADMINISTRATOR 1.41.

13.3 SAP Notes on SAP Service Marketplace

The SAP Notes section of the Service Marketplace is typically where SAP customers go when they need to troubleshoot an issue. This site, previously called OSS (Online Service System), provides important bug fixes for SAP customers and consultative advice on workarounds for known product issues. It is a lifeline for a lot of project implementations.

You can directly access the SAP Notes section of the Service Marketplace by going to *http://service.sap.com/notes* in your web browser. You will be prompted for a username and password because you will need to be a registered user.

All SAP E-Recruiting SAP Notes are categorized under application area PA-ER. Under the PA-ER application area, the following subapplications are available:

- PA-ER-ALE for ALE topics
- PA-ER-BSP for Business Server Page topics
- PA-ER-INT for integration topics
- PA-ER-IS for R/3 reporting topics
- PA-ER-LOC for localization topics
- PA-ER-SEA for search topics
- PA-ER-SEA-SES for search using SES topics
- PA-ER-WD for Web Dynpro for ABAP topics

Figure 13.2 shows the PA-ER application hierarchy from within the SAP Service Marketplace.

At the time of this book's writing, almost 1700 SAP Notes are available in the Service Marketplace. Although it is impossible to list all SAP Notes here, some of the more important ones include:

- SAP Note 711701 – Composite SAP Note: Security in E-Recruiting
- SAP Note 817145 – Composite SAP Note/Overview: TREX troubleshooting
- SAP Note 1300398 – General Recommendations for Search Related Issues in E-Rec

Searches for these and other SAP Notes is performed through the website *http://service.sap.com/notes.* Figure 13.3 shows the website's main search screen.

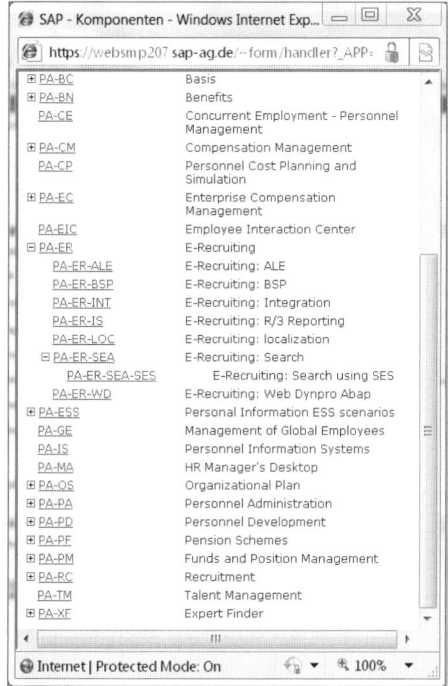

Figure 13.2 Application Area PA-ER and all Subordinate Application Areas

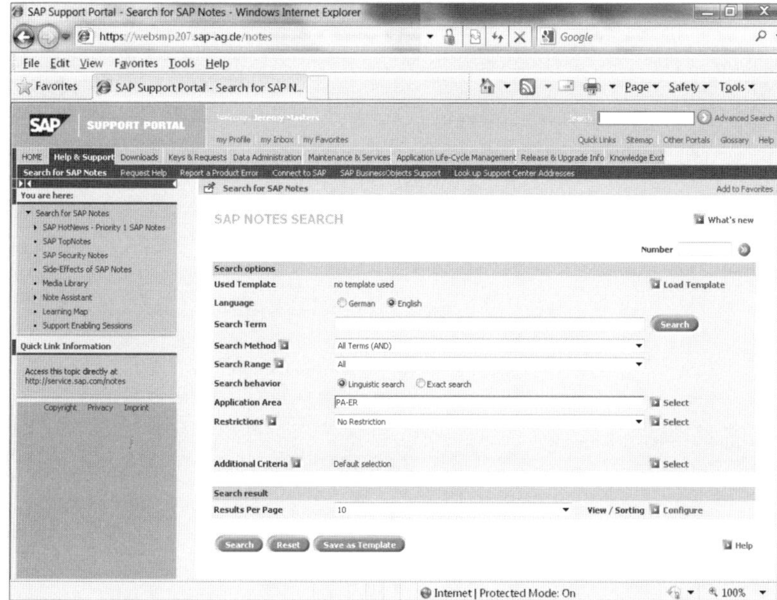

Figure 13.3 SAP Notes Main Search Page

13.4 SDN – SAP Community

The SAP Developer Network (SDN) is an online community and network of SAP practitioners — developers, configurators, and other project team members. SAP is now branding SDN within the larger SAP Community Network because the site has a lot to offer to other people besides developers. The website is *http://sdn.sap.com,* and registration is free. Members can post, respond to, and view questions found in the popular forum. Although the forum is the most popular spot on the site, other useful features include free eLearning classes, interesting blogs, and downloads.

The majority of the threads on SAP E-Recruiting can be found in the forum ERP HCM (HR). Figure 13.4 shows a screenshot of the ERP HCM (HR) forum with a search result for TREX.

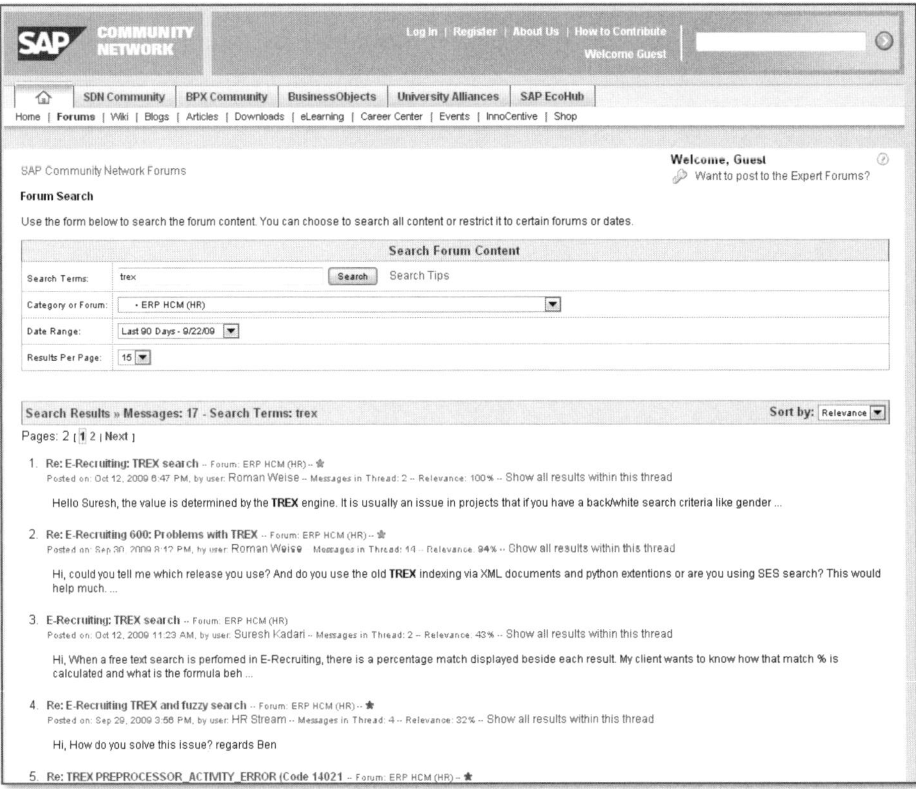

Figure 13.4 Forum Search on the SDN SAP Community Network Website

13.5 HR Expert

Wellesley Information Services, producer of SAP Insider events and publications, publishes *HR Expert*, a magazine that covers essential SAP ERP HCM concepts, tips, and best practices. There is a focus on case studies and real-world experiences in the articles. You can find a lot of good material on the website as well (it is a paid subscription). The website is *http://www.hrexpertonline.com/*. Figure 13.5 shows an example article from a three-part series on SAP E-Recruiting best practices.

Table 13.1 lists several articles in the *HR Expert* archive are relevant for E-Recruiting.

Article	Volume # / Issue # / Month
Best Practices: Plan for and Implement SAP E-Recruiting	Volume 03, Issue 05, June
SAP E-Recruiting Part 2: Eight Tips to Ensure a Smooth Implementation	Volume 03, Issue 06, July
SAP E-Recruiting Part 3: Source Talent Globally While Supporting Local Regulations and Business Needs	Volume 03, Issue 07, August and September
Talent Groups in SAP E-Recruiting Target the Right Candidate	Volume 07, Update 06

Table 13.1 List of HR Expert Articles Pertinent to E-Recruiting

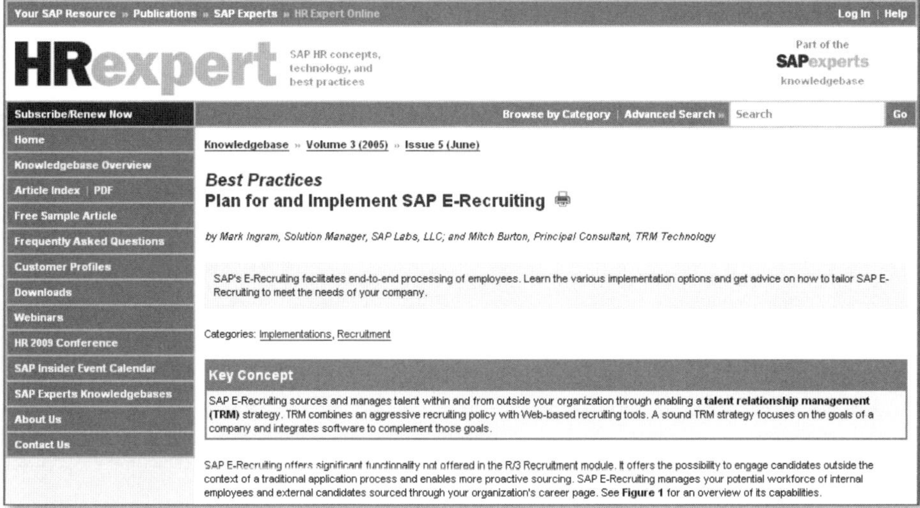

Figure 13.5 Example Article on the HR Expert Website

Next, we discuss some conference events.

13.6 Annual Conferences

Two conferences are the most popular for SAP ERP HCM practitioners — the annual SAP HR conference and ASUG/SAPPHIRE.

Every year, Wellesley Information Services sponsors the HR conference, where SAP partners, exhibitors, and customers come to listen to speakers, share best practices, and see what new functionality is coming available. The conference is a great place to network, hear what others are doing, and have fun. The website for the HR 2010 conference is at *http://www.sapinsiderhr2010.com.*

Also, SAP annually hosts a combined ASUG/SAPPHIRE event that is geared toward both current and prospective clients. It is an opportunity for SAP to show their cutting-edge solutions to their customer base. The ASUG/SAPPHIRE event includes speaker presentations, demos, and an exhibitor area. For more information on the conference, visit *http://www.sapsapphire.com/.*

13.7 User Communities

Two SAP ERP HCM user communities are popular for networking events, knowledge sharing and harvesting, and roundtable discussions:

ASUG (Americas' SAP Users' Group) is a customer-driven community of SAP professionals and partners. More than 75,000 individuals and 2,017 companies are represented within the community. It is a great place for networking. Visit their website at *http://www.asug.com/.*

SHRM (The Society for Human Resource Management) is the world's largest association devoted to human resource management. Founded in 1948 and representing more than 250,000 individual members, SHRM currently has more than 575 affiliated chapters and members in more than 140 countries. Visit their website at *http://www.shrm.org/.*

13.8 LinkedIn

LinkedIn (*www.linkedin.com*) is a business-oriented social networking site launched in May 2003, mainly used for professional networking. The site has some excellent groups to subscribe to for registered users. Membership is free. Of particular interest for SAP recruitment professionals is the subgroup E-Recruiting within the SAP Talent Management group at *http://www.linkedin.com/groups?subgroups=&gid=152688*. This group is dedicated to discussing "topics around SAP E-Recruiting and associated processes and technologies." Check it out!

13.9 Internet Search Engines

Don't forget about your Internet search engines! Google, Bing, and Yahoo, among many others, provide a great mechanism for answers to SAP questions. You know what to do. Simply type in your question or keyword and see what you get. You might be surprised. Just be sure to give proper credit if the material is not public domain.

13.10 Summary

There are many resources you can embrace to research answers to your SAP E-Recruiting questions. Some of these resources, such as the SDN SAP Community, SAP Service Marketplace, and Internet search engines such as Google, are absolutely free and provide a wealth of information at your fingertips. Just remember: If you are stuck on something, there are probably fellow SAP ERP HCM practitioners who are struggling or have struggled with the same or a similar challenge. Go out there and take advantage of all the wonderful resources at your disposal.

Appendices

A Talent Groups in SAP E-Recruitment Target the Right Candidates

This article, *Talent Groups in SAP E-Recruitment Target the Right Candidate*, was published in HR Expert in Jul 2009.

A.1 Abstract

SAP E-Recruitment provides talent group functionality to help companies build relationships with candidates based on their hiring criteria and recruiting strategies. Recruiters can customize services such as the job alerts, newsletters, and invitations to events to meet the needs of the talent groups.

A.1.1 Key Concept

Talent groups are a segmentation of the talent pool based on recruitment needs (both forecast and current). For example, if a company's recruiting strategy is to fill open positions with college interns, it would segment a talent pool for recent graduates or college students. Resumes from candidates looking for internships are then assigned to this particular talent group. These resumes can be easily matched with requisitions seeking recent graduates or college students.

A.2 Talent Groups in SAP E-Recruitment Target the Right Candidate

The talent group concept in SAP E-Recruitment (SAP ERC) makes recruiting proactive by having recruiters build a talent pool rather than recruiting on a just-in-time basis. When a recruiter is assigned to a requisition, he can check the talent group to see if any candidates fit the requisition prior to making a new posting. In the current economic climate, talent groups and customized talent services help organizations attract top talent in a crowded job-seeker pool. From my implementation experiences, I have noticed many companies lack a strategy for segmenting their talent pool. *Venki Krishnamoorthy, SAP (July 2009)*

Note

For this article, SAP 6.0 SP level is used as well as SAP E-Recruitment 6.0 and Enhancement Package 3. However, Enhancement Package 4 offers new functionality. For more information on the changes see the sidebar "Enhancement Package 4."

A talent pool is a common pool of candidates that all recruiters can access. The talent pool is at times referred to as the candidate pool or the recruiting pool. Many organizations restrict recruiters to certain talent groups or segments of the talent pool based on the recruiter's assigned requisitions or the departments the recruiter supports.

Note

Talent groups are available from SAP E-Recruiting 6.0 Enhancement Pack 1. In earlier releases, talent groups are referred to as target groups.

A.3 Enhancement Package 4

In Enhancement Package 4, the administrator and the recruiter start page is delivered with Web Dynpro for ABAP (WD4A) functionality. That means you can access both the administrator and the recruiter's role through the portal (manager portal/employee portal).

Also, in Enhancement Package 4, the administrator start page has a mini-dashboard that gives an overview of the administrative tasks for which the administrator is responsible. The recruiter start page has a new UI and introduces the concept of a work center, which gives the recruiter an overview of the current recruitment process he is responsible for. The recruiter can customize the work center to meet requirements. You can search for candidates by candidate type — internal or external, for example. SAP has enhanced the recruiter role considerably. This has a cascading effect of a reduced recruiting lifecycle and a greater savings in the recruiting budget.

For more information about the changes in Enhancement Pack 4, refer to SAP Note 1241014.

A.4 Talent Groups

In Figure A.1, I identified a few talent groups you could create from the talent pool. Some of these talent groups may not be suitable for every organization. For example, in the medical devices/pharmaceutical industry, I have found that past industry experience is rated very highly. You can further segment the business functions talent groups as sales, marketing, HR, or training.

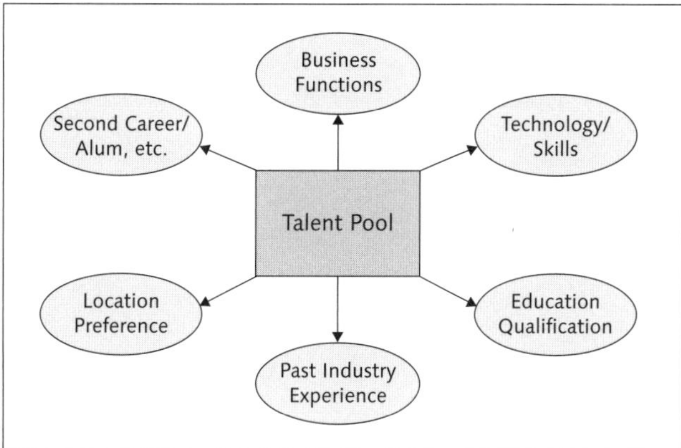

Figure A.1 Possible Talent Groups

Other segmentation of the talent pool can include:

- Level of experience – recent graduate, experienced professional, mid-level manager, executives
- High-potential candidate – based on industry or education qualifications
- Willingness for international assignments
- Rare skills/specific experience

Assigning candidates to a particular talent group is not a reflection on the quality of the candidate. What a talent group accomplishes is grouping together candidates with similar profiles so that talent services can be tailored to the specific needs of this talent group. For example, a candidate with mid-level managerial experience should not be grouped with a recent graduate; the candidates have different talent services needs. A candidate can belong to more than one talent group.

A.4.1 What Are Talent Services?

Figure A.2 shows some common talent services that I have implemented during some of my client projects. You can develop talent services to meet your organization's requirements. For example, you can start talent services to target former employees. You could create a web page where they can congregate to learn more about their former employer. You can post open requisitions in that website in case they are interested in returning or can make a referral.

Each of these services is customized to meet the specific needs and the requirements of the talent groups. Each is implemented from the respective start pages. If you are an internal or external candidate searching for a suitable position, you can create a job alert. When a requisition that meets your specific job requirements is posted, you receive an alert. You can then apply to the posted requisition or contact your recruiter to discuss the open requisition.

Figure A.2 Different Talent Services

Let me give you an example of something I saw during a past implementation. College students spend much of their time in the Web 2.0 world; therefore, it is so much easier to reach out to new graduates and college students through Web 2.0 applications such as Facebook rather than through email correspondence. If you are planning to recruit college graduates or if there is a recruiting event for college grads, you can send the notifications through Web 2.0 targeting them. You can customize the notifications to meet the interests of this talent group — details such as why the company is a great place to start your career and how the company is net savvy. You can even invite students to visit your company website and interact with the recruiter through Facebook or other social networking sites.

Without talent groups, your recruiter could have sent a global email to all candidates that exist in your organization's talent pool, but that casts a net that is too wide. A mid-level manager does not want to see an email informing him of a recruiting event for new graduates.

Figure A.3 An Example of Talent Services

Let me give you another example. Your organization has a requisition to fill the Manager-IT Projects position and posted it on web job boards. As shown in Figure 1.3, your recruiter can send a job alert to the talent group Business Functions – IT targeting mid-level professionals. The channel to send the job alert can be email or a personal contact by phone. Recently I have noticed recruiters sending job alerts by Twitter, though I do not have personal experience with this channel.

During my implementations, I have heard many of my clients mention that a significant portion of the budget is spent making job postings on job boards to target the right candidate. A potential candidate responds to your job posting, and later, the recruiter finds out the candidate is already registered in your talent pool. The candidate has not heard from the recruiter regarding this job posting. What this really means is that the organization has not created talent groups, and therefore talent services cannot target the right talent.

Note

Talent groups are different from application groups. Talent groups are groupings of people with similar profiles and are used for talent relationship management. Application groups are groupings of unsolicited applications for similar jobs. Talent groups help the recruiters in proactive recruiting, whereas application groups result in reactive recruiting.

A.5 Generate SAP E-Recruiting Access Links for Start Pages

To generate SAP ERC access links for the start pages from the SAP Easy Access screen, click System in the menu bar. In the displayed options, select Services and then Reporting. The ABAP: Program Execution screen is displayed. In the Program field, enter RCF_GENERATE_URLS and click the execute icon. Use RCF_GENERATE_URLS in every system for every time someone wants to create the access link for a start page. This displays the E-Recruiting: Generate All Relevant URLs screen. Alternatively, in the SAP Easy Access screen, enter Transaction code SA38, which displays the ABAP: Program Execution screen.

Select the option HTTPS (or HTTP, check with your portal administrator) and choose the language as EN (English). Click the execute icon to generate the URLs for the various start pages. You can click the local file icon and save the generated URLs to the local file.

A.6 How to Create Talent Groups

Talent groups are configured in the portal from the administrator's start page. The first step in creating talent groups is to launch the administrator page from the portal (see Figure A.4). There is no menu path; you need to click the URL. If you have not implemented manager portal/employee portal functionality, you can click the administrator URL that you have generated, as described in the section "Generate SAP E-Recruiting Access Links for Start Pages" to launch the administrator's start page.

The administrator is responsible for creating the talent groups, assigning the recruiters to the required talent groups, and assigning and restricting access to the talent pool. SAP has provided a standard role SAP_RCF_BUSINESS_ADMINISTRATOR for the talent administrator that provides access to the administrator start page.

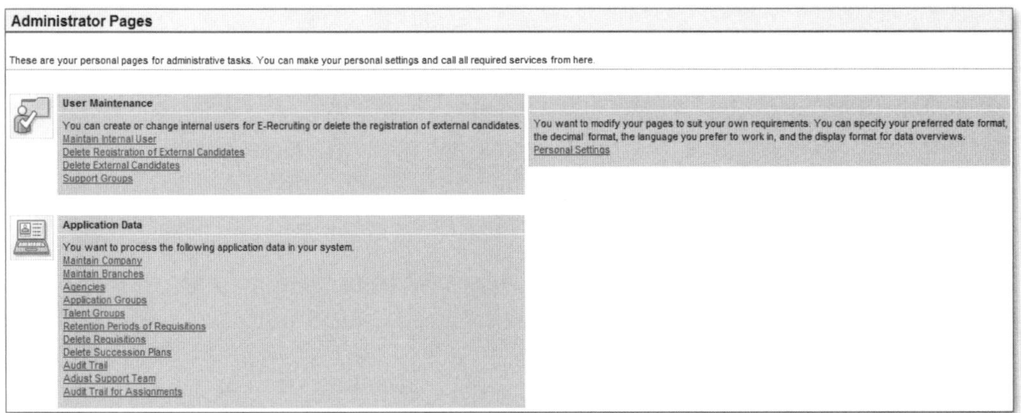

Figure A.4 Administrator Start Page

In the administrator start page (see Figure A.4), in the Application Data group, click the Talent Groups link to get to the talent groups list page. Follow the menu path ADMINISTRATOR PAGES • APPLICATION DATA • TALENT GROUPS. In the Talent Groups launch page, click the Create button. This takes you to the Talent Group Basic Data page (see Figure A.5). In Figure A.5, I have circled the SAP definition of talent groups.

The name mentioned in the Person Responsible field is the administrator of this talent group. On the Talent Group Basic Data page, enter the name of the talent group you are creating, enter the description of the talent group, and click the Save button.

In Figure A.5, if you notice, the basic data required to create a talent group is displayed in different tab pages. If you have completed and saved the data in a particular tab page, the green check mark icon is highlighted against the short text.

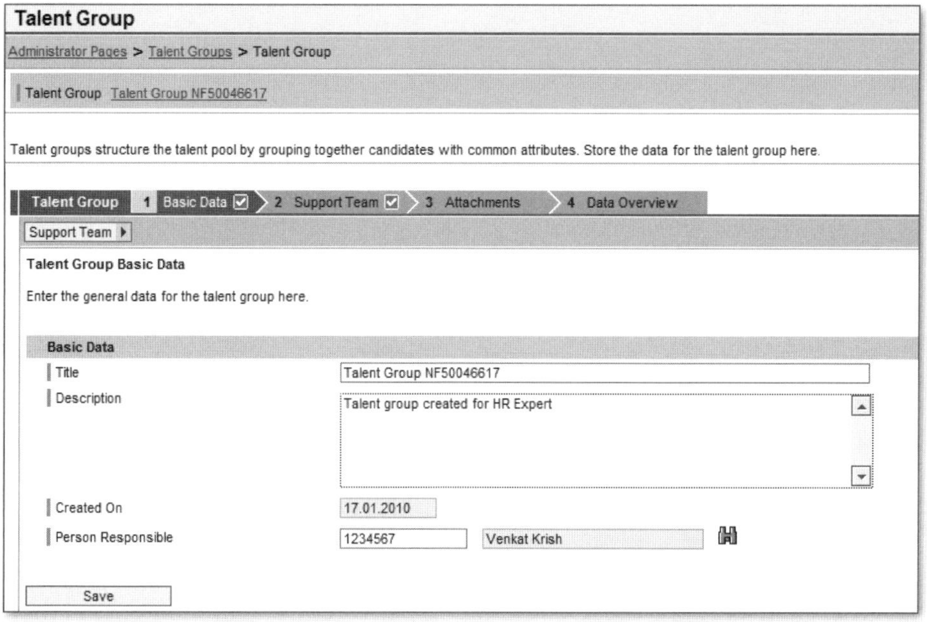

Figure A.5 Talent Group Basic Data Page

> **Note**
>
> You can create talent groups from the recruiter's start page if the recruiter is granted the role to create one. In many of my implementations, I have seen clients restrict the talent group creation to the recruiting administrator role.

If you want to add members to the support team for this talent group, click the Support Team tab (see Figure A.6)

Add members to the support team by clicking the Further Assignment button. You can assign the members either as an individual or you can add another support team to your talent groups. Members of the support team alone have access to the talent group and can add new candidates to the talent group.

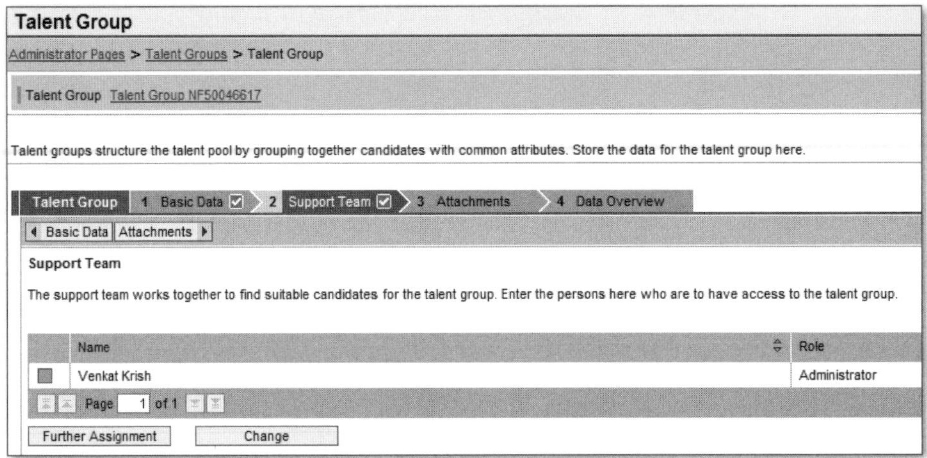

Figure A.6 Create a Support Team for the Talent Group

The support team for talent groups is different from the support team for requisitions. In the talent group, the support team has access to the talent groups they are assigned to and they work as a team to identify the talent available in the talent pool for this talent group. Some (or all of the) members of the support team (recruiters, for example) might be working on open requisitions and might be accessing the talent group to fill those requisitions.

In requisitions, the support team is responsible for the creation and approval of the requisitions. Some members of the support team might be responsible for interviewing the candidate who has applied to the requisition, and some might be involved in the consensus meetings. Some members of the requisition support team might be recruiters (who also might be members of the talent group support team) who are responsible for recruiting candidates to fill this particular requisition.

If you wish to add attachments to the talent group, click the Attachments tab (see Figure A.7).

For the attachment type to be displayed in the attachment tab, you should have defined the attachment type in the IMG and assigned the attachment type to the object NF-Talent Groups. You can define the attachments and assign the attachments to the HR objects in the IMG. Use Transaction code SPRO and access the IMG transaction. The attachments are stored in infotype 5134 (attachments). The attachment types can be Microsoft Word documents, text files, PDF documents, JPEG files, or TIF files. What attachment type is suitable depends on the server space you are willing to use.

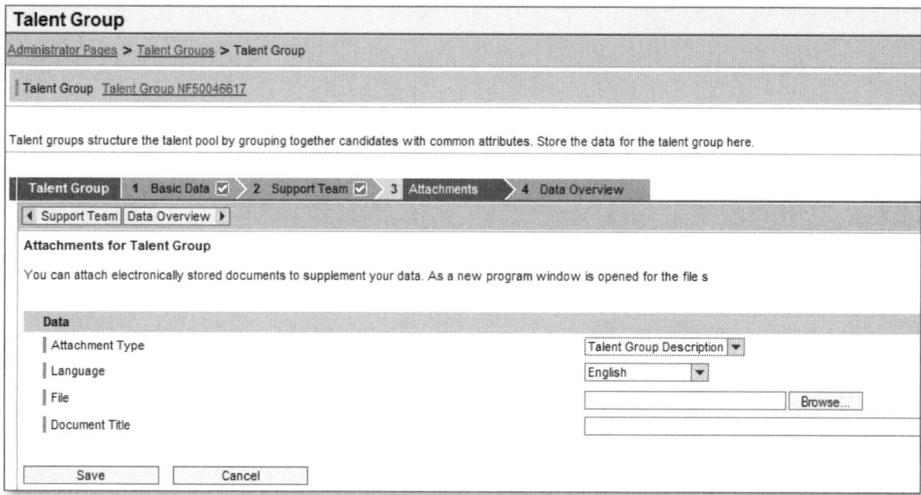

Figure A.7 Add Attachments to the Talent Group

You can customize the different attachment types in the SAP IMG. The menu path is IMG • SAP E-Recruiting • Basic Settings • Attachment Types. In the Define Attachment Types, you can configure the different attachment types such as resumes, reference letters, certificates, and talent group descriptions. In the Determine Use of Attachment Types, you assign the attachments (that you configured in the Define Attachment Types) to the HR objects such as NA-Candidate, NB-Requisition, NC-Posting, ND-Application, and NF-Talent Group.

You can use the Business Add-In (BAdI) HRRCF00_DOC_UPLOAD to upload the documents. The BAdI provides the following methods:

- CHECK_ATTACH_FILE_TYPE – This method checks the data types of the uploaded file. You can only upload file types that have been configured in the process step Determine Use Of Attachment Types.
- CHECK_ATTACH_FILE_SIZE – This method checks the file size of the uploaded file. You can configure the maximum file size of an attachment. Files that exceed this file size cannot be saved.
- CHECK_NUMBER_OF_ATTACH – This method checks the number of attachments. You can specify the maximum number of attachments or the maximum sizes of all the uploaded files.
- CHECK_ATTACH_VIRUS_VIA_VSA – This method scans the files for viruses.

The attachment can provide more details about the talent group. It can mention some of the top/high potential talent in the group. The attachment can provide details that you would like to share with your support team.

The data overview provides details (data overview) about the talent group (see Figure A.8). It is similar in concept to the data overview in the requisitions. You click the URL field to display the attachments. You can have the data overview in smartform or in PDF. I do not have a preference for either. Smartforms are displayed in HTML. Adobe Forms provides more interactive features such as online and offline viewing and enhanced printing solutions — for example, a display of your organization logo. Depending on the level of customization, you might need the assistance of a technical developer to develop Adobe Forms.

Personal Settings

Administrator Pages > Personal Settings

Here you can tailor your pages to suit your personal requirements.

Basic Settings

Specify the formats in which numbers and dates are displayed. Note that these settings do not apply until your next logon.

Date Format	DD.MM.YYYY
Decimal Notation	1.234.567,89

General Settings

You can display data overviews in HTML format or in Adobe Portable Document Format (PDF). You must have the Adobe Acrobat Reader installed to be able to display the overviews in PDF format. The preferred language specifies the language in which you want to receive and send your correspondence.

Display Format for Data Overviews	-- Select --
Preferred Language	-- Select -- / HTML / PDF

Printer Settings

Specify the printer you want to use to print your letters and documents formatted by the system.

Output Device

Save

Figure A.8 Personalization

In the recruiter start page, click the link Personal Settings available in the group Personal Settings. In the displayed BSP (see Figure A.8) in the group General Settings, click the Display Format for Data Overviews dropdown list box. Then you can choose how you would like your data overview to be displayed. Figure A.9 shows the data overview of the talent groups.

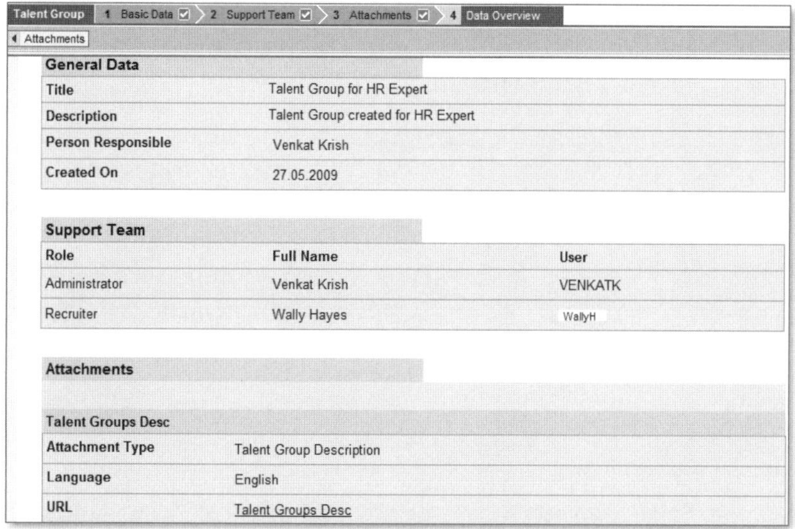

Figure A.9 Talent Groups Data Overview

A.7 Assign Candidates to the Talent Group

As shown in Figure A.10, you assign candidates to a talent group from the recruiter's start page. Refer to my earlier note on how to generate the URLs for the start pages.

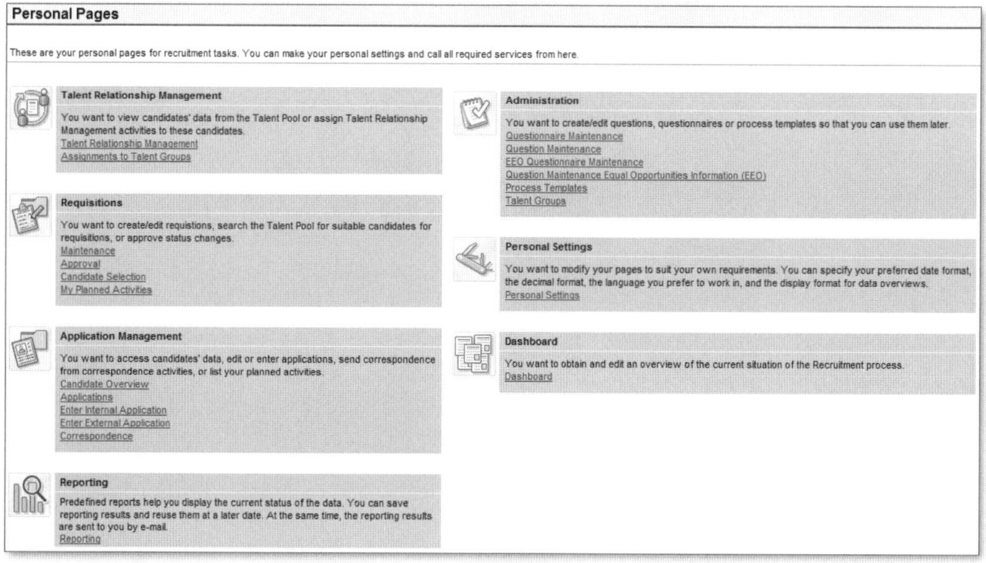

Figure A.10 Recruiter Start Page

In the recruiter's start page, click the Assignment to Talent Groups link. The Talent Groups assignment page (Figure A.11) displays all the talent groups that are assigned to you as a member of the support team.

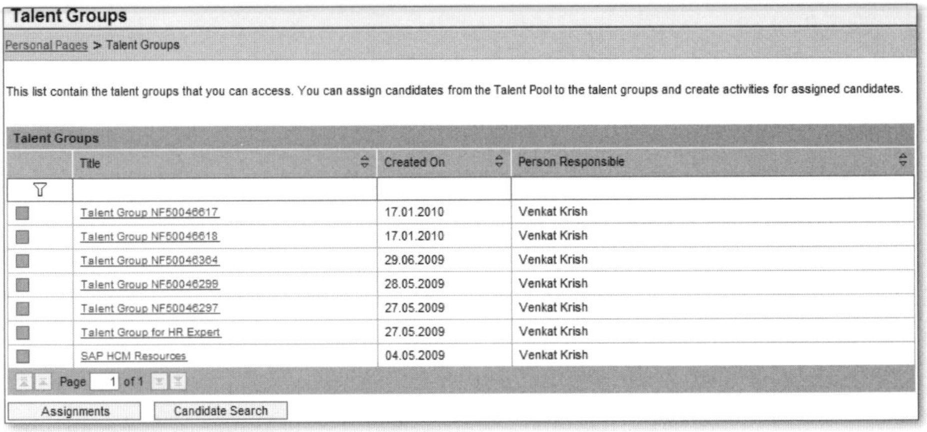

Talent Groups

Personal Pages > Talent Groups

This list contain the talent groups that you can access. You can assign candidates from the Talent Pool to the talent groups and create activities for assigned candidates.

Talent Groups

	Title	Created On	Person Responsible
	Talent Group NF50046617	17.01.2010	Venkat Krish
	Talent Group NF50046618	17.01.2010	Venkat Krish
	Talent Group NF50046364	29.06.2009	Venkat Krish
	Talent Group NF50046299	28.05.2009	Venkat Krish
	Talent Group NF50046297	27.05.2009	Venkat Krish
	Talent Group for HR Expert	27.05.2009	Venkat Krish
	SAP HCM Resources	04.05.2009	Venkat Krish

Page 1 of 1

Assignments | Candidate Search

Figure A.11 Talent Groups Assignment Page

Click the Candidate Search button and then enter the search criteria to be used to select and display candidates from the talent pool. From the displayed list, you can select the candidates and assign them to the talent group. When you click the Assignments button, it displays all the candidates that are assigned to the particular talent group. Select the candidate to perform talent relationship management activities.

As you can see, assignment of candidates to the talent groups is a manual process. This is beneficial since it helps the recruiter to know the candidates in the talent group. It helps the recruiter to understand the talent group better and customize the talent relationship management activities for the talent group.

B SAP E-Recruiting Terms

The following is a list of frequently used terms in SAP E-Recruiting and their descriptions.

Terminology	Description
Activity	The tasks and processes in SAP E-Recruiting. An activity is always attached to an SAP E-Recruiting object.
Activity category	In SAP E-Recruiting, activities are grouped into categories, for example, simple activity, qualifying event, simple correspondence.
Activity type	Activities in an activity category are grouped into activity types. The activity types contain data, and the system executes the steps using the data contained in the activity types. Examples of activity types in the simple activity category are add to referral list, contact with candidate, and find suitable requisitions.
Application	An application is an expression of interest by a candidate to accept new employment in your organization or change his current position in your organization.
Candidacy	Candidacy is an object created by SAP E-Recruiting when a candidate sends his application in response to a job posting.
Communication data	The candidate's contact details, including email ID, phone numbers, and the mailing address.
Data overview	Provides an overview of the data for a specific SAP E-Recruiting object. The overview is displayed in an SAP SmartForm or in Adobe Forms.
External candidate	A candidate who is interested in an employment in your organization. The candidate is currently not employed in your organization.
Favorites	The results of a job search can be selected and copied into a special folder. At a later date, the candidate can visit the folder and apply to the selected job posting or edit or delete the list.

Terminology	Description
Hiring manager	The manager who is looking to fill a position in his team. The manager is also a member of the support team for the requisition.
Interest group	Grouping of candidates with similar characteristics. When a candidate creates his profile, the candidate can choose the interest group to which he would like to be assigned. A requisition can be assigned to a particular interest group. Interest groups are different from talent groups.
Internal candidate	A current employee who is interested in a different position.
Mass processing	The same activity can be created for multiple candidates simultaneously.
Personal settings	In the portal, the user can adjust settings to suit his personal requirements.
Posting or job posting	Publication of a job announcement.
Posting channel	The medium where the job postings are published. The posting channel can be internal or external. Examples of a posting channel are corporate intranet, Internet job boards, and newspapers.
Process template	The process template consists of a defined set of processes and assigned activities to the individual processes. A process template can be attached to a requisition or to an application group.
Profile or candidate profile	A candidate profile consists of the candidate resume, education qualifications, interest group, and so on.
Questionnaire	A questionnaire consists of questions, assigned response options, and free text responses. The questionnaire can be responded to by the candidate or by the recruiter on behalf of the candidate.
Questionnaire category	Questionnaires are grouped into two categories — evaluable information and EEO. Questionnaires in the evaluable information category can be used to evaluate a candidate. Questionnaires in the EEO category cannot be used to evaluate a candidate. The data collected is for information only and is used for federal filing.

Terminology	Description
Ranking	The candidates are compared based on their responses to the questions.
Reference code	The reference code is system generated. You can customize the reference code by implementing a BAdI. The candidate can use the reference code to do a job search and to apply to a job posting.
Registered candidate	A candidate who is registered in the talent warehouse.
Requisition	A requisition is an internal document containing a formal request by the manager to fill a position. The requisition contains details about the position, the salary offered, and the requirements the candidate must fulfill to be considered for the position.
Search criteria	The parameters that are used to construct a search query and that are used by TREX to conduct a search. The search criteria are entered by the user and can be saved for future use.
Support team	Groups of people (employees of the organization) with assigned roles who work together to fill a position. A support team is assigned to a requisition, to an application group, or to talent groups.
Talent group	Segmentation of a talent pool. You can define the criteria for segmentation and assign candidates to the talent pool. A candidate can be assigned to multiple talent groups simultaneously.
Talent pool	A database of candidates.
Talent warehouse	Consists of talent pool and talent relationship management services that are available.
Talent Relationship Management (TRM)	Services that are offered to develop and maintain relationship with the talent (candidate).
TREX	SAP E-Recruiting search engine.
Unregistered candidate	A candidate who is not registered in the talent warehouse.

C Business Function HCM_ERC_CI_3

In this section we will explain about the new business function HCM_ERC_CI_3 released by SAP and available as of enhancement pack 4 (SP04).

To implement HCM_ERC_CI_3 you should have activated the business function HCM_ERC_CI_2.

The following components should be installed and are a pre-requisite:

- Business Function HCM_MSS_ERC_CI_1
- Business Package for Recruiting Administrator 1.41
- Business Package for Recruiter 1.41

C.1 New Functionalities in SP04

The new functionalities available in SP04 include:

C.1.1 Requisition Management

- There is a new *Restricted Recruiter* authorization role. Recruiters with this assigned role can create and edit requisitions but cannot release the requisitions. The requisitions created by a Restricted Recruiter need to be released by a recruiter with the required authorizations. Restricted Recruiter cannot release publications or withdraw job postings.
- There is a new standard delivered workflow, which sends the requisitions created by a Restricted Recruiter to the appropriate recruiter for verification and approvals. The requisition created by the Restricted Recruiter will be in *Draft* status, and on approval by the appropriate recruiter, the status is set to *Released*.
- Job Postings can now be published in two steps
- The qualifications assigned to the position are automatically transferred from HCM to the requirements of the requisition, when the requisition is created.
- The requisitions created in Management Involvement (*Create Requisition Request* MSS scenario) after approval of the request, appears in the dashboard of the lead recruiter (recruiter assigned to the support group of the requisition, and has the role *Lead Recruiter* assigned to him in the support group). The recruiter can access the requisition in the *My Draft Requisitions* query.

C.1.2 Recruiter Work Center

The following queries are new and are available in the dashboard of the Recruiter Work Center:

- My New Applications
- New Team Applications
- **My Planned Activities:** All activities where the recruiter is the creator or the processor are displayed. The activities that belong to the Simple Correspondence category are not displayed.
- **My Planned Correspondence Activities:** All planned activities where the recruiter is the creator or the processor are displayed.
- **Talent Groups:** All talent groups where the recruiter is assigned to the support team of the talent group are displayed.
- **My Planned TRM Activities:** All TRM activities where the recruiter is the creator or the processor are displayed.
- **New Registered Candidates:** Candidates who have registered in the last 7 days are displayed by default.
- In SP04, mass processing of candidates for TRM related activities are possible.

C.1.3 Search Functions

In SP04, both structured and unstructured data are indexed. All attachments are now included in the search profile. SAP E-Recruiting uses Search Engine Services (SES) for indexing and searching.

C.1.4 Important SAP Notes

Review SAP Note 1394119, which describes the changes and new functionalities available in enhancement pack 4 SP04.

D The Authors

Jeremy Masters is an author, speaker, and SAP ERP HCM subject matter expert. Mr. Masters is also the cofounder and managing partner of Worklogix, which provides SAP ERP HCM professional services and software solutions to Fortune 1000 companies. Mr. Masters has been an SAP ERP HCM practitioner for over 12 years, spending his early years with Price Waterhouse, PwC Consulting, and IBM Global Business Services. He has been involved in over 20 projects, many of them global in scope. Mr. Masters has been helping clients implement HCM talent management including e-recruiting solutions for over a decade. Besides implementing SAP E-Recruiting, he has worked with much of the new talent management functionality, including performance management, succession planning, and enterprise compensation management, as well as self-service functionality including Employee Self-Service and Manager Self-Service. You can reach him via email at *jmasters@worklogix.com.*

Christos Kotsakis is an author, speaker, and subject matter expert on HR processes and systems. Mr. Kotsakis has been working on transformation projects for over 12 years and has extensive knowledge of self-service applications and related technologies. Mr. Kotsakis was an associate partner in the human capital management practice at IBM Global Business Services, where he led the design and implementation of largescale, global HCM transformation projects using SAP ERP HCM. Over the past 10 years, Mr. Kotsakis has managed more than a dozen project teams, spanning across HCM functionality, including performance management, compensation management, and e-recruiting. He also has extensive experience in software development and enterprise portal implementations including the SAP NetWeaver Portal technologies. You can reach him via email at *christos.kotsakis@emedianet.com*.

Venki Krishnamoorthy is an author, speaker, and SAP ERP HCM talent management solutions subject matter expert. Venki is currently an SAP ERP HCM functional consultant with SAP America. Venki Krishnamoorthy has over 10 years experience as a functional lead, project manager/program manager in the HCM space. Besides implementing SAP E-Recruiting, he has implemented and acted as a trusted advisor on SAP ERP HCM talent management implementations including performance management, succession planning, SAP Talent Visualization by Nakisa, and Employee Self-Service and Manager Self-Service. You can reach him via email at *venki.krish@ymail.com*.

Index

A

B

C

D

E

F

G

H

I

P

Q

R

U

V

W